Ethical Dilemmas and Social Science Research

An Analysis of Moral Issues
Confronting Investigators
in Research Using Human Participants

Paul Davidson Reynolds

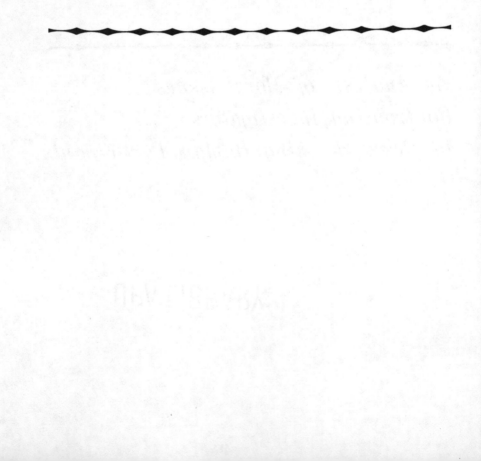

Ethical Dilemmas and Social Science Research

 Jossey-Bass Publishers

San Francisco • Washington • London • 1979

ETHICAL DILEMMAS AND SOCIAL SCIENCE RESEARCH
*An Analysis of Moral Issues Confronting Investigators in Research
Using Human Participants*
by Paul Davidson Reynolds

Library of Congress Cataloging in Publication Data

Reynolds, Paul Davidson.
  Ethical dilemmas and social science research.

  Bibliography: p.
  Includes index.
  1. Social science research—Moral and religious
aspects. 2. Social science research—Political aspects.
3. Social scientists. 4. Social ethics. 5. Civil
rights. I. Title.
H62.R468   179′.7   79-88110
ISBN 0-87589-422-4

Manufactured in the United States of America

JACKET DESIGN BY WILLI BAUM

FIRST EDITION

Code 7927

The Jossey-Bass
Social and Behavioral Science Series

To my wife
Anne-Marie;
may this work be worthy of her

Preface

This volume has two objectives: to provide an overview of the major moral dilemmas associated with the social science enterprise and to assist investigators in developing the confidence to resolve such quandaries on their own.* Several important assumptions underlie the discussion:

1. Serious, thoughtful pursuit of social science will be associated with an awareness of moral, ethical, or value dilemmas.

*Many social scientists are seriously concerned with acting in accordance with accepted notions of right and wrong, which is the major connotation of *moral;* few seem to be as concerned about the "rules of good behavior" established by the various professional associations (the term *ethical* connotes conformity to a code or set of principles). Since the major problem confronting most social scientists is determining what is a correct or good action, rather than deciding how the "professional codes" apply to their situation, the term *moral* will be emphasized.

2. Each social scientist will resolve these dilemmas in some form, even if only by avoiding them.
3. The inability to predict the future orientation of social science endeavors, the development of new research techniques, and shifts in the norms and values of societies make the formulation of universal, precise, and permanent guidelines for resolving most moral dilemmas impossible (except for extreme or trivial cases).
4. Since the social science enterprise is an important feature of society, analysis of moral dilemmas should emphasize societal contributions as much as it does the relationships of investigators with colleagues, participants, students, institutional representatives, clients, patients, and the like.

Ethical Dilemmas and Social Science Research is organized around a review of three dilemmas, with major attention given to the dilemma associated with the use of human participants in research, a recurrent problem for most investigators. Attention is also given to the social scientist's role in society (the citizen-scientist dilemma) and to his or her ability to affect the practical application of scientific knowledge.

Although published work on moral, legal, and political philosophies is voluminous and a number of statements exist regarding the ethical behavior of social and medical investigators, they do not provide serious social scientists with a useful framework for making their own decisions. Those available works tend to be personal statements or philosophies (Kelman, 1968; Kennedy, 1975; Smith, 1969), reviews of situations where individual social scientists confronted a personal ethical dilemma (such as the several thousand cases systematically assembled and consulted in developing the principles for the American Psychological Association, 1973; Rynkiewich and Spradley, 1976), treatments of special research activities or specific studies (Bermant, Kelman, and Warwick, 1978; Rivlin and Timpane, 1975; Sjoberg, 1967), or discussions of the rules that will promote "ethical behavior" of social scientists—by the standards of the authors (Diener and Crandall, 1978). Even the major review of case materials related to research with human participants (Katz, 1972) fails to provide an explicit strategy for analysis of potential problems.

This book differs from these others in several important aspects. First, it is deliberately designed to provide assistance to a social scientist seeking guidance in analyzing a moral dilemma; the emphasis is on the major factors, arguments, and issues generally considered relevant to completing an analysis and arriving at a decision. Second, there are no prescriptive statements, no discussions of what is required or prohibited if a social scientist is to be morally correct or a "good person." Third, there is no evaluation of any research activity or individual social scientist. Although numerous examples emphasized in ethical controversy are discussed (a balanced treatment requires that some be analyzed in detail), the objective is to review the factors that are important to the moral dilemmas rather than to provide examples of commendable or reprehensible behavior. Finally, while many references are taken from biomedical investigations, the major focus is on the social science enterprise. The fundamental issues may be the same for both social science and biomedical research, but the applications are somewhat different, primarily because of the more dramatic, unequivocal effects—positive and negative—for both research participants and society associated with biomedical investigations.

The complexity of mechanisms for satisfying nonscientists (or their representatives) that the rights and welfare of participants are given appropriate consideration will be clear to any investigator actively engaged in research (or from a review of this book). Although designed to assist social scientists in understanding the rationale and justification for these mechanisms, the following discussion cannot provide a current treatment on the details of administrative or legal requirements—they change too fast for any description to be current. The most recent information will be available from the administrative units handling federal requirements, the Office for the Protection from Research Risks (or its current equivalent) within the Department of Health, Education, and Welfare, or from legal counsel specializing in this area.

Completion of this work has involved the study of a multitude of complex issues and abstract intellectual frameworks. Confidence to pursue the problem has come from the recurring controversies over "ethical" issues in which combatants often seem to have nothing in common except emotional agitation. Encouragement to complete the work has come from several sources, including Pauline and Thomas Bouchard, Don McTavish, Ira Reiss, Roberta Simmons, and June and Robert Tapp, as well as various graduate seminars and faculty groups where parts of the analysis were presented. The speed and conscientiousness of Helen Keefe in typing various drafts of the work were of considerable help.

Portions of this work, particularly Chapter Twelve and Appendices 4, 5, and 6 (which are composites developed from a review of a number of ethical codes) were originally prepared by the author for a report for the United Nations Economic, Social, and Cultural Organization (UNESCO) in 1975 under the title "Value Dilemmas Associated with the Development and Application of Social Science." They are included with the permission of UNESCO.

Minneapolis, Minnesota   PAUL DAVIDSON REYNOLDS
August 1979

Contents

Tables

The Author

PAUL DAVIDSON REYNOLDS is associate professor of sociology at the University of Minnesota in Minneapolis. He previously taught at the University of California, Riverside, and at San Francisco State.

Reynolds completed his undergraduate education (in engineering) at the University of Kansas (1960) and was awarded three graduate degrees from Stanford University: the master's of business administration degree (1964), the master's degree in (social) psychology (1966), and the doctoral degree in sociology (1969).

Reynolds is the author of *A Primer in Theory Construction* and of several journal articles. He has directed experimental research on small group processes and supervised an evaluation of neighborhood service agencies for youth, which included survey-based estimates of victimization. Since 1971, he has pursued writing, research, and consulting on ethical issues (the latter two for UNESCO and the International Social Science Council).

At the University of Minnesota he is helping to develop graduate training in applied sociology and attempting to determine the extent to which social science provides an "understanding of everyday life."

Ethical Dilemmas and Social Science Research

An Analysis of Moral Issues
Confronting Investigators
in Research Using Human Participants

The true and lawful goal of the sciences is none other than this: that human life be enriched with new discoveries and powers.

Francis Bacon
Novum Organum
Aphorism LXXI

1

Ethical Dilemmas:
The Issues and
Sources of Solutions

The development and application of social science appears to be more complex than Bacon's suggestion. A variety of issues, often referred to as moral or ethical problems, have led to controversy and ambiguity regarding the best way to enrich human life with social science. These questions include:

- Is it unethical not to acquire participants' informed consent for all research? Are there any exceptions?
- When is potential stress or discomfort for research participants justified?
- What are the limits of an investigator's responsibility for participants?
- Should promises of confidentiality always be kept or should investigators divulge information obtained in confidence from

1

participants if they feel this would discourage public wrongdoing by others?

- Should investigators provide willing cooperation with the human subject committees (or institutional review boards) that evaluate and approve research? What are the benefits of such procedures?
- If social scientists are providing valued contributions to society, should not their research data have legal protection (similar to that of other professionals)?
- What type of relationship should a social scientist attempt to develop, as part of the scientific enterprise, with society? Are societal reactions to different professional orientations likely to vary?
- Should social scientists take responsibility for the applications of scientific knowledge? Is responsibility increased when the investigator has contributed directly to the creation of the knowledge?
- What can a social scientist do when he or she anticipates an application of scientific knowledge that will not be in the public interest? What might be the personal repercussions of different actions?

These and similar questions can be subsumed within three general dilemmas encountered by social scientists:

1. *Research Dilemma:* How to proceed when the development of knowledge—that may benefit mankind—involves research procedures that may infringe upon the rights and welfare of individuals?
2. *Scientist-Citizen Dilemma:* What orientations help to minimize complications associated with incongruencies between scientific obligations and the responsibilities of citizenship?
3. *Application of Knowledge Dilemma:* What responses are available to scientists when scientific knowledge may be utilized to achieve goals inconsistent with their personal values?

A fourth problem, a major concern for both the scientific community and society as a whole, is related to the first dilemma:

4. *Conduct of Research Quandary:* What societal mechanisms or collective guidelines provide assurance to the general public and

scientific investigators that the resolution of the research dilemma will be morally acceptable?

These four issues provide the framework for this book; much attention to specific instances of these problems is involved.

Social scientists may encounter moral dilemmas in their own work infrequently; most professional and research decisions are probably made without conscious attention to their usually inconsequential moral implications. If, however, a social scientist did confront a moral dilemma and wished assistance in resolving it, it is not clear where or how he or she could find assistance in developing a solution or gaining confidence that the decision was correct or at least acceptable. He or she might look to the ethical commentaries within the social science literature, to social science research on values and moral orientations, or to writings on moral, legal, and political philosophy.

Discussions of moral or ethical dilemmas in the social science literature seem to have several dominant features. Foremost is the wide range of positions and judgments expressed by social scientists, the following comments reflect this lack of consensus:

A popular mode of social-psychological research ... centers on trickery that ranges from harmless clownery to the downright diabolical (Rubin, 1970, p. 18).

Although for everything there is a season and a time and for every purpose under heaven, for a given season and time an action can be judged as evil. ... The influence of the research psychologists, such as it is, great or small, should be used as a positive moral vector and not a negative one (Baumrind, 1971, p. 890).

Whenever someone is oppressed, an "establishment" sociologist seems to lurk in the background, providing the facts which make oppression more efficient

Misinformation is employed ...; illusion is used when necessary in order to set the stage for the revelation of certain difficult to get-at truths (Milgram, 1974, p. 198).

Concern about "professional integrity" ... is symptomatic of a dying discipline. Let the clergy worry about keeping their cassocks clean; the scientist has too great a responsibility for such compulsions (Humphreys, 1970b, p. 168)!

Many sociologists would rather engage in rhetoric than in research, in political moralizing than in rigorous study related to social problems, and in ... criticism

and the theory which makes it legitimate to the larger constituency
(Becker and Horowitz, 1972, p.
48).

of peers rather than in critical
analysis of major social problems. . . . Such deportment dilutes
the . . . strength of the discipline
by confusing ideological special
pleading with the labor of developing and disseminating basic
knowledge . . . requisite for the
emergence of a new and better
society (Larsen, 1975, p. 10).

Unfortunately, the more critical the dilemma—the greater the uncertainty about the appropriate course of action—the less agreement can be expected among social scientists.

Discussions of moral or ethical issues by social scientists appear to reflect something other than intellectual analysis or simple
expressions of opinion. Those who speak or write about these
problems frequently voice considerable anguish over situations
they have confronted or the behavior of other social scientists and
then strongly recommend that certain actions be taken—if only to
relieve personal feelings, occasionally acute, of guilt. This personal
identification and emotional intensity give discussions of moral
dilemmas a special character; it often appears that the analysis is
developed to justify predetermined subjective judgments. One
strategy for accomplishing this is to specify rules or standards, inconsistent with the events creating the moral guilt, and then claim
these guidelines represent the accepted principles for professional
behavior, "proving" the actions immoral or unethical, given their
dictionary definition (actions inconsistent with accepted norms or
practices). Such discussions are usually so personal and deal with
such idiosyncratic situations that a general strategy for resolving
other dilemmas cannot be developed.

Another potential source of assistance is social science research on values or moral orientations. A major research program
on values (interpreted as desired states of existence or modes of
conduct) involved measures of value hierarchies of typical American adults and members of scientific faculties (Rokeach, 1973).
Faculty in biological, physical, and social sciences give about equal
emphasis to the values of wisdom, freedom, and equality; thus, if

attaining scientific wisdom required unequal treatment and constraints on the freedom of research participants, a serious dilemma
could arise. Academic scientists also gave about equal emphasis to
the values of wisdom and world peace; they might then confront
a dilemma if they felt that an increase in scientific wisdom would
jeopardize opportunities for attaining world peace. While such interpretations have a bearing on the dilemmas selected for attention
in this book, summary measures of value hierarchies (rank orders
of eighteen values) for aggregates of individuals may or may not
reflect incongruencies confronted by specific individuals.

Several programs of research have dealt directly with the
moral orientation or social philosophy of individuals. The six
moral development stages (organized into three levels) proposed
by Kohlberg (1976) are designed to describe the natural development of individuals as they reach the maximum level of moral
maturity (based on Tapp and Kohlberg, 1977):

- The *preconventional level* emphasizes "good" and "bad" in terms
  of physical consequences; stage one focuses on punishment (or
  its avoidance) and stage two on a hedonistic strategy that maxi-
  mizes immediate rewards and minimizes suffering of any kind.
- The *conventional level* emphasizes support of the rules or authority in any social system; stage three focuses on conformity
  to the wishes of immediate associates to gain approval and stage
  four on respect and obedience to the standards and laws of the
  greater society.
- The *postconventional level* emphasizes conformity to principles
  apart from the individuals involved; stage five (social contract)
  focuses upon adherence to rules developed by the whole society
  because the procedures were acceptable and stage six (universal ethic) on decisions of right based on culture-free principles
  that appeal on the basis of logical comprehensiveness, univer-
  sality, and consistency.

Although Kohlberg (1971) has suggested that this hierarchy
of development is a cultural universal and represents the "morally
correct" sequence, the argument suffers from a number of problems. First, there are the complications associated with the "natu-

ralistic fallacy"—an assumption that the patterns repeatedly found in nature represent moral good—reviewed by Alston (1971) and Peters (1971). Second, there is very little evidence in the public domain (much of the research on the Kohlberg perspective is unpublished) regarding the empirical support for the sequence of moral stages and almost no evidence regarding the distribution of moral orientations among typical adults. Some suggestive evidence indicates that the factors most highly related to level of moral orientation are educational attainment and intelligence (Rest, 1976); for example, graduate students in moral philosophy and political science tend to use more advanced moral justifications than those with less formal education, even mature adults. Third, this perspective assumes that the sole source of variation in the analysis of moral dilemmas will be a characteristic of the individual (an assumption shared with Hogan, 1973); there is very little analysis of variation associated with different types of moral dilemmas. This leads to substantial problems in achieving interobserver agreement on the moral stage of individuals (Haan, Smith, and Block, 1968; Holstein, 1976; Kurtines and Greif, 1974; Leming, 1974; Podd, 1972). Fourth, available evidence suggests the existence of unusual relationships between moral orientation and the behavior of individuals (Haan, Smith, and Block, 1968; Leming, 1974). The empirical patterns are also causally ambiguous: the moral orientation may have developed after the behavior occurred. Other evidence suggests—at least for children and adolescents—that the characteristics of the situation are at least as important as any personal trait or orientation in dealing with a fundamental moral behavior like honesty (Burton, 1976). This is consistent with the substantial evidence indicating an ambiguous relationship between individual attitudes and behavior (Deutscher, 1973; Liska, 1975; Wicker, 1969).

Perhaps the most fundamental problem with applying the stages of moral development (Kohlberg, 1973a, 1973b), moral judgment as a personality dimension (Hogan, 1970), or various value hierarchies (Rokeach, 1973) to dilemmas in the social sciences is that all are described in such ambiguous terms that almost any action or behavior in a specific situation would be consistent with one or more stages, personality traits, or values. In fact, the basic research strategy in studies of moral orientation focuses upon the justification for a particular decision, not the actual decision itself (Piaget, 1932; Kohlberg, 1958). In sum, this knowledge on moral or value orientations cannot be used as a guide for resolving serious dilemmas, although it may suggest alternative justifications or issues for consideration.

The types of dilemmas now being confronted by social scientists have received attention for centuries by those concerned with general problems in moral, legal, and political philosophy. Confidence in the strategies and guidelines for developing solutions to moral dilemmas will be substantially increased by an understanding of the basis for various philosophical orientations. For this reason, the book begins with a review of these orientations (Chapter Two), illustrating their importance in applications to the specific problems confronting social scientists. Those who wish to move immediately to a discussion of specific dilemmas could skip to Part One, but the rationale for the analysis is presented in Chapter Two.

An extensive discussion of research dilemmas related to different types of research procedures is the focus of Part One; five issues are developed to aid in analysis of specific research activities. Because of the importance of the research dilemma and the public's lack of confidence in the ability of investigators to provide acceptable solutions, a number of mechanisms have developed for creating "societal solutions" to dilemmas associated with specific research projects; such mechanisms are the focus of Part Two. Both the scientist-citizen and application of knowledge dilemma involve the relationship of scientists to the greater society, and considerations associated with their resolution are reviewed in Part Three. All discussions are designed to provide a review of the factors or issues that might be considered by social scientists in developing a personal solution to these dilemmas; no attempt is made to dictate either behavior or perspectives. The right answer for each individual is the one that he or she finds personally acceptable.

2

Moral, Legal, and
Political Issues

The ethical arguments of social scientists involve the application
of ideas developed in response to more general issues in moral,
legal, and political philosophy. This chapter therefore provides a
background to the analysis pursued in the remainder of the book
by discussing these more general issues, the most widely accepted
resolutions for them, and how they are related to the three major
dilemmas confronted by social scientists. Because of the importance associated with the involvement of individuals in research,
special attention is given to the explication, justification, and application of human rights.

Major Issues in Moral and Legal Philosophy

Three major issues, relevant to the focus of this book, are
treated in moral and legal philosophy. They are (1) the justification
for various political systems; the rationale that is, or should be, the

basis for arrangements between the citizens and the state; (2) the criteria to be used to evaluate government legislation, programs, and policies within a political state; and (3) the standards an individual should follow in order to be moral, good, or ethical. A review of the most widely accepted solutions to these issues is complicated by two "meta-issue" problems, not directly related to the issues themselves.

For the first of these metatheoretical problems—lack of consensus on criteria for an acceptable solution—three strategies seem to dominate. One is to develop fundamental principles or basic assumptions that can or should be shared by all. From these principles a number of specific directives are deduced, that is, are adopted as standards on the basis of acceptance of the initial assumptions. Those highly committed to this strategy tend to emphasize "fundamental values" and to suggest that the "ends do not justify the means" (Kant [1797], 1965; Nozick, 1974; Rawls, 1971). An alternative strategy is to consider the effects of different actions and policies, each situation being seen as a separate case. Those actions or procedures that provide the most satisfactory solution, by some criteria, are considered the most important. The focus is upon the effects of the action rather than adherence to a set of principles developed from basic assumptions and universally applied (Mill [1863], 1971; Fletcher, 1966).

Still another strategy, particularly associated with legal philosophy, is to develop a framework that is consistent with personal, intuitive judgments about right and wrong (or the "reflective equilibrium" of Rawls, 1971). It may include appeals to evidence about the standards accepted in society—reference to legislation or legal decisions is very common. However, for those who wish to develop a set of moral principles that are both logically consistent and congruent with accepted standards regarding morality, this strategy could prove frustrating. Evidence from the empirical study of individual values (Rokeach, 1973, p. 58) suggests that not only do individuals adopt value structures that are inconsistent but they do not consider logical consistency as particularly important, ranking it low as a desirable personal attribute. Hence, an explicit, internally consistent moral philosophy compatible with the intuitive judgments of a majority of ordinary individuals may be an unattainable ideal.

The second major problem—application of the same philosophical framework to different issues—is clearest in relation to the questions of criteria for societal action and standards for individual morality. There are many situations where an individual is expected to take actions for the benefit of the greater society—for example, restraining and incarcerating criminals—that may be inconsistent with various moral guides for individual behavior. While a single philosophical framework that could provide solutions (by whatever criteria) to both types of issues might have some advantages, it has not yet been developed and could result in an unwieldy intellectual structure that would be impossible to comprehend or apply. The absence of a "grand theory" to resolve all issues does, however, encourage the development of "issue specific theories" that may—for actions or procedures relevant to more than one type of issue—result in inconsistent moral directives. The result can be uncertainty about the right or moral response to the situation, and this particular type of dilemma is a major problem for many social scientists. Following a review of widely accepted solutions to the three major issues outlined at the beginning of this chapter—justification for a political system, criteria for societal action, and standards for individual morality—inconsistencies between solutions and their reflection in the dilemmas confronted by social scientists will be considered.

Justification for a Political System

A fundamental issue associated with the political organization of any society is the justification for that particular political order. One approach is to assume that the existing system is a reflection of "God's will" or a "natural order" (Olafson, 1961). A major alternative, at least in the history of Western societies, has been social contract theories that emphasize the agreements among the individuals involved—the citizens and/or the rulers. The major thrust of these theories of political obligation has been "to explain the nature and limits of allegiance owed by subjects to the state, and of the right on the part of the state or its government to control the lives of its citizens" (Gough, 1957, p. 244). Two major types of analyses are associated with social contract theory.

The first considers the agreements developed among un-
affiliated individuals who join to form a new society—those in the
"original position." It involves speculation on the nature of the
joint agreement that would be made among these individuals,
more properly called a "compact" or "articles of association" than
a contract (which implies a means to force compliance). In such
analyses the assumption is usually made that the final form of the
compact or agreement should be universally accepted—no dis-
senting votes—although the agreement might include the condition that future decisions regarding details be made by a majority.
An issue central to all such analyses is the nature of the liberties,
rights, or privileges forgone by the citizens and assigned to the state
(either a monarch or representatives of the people). The social contract theory as a literal interpretation of the origin of organized
societies has long since been abandoned, and the analysis of the
"original position" is now considered purely speculative.

A second form of the social contract analysis concerns the
relationship between the citizens and the legislative group or monarch responsible for the administration of the political state. In this
form it emphasizes the reciprocal rights and obligations associated
with each role—subject and ruler. The general strategy is to specify
the privileges and responsibilities forgone by the citizens (and
placed in trust with the governing agency) and the benefits they
would receive in return, usually good government and protection
from external threat. The argument goes that if the citizens do
not honor and respect their obligations, they can be punished. If
the rulers do not honor and respect their obligations, the citizens
need not acquiesce to their demands—the people need not obey
a tyrant.

Whatever the form of the social contract analysis, a major
issue is the apportionment of liberties (or rights) between the individual and the state (Coleman, 1974). Practically the entire range
of alternatives is represented here. Some writers suggest that all
individual rights and liberties should be given up to the state in the
original contract, but for different reasons. Rousseau ([1762], 1972)
and Rawls (1971) assume that the state would be administered by
responsible individuals who would not abuse their position or privilege but would use their power to the best interests of all con-

cerned. (Whether the citizens would share this perspective is not clear.) In contrast, Hobbes (1651) assumed that man is naturally violent, destructive, and competitive and that a "war of all against all" can be prevented only if the state has maximum control over the individual.

Others would limit the responsibilities of the state more severely. Locke ([1690], 1966) proposed that the government should have the responsibility for guaranteeing the right to life, liberty, and personal property for individual citizens, but should also retain control over the regulation of force within the society and the negotiation of war and peace with other political units. (Because the philosophy of Locke was widely known and accepted among English-speaking peoples by the early part of the eighteenth century, his ideas had a major influence upon many of the constitutions created in the original American colonies, including the Constitution of the United States.) Nozick (1974) would also restrict the state to a monopoly on regulation of force, negotiation with other political states (or "protective associations"), and the redistribution of property if the process of acquisition was somehow unjust. All persons would be entitled to the benefits of property achieved through the voluntary contributions of others (the "entitlement theory"), even though inequities of wealth might develop.

Concern with the problem of how individuals can protect themselves against unjust actions of a government with substantial power leads to a different perspective on this problem. Coleman (1974) suggests that not only should the allocation of responsibilities over rights be carefully delineated but multiple political corporations should be developed to represent unique collections of individuals—multiple social contracts. This would provide the citizen with some form of protection against the despotic actions of any one "corporate administration," although it is not clear what mechanisms would prevent collusion among various "corporate administrators."

The importance of the various analyses related to social contract theory lies not only in their attention to the problems associated with the legitimation or justification of the political state but in their concern with the "natural rights" of the individual citizens, rights they hold in their "natural" state before the social contract is established. The notion that such rights are absolutely inviolate, not to be abridged for any reason or purpose, no matter how worthy, becomes very important with respect to the constraints that may be placed upon activities that will benefit all citizens in a society.

Criteria for Societal Programs

Assuming that people have accepted a form of political organization as legitimate, either because a satisfactory social contract has developed or because they believe it is "God's will," a separate issue is the nature of the criteria to be used in the development of legislation and government programs. One major orientation—utilitarianism—was created specifically to deal with this issue. Widely known because of its applications to economic decisions, the utilitarian approach has a considerable history (Bentham, 1789; Frankena, 1963; Fried, 1974; Mill [1863], 1971; Rawls, 1971; Rescher, 1966). Utilitarianism in general emphasizes maximization of some type of value or utility for all members of society the maximum good for the greatest number, or the "greatest happiness" principle. Application of this strategy involves attention to two critical issues; for each alternative (legislation or program) it is necessary to estimate the net value (benefits less costs) and distribution (homogeneous versus heterogeneous) of the effects for members of society.

In elementary form, application involves identification of the effects of a particular course of action, estimating both the total benefits and total costs to all members of the social system and, if benefits exceed costs, recommending that the action be initiated. When a utilitarian strategy is used to develop a general set of standards or principles, it is referred to as "rule-utilitarianism"; when adopted as a guide to specific actions or behaviors that an individual might consider as alternatives, it is called "act-utilitarianism." A utilitarian analysis has its greatest appeal in situations where the costs and benefits can be identified, measured with little difficulty, and algebraically summed to allow calculation of the total benefit (or cost) expected from a particular course of action. For example, the value of a public works project (such as a new highway) can be estimated by using this procedure. Further, if there are several alternatives (different routes for the highway), the benefit-to-cost ratio of each alternative can be calculated to determine which of the alternative routes will lead to the greatest net benefits.

Even with relatively straightforward public works examples, however, many problems are apparent—identifying and measuring all possible costs and benefits, determining the individuals who will be affected by the action to be taken, and—most crucial of all—being able to aggregate the measures of costs and benefits so that one figure represents the net utility, or good, associated with the action. It is true that there are some situations where translation of all effects (positive and negative) into one measure is not absolutely necessary. For example, when comparing the effects of alternative solutions to the same problem, it may be sufficient to show that one solution produces more benefits and lower costs than any other alternative, considering each specific benefit and cost separately; this is a variation of the "Pareto optimum" (Koopmans, 1957, p. 42). In such situations the need for a common measure of utility is an elegant, but unnecessary, requirement. However, if a pattern of benefits and costs is inconsistent among alternatives, or the issue is one of comparing completely different programs—each designed to deal with a different kind of problem—then a benefit-to-cost ratio requiring that all effects be aggregated into a single value is a useful summary measure.

There are other problems on the philosophical level, the most important of which refers to the distribution of the costs and benefits among those affected by a given action since the major emphasis of utilitarian analysis is on increasing the total amount of net benefits to the entire aggregate. This problem of selecting a satisfactory distribution of benefit—honor, economic benefits, privileges—is often referred to as the problem of justice or distributive justice when specifically related to divisible goods. General acceptance of a utilitarian analysis appears to be greatest when each individual suffers a small cost and all individuals receive benefits greater than their costs. For example, if a water distribution system is to be installed in a community, each property owner must contribute tax money and tolerate some inconvenience in return for an adequate supply of sanitary water for everyday use and emergencies (such as fires). The contributions of each individual are considerably less than if he or she attempted to achieve similar benefits acting independently.

The problem of justice arises when costs and benefits are distributed unevenly, with a small group either bearing unusually high costs or receiving unusually large benefits. For example, in the construction of a new highway some individuals may lose their homes—a high cost for a small number of individuals—and others, those with property adjoining the freeway, may experience unusually high benefits in increased land values. A sense of injustice may develop in either case, even though the total "utility" for all affected individuals may clearly be positive.

There are a number of ways to respond to this problem:

1. Restrict analysis to the problem of maximizing the total utility and let others take responsibility for solving the problem of distributive justice.
2. Attempt to modify the utilitarian strategy so that the "maximization of utility" principle can be integrated with other criteria that will lead to satisfactory solutions of both problems—increasing total benefits and ensuring a just distribution.
3. Abandon the utilitarian orientation completely and attempt to develop another philosophical perspective that will solve the distribution problem.
4. Explicate the important values or principles to be promoted by a decision and work out necessary compromises intuitively, on a case-by-case basis, without attempting to develop general principles that can be applied to a wide range of similar situations.

The first strategy, to ignore issues of distribution of benefits and costs, has been seriously proposed by the economists Kaldor (1939) and Hicks (1939) and may be a suitable solution for this professional group, since they have developed numerous elegant techniques for maximizing economic values. But no such techniques have been developed for ensuring a just allocation of effects or even measuring the distribution of utility.

To give one example of the second strategy, Rescher (1966) concludes that a modified form of a utilitarian analysis, maximizing the "effective average" (as represented by a formula), is appropriate when (1) there is a utility economy; (2) it is not an economy of scarcity (resources are at least adequate to support all members of society); (3) there is a fixed amount of utility that is divisible; (4) all recipients have equal claims to a share of the "goods"; and (5) all recipients are deserving (none is morally unredeeming). The "effective average" is one of several schemes, referred to collectively as "average-utilitarianism," that emphasize a more equal distribution of effects than might be anticipated from strict utilitarianism. Both the distribution of effects and the total net benefits are considered in such analyses.

Rawls (1971) provides a serious attempt at the third alternative, development of a philosophical orientation to replace the utilitarian strategy. Realizing that the utilitarian strategy has been the most widely adopted perspective for evaluating economic and social programs that affect entire societies, Rawls has attempted to develop an analysis that will lead to alternative solutions. His analysis starts with a sophisticated version of the "original position" in social contract theory—the decisions to be made by a group of rational, mature individuals planning to form a society.* These persons, it is assumed, expect to form a society to which all will contribute. But in advance of a final joint commitment, they must formalize not only the principles used to assign the rights, duties, and liberties associated with the basic institutions but also the appropriate distribution of benefits and burdens associated with social cooperation. Furthermore, in order for the original situation to be "fair," it is also assumed that these individuals are ignorant

*Speculation on the agreement reached in the "original position" is only one standard used to evaluate the principle of justice. Rawls (1971, p. 579) comments that "justification rests upon the entire conception and how it fits in with and organizes our considered judgments in reflective equilibrium. As we have noted before, justification is a matter of the mutual support of many considerations, of everything fitting together into one coherent view." In short, the results of the analysis of the rational decision in the "original position" are tempered, in some subjective fashion, by other judgments based on any number of factors. This leads to a suspicion that the entire structure is a rationalization of a personal philosophy adopted by Rawls prior to the analysis of the "original situation," particularly in view of the complexity and ambiguity of the presentation in *A Theory of Justice* (1971).

of their role in the new society, the degree of their natural endowments or abilities, and the generation—initial founders or descendants—in which they will participate in the society. (This last assumption helps to resolve the ambiguities that arise when individuals have to honor agreements made by previous generations.)

Rawls concludes, on the basis of introspection, that "rational" individuals in the original situation would arrive at two principles:

1. Each person is to have an equal right to the most extensive total system of equal basic liberties compatible with a similar system of liberty for all.
2. Social and economic inequalities are to be arranged so that they are both to the greatest benefit of the least advantaged and attached to offices and positions open to all under conditions of fair equality or opportunity.

In addition, these individuals would agree that the first principle takes priority over the second (liberty can be restricted only for the sake of liberty, presumably of another kind) and that both principles take priority over a criterion of efficiency (utilitarianism).

Rawls (1971, p. 303) summarizes his general conception as follows: "All social primary goods—liberty and opportunity, income and wealth, and the basis of self-respect—are to be distributed equally unless an unequal distribution of any or all of these goods is to the advantage of the least favored." Rawls chiefly devotes his analysis to showing how this strategy would affect the form and procedures of social institutions in a "well-ordered society" in ways that are different than if those institutions were based on other moral or political philosophies, primarily utilitarianism.

A major problem in Rawls' scheme, however, is the nature of the administration of society (Coleman, 1974, 1976). Rawls does not consider the problem of how to ensure that those individuals administering the institutions could be trusted or would be responsive to the wishes of the citizens. Further, it is an empirical question whether or not an unorganized aggregate would adopt principles that reflect a desire to minimize potential costs rather than to maximize potential gains; most individuals do not take such a pessimistic attitude toward the future. It is also quite likely that the first issue for consideration among such a group would be the determination of the rights to be given to the state and those to be retained by individuals, the very issue that was dominant in the construction of the United States Constitution and the Bill of Rights.

What is important for present purposes is that Rawls' analysis results in a rank ordering of three basic criteria: equality of liberty; social and economic equality, or improvement of the situation of the least advantaged (most disadvantaged); and maximization of value or utility (efficiency). Rawls never makes it clear just what is included in his conception of "liberty," but it seems fair to assume that it is quite similar to the "natural rights" that other contract theorists have considered to be important for individuals.

The final strategy for solving the problem of justice, namely, intuitionism, is described by Rawls (1971) as the creation of explicit principles—for example, the maximization of utility (efficiency) and the achievement of justice (in distribution)—in the absence of clear rules for determining the priority of these principles. As a result, there is no way to establish a clear preference for specific alternatives when a choice is available. While this strategy may lack a satisfactory intellectual structure, it may not be inaccurate as a general description of the judgments produced within the legal system, as reflected in legislation and court decisions.

Whatever strategies should be used to develop criteria for evaluating societal problems, it is clear that the most widely used strategy has been utilitarianism, tempered by concerns that have limited the kinds of problems to which it has been applied (such as problems of criminal justice) and its extreme effects in some cases (an intuitive form of average utilitarianism is often found).

Standards for Individual Moral Behavior

The issue of individual morality, or those standards a person should accept to have confidence that he or she is living a good or moral life, is the third major problem area; the general issue is one of selecting criteria (or standards) for determining the actions an individual should take when confronted by a moral or ethical decision. Three general strategies have been developed for resolving this problem: (1) adherence to a set of specific, abstract rules (deontological theories); (2) evaluation of the effects of alternative actions (teleological theories); and (3) rejection of any sort of formal principles or analysis, relying on instinctive responses to specific situations.

Adherence to Rules (Deontological)

Of the two major types of deontological theories, one is closely associated with the work of Kant ([1797], 1965). The basis of Kant's moral views is an emphasis on collective rationality and on the importance of moral laws as "categorical imperatives" (Brandt, 1959; Frankena, 1963; Fried, 1974; Macklin and Sherwin, 1975). A categorical imperative is a principle or statement that defines appropriate action in all situations and to which adherence is expected as a matter of duty.

Kant suggests that three principles should guide individual adoption of categorical imperatives. First, only principles that one would wish to have universally implemented should be followed, "Would I . . . be satisfied to have my maxim considered a universal law?" (Kant, [1785] 1938, p. 18), or in other words, do as you would have all others do. Second, "act so that in your own person as well as . . . every other you are treating mankind . . . as an end, never merely as a means" (Kant, [1785] 1938, p. 47); in other words, an individual should never be "used" to achieve goals that do not give primary consideration to the individual's own goals. Third, all individuals, acting rationally on these first two principles, will make similar analyses in similar situations and come to the same conclusions. Therefore, an isolated individual, acting logically and utilizing the two major principles, can assume that any principles that he or she develops would be shared by others and, hence, should be considered equivalent to principles formally adopted by a legislature. Just as individuals have a duty to follow formally developed laws, they also have a duty to follow any categorical imperatives that they develop on their own, because they can assume that the same principles would be adopted by people in general.

So rigid was Kant's original position that he even suggested that commitment to principles was more important than the survival of humanity. In considering the reduction of punishment for criminals who consent to participate in dangerous experiments, Kant ([1797], 1965, p. 100) comments that this would amount to the destruction of legal justice, and that "if legal justice perishes, then it is no longer worthwhile for men to remain alive on this earth." Kant's position of an "eye for an eye" is in marked contrast to the suggestions regarding punishment derived from utilitarian considerations. According to Mill ([1863], 1971, p. 52), punishment should be "the least that will suffice to prevent [a criminal] from repeating, and others from imitating, his misconduct." Current adherence to such a position is represented by Fried (1978, p. 2): "We must do no wrong—even if by doing wrong, suffering would be reduced and the sum of happiness increased."

Utilitarianism is in fact the second major orientation for producing a set of rules for individual behavior. Presumably individuals who have confidence in the process used to create the rules and to ensure widespread adherence to such standards will follow them. (Stopping for stop signs at empty corners, and so forth.) While the source of such principles is somewhat different from that of the categorical imperatives, the result is not much different in terms of specific actions in specific situations.

A more subtle orientation, in the form of a set of constraints rather than rules for action, develops from a social contract matrix. This analysis implies that individual rights should be respected by other members of the society and that the state has an obligation to ensure that this will occur. Hence, respect for the rights of others can act as a constraint upon actions one might take; for example, refraining from physical assault, invasion of privacy, and use of property without consent. While such constraints do not allow one to predict the actions of a moral person in a specific situation, they do allow one to predict what a moral person *will not do*—he or she will not infringe upon the rights of others.

Evaluation of Outcome (Teleological)

The second major strategy for resolving the problems associated with individual behavior is to consider the possible out-

comes and then to act in such a way that some outcome or benefit
will be maximized. At least two different frameworks share this
orientation, act-utilitarianism and situation ethics.

If utilitarianism is applied to specific situations, where the
directive is to maximize the net good resulting from specific actions,
it is referred to as act-utilitarianism. This is different from rule-
utilitarianism in that it is the individual confronted with a problem
who is expected to make a judgment based on comparisons of total
costs and benefits associated with different alternatives. (Rule-
utilitarianism assumes that this calculation will be completed by
others, whether legislators, moral leaders, or administrators.) For
some situations, act-utilitarianism might be too complex to be prac-
ticable, particularly where the consequences of an action are subtle
or unpredictable (as in many research situations); the "cost" of calculation may result in the abandonment of a utilitarian analysis,
except in a very cursory form.

Another approach for dealing with unique sets of conditions
is found in situation ethics (Fletcher, 1966, 1967; Cox, 1968; Cunningham, 1970). Proposed by and widely discussed among religious ethicists, it emphasizes the importance of "love"—in the
sense of a mature compassion for humanity—as a dominant value
more important than specific principles. While not insisting that
universal standards or rules should be abandoned, the thrust of
the argument is that the range of real life situations is too great
for rigid application of rules and that some other criterion should
be available, one that allows individuals to act in good conscience
and with respect for others as individuals. Like act-utilitarianism,
situation ethics opposes the popular notion that "the ends do not
justify the means." Attempts to evaluate the outcome of effects of
different actions are oriented toward the idea that "only the ends
justify the means; nothing else" (Fletcher, 1967, p. 21). There are
numerous situations, however, where the thoughtless application
of such principles could lead to unsatisfactory or, at the very least,
inconsistent results.

Instinct

A third strategy, referred to as instinctual reaction, is presented by Prichard (1912). He suggests that most moral philoso-

phies (regardless of their form) are designed to provide a "proof"—
in the sense of a relevant, abstract intellectual structure—that will
satisfy the individual's need to justify his or her instinctive realization that a given action is appropriate. Because they do little to
provide such an instinctive satisfaction, elaborate, explicit, intellectual frameworks are superfluous. In concluding his argument, Prichard (1912, p. 37) suggests that "if we do doubt whether there is
really an obligation to originate (action) A in a situation B, the remedy lies not in any process of general thinking, but in getting face
to face with a particular situation B, and then directly appreciating
the obligation to originate (action) A in that situation."

It seems clear, then, that there are a variety of strategies an
individual might use to help develop alternatives to problems of
individual morality—or use to justify actions already taken. Some
of these strategies, however, might lead to alternatives that are inconsistent with the solutions to the societal problems; this is reviewed in the concluding section of this chapter.

Human Rights: Justification

The most fundamental reason for a clear, unequivocal formal statement of human rights presented by those involved in political affairs is a concern that, without such a statement, individuals
in positions of public trust—responsible for governing society in
the public interest—will have a tendency to ignore, abuse, or fail
to defend the rights of ordinary citizens. Statements of human
rights reflect an attempt to provide a practical solution to the problem expressed by Lord Acton (1887): "Power tends to corrupt;
absolute power corrupts absolutely." Specification of the rights of
individuals provides a restriction on the privileges associated with
political power and may restrain the exercise of such power.

The development of constitutional guarantees of freedom
in Anglo-American law is marked by numerous examples of legal
documents that represent responses to both real and anticipated
abuses of political leaders. For example, the Magna Charta, signed
by the English King John in 1215, consists of sixty-three articles
representing a considerable range of "guarantees" designed to in-
hibit future abuse; these represent a mixture of the very general

and very specific. Two examples can be provided (Pound, 1957, pp. 117–129):

> 28. No constable or other bailiff of ours shall take corn or other provisions from anyone without immediately tendering money therefore, unless he can have postponement thereof by permission of the seller.
> 40. To no one will we sell, to no one will we refuse or delay, right to justice.

A comparable development was associated with the adoption of the Constitution by the thirteen former colonies. While the initial version of the Constitution referred to the right of life, liberty, property, and the pursuit of happiness, these were not considered sufficiently specific or complete (Findlay and Findlay, 1952); the result was the first ten amendments to the Constitution, the Bill of Rights. On the one hand, the Bill of Rights contains statements related to abstract rights, as in the First Amendment:

> Congress shall make no law respecting an establishment of religion, or prohibiting the free exercise thereof; or abridging the freedom of speech, or of the press; or of the right of the people peaceably to assemble, and to petition the government for a redress of grievances.

On the other hand, it contains specific prohibitions, as in the Third Amendment:

> No soldier shall, in time of peace, be quartered in any house without the consent of the owner; nor in time of war, but in a manner to be prescribed by law.

Both the Bill of Rights and the separation of power in the Constitution of the United States, also present in the constitutions of the various states, were attempts to ensure that respect for individual liberties would be maintained in the new governments. This reflects the familiarity of American colonial lawyers with English monarchs and the workings of centralized governments, where individual rights were frequently ignored (Pound, 1957).

Justifications for human rights provided by philosophers present a marked contrast to the practical, specific emphasis of legislators and politicians. One reason for this is the desire for an intellectual structure that can be used to justify (or explain) a variety of specific political systems, which may emphasize different individual rights. A second reason is the concern for an independent check on the "moral correctness" of an existing legal or political system; such an independent standard facilitates determination of the conditions under which civil disobedience or revolution is justified (Olafson, 1961). At least three types of justification for human rights have been developed by social philosophers: the "natural rights" argument, the social contract analysis, and application of utilitarian criteria.

The earliest justification for individual rights assumes that there is a system of rights that are "natural"; that is, they are part of the natural order and can be discovered—as if they were laws of physical phenomena—if the appropriate techniques are utilized (Olafson, 1961). A method for discovery was the comparison of positive laws (formal laws or laws widely accepted as valid) among various communities; those present in most communities were assumed to reflect universal natural laws. This type of analysis could then be used to evaluate the status of specific positive laws (those that were universal were seen as more congruent with natural laws and hence worthy of a higher degree of compliance) and to determine when civil disobedience or rebellion was justified—for example, when a sovereign imposed laws that could not be derived from natural laws.

Perhaps because of the problems in establishing natural laws or natural rights, an alternative strategy for determining the actual rights of individuals has been to speculate on how political systems are formed and on the nature of the contract that would emerge among those who participated in such a process. This analysis emphasizes an equitable exchange between individuals and the political state, focusing on a just allocation of rights and responsibilities between individuals and the political entity (or those who act for the political entity). Comparison of this analysis with actual political documents provides an empirical check on the usefulness of this argument. However, the use of a social contract analysis to speculate on what rational individuals "should do," as developed by Rawls (1971), can lead to more controversial conclusions, such as assuming that the potential citizens would agree to adopt programs that would infringe upon the rights of those with advantages if they would benefit the disadvantaged.

A utilitarian justification for rights and liberties is relatively easy to develop, although it might be difficult to realize in practice (Blake, 1925; Olafson, 1961). In brief, this view suggests that if the total "happiness" in a society is increased by allowing individuals freedom and autonomy with respect to certain matters (such as choice of occupation), then such rights should be guaranteed by legislation. If, on the other hand, individual autonomy with regard to a specific type of activity (such as environmental pollution) leads to a reduction in total "happiness," then legislation should be passed to restrain autonomy (reduce individual liberty) in this specific area.

A review of the arguments that might be used to justify a particular set of human rights suggests two important conclusions. First, there is considerable agreement on the nature of those human rights that should be established as universal. This is clear from the agreement among individuals with diverse philosophies on the rights stated in the Universal Declaration of Human Rights (See United Nations Economic, Social, and Cultural Organization, 1949). Second, the arguments for justification that are most likely to be accepted as valid in the United States and other developed countries are those associated with attempts to prevent abuses of power—the practical justification—in combination with some version of a social contract analysis—the philosophy reflected in the federal and state constitutions and widely accepted by many decision makers and ordinary individuals.

Human Rights: Specification and Application

The most explicit statements regarding the status of human rights are usually constitutions or similar documents formally adopted by governments and other political organizations; one such is the already mentioned Universal Declaration of Human Rights, adopted by the United Nations General Assembly on December 10, 1948. This document (see Appendix 1) is useful because it focuses exclusively on human rights instead of discussing them as one aspect of a political structure for a society. Two historical trends have been recognized in the development of this declaration (United Nations Economic, Social, and Cultural Organization, 1949). The first was the development of civil and political rights—freedom of thought, expression, conscience, worship, speech, assembly, association, and of the press—reflected in British, American, and French political documents as well as in Articles 1 through 21 of the UN declaration. The second trend, following the Industrial Revolution—which led to speculation that minimal standards of existence for all men might be feasible—involved development of the economic and social rights that are reflected in the constitutions of nations (many of them socialist) formed in the twentieth century and in Articles 22 through 29 of the UN declaration.

While this more recent orientation includes a shift in the right of property ownership from the individual to the state (a major change from the earlier emphasis upon individual property rights), it also includes an emphasis upon rights to education, health care, and a useful occupational role in society. Furthermore, much of the recent legislation in nations with constitutions emphasizing civil and political rights (in particular, England and the United States) has been designed to promote the social and economic rights that are incorporated as basic in the constitutions of the newer (socialist) nations. Regardless of the emphasis of their original constitutions, many nations—especially those that are industrialized—seem to be developing a broad range of rights for their citizens.

While the most useful evidence available regarding agreement on universal human rights, at least in terms of an ideal, is the United Nations declaration itself, the extent to which these rights can be realized by all citizens of the world—even in countries that promoted the adoption of the declaration—is a separate question. Two types of complications are apparent. First, the economic costs associated with some rights may require compromise. The universal right to adequate medical care, for example, may be difficult to realize in an overpopulated, developing country. Second, there is the question of the desirable characteristics of a complete, viable statement of human rights as an intellectual product. These would have to include completeness, incorporation of all rights considered important, precision of exposition to minimize confusion over the extent to which an individual's rights are realized in any particular situation, and consistency in application to avoid conflict between the rights of any two individuals. Even if the issue of economic feasibility is ignored, it is not clear that all these other desirable features are present in the United Nations declaration.

It seems reasonable to consider this declaration as an example of a relatively complete document, one that has the advantage of being approved by representatives of the majority of the world's population. But the second issue, that of unambiguous application of specific rights, is somewhat harder to resolve. There is no obvious way of ensuring that all individuals will interpret various rights in the same way other than clarity in the initial specification of the rights and their application to specific situations.

Philosophers in particular have given considerable attention to the third criterion, that is, consistency. Perhaps the simplest solution to the problem of potential inconsistencies among rights is to favor a very short list of rights. For example, Hart (1955) examines those rights that would exist for individuals in the absence of a political system and proposes that only one—the right to be free—satisfies all necessary criteria for a "natural right." More precisely, any human being capable of choice has the right to forbearance on the part of all others from the use of coercion or restraint against him or her save to hinder coercion or restraint, and is at liberty to do any action that is not one coercing or restraining or designed to injure other persons. Brown (1955) proposes that the only inalienable right—a right that cannot be voided or transferred to another—is the right to the protection of moral interests (life, liberty, property, and the pursuit of happiness) by the state. While this provides an unambiguous solution to the problem of specifying a basic right in the abstract—state protection of moral interests—it becomes somewhat less straightforward when applied to specific rights, many of which may be transferred or voided under special conditions (people may sign a contract to forego property rights or give up certain liberties when accepting occupational or martial responsibilities).

Another solution is to define rights as having different statuses, some being considered prima facie rights that a person has unless a more important right is present, in which case the more important right is to dominate (Frankena, 1952). For example, an individual has the right to be told the truth, but if the truth might inflict severe damage to his or her well-being (such as some unpleasant information about illness), the right to be protected from damage might take precedence and the person would not be told the truth. However, such a shift in the conception of rights tends to undermine the entire notion of "universal, inalienable human rights," particularly when no clear criteria for determining the relative importance of different rights are developed. It is hard to consider rights as guaranteed when a specific right may be set aside on the basis of a personal and possibly controversial judgment.

The practical problems involved in resolving potential inconsistencies between individual rights can be demonstrated by considering the statements in the Declaration of Universal Human Rights (Appendix 1) that are relevant for those groups affected by the scientific enterprise. For this analysis, three categories of individuals can be considered: research participants (experimental subjects, interview respondents, those subject to observation, and so forth), scientific investigators, and the public-at-large. The articles of the United Nations declaration have been used to derive major rights associated with these three categories of individuals in Table 1.

One potential inconsistency between rights for individuals depends upon the interpretation of Article 27–1. If interpreted in a narrow fashion, the article becomes a statement regarding the right of individuals to share in the benefits of scientific research. Since, however, the statement itself assumes that scientific advancement will occur, it can be interpreted as a "right to scientific advancement." Given such an interpretation, no problems will arise if scientific advancement does not require the involvement of human participants—as is the case in the physical sciences. However, if research with human participants is required, there is a substantial potential for incongruencies, since the research techniques necessary for scientific advancement may infringe upon a number of basic rights, such as the right to privacy or freedom from risk to

Table 1. Interpretations of Human Rights Relevant to Participants in Research Enterprise

	UN Declaration Article Number	Basic Emphasis	Interpretation/Application
Research Participants	1	Humans should treat each other with dignity, spirit of brotherhood	Individuals should not be manipulated or deceived unnecessarily
	2	Equal treatment of all individuals by their governments	No category of individuals can be considered to have foregone rights for any purpose, including research
	3	Right to life and personal security	Consideration of personal physical security and safety
	3	Right to liberty	Right to self-determination with regard to participation in research
	4	Prohibition of slavery in any form	
	5	Prohibition of torture, cruel, inhuman, or degrading treatment	Right to personal respect, treatment with dignity in research
			Right to expect minimization of personal stress or pain
	12	No arbitrary interference with personal privacy	Respect for individual privacy in the collection and maintenance of information
	17	Right to own property	Respect for personal property, including the time required of participants
	21–2	Right of equal access to public service	Right to participate in research beneficial to participants (especially if publicly supported)

Table 1. Interpretations of Human Rights Relevant to Participants in Research Enterprise (cont.)

	UN Declaration Article Number	*Basic Emphasis*	*Interpretation/Application*
Scientific Investigators	18	Freedom of thought	Freedom to explore any set of ideas or issues
	19	Freedom of opinion and expression	Freedom to openly publicize ideas and analyses
	20	Freedom of voluntary assembly	Freedom to pursue discussions with other investigators
	23	Right to work, free choice of employment	Privilege to disassociate from any research project
	4	Prohibition of slavery	(Right to work as a scientist is not clearly implied)
	27–2	Protection of the moral and material interests resulting from scientific contributions	Credit and recognition for scientific contributions
All Human Beings	21–1	Right to take part in governing of society	Right to affect distribution of public resources
			Right to affect extension of special privileges to unique occupational groups, that is, scientific investigators
	27–1	Right to share in benefits of scientific achievement	Right to share in benefits of scientific achievement

personal safety. This is another reflection of one of the basic dilemmas selected for attention in this book—the dilemma between the rights of research participants and the potential advantage associated with the conduct of scientific research.

Article 3 of the UN declaration, regarding liberty, clearly implies that no individual should be coerced into participation in research—participants should have a free choice of involvement in any project. But this tends to overlook the obligations or responsibilities that go with any rights. If individuals have a right to participate in the benefits of scientific advancements, and these advancements were based upon past research that involved participants, it might be argued that unless current individuals are making a contribution—through participation—they are not meeting a responsibility to facilitate the continuous development of scientific knowledge. Thus, future generations will not be able to share in the benefits of scientific advancement if current generations do not participate in the research process.

Several problems can be considered from the perspective of scientific investigators. For example, it is clear that the United Nations declaration intends that no individual's freedom of thought shall be infringed, but if the advancement of scientific thought requires resources, then this freedom is similar to numerous other rights (such as adequate medical care) whose implementation depends upon the availability of resources. Further, there is some ambiguity surrounding scientists' moral interests in relation to their creative products; Article 27-2 suggests that such moral interests should be "protected." If this means that scientists responsible for an idea should have some control over its application in practical affairs, there is considerable potential for inconsistencies. For example, a scientist may wish to influence the application of a scientific achievement in such a way that all individuals will not share in its benefits—a clear conflict of rights. There may also be controversy over the extent to which application of scientific knowledge actually creates benefits, such as intelligence testing in schools or nuclear power. It is not clear how resolution of such conflicts can avoid violating individual rights; the specification of rights assumes that there will be no ambiguity involved in their realization.

Some writers (Kelman, 1972) have emphasized the asymmetrical nature of the power relationship between research participants and scientific investigators, implying that research participants are powerless (without rights) in these situations. But if the rights of research participants as ordinary citizens are fully realized, then they should have the power to affect the governing process, which includes the distribution of public resources for research and development of special privileges for professional groups (such as the right to conduct research with human subjects). If this is the actual situation, ordinary citizens clearly have the upper hand, even though the investigator may have more influence in specific research settings. (The same point could be made about such other professional groups as physicians, lawyers, and college professors.)

The specification of a set of rights that is unambiguous, complete, consistent, and acceptable to all individuals affected is thus a quite difficult task. The usual solution appears to be one of stating "fundamental" rights *and* providing a legal or administrative mechanism for resolving not only problems that stem from the inability of societies to afford the economic cost of meeting all rights but also ambiguities in application to specific situations and inconsistencies between rights.

Dilemmas Posed by Conflicting Solutions to Moral Problems

Several problems have developed from attempts to resolve the major issues—justification for a political state, criteria for societal actions, and standards for individual morality:

- An accepted solution to one issue may be inconsistent with accepted solutions to another. For example, solutions to the first two issues—legitimation of a political order and criteria for societal action—may be inconsistent. Again, solutions to either of the first two issues must be implemented by individual action, but this action may be inconsistent with accepted standards of individual morality.

- Lack of agreement on the moral or political philosophy appropriate as a source of solutions to an issue can make it unclear which of several incompatible responses should be adopted.
- The specification of a particular moral or political philosophy may be so imprecise that application to a particular problem becomes ambiguous. (Relevant experts may disagree on the appropriate behavior.)

These problems have led to a substantial number of mechanisms for resolution, including political legislatures, court systems, and many types of activities designed to help resolve individual dilemmas (such as religious counseling).

The first conflict—between justification for a political structure and the criteria for societal action—may be the dominant problem in political and moral philosophy. It is a major problem because its accepted solutions—social contract theory (emphasizing human rights) and the utilitarian analysis (focusing upon the net benefits to an aggregate of individuals)—provide for a wide range of specific situations where conflicts may occur. These include (Fried, 1974, p. 5) "areas of criminal law, procedure, and corrections, in the control of bureaucracies concerned with housing, education, employment, land use, the environment, and technology." In short, in every aspect of social life where the government (or the state) attempts to exercise some control over the citizens, respect for individual rights may conflict with demands of efficiency or benefits to the aggregate. In discussions regarding research with human participants, concern for individual rights is reflected in an emphasis on obtaining informed consent, while utilitarian analysis is reflected in the emphasis on risk-benefit evaluations of specific projects.

The issue can be rephrased as a personal problem for scientific investigators by using categories from Chapter One:

Research Dilemma: How to proceed when the development of knowledge that may benefit mankind involves research procedures that may infringe upon the rights and welfare of individuals?

All social scientists responsible for research involving human participants have resolved this dilemma in one way or another, but some have been more conscious of the relevant issues than others. A framework for analysis and examples of applications to different types of research are thus the focus of Part One. The need for procedures to provide systematic resolutions to this dilemma has recently become apparent; it can be expressed as follows:

Conduct of Research Quandary: What societal mechanisms or collective guidelines provide assurance to the general public and scientific investigators that the resolution of the research dilemma will be morally acceptable?

A discussion of the current solutions to this problem (provided by professional associations, government agencies, and the legal system) is provided in Part Two.

The second general dilemma—conflict between solutions to societal issues and accepted standards of individual morality—takes several forms as it relates to social science investigators. As noted earlier, one involves concern over the relationship between the scientist and society:

Scientist-Citizen Dilemma: What orientations help to minimize complications associated with incongruencies between scientific obligations and the responsibilities of citizenship?

At the most fundamental level, this involves the scientist's perception of the position of the scientific enterprise in society and how it should be related to societal and human problems. One solution is to assume that scientists are autonomous, independent from society, and not responsible for the conduct of practical affairs in their professional work (their obligations as citizens have no relation to their professional obligations). Other approaches may emphasize their involvement in practical matters as social scientists, with different effects upon scientific work, depending upon the relative importance attributed to their obligations as scientists or citizens. Strategies may in fact shift, depending upon a scientist's professional position or the current issue. Alternatives are reviewed in Chapter Eleven.

A second variation of this problem—conflict between solutions to societal issues and accepted standards of individual morality—is the potential conflict between the perceived responsibility for producing knowledge and the felt responsibility for ensuring that the knowledge is used only for desirable purposes:

Application of Knowledge Dilemma: What responses are available to scientists when scientific knowledge may be utilized to achieve goals inconsistent with their personal values?

The occurrence of this dilemma is related to the high degree of identification that investigators often develop with their work and the knowledge that may result. Since they feel responsible for the creation (or discovery) of an idea, they would like to think that they are responsible for its application, particularly when important benefits result. Alternatives available to investigators for influencing the application of knowledge, along with the possible consequences of various actions, are reviewed in Chapter Twelve.

An overview of the relationship between basic moral and political issues, the most widely accepted solutions, and the dilemmas confronted by social scientists is provided in Table 2. Dilemmas receiving recent attention by social scientists can be subsumed under the more general issues and solutions that have occupied moral and legal philosophers for hundreds of years. And if the resolution of these problems is ambiguous even in the context of abstract philosophical discussions, it is far more complicated when specific human rights, specific legislation, and specific research programs are involved. The remainder of this book reviews the problems confronting social scientists as well as the mechanisms for resolution. In most cases there is no simple solution; if a solution can be identified, it is usually an uneasy compromise.

Table 2. Overview of Philosophical Issues, Accepted Solutions, and Major Dilemmas

Basic Legal, Moral and Philosophical Issues		Summary of Widely Accepted Solutions		Dilemmas Confronting Social and Behavioral Scientists	
I)	Justification for the formation of a political system (or state).	A)	Individuals are better off in a social system where they relinquish rights to use force and negotiate with other political states in exchange for a guarantee of basic rights and liberties (for example, life, liberty, pursuit of happiness) not to be curtailed without due process and equal treatment (social contract theory).	1.	How to proceed when the development of knowledge that may benefit mankind involves research procedures that may infringe upon the rights and welfare of individuals?[a]
II)	Criteria for evaluation of public programs and legislation.	B)	Assess the aggregate costs and benefits to the society as a whole and select the alternative that will produce the greatest aggregate benefit (or least aggregate cost); attempt to ensure that the distribution of costs and benefits is not inequitable (utilitarian analysis).	2.	What orientations help to minimize complications associated with incongruencies between scientific obligations and the responsibilities of citizenship?[a]
III)	Criteria for leading a moral or good life as an individual.	C)	a) Follow rules that are, or should be, widely accepted. b) Respond in such a way to any situation that the negative effects are minimized and/or the positive effects maximized.	3.	What responses are available to scientists when scientific knowledge may be utilized to achieve goals inconsistent with their personal values?[a]

Meta-Issues:

IV) Criteria for a consensus on standards for accepting solutions to these basic issues.

V) Unambiguous application of general philosophical positions to specific problems.

c) For any choice, select an alternative that appears to be—on an intuitive basis—correct and personally satisfying.

Meta-Issues:

E) How to resolve incongruencies that occur when:
  a) More than one solution strategy applies to a specific problem.
  b) A single-solution strategy provides ambiguous results.

F) How should an individual respond when the solution to a societal problem requires violation of the criteria for a good or moral personal life?

4. What societal mechanisms or collective guidelines provide assurance to the general public and scientific investigators that the resolution of research dilemmas will be morally acceptable?[b]

---

[a]Individual moral dilemmas.
[b]Social response to Dilemma I).

Part One

This part analyzes the philosophies and issues associated with the research dilemma: How to proceed when the development of knowledge that may benefit mankind involves research procedures that may infringe upon the rights and welfare of the participants? This possible encroachment upon the rights and welfare of participants does not stem from the insidious impulses of misanthropic investigators but from the technical and methodological demands of creating knowledge, briefly reviewed below.

Selected Considerations in Research

Conducting research that may encroach upon the rights and welfare of participants is not the major interest of most investigators. The objective of most scientists is to contribute to the development of intellectual structures—accepted in the community

The Research Dilemma: Investigators' Responsibilities and Participants' Rights

of scientists—that are useful (Reynolds, 1971) for providing: (1) typologies and descriptions, (2) explanations and predictions, (3) a potential for control (if the appropriate variables can be manipulated), and (4) a sense of underatanding (an intuitive feeling that one knows how or why something affects or produces a phenomenon). In some cases the phenomenon will be selected because of its importance as a practical problem and the scientist's objective may be to develop an intellectual structure that will help to resolve the problems. At other times the focus may be upon an "interesting" scientific issue, where the major goal is the satisfaction of curiosity, although important practical applications may sometimes result from such endeavors.

Any number of different intellectual structures—religion, folk wisdom, common sense, societal tradition, mysticism—may provide a basis for the resolution of practical problems, but they can be differentiated on the basis of how confidence in the knowledge is developed. One of the oldest mechanisms for providing such confidence is reliance upon the shared opinion of "experienced elders" or "wise old men," a technique still used when individuals cite historical authorities in support of their arguments. Another alternative is to accept "common knowledge" or the unsystematic aggregation of the personal observations of a group of people, usually in frequent personal contact; this may be the basis for most of the knowledge or cultural folklore that governs everyday life.

A somewhat different strategy is to base confidence in an intellectual structure on its coincidence with systematic, shared observations of reality—empirical data. Ideally, each individual can personally examine the congruence between an abstract intellectual structure and these special descriptions of the "real world." They may decide for themselves whether or not the intellectual structure is useful for the goals of science—especially providing a sense of understanding—and worthy of their confidence. It is this objective, developing confidence in abstract knowledge that is pursued when research is conducted—research itself is generally a tedious, frustrating burden, and it is the excitement and challenge of developing new knowledge or solving a significant practical problem that provides the incentive for most scientific investigators. Several features of research activity, conducted in an attempt to contribute to the development of knowledge, are relevant to the involvement of participants: (1) the choice of phenomena for study, (2) the complex character of knowledge related to social and human phenomena, (3) the concept of understanding that dominates the scientific enterprise, and (4) the scope of phenomena that must be studied to develop a complete understanding.

Two aspects of the first issue—selection of phenomena for study—are of importance, namely, the extent to which the phenomena is of consequence and the extent to which it involves a risk to the rights or welfare of the participants. For most phenomena these two characteristics are closely related: the more important the subject matter, the more likely it is that the rights or welfare

of the participants will be affected by the research; the more trivial
the problem, the less the welfare of the participants is an issue.
Given the infinite range of phenomena for consideration and the
limited resources (time or financial support) available to investigators, it is not surprising to find that many will choose to study
important phenomena. Further, it may be that the interests of society-at-large are best served by this strategy, given the investment
in the training of scientists and the societal costs of research.

Assuming that an investigator has chosen the study of an
important phenomenon, the next issue is the extent to which human participants must be involved. The current status of knowledge about most human phenomena—biomedical, psychological,
or social—suggests that there are often a large number of variables
and processes, usually subtle and interrelated, that will influence
major research interests, particularly for significant societal problems such as illiteracy, crime, violence, and poverty. Empirically
based knowledge related to such phenomena requires research
that systematically examines the interrelationship among many
variables, a process that can only be carried out when a large number of "units of analysis"—usually human participants—are involved. While presenting a dramatic challenge for those attempting
to organize and develop scientific knowledge, this process has important implications for the type of research that must be conducted to provide appropriate empirical data. Research programs
adequate for developing confidence in scientific knowledge related
to medical, human, or social phenomena may require numerous
projects involving a multitude of human participants, a need that
can be attributed to the process itself rather than to the desire of
investigators to supervise research.

The third major problem is related to a conception of "understanding" shared by most scientists—confidence that the causal
relationship among the major variables is known. The most widely
used techniques to provide such confidence involve experimental
strategies in which the investigator controls, either through the
manipulation of variables or the selection of units for study, the
characteristics of the independent variables and examines their
effect upon the dependent variable(s). Since the investigator has

controlled some aspect of the environment of the human participants, he or she is seen as responsible for effects they may experience. When a risk of negative effects is associated with the variables under control, the "cost" of gaining confidence in knowledge
of causality becomes the possible negative effects to be experienced
by the participants.

An alternative procedure is frequently used in social science
to establish causal relationships; that is, repeated surveys of the
same individuals, frequently called panel analysis, are often taken.
This allows development of a systematic history of individuals with
different characteristics, providing confidence that differences at
one point in time may be systematically related to differences at
later points in time. For participants, this involves the tedium of
being asked similar questions at different points in time, although
this may not be a burden in all cases.

A final and more subtle problem is the need to study a wide
range of phenomena to develop useful descriptions related to atypical, unique instances, particularly when societal or human problems are involved. For example, it may be necessary to study the
healthy to understand illness, examine happy marriages to understand divorce, and study successful learners to understand learning
disabilities. In such situations, the research participants are encouraged to contribute to the research activity to help others rather
than derive direct personal benefits. The value dilemma with regard to the "normal" research participants becomes significant
when some risk is associated with the research procedure, and it
is almost impossible to eliminate all risk.

In sum, there are four factors that have a major effect on
the research procedures employed by scientists and, consequently,
on the potential effects for participants:

1. Preference for the study of significant problems and issues of
   importance to participants;
2. The frequent presence of multiple causal mechanisms and variables that necessitate research with a large number of individuals;
3. The concern for developing confidence in causal relationships
   among variables, which results in the conduct of experiments

where the environment or characteristics of participants may be controlled; and

4. The need to study typical individuals, as controls, to gain information about those who are unusual or unique.

Such research is completed in the hope that it will lead to greater confidence in abstract (or scientific) knowledge—not to control participants and "play God" with their lives.

Resolution of the Research Dilemma

Once an investigator has selected a significant phenomenon and determined the crucial and unresolved scientific issues, working out a procedure to guide the analysis of specific programs or projects that might involve human participants has many advantages. Problems associated with the research dilemma can be organized around five issues and stated as questions:

1. *Research program effects:* What are the positive and negative effects associated with a particular research program—achievements of an intellectual objective?
2. *Research project effects:* What are the positive and negative effects associated with the conduct of a specific research project—as a contribution to a research program?
3. *Participant effects:* What are the positive and negative effects associated with an individual's participation in (contributions to) a research project?
4. *Distribution of effects:* Are the major positive and negative effects of research distributed unevenly among different social categories or social groupings? If so, is the distribution unjust?
5. *Consideration of participants' rights and welfare:* What features of the research procedure provide confidence that the rights and welfare of the participants were (or will be) respected?

It might be argued that the issues should be examined in the reverse order, giving priority to the analysis related to the participants' rights and welfare and the effects they may experience by virtue of participation in the research. This order was chosen because of the greater generality of the first and second questions. The positive and negative effects related to a research program—or a general area of research—are somewhat different from those related to a specific research project; there may be a number of different research projects that contribute to a particular research program or general objective. Further, once a research project is developed, different aspects or conditions in an experimental study may have different effects on the rights and welfare of the participants. In short, while the advantages and disadvantages to participants of pursuing a particular project may affect the design of the project, a general research objective will not be dramatically affected by such considerations.

  Nevertheless, the results of the analysis of the effects for participants cannot be ignored in the selection of research programs (areas of emphasis) or specific research projects, for if the effects for the participants are overwhelmingly negative, this may have a major effect on the evaluation of a research project or program. There are numerous research projects that will never be initiated, despite the importance of the issues involved, because of concern for the effects on participants. For example, a long-term experimental study comparing the effects of genetic composition and socialization experiences on intelligence in human beings is clearly unacceptable; no investigator would want to be responsible for deliberately creating unintelligent "participants." The need to rely on alternative sources of data, such as the results of "natural experiments," has increased the complexity of research and the ambiguity associated with the resolution of this issue.

  The value of these issues as a guide for analysis of research projects is mixed. While they do provide a useful method for organizing the effects and concerns associated with the conduct of research, it is difficult to resolve each question independently. The value of pursuing a research program cannot be decided without reference to both the balance of effects for participants and the overall research objectives. This interrelation of effects is only one factor that precludes independent resolution of issues at these different levels; the other is the inability to predict (for a substantial proportion of research) the effects (positive or negative) of research or the potential implications (or value) of the resultant knowledge. It is unlikely there will ever be a single way to analyze research endeavors, although any procedure for systematic review is likely to lead to more confidence in the appropriateness of the final resolution than is an ad hoc analysis, focusing upon a subset of issues or using intuitive, instinctive reactions.

In summary, the following chapters in Part One are designed to provide a framework for resolving the research dilemma. Chapter Three reviews the various effects of research, crucial to the completion of cost-benefit (or risk-benefit) analysis, required when a utilitarian analysis is pursued to evaluate programs with societal impact. Chapter Four reviews procedures used to ensure that relinquishing rights is an informed, voluntary act—the conditions when it is considered "just." The remaining chapters provide applications of the analysis to three different types of research that involve human participants: overt research in the context of experimental projects; overt research that emphasizes descriptions of natural phenomena; and covert research, where the participants are unaware of the existence of the endeavor. (Cassell, 1978, pursues an alternative strategy; the issues are reviewed in relation to one research technique, fieldwork.) The examples of research chosen to illustrate the analysis have several important features: they are based on published reports, have been the source of ethical controversy, and often involve phenomena of significance, both to the participants and the public-at-large.

Reliance upon published accounts of studies represents a clear bias, a focus upon projects where the final decision was to initiate the study and the consequences were significant enough to warrant publication and "being noticed." Those situations where an investigator concluded that the complications involved in the research (to protect the participants) or the risks to the participants were so great that the research was not initiated (or it was completed and unpublished or published and unnoticed) are not included in the discussion. Conversely, situations where there was an overwhelming case for conducting the research—trivial or insignificant negative effects for participants, large potential benefits, or high confidence that the rights and welfare of the participants were given full consideration—are not generally emphasized. The examples are illustrative, not representative of a well-defined population of research studies.

The following discussion is not designed to evaluate particular research projects or decisions as to whether they should be, or should have been, conducted. The basic purpose is to review how research may be analyzed rather than to categorize research as "good" or "moral" versus "bad" or "unethical." Much of the research that is discussed is controversial, and an attempt has been made to review the differing viewpoints; it is for individuals to consider which effects they wish to emphasize in arriving at their own cost-benefit ratio.

3

Effects of Research for Participants and Society

━━━◆━━◆━━◆━━◆━━◆━━◆━━◆━━◆━━◆━━◆━━

Utilitarian or cost-benefit analysis was developed to help resolve decisions with multiple, complex effects for society. The research dilemma, attending to both the benefits of scientific investigation and the potential negative effects for participants, provides a typical example of such decisions. This issue can be analyzed at several levels: decisions regarding the support of science itself (which may involve a number of research programs), the decision to promote and encourage a research program (which may involve a number of specific projects), the decision with regard to the initiation of a project (which may involve a number of individual participants), and the decision of an individual to become involved in a specific project.

To complete a utilitarian analysis of a decision at any level requires an identification of all positive and negative effects, esti-

mates of their severity or importance, and some procedure for
determining the balance of effects: Do the positive effects outweigh
the negative, or vice versa? Since research involves examination of
unknown relationships and effects, it is frequently not possible to
predict the effects (positive or negative) or their magnitude with
certainty. In many cases it is only possible to provide estimates of
the probability of occurrence; this ambiguity is recognized in discussions regarding the value of research by the adoption of the
phrase "risk-benefit analysis," which implies that the disutility of
unpredictable negative effects will be compared with the utility of
predictable positive effects—a misleading orientation, to say the
least. This chapter reviews information useful for utilitarian (cost-
benefit) analysis at two levels, the individual's participation and the
decisions regarding initiation of projects.

Individual Effects: Identification

Numerous effects may be experienced by individuals involved in research. Cost-benefit evaluations are facilitated if the
same general scheme is utilized for both positive and negative effects and if it reflects a major feature of much research—deliberate
intervention with natural processes or activities—as well as allows
for the incorporation of new and previously unidentified effects.
The use of four general categories of effects seems to satisfy
these constraints:

1. Temporary, direct effects that are readily reversed or modified
   by natural processes or professional intervention; the individual
   can be returned to the preresearch state with a minimum of
   problems, although there may be some costs.
2. Permanent, direct effects that cannot be eliminated, at least not
   efficiently or with certainty; these effects may persist for a considerable time after the research experience has terminated.
3. Socially mediated effects that are experienced by virtue of the
   impact of the research upon societal processes or social characteristics, having, in turn, subtle, indirect effects on the research participants.

4. Societal rights effects upon various concepts of individual rights; these effects may be present without the knowledge of the participant.

Effects in any of these categories may be seen as positive or negative for the individual participant, although existing research and discussions tend to emphasize the negative.

The categorization of direct effects related to biomedical, psychological, and social research are a useful subset of the first two general categories, temporary and permanent direct effects. Biomedical effects cover the wide range of conditions or processes associated with changes in health, occurrence of disease, and so forth. Psychological or mental changes include characteristics of personality and perhaps cognitive skills or abilities. Social effects would involve an individual's position, status, or relationship in any social system (interpersonal or societal). These three categories are important because the major measures employed in research to estimate effects are usually associated with phenomena in these areas. In one sense, however, this "disciplinary" categorization is artificial, for a change in one area—the focus of the research—may result in changes in other areas. For example, a person who is physically disabled may improve, creating changes in his self-concept or relations with others on whom he has been dependent.

An additional category of temporary, direct effects resulting from most research is composed of the transitory economic or situational effects upon the individual. These would include cash payments for participation in research or for additional personal expenses, unusual privileges and use of special facilities or denial of same, free professional services or the need for additional professional services (as when the research project creates legal complications for the individual), and time taken from other activities (gainful employment, for example). Many of these factors are present in all research, such as time taken from other activities; others are associated with only certain types of projects or individuals in special situations, such as additional privileges or denial of use of facilities. There may also be miscellaneous temporary effects, such as the pleasures of a novel, interesting experience, a

sense of moral uplift at being involved with a project that is useful
for society, or even resentment at being treated as an object for
research.

One important permanent effect, not directly related to the
phenomenon being studied, would be the educational benefits that
may accrue to some participants, particularly students who take
part in research during their educational activities. Students in a
number of areas—medicine, dentistry, psychology, sociology, for
example—may be asked to become involved in research as participants and may thereby gain important insights into the conduct
of research. While this can be considered a permanent benefit, it
is one that may be present for only the first few such experiences;
there may not be many additional educational benefits for the
tenth, twentieth, thirtieth . . . such experience.

Effects mediated by society fall into two major categories.
The first are those that result from changes in attitudes, norms,
or policies specific to unique social categories of individuals. For
example, the participant may have taken part in a research project
on the effects of a "soft drug" such as marijuana: the results of the
research may affect the legal status of the drug, and this may be
considered a positive or negative outcome by the participant, depending upon the nature of the change and his or her attitudes
toward the use of such drugs. A similar change in official policy
or unofficial attitudes, following a research project, may affect
other social categories—minorities, handicapped, the elderly—and
participants may experience such effects for some time after the
research is completed.

The conduct of research may be associated with several
types of undesirable changes in societal values. The treatment of
individuals as objects rather than as unique persons, the tolerance
of deceit, or the acceptance of misleading presentations by those
in positions of authority may be promoted by certain types of research techniques. This could contribute to an increase of suspicion
of professionals and a reduction in mutual trust among societal
members. While such effects are conceivable, it is not clear that the
conduct of research will have a significant or important impact
upon such societal norms.

The final category of effects is the most difficult to review, for it has no clear empirical referent, even in the subtle sense of socially mediated effects. This involves the impact upon societally defined rights, including the rights to privacy, liberty, and self-determination—all legally protected in many societies—as well as other rights, such as the right not to be deceived or the right to routine professional attention (which may be denied when a participant is assigned to a control or a comparison group). Several less well-established rights with positive features may be realized in research, such as the right to share in scientific benefits (a participant in research on a new therapy may be one of the first to benefit from it) and the right to scientific progress (which is promoted by participation in any research project). Nonetheless, this last category—impact upon rights—is a major source of the negative effects that form the basis for the implementation of the informed consent procedure discussed in Chapter Four.

An overview of effects is presented in Table 3. A utilitarian (cost-benefit) analysis of the effects of participation on a single individual in a specific project would require identification of all possible effects, along with estimates of their probability of occurrence and severity (seriousness, if negative; value, if positive); the net utility for the specific individual could then be estimated. A decision regarding the conduct of a research project, which may involve many participants and benefit many individuals, would require similar estimates for the effects on the participants, as well as an additional estimate of the value of the knowledge to be obtained (both as "pure" knowledge and as potentially beneficial to society). A decision regarding a program of research would emphasize not only the effects on successive groups of participants but the general effects of the research program on knowledge and society.

Some very general effects for society as a whole are indicated at the bottom of Table 3. Major positive effects, those most frequently cited in support of scientific research, are the increase in knowledge—knowledge being the most valued objective—and an increased capacity to control biomedical, psychological, and social phenomena. Negative effects would include the financial costs

Table 3. Overview of Effects for Individual Participants in Research

Major Categories of Effects	Positive	Type of Effect	Negative
Temporary, Personal			
Direct	Biomedical Psychological Social Context		Biomedical Psychological Social context
Economic, Situational	Cash payments Use of facilities, privileges Professional services		Personal expenses Denial of facilities, privileges Additional professional services Time taken from other activities
Miscellaneous	Novel, interesting experience Altruistic satisfaction		Resentment of treatment as "object"
Permanent, Personal			
Direct	Biomedical Psychological Social relations Educational		Biomedical Psychological Social relations
Miscellaneous			
Mediated by Society	Benefits of new programs based upon the research		Harm from new norms that are established or enhanced by research: Appropriate to treat individuals as objects Legitimation of deceit
	Benefits to a social category, which includes the participant, based upon the research		Discrimination or harm to a social category, to which the participant belongs, based upon the research

		Infringement upon rights of:
"Rights" Specified by Society	Right to scientific progress	Privacy
	Right to share in scientific benefits	Self-determination
	Right to efficient and effective government	Liberty
		Not to be deceived[a]
		To be left alone[a]
		Benefits of science when assigned to a control group
Society in General	Increase in objective, empirically based knowledge (science)	Financial costs of research
	Potential increase of capacity to control biomedical, psychological, and social phenomena	Time of trained professionals
		Potential costs and disruption associated with restructuring society in response to research findings
		Cost of reorganizing society so those with the responsibility for control of phenomena, previously considered uncontrollable, can be trusted to act in the best interests of society.
		Reduced sense of individual autonomy or personhood as more phenomena are considered controllable.

[a]No legal status; mentioned by some commentators.

of the research—not inconsiderable for some projects—as well as
the potential disruptions that may occur if the research suggests
that new procedures or structural arrangements are required.
(The decision to initiate such changes would require a separate
cost-benefit analysis, unique to each suggested modification.) A
more subtle consideration is the reduced sense of personal autonomy that may be experienced by individual members as knowledge
of ·phenomena increases. Questions may also arise about the trust-
worthiness of those responsible for applying the new knowledge.

Individual Effects: Perceived Intensity

While it is useful to identify different effects, positive and
negative, the magnitude of their impact upon participants is a distinctly different issue. In economics, it is well accepted that different amounts of money have different degrees of utility for individuals: twice as much money is not considered twice as useful (the
incremental value of additional units of money decreases). In a
similar fashion, the intensity of different research experiences,
particularly those predominant in social science research, may not
have a direct, linear relationship to increased demands upon participants. For example, asking participants to hold their hands in
ice water for ten minutes may be more than twice as uncomfortable
as a request for five minutes; two questions about sexual behavior
may not be twice as embarassing as one such question.

Ideal descriptive data would utilize a common measure of
effect—similar to the concept of utility—and provide estimates of
a wide range of positive and negative effects for a diverse range
of research experiences from a variety of respondents. While there
is some doubt whether such an analysis would ever be possible—
the development of a common measure of "effect" seems quite
remote—it may be possible to develop measures related to different categories of effects. A few studies have evaluated standard
research procedures, concentrating upon the type of research
completed by social psychologists. While these studies do not cover
the complete range of research effects and tend to ignore positive
effects, they are substantially more useful than speculation from
published descriptions of research procedures.

Eighty undergraduate students from an introductory psychology course (Epstein, Suedfeld, and Silverstein, 1973) were asked to rate selected negative events associated with social-psychological experiments in terms of three characteristics: expectation of occurrence, desirability, and appropriateness, each on an 11-point scale. Negative evaluations were most frequently associated with administrative features of research—unclear instructions (averages of 9.2; 9.0; 8.2), late experimenter (8.6; 9.0; 8.8), incompetent (9.6; 9.0; 9.8) or disrespectful (9.9; 9.8; 9.3) experimenter—rather than aspects of the research experience: purpose concealed (3.6; 6.5; 4.8), deception (6.1; 7.6; 4.7), or possible electric shock (7.9; 9.0; 5.0). Analysis of the expectations of potential participants (also college undergraduates) about experimental research suggested that they approached the role of subject as though it were a job, one where a "supervisor" (that is, the experimenter) is expected to act as a responsible, competent bureaucratic official and receive willing, conscientious cooperation in return (Epstein, Suedfeld, and Silverstein; 1973, pp. 213 216).

A comparison of the evaluation by college undergraduates and professional psychologists of four experiments was based on the respondents' evaluation of the ethical characteristics of a written description of a study; descriptions of four different studies were used among the respondent populations (Sullivan and Deiker, 1973). The results indicate that, for almost every issue and every study, the psychologists were two to three times more likely to condemn the study than were the students, suggesting that psychologists are more conservative or less tolerant than students regarding acceptable negative effects in social-psychological research.

Two studies have examined the intensity of discomfort attributed to various research procedures by asking samples of undergraduates to rate brief descriptions on a 5-point scale (Farr and Seaver, 1975; Meglino, 1976a, 1976b). The Farr and Seaver study utilized brief statements representing experimental procedures developed from an examination of the literature and evoked responses from eighty-six students in an introductory psychology class. Virtually no items received average ratings near the maximum discomfort end of the scale (5.0); the highest was an average of 4.2 for "maximum tolerable" electric shocks. The authors com-

ment on their surprise at finding a high tolerance for an invasion
of privacy—the undergraduates appeared willing to complete and
sign a questionnaire about past sexual experiences (average rating
of 2.9), although they indicated that they might give careful consideration before cooperating. (Items on an anonymous questionnaire were rated as less of an invasion of privacy than those on a
signed questionnaire.)

A useful improvement is provided by a comparison of judgments on the "severity" of research procedures with similar judgments about everyday life events for college students (Meglino,
1976a, 1976b). A sample of eighty-three undergraduates rated
only everyday life events; a comparable sample of sixty-nine students rated both everyday life events and descriptions of research
procedures. The general pattern suggests that, while some research procedures were seen as potentially more "severe" than
common everyday life events, they were usually related to physical
discomfort; the research procedures related to psychological stress
or an invasion of privacy were considered no more serious than
the everyday life events chosen in comparison.

The apparent tolerance for invasion of privacy in natural
situations is represented by a comment on the study of behavior
within households in a crowded urban neighborhood (Ashcraft
and Scheflen, 1976). With the consent of the families, video cameras were placed in the hallway, living rooms, and kitchens of
apartments; a nearby apartment was rented for monitors and recording machines. Since the cameras were "unobtrusively" recording from "very early morning until late into the night," each family
was allowed to review the video tapes and erase what they did not
wish to be preserved. "To our surprise, not one family ever chose
to erase a tape" (p. 162).

Concerned that survey researchers may be wearing out their
welcome, investigators at the University of Michigan Institute for
Social Research, working with the U.S. Census Bureau, interviewed
a representative national sample of U.S. citizens about their attitudes toward being interviewed. While half had been interviewed
within the past four or five years and 40 percent more than once
in that time, 68 percent said they would be "somewhat" or "very"
interested in participating in another interview. Those with more

experience were more willing than others to be involved again; 80 percent of those who had participated in as many as four or more surveys said they would like to do so again (Scott, 1978).

Related evidence on the impact of questionnaire research is provided by a report on a review of all questionnaires (109) received by the U.S. Office of Education Internal Clearance Committee over five continuous weeks in 1967. Of the more than fifty-three hundred items included, only ten items (0.2 percent) from five questionnaires (5 percent) were seen as potentially embarrassing, self-incriminating, dealing with very private matters, or in some other way inappropriate (Conrad, 1967); clearly, the vast majority of the questionnaires (95 percent) and items (99.8 percent) were not considered a threat to the rights or welfare of the respondents.

These studies seem to justify several tentative conclusions. First, there is little systematic data on the evaluation of positive effects of research experience; the available evidence stresses the negative effects. Second, most of the evidence is related to highly controlled research situations—experiments or the administration of questionnaires—and thus to activities typical of social psychologists. There is less evidence related to the general administration of survey instruments or the responses of those observed in natural or field settings. Third, judgments from the population that represents the participants—college students—suggest that they do not consider the effects of research experiences especially serious when compared to everyday life events (except for physical stress). Fourth, investigators appear more concerned over the intensity or severity of the effects than do the participants, a concern that may lead investigators to be more conservative in research administration than students would be. (This latter finding would lead to predictions of controversy between students designing and conducting their own studies and their faculty advisers.)

Future research on this issue would be of considerable value, especially if it continued to utilize a wide range of research effects and comparisons with everyday life experiences, while expanding the scope of the studies in several ways. First, it should include respondents who represent a wider variety of participants (patients, general population, children, and so forth). Second, it should

utilize a wider diversity of negative effects and include examples
for all areas of research, including medical studies. (How threatening is giving a blood sample compared to a mild electric shock?)
Further, evaluations should also include ratings of positive effects
of research experiences. Estimates of participants' judgments about
taking part in research with different types and combinations of
positive and negative effects would be a more complicated, but
valuable, contribution. Finally, evaluations could be collected from
participants after actual research experiences, perhaps asking them
to compare the effects with common everyday events.

Individual Effects: Occurrence

Speculation on the nature of effects and participants' estimates of their magnitude or severity leads directly to concern about
the actual occurrence of positive and negative effects in research.
Anecdotal information provides an image of a substantial number
of effects. For example, the reference work compiled by the American Psychological Association (1973), the many popularizations on
the abuse of subjects (Baumrind, 1971; Jung, 1975; Rubin, 1970;
Warwick, 1975), and several books on abuse in medical research
(Pappworth, 1967; Beecher, 1970) give the impression that abuse,
or the risk of abuse, is widespread. Interestingly enough, there is
much less emphasis upon the occurrence of desirable effects, which
are taken for granted in therapeutic research and difficult to document for nontherapeutic research.

Estimates of the effects upon participants attributable to research can be organized into two general categories, based upon
the unit of analysis. The largest group of studies emphasizes the
actions of investigators, using the study or project as the unit of
analysis. These lead to statements about the percentage of studies
that are unethical or have undesirable effects (or risks). The smaller
group (one study of medical research) consists of a project that
estimated the probability that a participant would experience negative effects by virtue of participation in a research project in comparison with risks of other, everyday activities.

Measures of effect in this research are very imprecise, and almost no study provides a review of all possible effects. The majority focus upon simple counts of any unethical or undesirable effect; very few attempt to scale the magnitude and/or severity of effects. Further, there are very few studies related to the major effects associated with social science research; the data on medical effects will be presented to demonstrate the type of evidence that may be available and as a basis for comparison with psychological and social effects. Studies emphasizing the project as the unit of analysis will be reviewed first.

Frequency Among Projects

Two strategies have been used to estimate the occurrence of risk or unethical behavior of investigators. The first is to review published research reports and evaluate their procedures or effects; the second is to interview investigators about the characteristics of their current research. The latter strategy provides more specific information about projects and their potential effects.

One of the most influential analyses of the use of participants in medical research (Beecher, 1966) estimated that 12 of 100 consecutive articles in an "excellent" medical journal were considered unethical. "Unethical" included a wide range of actions (known effective treatment withheld, subjecting participants to unknown or substantial risks to improve knowledge of diseases or bodily functions, experimental therapies continued after evidence of substantial negative effects appeared, and failure to follow the spirit or letter of informed consent procedures). There were studies where serious medical harm had occurred (death) and some that involved high risks for the participants (even when they did not suffer negative effects). The analysis, based entirely upon the descriptions from journal articles, did not include any systematic attempt to evaluate the severity of effects for the participants or the extent to which there were benefits that compensated for the risks, either to the participants or society in general; it was very successful in bringing attention to the issue.

Several surveys of prestigious journals that publish research on social-psychological phenomena have attempted to analyze the occurrence and nature of deception (Stricker, 1967; Seeman, 1969; Menges, 1973). Use of deception over a period of time was estimated by analysis of the percentage of studies (one article may report on several studies) utilizing deception that appeared in the *Journal of Personality and Social Psychology* between 1948 and 1971. These data suggest that a sizable increase in the percentage of published studies reporting the use of deception—from 14 percent to 37 percent—occurred between 1961 and 1963. But this increase in the use of deception may be related to changes in phenomena selected for investigation. An analysis of the relationship between the use of deception and the nature of the phenomena under investigation is reported by Stricker (1967); the two categories with the highest levels of such use, studies related to conformity (81 percent) or cognitive dissonance and cognitive balance (72 percent), became popular during the early 1960s, coinciding with the increased percentage of studies utilizing deception between 1961 and 1963.

The nature of deception utilized in research is explored by both Stricker (1967) and Menges (1973); deception about the nature of the "instruments" (personality tests, problems, tasks, and so forth) utilized in the studies decreased (from 76 percent of studies published in 1964 to 20 percent published in 1971), while deception about other participants in a study increased (from 29 percent in 1961 to 38 percent in 1971). There may have been a dramatic increase in deception about the purpose of the research in the middle 1960s (to 51 percent of the studies), but that appears to have diminished in the late 1960s (to 10 percent of the studies). Misinformation about the participants' own behavior appears to have occurred at a constant rate (30 percent of the studies) across the ten years covered in this analysis.

The strategy of examining specific projects is usually implemented by using some procedure for identifying a group of projects and then asking the principal investigator to estimate the extent to which positive and negative effects are present. In most cases the projects are selected because they have received support from the federal government or approval from a human subjects committee and so do not represent a random selection of all research projects—just as published research does not represent a random selection of all research that involves human participants.

A survey of biomedical investigators asked them to describe any studies they were conducting that involved human participants and to evaluate the risk to the human subjects (Barber and others, 1973). Risk was defined as "danger to the subject above and beyond that to which he is already exposed as a patient or as a normal, healthy person" (p. 44). "Risk . . . , approximately that which is associated with a venipuncture, should be placed in the 'very little risk' category" (p. 45); 45 percent of the 422 studies were so placed, and 44 percent were considered to have no "additional risk." It is clear that the number of studies involving more than minor risks was very small (11 percent), and only 1 percent (4 out of 422) were judged to involve a large amount of risk. Unfortunately, the respondents were not provided with a standard of comparison for the "large amount of risk" category.

Two types of benefits were estimated by these investigators: increased medical knowledge and therapeutic benefits for both present patient-participants and future patients. It was estimated that over two thirds (69 percent) of the present patient-participants would receive "some" or "great" benefits and that almost all future patients (93 percent) would receive "some" or "great" benefits. All projects were seen as having a potential for contributing to medical knowledge, but slightly less than one half were seen as providing "highly significant" or "outstanding" contributions.

A series of studies have been conducted on the effects of projects that used human participants from a number of different populations—general research populations (students, patients, survey respondents), prisoners, children, and mental patients (Institute for Social Research, 1976a, 1976b, 1976c). In all cases the institutional review board is assumed to have approved the projects as "ethically acceptable."* While the results may not be representative of all research, these studies represent a careful attempt to

---

*The projects from the major sample were selected from among those approved by institutional review boards; the institutional review boards were selected at random from among those with assurances (formal statements of intention to comply with federally imposed procedures) filed with the Department of Health, Education, and Welfare (Institute for Social Research, 1976c). Approximately 2,880 projects from 4,150 were considered eligible; 2,120 interviews with principal investigators were completed (the response rate was approximately 74 percent). A special subset

evaluate the types of effects—estimated and realized—among participants in research. The survey of projects involved interviews of the principal investigators as a source of information on the estimated effects—both positive and negative—of the project on the participants. The severity of medical and psychological negative effects were incorporated into the scheme by utilizing several levels of effects; "minor" and "major" psychological effects, and "minor," "major," and "fatal" medical effects.

The major results, summarized in Table 4, review data on four subject populations. Data from the sample of general research are divided into two categories, beneficial (to participants) and nonbeneficial; the pattern suggests that positive effects are expected more frequently in the former category. The presentation is designed to provide information on the percentage of projects in which a probability of a particular effect may occur as well as the level of the probability—the principal investigators could classify their judgments into very low, low, medium, and high probability of occurrence (or risk). Since one project could involve more than one risk, no precise statements can be made about the distribution of risks across projects, that is, the number or types of risks associated with a typical project.

Statements regarding the types of risks associated with broad categories of projects—biomedical, behavioral intervention, other behavioral, and secondary analysis—are, however, available from the study of general research (Institute for Social Research, 1976c). The probability of effects—positive and negative—is highly consistent with the focus of the research, with the highest estimates for biomedical, lower for behavioral intervention and other behavioral, and virtually no effects associated with secondary analysis (of information or human products). No category of research,

of institutions was selected to study the research on children and the mentally infirm; projects were selected from those approved by review boards at these institutions (Institute for Social Research, 1976b, pp. 4–5). The projects in prisons with prisoners were selected from those approved by review committees for five prisons; although not a random sample of all prison research, this group of projects does compose a substantial proportion (one half) and can be considered representative of prison research (Institute for Social Research, 1976a, pp. 4, 13).

Table 4. Percentages of Investigators' Estimates of Effects of Research: Participants from Four Populations

	General Population Beneficial (1) 902			General Population Non-Beneficial (2) 822			Prisoners (3) 40 (approx.)			Research with children (4) Hospital/Other 43	126	Research with Mentally Infirm (5) 76
	Occurrence[a]	Mode Prob.[b]	High Prob.[c]	Occurrence	Mode Prob.	High Prob.	Occurrence	Mode Prob.[d]	High Prob.[d]	Occurrence	Occurrence	Occurrence
Positive Effects												
Medical	81	M	32	19	L	—	—	—	19	61	46	21
Psychological	63	M	18	20	VL	—	—	—	17	41	46	54
Other	20	H	12	3	VL	—	—	—	—	23	35	25
Negative Effects												
Minor psychological	70	VL	2	42	VL	1	92	VL	—	66	54	55
Major psychological	28	VL	—	7	VL	—	29	VL	—	19	9	13
Minor medical	61	VL	3	28	VL	—	85	VL	—	64	37	20
Major medical	39	VL	1	13	VL	—	50	VL	—	—	16	9
Fatal	27	VL	—	7	VL	—	40	VL	—	17	9	4
Embarrassment	22	VL	1	19	VL	1	13	VL	—	18	21	21
Legal	12	VL	—	9	VL	—	10	VL	—	3	10	10
Other	6	VL	—	4	VL	—	—	VL	—	13	6	4

[a] Refers to the percentage of projects where the effects are expected to occur with a very low or greater probability.

[b] Refers to the modal category (most projects) in terms of estimated probabilities of occurrence: VL = very low, L = low, M = medium, and H = high.

[c] Percentage of projects in which there was a high probability of the effect.

[d] All studies were related to drug toxicity, and available information related only to percentage of projects rated as having medium or high probability of beneficial effects. See Institute for Social Research (1976a, p. 19).

Sources: Institute for Social Research, 1976a, 1976b, and 1976c.

whether biomedical or behavioral, was associated with more than a very low probability of any type of negative effect.

A quite different issue, distinct from the "estimates of the probability of effects," is the actual occurrence of effects. For projects using a general subject population, harm (not predictable as an integral part of a relevant therapy or procedure) occurred in 3 percent of 2,052 projects; on average, two individuals in each project were affected. These effects were usually considered trivial or only temporarily disabling. Assumptions about the number of participants allow a rough estimate of the rate of injury to participants—one in every 581 (0.172 percent). Little data are available on serious effects; five deaths were reported on three projects, all related to cancer research and patient-participants in a terminal status when incorporated into a research project. Three projects reported a breach of confidentiality that harmed or embarrassed a subject (Institute for Social Research, 1976c, pp. 26–27). During the review of research conducted with prisoners (all were studies of drug toxicity), one investigator reported that one participant was temporarily disabled (Institute for Social Research, 1976a, p. 19). There was no mention of negative effects experienced by children or mentally infirmed participants (Institute for Social Research, 1976b).

What causes this rather dramatic difference in the occurrence of negative effects among the participants—which are difficult to find except for projects involving terminal cancer patients—and investigators' estimates of risk? The difference may be attributable to the conservative, that is, high estimates of risk provided by the investigators rather than to the usually low frequencies of actual damage. These high estimates may be due to a concern for the welfare of the participants, a concern that is reflected in a readiness to detect and cope with potential problems (negative effects for participants). Such concern may result in preparations for response to a wide range of negative effects, no matter how remote the possibility of their occurrence; estimates of the probability of occurrence may then be inflated because such precautions have been taken. While it is to the benefit of the participants to have a conservative, prepared investigator responsible for a project, there is considerable question whether these estimates can be used as a basis for an objective description of the effects of research.

Experience of Participants

One study has attempted to provide estimates of the occurrence of negative effects among research participants in biomedical research (Cardon, Dommel, and Trumble, 1976), and its results seem to have important implications for research in general, including research in social science. Five hundred and forty-seven principal investigators from among 2,904 research project grants awarded by two federal agencies were selected for interview; they were asked to provide data for all research supervised over the previous three years. Questions were asked about the total number of participants involved in the research (if a specific individual participated in more than one project, he or she was counted once for each project), the type of project (therapeutic or nontherapeutic), and any injurious effects upon the participants. Eighty-five percent of the principal investigators were willing to provide information, but after those with incomplete responses, no direct contact with research, no research with human participants, or those who could not be contacted in the available time were eliminated, only 331 provided relevant information (on a total of 415 studies).

Effects upon the participants were estimated in five categories: none, trivial, temporarily disabling, permanently disabling, and fatal. The major results, organized in relation to the distinction between therapeutic and nontherapeutic research, are presented in Table 5. It should be mentioned that there was only one permanently disabling injury reported for ninety-three thousand participants in nontherapeutic research, and even this injury was a "probable"; the cause of a stroke that a patient suffered three days after participation in the research project was uncertain. Most of the temporarily disabling effects from nontherapeutic research were adverse drug reactions, corneal abrasions, injuries from needle insertions, and miscellaneous effects, including an injury that one participant sustained after an assault by a patient.

An attempt was made to estimate the risk of research in relation to other types of activities or therapeutic treatments. The

Table 5. Occurrence of Negative Effects for Participants in Therapeutic and Nontherapeutic Medical Research

| | Nontherapeutic Annual Rate 1,000 Participants | | Comparison (Accident Risk—Typical Americans, Annual/1,000)[a] | Therapeutic | |
	Incidence			Incidence	Comparison (Risk of Injury in Medical Service of Teaching Hospitals)
Total number of projects	255			160	
Total participants	93,399			39,216	
Effects on participants					
No Injuries	99.2%			89.2%	
Injuries[d]	0.8			10.8	
Types of Injuries					
Number	711			4,246	
Trivial	0.7%			8.3%	
Temporary Disabling	0.1	37	50	2.4 }	
Permanently Disabling	<0.1	1	2	<0.1	4.5%[b]
Fatal	0.0	0	0.6	0.1	1.3%[c]

[a]Includes the rates for accidental injuries to all Americans presented in National Safety Council (1972).
[b]Based on estimates prepared by Barr (1955) and Schimmel (1964).
[c]Based on estimates prepared by Schimmel (1964).
[d]Injuries emphasized medical problems but also included "psychological condition requiring treatment after participation in a research study."
Source: Body of table based on presentations in Tables 3 and 4 and pp. 653–654 in Cardon, Dommel, and Trumble (1976).

annual rate of injury for participants in nontherapeutic research was estimated (assuming each participant was involved in research activities for three days) and then compared to the annual rate of injuries from accidents (in the United States). The results, shown in Table 5, indicate that the risk of research is slightly lower than the risk of accidents, although the risk of research is added to the risk of accidents in everyday life. The risk for participants in therapeutic research was estimated by comparing the percentage of participants experiencing each type of injury with estimates for all types of therapeutic treatment, also presented in Table 5. In both cases, the risks of research appear to be equal to, or less than, the basis for comparison, accidents in everyday life or routine therapeutic treatment.

Some evidence on the distribution of injuries to participants among research projects is provided by this study; the distribution appears to be quite heterogeneous or skewed. In part, this is related to the phenomena under investigation. For example, eight investigators (6 percent of the sample) accounted for 65 percent of all reported injuries in therapeutic research, and thirty-seven of forty-three fatalities (86 percent) occurred among patients receiving chemotherapy for cancer. Among investigators conducting nontherapeutic research, 12 percent account for all trivial injuries, 5 percent for all temporarily disabling injuries, and 0.4 percent for the single permanently disabling injury—the "probable." The same pattern can be described by pointing out that at least 83 percent of the investigators reported *no* injuries in nontherapeutic research. In brief, while there is virtually no probability of permanent damage to participants who engage in nontherapeutic research, the probability of any injury is not evenly distributed among all projects. Systematic review of the phenomena or procedures that are associated with injury may thus provide useful leads to mechanisms for reducing injuries.

Summary and Comments

Inference about the effects actually experienced by research participants is affected by the different research procedures used in studies. Studies that focus upon the ethical or unethical aspects of published reports of research can be used to support the argument that a substantial amount of unethical research occurs, but they have not provided estimates of benefits that might offset negative effects, particularly estimates of the importance of the intellectual issues to be resolved by the research. Studies that focus upon the investigators' estimates of the effects of their projects provide a more useful range of information, but the estimates of occurrence of positive and negative benefits are not very precise and seem to be quite inconsistent with evidence on the actual occurrence of negative effects—these occur for substantially less than one percent of the participants, or approximately 0.2 percent when all effects, trivial and temporary, are included. Investigators' estimates of negative effects are extremely inaccurate—much too high—when compared to the actual occurrence of such effects. One study that attempted to estimate the actual occurrence of negative effects in medical research found a rather low rate of occurrence, lower than risks of accidents in everyday life or negative effects of routine therapeutic treatment. Further, there is some indication that most of the negative effects occur among a small percentage of the projects; in other words, there seems to be a highly skewed distribution of risk across projects.

Several tentative conclusions can be drawn from this review of the available studies of effects on research participants. First, existing research is a valuable source of information, but the scope and precision of estimates could be substantially improved. Future research should utilize more precise measures of both the magnitude of effects and the probability of occurrence. Substantial attention should be given to the actual occurrence of effects, both positive and negative, since the estimates of investigators appear to be quite inaccurate. Second, these patterns have major implications for mechanisms designed to control research activities and investigators. Although the sample of projects was not random—projects were chosen from those receiving committee review and approval—there is no evidence to indicate that the investigators had been callous or indifferent to the possible negative effects upon the participants. In fact, the evidence is just the opposite: investigators seemed to estimate higher levels of risk than actually existed. Further, some evidence suggests that risks are highly concentrated among a few projects. This suggests that control of participant risk would probably be more efficient if future efforts were directed toward identifying those characteristics of projects that seem to account for the greatest percentage of negative effects rather than attempting to increase supervision of *all* research activity.

Individual Effects: Cost-Benefit Ratio

The final stage of a utilitarian analysis is the comparison of the anticipated costs and benefits of a particular course of action. In the ideal case, all effects would be clearly identified and measured with the same standard (such as money for economic analysis); this would allow a direct comparison of the utility of costs and benefits. But several features of research projects complicate such a comparison.

First, the type of effects to be considered will vary by categories of research activity. If the participant alone will benefit from the activity, there may be no contribution to a body of knowledge that could help others, and research benefits need not be considered. If others might benefit along with the participant, additional estimates become involved in the comparison, although the major factors may still be the effects for the participants. If there are no direct benefits to the participant, then the major positive effects must be sought in contributions to knowledge and possible benefits to others. In short, three different types of situations require the identification and estimation of somewhat different types of effects.

A second complication stems from the wide range of effects to be considered and the resulting inability to use a common standard for all effects. This makes it impossible to directly compare the utility of many of the effects, such as the "cost" of an invasion of privacy or the "benefit" of increased self-knowledge. One alternative is to make a subjective judgment regarding the balance of positive and negative benefits. This can be done on two bases, emphasizing the total effects for individuals and society as a whole—the perspective for most nontherapeutic research—or emphasizing only the effects for the research participants.

A serious study of the cost-benefit balance of projects for the participants would involve a sample of participants and some attempt to measure the number and magnitude of the positive and negative effects. These data might then be used to estimate the percentage of participants who "lost," "gained," or "balanced" the utility of effects. There appears to be no research that bears directly upon this issue; the studies that come closest are those that focus on effects for participants, reviewed above. There have been several attempts to estimate the cost-benefit balance for all participants in projects, using the judgments of the principal investigators as the basis for estimates of the balance.

A third major problem is the unpredictability of the effects—if the effects were predictable, the activity would of course not be considered research but simply a routine application of knowledge. One solution in such situations is to develop estimates of the probability of occurrence of effects and try to estimate the expected utility (or expected disutility) associated with each effect. A low probability of a highly valued effect would be considered equivalent to a high probability of an effect with a low value. Such a computation requires precise information on both the probability of effects and the utility or importance attached to each effect, measured on at least an internal scale; it is not surprising that few cost-benefit analyses have been able to utilize such computations. In contrast, several studies have developed estimates of the cost-benefit balance (or risk-benefit ratio) associated with research projects, using procedures that ignore the problems associated with a precise analysis. The general procedure has been to develop subjective estimates of all costs and benefits or of the risk-benefit ratio, without attention to careful measurement of each type of effect and probability of occurrence.

Estimates related to the positive and negative effects of biomedical projects assembled by Barber and others (1973) were used to classify projects on the basis of the estimated balance of effects for patient-participants. The scale for positive and negative effects was reduced to three way classifications; this procedure assumes that it is appropriate to compare directly the measures of positive (therapeutic benefits) and negative (risks) effects for the participants. But these may be incommensurable dimensions, and the authors present no evidence to support their assumption. A distribution of projects in relation to the balance of positive and negative effects was developed in the study, and it appeared that the potential effects for the patient-participants were either balanced or favorable for 80 percent of the projects, possibly unfavorable for 18 percent, and probably unfavorable for 2 percent. Given the tendency of investigators to overestimate the risk associated with research, it would be difficult to argue that a substantial proportion of projects will "cost" the participants.

The studies of projects approved by institutional review boards (Institute for Social Research, 1976b, 1976c) included estimates provided by the principal investigators of the risk-benefit ratio for participants. These differ from the study by Barber and others (1973) in that the investigators provided an estimate of the cost-benefit ratio per se; the ratio was not estimated by comparing the investigators' separate estimates for the probability of positive and negative effects. Investigators estimated more risk than benefit for 4 percent of all projects, with 2 percent considered as having substantially more risk than benefit; 39 percent were seen as having a balanced risk benefit ratio, and 56 percent as providing more benefit than risk.

Projects were also classified on the basis of whether or not they were expected to have a substantial direct benefit for the participants. While the percentage of projects expected to have a greater risk than benefit was approximately the same for these two categories (4.7 percent), the percentage expected to provide greater benefits was dramatically affected; 85 percent of the beneficial projects were expected to provide participants with more benefits than risks, compared to 22 percent of the nonbeneficial projects. However, since the classification of projects was based, in part, on the expected benefits for the participants, this result should not be unexpected.

Investigators supervising research with children and the mentally infirmed provided similar estimates, although a much smaller percentage of projects was considered to have greater risks than benefits (2 percent); the percentage of projects expected to have equal risks and benefits or greater benefits were of the same order of magnitude for the three categories of research populations—children, mentally infirmed, and general. No such estimates were developed for research with prisoners (Institute for Social

Research, 1976a), perhaps because all studies were related to drug research with minimal direct benefits to the prisoner participants.

In general, the available evidence suggests that while there are a number of studies that involve high risks for the participants, the percentage of such studies is very small, from 4 to 20 percent. Perhaps more significant is the inadequacy of the available information for resolving issues or problems of policy related to the use of human participants in research. This is due to the imprecise estimates of costs and benefits—there is no evidence to distinguish between the magnitude of the effects and the probability of their occurrence—and a lack of confidence in investigators as accurate sources of estimates. While investigators would seem to have a vested interest in making projects appear benign, evidence in the previous sections suggests that they provide high estimates of the probability of negative effects. Further, it is not clear which benefits were incorporated into their estimates of the cost-benefit ratios in the second set of studies (Institute for Social Research, 1976b, 1976c): benefits to participants, science, society, or all three. If more precise information about the characteristics of projects with unfavorable, balanced, or favorable cost-benefit ratios—from both the perspective of the participants and society—were available, identification of projects that required special attention or less surveillance would be facilitated.

Individual Effects: Distribution

A major problem with the direct application of a utilitarian analysis for making decisions involves the distribution of effects among members of society. In terms of an individual's decision to participate in a project, this is not a problem; a utilitarian analysis would emphasize the positive and negative effects for each individual participant. But for decisions regarding the initiation of projects that may have substantial effects for others besides the participants, the analysis becomes quite different; concern may develop over the distribution of both costs and benefits. For example, the costs of a research project may be considerable, requiring substantial financial resources and professional commitment. If these costs are borne by society, each person incurs a small

negative effect; if a few research participants with complex problems receive dramatic, significant benefits, there is a substantial imbalance in the distribution of costs and benefits. Some medical research, such as studies of organ (heart, kidney, bone marrow)
transplants seem to have this characteristic. Such research can be
justified if the high value of the positive benefits to the few is seen
as outweighing the small increase in the tax burden borne by the
general population. It may be further justified by the argument
that the patient-participants cannot be blamed for their problems
and that society should be organized to help those suffering such
"accidents."

The converse situation occurs when participants are exposed to a high risk of negative effects for projects that may produce small benefits for all. Here the concern might be that social
scientists study the disadvantaged (poor, prisoners, factory workers) because they are convenient and the resulting information will
be of value to the "elite" who want to "control" the disadvantaged.
There may also be concern that risky research is conducted on
those who are not free to refuse (charity patients, the mentally infirmed, prisoners) in order to provide knowledge that will benefit
the privileged.

A serious attempt to determine the distribution of positive
and negative effects of research activity on various categories of
citizens should involve either a random sample of the general population (to measure such effects) or a careful sample of individuals
participating in research. Since neither of these appear to have
been completed, it is necessary to utilize the evidence available
about the characteristics of those participating in research and
about the extent to which projects with different cost-benefit ratios
utilize participants with different characteristics.

Evidence on the nature of participants utilized in general
research is provided by the Institute for Social Research (1976c,
p. 103) study mentioned earlier. It appears that patients are used
in a higher percentage of projects (67 percent) than are other types
of participants, although staff members (8 percent), students (11
percent), and members of the general population (33 percent) are
all used in a substantial proportion of projects. There is no great
difference between beneficial (for the participants) and nonbene-

ficial projects in this regard. Examination of the relationship between the type of research and the characteristics of the participants indicates substantial differences. Seventy-nine percent of biomedical projects involved patients, 6 percent staff, 7 percent students, and 23 percent other types of participants (mostly from the general population). In contrast, 41 percent of behavioral research (intervention and "other") projects utilized patients, 12 percent staff, 21 percent students, and 54 percent other types of participants. Perhaps the major importance of these descriptions is that they tend to disprove the notion that any particular category of citizens is being used to provide advantages for others, unless there is something unique about the research involving patients or the patients themselves.

Additional evidence on this point is provided from these studies by a comparison of the expected effects of general research with the effects of research utilizing children, the mentally infirmed, and prisoners (Institute for Social Research, 1976a, 1976b, 1976c). There was no indication that the probability of negative effects for participants was substantially higher for either of the incarcerated groups—mentally infirmed and prisoners—and there even seem to be minor direct benefits for the prisoners. A similar pattern is present in comparisons of the cost-benefit ratio of projects utilizing different populations of participants; the cost-benefit ratio was approximately the same for general research and for research utilizing children and the mentally infirmed.

Another study of research supervised by medical investigators classified projects on the basis of the nature of participants, distinguishing between private patients, assumed to be affluent enough to provide for their own medical expenses, and ward or clinic patients, assumed to be receiving medical care financed by other sources and, hence, to be less autonomous with respect to choice of medical treatment (Barber and others, 1973, p. 54). The investigator's estimates of risks to the participants suggested that there was no substantial pattern of higher risk projects that used a larger percentage of ward or clinic patients.

An alternative analysis involved classification of the same projects on the basis of the estimated cost-benefit balance and the nature of the participants (Barber and others, 1973, p. 56). Among projects with a probably or possibly unfavorable cost-benefit balance, 58 percent involved from 75 to 100 percent ward or clinic patients, whereas only 31 percent with a balanced or possibly favorable ratio utilized such a high percentage of ward or clinic patients (all remaining participants were private patients). While this finding may suggest that low-income patients were being exploited, two points should be made. First, as already mentioned, there are some problems with the cost-benefit estimates produced for this analysis. Second, the ward or clinic patients received medical care they might not have been able to receive unless they were involved in research projects—this was particularly true in the early 1970s when the data were collected. If, however, one assumes that all citizens are entitled to medical care as a basic right, it is hardly possible to argue that these individuals should bear an unfavorable cost-benefit ratio compared to more affluent patients.

While evidence from past research practices (Ivy, 1948; Katz, 1972)—with slaves, prisoners, the poor, and so forth—clearly suggests that certain categories of individuals *were* more likely to be subjected to research risk than advantaged and influential social groups, the available evidence on research practices in the United States in the 1970s does not provide strong support for the conclusion that the disadvantaged bear research risks for the benefit of the advantaged. Bearing research risks and experiencing their benefits may not be distributed homogeneously throughout the population, but there is not enough reliable data to determine the actual form of the distribution—a problem that could, however, be overcome.

Effects Associated with Research on Social Systems

Research that involves social systems is a basic focus of many social science disciplines, including anthropology, economics, political science, and sociology. It is useful, in a discussion of the effects of research, to consider the application of the utilitarian strategy to those situations where the unit of analysis is an interrelated collection of individuals—a social system. While a cost-benefit analysis does not have the same implications for the decision of a "social system" to participate in research, it does have implications for the decision to initiate research, because the effects upon the social system may be considered either positive or negative.

The major emphasis is slightly different when social systems rather than individuals are the focus of study, for not only are the types of effects different but confidence that a research activity *can* produce changes in social systems may be lacking. For example, a political survey conducted among several thousand voters may stimulate discussion of issues, but there may be little reason to expect that it will have a major influence on the voting preferences of an electorate of millions. At the same time, there may be substantial confidence that research on social systems has had marked effects upon individuals associated with a particular social system. These might include: (1) effects upon individual relationship to the social system (involvement or inclusion, structural position, informal reputation, and so forth); or (2) effects upon individual behavior, performances, or activities within the social system, actual or as perceived by other members. Such effects may be positive or negative from the perspective of the individual involved or in terms of the "interests" of the social system. For example, a promotion may benefit both the individual and the social system. Further, there is no reason to expect that the effects for the individual and the social system will be congruent; those considered negative for the individual may be seen as positive for the social system, or vice versa. For example, an individual may wish to retain his position in a formal organization, which might benefit if he left; a person providing crucial contributions may leave an organization for a better opportunity.

Research activities involving social systems fall into three general categories, regardless of the focus of the study:

1. Experimental activities—deliberate attempts to modify a set of variables to determine the causal effect on another set of variables.
2. Active, overt data collections—generally requiring the active cooperation of others (as in surveys), although there is no attempt to systematically affect any phenomena or variables.
3. Passive, covert data collection—generally involving the development of descriptions of natural phenomena using informa-

tion that is provided as a matter of normal activity, either through public performances (courtroom proceedings, press conferences, work of salespersons, and the like) or for administrative purposes (decennial census, official public reports, and so forth).

These categories parallel the major research procedures used in the study of individuals, although they may require a new perspective (in terms of impact for the subject of research) when considered in terms of research on social systems.

The use of an experimental research procedure in studies that involve social systems has two important features. First, confidence that the research has had an effect upon the social system will be at a maximum; indeed, this is one of the major advantages of experimental research. Second, the complexities associated with such research—particularly the need for systematic control of variables—considerably restrict the scope of application. Occasionally it is possible to conduct an experimental study with some of the structural features or processes in aggregates (such as different types of channels for crowd movement), formally established organizations (such as the work procedures to be followed in a subunit of a corporation), or self-contained social systems (variations in the treatment of individuals on welfare, for example), but it is almost impossible—because of the cost alone—to utilize experimental procedures for study of the characteristics of an entire social system, except for some possible applications with interpersonal groups (families, work groups, and the like). And for most research with social systems, there can be little confidence that the research activity will have a major impact.

Overt data collection—for example, observations of behavior and surveys—is frequently used in the study of social systems. Aside from considerations associated with individuals, the scope and momentum of processes in most social systems suggest that such procedures will have little effect. However, there may be some small, less cohesive social systems—such as an engaged couple or a counselor and a client—that will be seriously affected by the nature and form of such data collection. For example, the questions raised may introduce factors into the relationship that were absent prior to the initiation of the research, such as a question for an engaged couple about the "ideal family size" or a question for a counselor and client about a "just fee."

Passive, covert data collection can take at least two forms, collection of new information and review of existing public data. If a project is confined to the review of existing public data, whether public performances or data collected for public distribution through existing procedures, then there is little chance that major new effects on the social system will occur. In the event that new data are collected in a covert fashion (no action is required on the part of the social system or its participants, who are unaware of the research activity), it is again unlikely that any direct effects will occur. However, it should be mentioned that a major controversy over research with a social system—the study of real juries in the legal process—involved use of such a technique; the controversy stemmed from concern that knowledge that such research was permitted might affect the deliberations of juries in the future, causing the members to be less open and unbiased in their discussions and reducing confidence that their decisions represented justice.

In summary, substantial, direct effects upon social systems—apart from any effects upon the individual members—are likely to be associated with experimental research on interpersonal groups. Direct, overt observations may produce some effects, but it is unlikely that passive covert research activities will influence social systems in a direct fashion. All research strategies may influence the social system in an indirect fashion, depending upon how such reports are utilized by those with influence on that system.

Once the possible effects of research upon a social system are identified, it is a major problem to determine the extent to which they are good or bad from the perspective of society as a whole. While there is some general agreement regarding desirable outcomes for individuals—good health, education, improved social position, pleasant job, and the like—this is somewhat less true for social systems, particularly for those that are not self-contained. For example, while it may be considered good to enhance the task effectiveness of a social system, some may not consider this desirable if it is done at the expense of individual rights or promotes the growth of organized crime. While it may be considered good for a social system to survive, not all may consider it good for an unsatisfying marriage to continue.

The purpose of developing a cost-benefit analysis is to ensure that the net impact of a research project is positive, a benefit to society. The problems associated with applying a cost-benefit analysis to research involving social systems—particularly the ambiguities associated with determination of good effects—lead to serious consideration of an alternative. The most defensible position may be to conduct the research in such a way that there will be no effect upon the social system—survival, task effectiveness, social characteristics, and the like will not be affected in any way. This would minimize complications associated with controversy over what is a desirable effect. As social systems, unlike individuals, are not considered to have rights that may be abridged, there are few other issues of significance.

Summary

The utilitarian analysis provides a procedure for analyzing and comparing alternatives that have multiple, inconsistent effects. The important decisions related to research are made by (1) individuals confronted with an opportunity to participate in research and (2) investigators considering the initiation of a research project. A utilitarian analysis requires a number of basic steps, including identification of important effects, estimates of the intensity or utility of all positive and negative effects, estimates of the probability of occurrence and expected utility, and the final step—calculation of the cost-benefit balance. Presumably, if the total benefits are greater than the total costs, the decision will be to initiate the action—that is, to become involved as a participant or to implement a project. A major difference between the analysis regarding an individual decision to participate in a project and that regarding initiation of the project is consideration of the possible effects that the latter decision will have for society.

Individual Decision to Participate in Research

Identification of the major effects for individuals, the first step in the analysis for either decision, was pursued by classifying effects, both positive and negative, into four categories: temporary direct effects, permanent direct effects, effects mediated by society, and effects upon rights (specified for a particular society). Temporary and permanent direct effects were further subdivided into biomedical, psychological, and social contextual effects.

Available research seems to indicate that estimates of the magnitude of some negative effects are possible; the emphasis has been upon effects common in social science research, both in experiments and in questionnaire administration. College undergraduates seem to consider some potential effects—related to physical pain, psychic stress, invasion of privacy, and deception—less desirable than others, but these effects are not seen as more distressing than disorganized or inconsiderate administration of research or unpleasant everyday experiences in college life. In contrast, psychologists evaluate certain effects of research as much more undesirable than do representatives of the student population.

Two procedures have been used to measure the occurrence of unethical practices or research effects. The studies of the descriptions of research projects indicate that a substantial percentage of social-psychological experiments (as described in leading journals) involve deception of some kind, deception being defined as failure to provide complete and accurate information to the participants. Interviews with investigators find that they anticipate negative effects in a substantial proportion of research, although these are usually minor effects or expected with a very low probability. The few attempts to systematically estimate the actual occurrence of negative effects for participants find such occurrences to be very rare—much less frequent than indicated from estimates based on investigators' judgments. Some evidence indicates that actual damage is distributed among projects in a quite skewed fashion; a very few projects account for a substantial proportion of the participants who experience negative effects.

Estimates of the cost-benefit balance for individual projects have been developed, but none warrant high confidence. One procedure has been to compare investigators' estimates of negative and positive effects—using scales that may be incommensurate—to develop an estimate of the percentage of projects with an unfavorable balance (approximately 20 percent). Another procedure has been to ask investigators to estimate the risk-benefit ratio for projects they are conducting; approximately 4 percent of a sample of projects had unfavorable balances based upon this procedure. Unfortunately, it is not clear what effects were included in the investigators' subjective judgments, although benefits to society may have been stressed in the projects where there were no direct benefits expected for the participants.

The available information suggests that it is useful to assemble the information required to complete a cost-benefit analysis of individual decisions to participate; it would appear that in most cases negative effects of research are innocuous or absent (except for the participant's investment of time) and far less of a threat (considering either severity or probability of occurrence) than might be expected. A major problem, obscured by the emphasis on studies of aggregates, participants, or principal investigators, is the substantial individual differences that may exist among participants with regard to the value or severity attached to the various effects. Some may consider a mild shock more threatening than an invasion of privacy, while others may consider a token cash payment less valuable than increased self-knowledge.

This problem, as well as the problems associated with comparing estimates of the utility of various effects, is to some extent resolved by allowing *each* individual participant to make a decision regarding involvement in a project—the informed consent procedure. While the basic justification for the use of informed consent is a respect for individual self-determination, it can also be considered a mechanism that allows each potential participant to complete a cost-benefit analysis and develop his or her own individual judgment about participation.

Research with Social Systems

The application of a utilitarian analysis to research with social systems is complicated by the ambiguity of the "status" of social systems—they are not considered to have rights in the same sense as individuals—and by low confidence that research activity can have a major effect upon social systems. (One exception is experimental research conducted with natural interpersonal groups, such as families or work groups, and with groups created for a research project, such as discussion groups of students or mock juries.) The major impact of a research project upon a social system may be indirect, as when a research report is utilized by the normal political processes that modify and change the structure and membership of social systems. Any research project involving social systems may have substantial influence upon the members; analysis of the potential effects upon these participants should be separated from analysis of effects on the social system itself.

An unresolved problem in evaluating the impact of a research project on a social system, such as an aggregate, an established, structured organization, or a self-contained society, is determining whether a potential effect is desirable or not. But such problems can be avoided if the project is conducted in a way that minimizes any lasting effects upon the social system. While this does not solve the problem of establishing what is "best" for the social system, it does allow research to proceed. Such an orientation is probably not feasible for research with individuals, since there is more general agreement on what constitutes benefit and harm to individuals than to society.

Decisions Regarding Initiation of Projects

Use of a utilitarian analysis for the major research decision of investigators—whether or not to initiate a specific research project—requires consideration of the effects (positive and negative) for participants, as well as several additional factors. One of these is the distribution of effects—if the positive and negative effects are distributed unevenly, questions of distributive justice will arise. Another involves the effects (positive and negative) for society (or its members), distinct from the effects for the participants. Positive effects for society are usually considered in two categories: the benefit of an increase in knowledge—knowledge itself being the desired objective—and benefits that result from application of the knowledge. The second category includes any new technique or procedure that directly or indirectly increases the welfare of the members of society.

There may, however, be disagreement on the value of potential applications of successful research. If all possible applications of a successful research project are considered to have only negative outcomes for society, an argument may be made that the cost-benefit balance—for society—can only be unfavorable and, hence, the research should not be conducted (Block and Dworkin, 1974b). This argument may be difficult to apply to those projects that have no direct, obvious applications to societal problems or decisions—the essence of pure research. More subtle would be those negative effects attributed to the conduct of research, irrespective of direct applications. These might include a shift in values toward acceptance of procedures that incorporate individuals as "things" or "units," consistent with the view that participants are "research material." Further, research procedures that involve deception, invasion of privacy, or a reduction in individual autonomy might lead to an increased acceptance of such activities as legitimate, particularly if they are initiated by scientific investigators, who are usually prestigious persons in positions of influence and authority.

Analysis of the cost-benefit balance for society may involve concern over the allotment of positive and negative benefits—the distributive justice issue. Review of the available studies suggests that research does not systematically involve abuse of one social category of participants, unless it was those individuals associated with universities and medical research institutions. Studies of drug toxicity utilizing prisoners provided a major exception to this generalization, but only because there were no direct benefits possible to these participants; direct negative effects appeared to occur very infrequently. Analysis of the character of the patient-participants in one study of medical research seemed to indicate that charity patients were more heavily involved in projects with a low cost-benefit ratio, but the calculation of this ratio was not without problems.

Research Suggestions

Discussion about processes and activities within society—including the conduct of research—will continue as long as knowledge increases and societal values and objectives evolve. The most widely used procedure for analyzing the desirability of various courses of action has reflected, and will probably continue to reflect, a utilitarian perspective. A precise application of this procedure is not possible for decisions regarding individual participation in research and may not be possible for decisions regarding the initiation of research projects. But no other procedure has been developed that will provide as useful a structure for the analysis of such decisions (Rawls, 1971, provides alternative criteria, not an alternative stragegy for analysis). Until such an alternative is provided, the utilitarian analysis will probably be the dominant procedure emphasized for all decisions.

While it is unlikely that it will ever be possible to employ a fully developed, quantitative utilitarian analysis—due to the incommensurability of the different effects, if nothing else—the precision of the analysis and confidence in its accuracy would be improved if additional research were completed on a number of problems, including:

• Improved information on the participant's evaluation of the intensity (or utility) of various effects; this should include all major categories of positive and negative effects.
• Additional information on the actual effects on participants from exposure to various research procedures; this would include a wide range of studies, participants, and types of effects. There is virtually no reliable evidence on these effects at present.
• Better measures for estimating the significance of research; standardized measures based on the judgments of investigators, knowledgeable lay individuals, and typical citizens should be established.
• Evaluation of the product of utilitarian analyses by various persons and groups including investigators committed to the projects, investigators not associated with the projects, and committees of varying composition.

There is some reason to doubt that such studies will be completed, since the major emphasis, which reflects a legal perspective, has been on developing acceptable *procedures* for resolving differences related to the conduct of research rather than on the actual consequences of research.

4

Waiving Rights: Application of Informed Consent

━━━◆━◆━◆━◆━◆━◆━◆━◆━◆━━━

Most research does not involve risks of negative effects for participants, but research that does—and that also has a potential for substantial positive benefits to society—requires two decisions. If the first issue, whether or not the project should be initiated, is settled in the affirmative, the second—the selection of individuals to bear the risk of negative effects—must be resolved. The most widely accepted solution has been to allow potential participants to make their own decision regarding involvement—this is the criterion of informed consent. In essence, this assumes that allowing each individual to make his or her own utilitarian (cost-benefit) analysis and arrive at a personal decision reflects a respect for the right of self-determination and shifts part of the responsibility to the participant for any of the negative effects that might be experienced.

Discussions of the implementation of the informed consent procedure focus on the nature of the conditions under which there is confidence that an individual's decision is truly self-determined: (1) competence to make decisions about one's future, (2) receipt of full and complete information about possible effects, (3) comprehension of information, and (4) a situation that allows a voluntary choice. Considerable attention has been given to the specific implementation of these four characteristics and to complications when they are implemented in atypical research situations.

Justification for Informed Consent

The increased emphasis on informed consent appears to have occurred concurrently with two major shifts in the values and norms of advanced societies. The first is the gradual elimination of categories of individuals not entitled to full consideration as human beings. For thousands of years, research with human beings involved categories of individuals thought especially suitable as research material; prisoners, slaves, the poor, charity patients, peasants, and others considered less worthy by the investigators, who tended to belong to the privileged classes in society, were utilized as research subjects, often carelessly and with little regard for the consequences to them. In modern times it has generally been assumed that no category of individuals is less worthy than any other, despite differences in personal characteristics, abilities, or experiences; this is clearly the emphasis of the *universal* declaration of human rights (see Chapter Two).

A second major shift has been the elaboration and increased emphasis upon various individual rights, the rights that individuals are assumed to have regardless of the form of the political or other institutions in society. These two trends were explicitly recognized in the Nuremberg trials with the creation of the first legal principles related to the conduct of medical research (Appendix 2); these principles were developed to assist evaluation of the research conducted by medical investigators in the concentration camps of Nazi

Germany.* The four major elements of informed consent—competence, voluntarism, full information, and comprehension—were first explicated in this document; they are now generally considered the conditions under which the individual is assumed to be able to exercise self-determination. And, presumably, individuals able to exercise self-determination would not agree to become involved in procedures that would lead to severe pain, bodily damage, or death.

Justification of informed consent as a mechanism for ensuring that the individual shares responsibility for infringements upon his own rights and welfare is widely reflected in legal standards, discussions of moral philosophers, research agency guidelines, and a large number of codes adopted by professional associations representing investigators (medical and social scientists). Less well known are the other justifications for informed consent procedures, some of which are listed below:†

1. Promotes respect of the participant's right to self-determination in control of other basic rights (freedom from bodily harm, privacy, freedom of movement, and the like).

*It is difficult to envision the context in which the Nuremberg Code developed without acquaintance with the transcripts of the original trial. The research conducted by physicians on prisoners included tests of reactions to simulated high altitudes; experiments on the effectiveness of various treatments for frozen body parts and different types of wounds (emphasizing sulfanilamide); research on diseases (malaria, epidemic jaundice, spotted fever) given to healthy persons for research purposes; studies with poisons; and the photographing, measurement, execution, and defleshing of "one hundred twelve Jews . . . for the purpose of completing a skeleton collection for the Reich University of Strasbourg" (Katz, 1972, p. 294). The defendants represented the entire range of the medical profession in Germany, from world-renowned scientists to the most marginal of professionals. A review of the "highlights" of the trial (*United States* v. *Karl Brandt*) is provided by Katz (1972).

†There has been one serious suggestion about the conditions when informed consent may be deemphasized. Making the assumption that individuals have an obligation to promote justice in society and defining justice as advantages for the "less fortunate" at the expense of the "more fortunate," Veatch (1978, p. 50) has suggested that, if research requires

2. Promotes respect of participants as unique individuals, as persons (Katz and Capron, 1975, pp. 82–85; Veatch, 1978, p. 9; Fletcher, 1967, p. 632; Fletcher, 1973, p. 41).
3. Minimizes fraud and deceit (Katz and Capron, 1975, pp. 85–87; Fletcher, 1973, p. 41).
4. Minimizes coercion and duress (Katz and Capron, 1975, pp. 85–87; Fletcher, 1973, p. 41).
5. Encourages self-scrutiny by investigators (Katz and Capron, 1975, pp. 87–88; Katz, 1972, p. 524).
6. Promotes responsible (legal-rational) decisions by participants (Katz and Capron, 1975, pp. 88–90; Katz, 1972, p. 524).
7. Reduces the possibility of criminal or civil liabilities for the investigator(s) (Levine, 1978b, p. 3; Gray, 1975, p. 239).
8. Promotes an egalitarian relationship between investigator and participant (Fletcher, 1967a, p. 646; Katz, 1969, pp. 486–487).
9. Allows participants to have an interesting experience (Gray, 1975, pp. 238–239).
10. Promotes involvement of the public and increases public support and trust in the research enterprise (Katz and Capron, 1975, p. 90; Veatch, 1978, pp. 9–14; Gray, 1975, p. 240).

These additional justifications reflect a number of concerns about the actual procedure for acquiring informed consent, particularly with reference to the situation, common in clinical medical research, where the physician-investigator is involved with patient-participants. For example, it has been widely observed that patients provide consent automatically, often unaware of the distinction between treatment, therapeutic research for their own benefit, and nontherapeutic research for the benefit of others or of science. This may lead to a suspicion that the entire procedure is not taken seriously by physician-investigators and attempts to convince such medical scientists that they should be conscientious about utilizing informed consent.

---

the contributions of more advantaged members of society and will promote the interests of the less advantaged (although not necessarily society in general), respect for individual self-determination may be "sacrificed." This, of course, shows the influence of Rawls (1971).

A second concern is associated with the social relationship that frequently exists between the investigator and the participant. This is almost universally one of differential authority and influence, although in medical research it may be modified by the physician-patient relationship of benefactor and recipient. This kind of relationship is strongly reinforced by medical educations that emphasize the physician's responsibility for the well-being of the patient (Katz, 1969). It is frequently suggested that such an orientation may result in a condescending attitude toward participants and thus may reduce their conception of self-worth as persons. Many suggest that the ideal relationship is one of equality (Mead, 1969); that is, an egalitarian partnership for exploring the unknown rather than a relationship in which one of the participants agrees to become "research material" for the investigator's purposes, albeit after receiving complete information regarding the procedure and possible effects. It is not always clear whether the concern is for a social relationship that will facilitate a voluntary commitment—or withdrawal—by the participant or whether the major goal is to promote equality per se.

A third reason for additional justifications for informed consent centers on the nature of the decision procedure utilized by those providing consent. While the legal model assumes a careful, conscientious evaluation of all the relevant information, it has been widely observed that many respondents, particularly in medical settings, agree to participate without a complete review of all factors, frequently relying upon the recommendations of an applied professional (such as a physician), who may also be the investigator. Emphasis upon the details of the informed consent procedure is associated with a desire to "improve" the quality of the decisions made by the participants, ensuring that they will be more autonomous and conscientious in making their decisions; that is, that they will adopt a legal-rational strategy.

Since there is no "right" answer to the question of whether or not an individual should participate in a particular research project, the focus on the features of informed consent is meant to provide confidence that all potential participants will be able to make a decision that allows their best interests to be fully and objectively considered in the decision. It may be that the attempts to promote these additional features—serious implementation by applied professional investigators, a research partnership between investigator and participant, and a responsible (rational) judgment by the participant—will provide some observers with confidence that the participant has provided voluntary, informed, and considered consent. Further suggestions have been made about the implementation of informed consent, including procedures for monitoring investigators and their approach to the procedure. These suggestions reflect a lack of confidence that every investigator will allow every participant to exercise self-determination.

Suggestions for Implementation

Informed consent procedures provide a solution to those situations where there is a conflict between desirable societal objectives and the rights of the individual. It is a specification of conditions—competence to make a decision, a setting void of coercion or undue influence, complete information, and comprehension of that information—that provides confidence that an individual has made a voluntary, rational judgment to forgo personal rights or accept the risks of negative effects. The following discussion reflects various suggestions that have been made about the implementation of the informed consent procedures; they appear to be based on different observers' judgments as to what provides *them* with confidence that a voluntary choice can be made.

Capacity to Make a Decision

A basic assumption associated with informed consent is that the decision made by a responsible, rational, and mature individual who is given the available information will be the correct decision. Since it is obvious that there are numerous persons who are not mature, responsible, and rational, the problem becomes one of systematically identifying them. Several solutions are possible: (1) providing criteria that can be applied to any individual to determine if he or she is competent, (2) identifying social categories of individuals who can be considered competent, or (3) identifying social categories of not competent individuals (who are to be treated in special ways). Almost all the serious discussion has been directed to the third alternative, selection of social categories of individuals who are considered not competent.

For the most part, individuals are said not to have the capacity to provide consent on the basis of two criteria—either they have inadequate mental capacity or they are in situations where there is some question about their ability to exercise self-determination. Those considered not competent usually include fetuses, young children, comatose medical patients, and formerly competent adults who are now mental patients. Other categories are less clear-cut, such as older children (teenagers), those institutionalized as mentally infirm but who are not necessarily mentally incompetent, prisoners, and individuals who are so distracted by their own illnesses that they are unable to consider the implications of involvement in a research project in a rational, objective fashion.

The distinction between two types of research—therapeutic (the participants are expected to benefit) and nontherapeutic (benefits accrue to others)—is related to an important variation of the informed consent procedure. Many consider it appropriate for parents, guardians, and others responsible for participants to make decisions for them when the participants may receive direct benefits and are considered not competent. (Military personnel have been disciplined for failure to submit to routine therapeutic procedures. See Johnson, 1953.) If there is no potential benefit but little or no risk, it may also be considered acceptable for the guardians to make the decisions. But, if there is no possible direct benefits and some risk of negative effects for participants who are considered not competent to make a rational decision, many would suggest that the research be prohibited altogether. This may reflect a lack of confidence in the judgment of the guardians or doubt that the social benefits of research could ever be great enough to justify such research (National Commission for the Protection of Human Subjects of Biomedical and Behavioral Research, 1977c).

Voluntary Choice

Perhaps the major issue related to relinquishing rights and accepting risks (or accepting another as a trustee of one's care) is the degree to which this is a voluntary decision; indeed, the notion of basic rights was developed as a guarantee against abuse of influence and privilege by those in positions of power. Establishing the conditions under which an individual is considered to be acting on the basis of free will—and not responding to some process or set of processes he or she cannot control—is a complex issue with little or no satisfactory resolution. Discussions about moral dilemmas in research tend to avoid the central issue, that is, the voluntary decision of a "typical" individual, and emphasize instead those situations where an individual is not free. These situations are usually ones that involve substantial influence from a person in authority—for example, a physician-investigator—or an institutional setting of some type—a prison, mental institution, hospital, public school, university, or the like.

Perhaps the most difficult situation for consideration—and one of the most prevalent—is that of the individual in the care of a physician-investigator. He may be asked to consent to routine, but complicated, treatment for his own benefit, novel and experimental therapy for his own benefit, or research procedures that will provide no direct personal benefits but may benefit others. When the individual is physically weak, concerned for his own health, desirous of being a "good patient," wishing to encourage attention from his physician, and confused by hospital administrative procedures, there is some question whether he will be able to distinguish among these various requests.

To give one example of this type of confusion, a study of the clinical effects of four drugs on neurotic outpatients was conducted without informing the seventy-two individuals that they were participating in a research project (Park and others, 1966). During the procedure the participants were subjected to multiple research procedures, including double-blind prescriptions (neither physician nor patient knows who receives the active agent or the inefficient placebo), evaluations by several interviewers, role playing by treating physicians, unexpected change of treating physicians, completion of multiple forms, and observation and recording of interviews. The majority of the patients (76 percent) considered all procedures diagnostic and had no notion whatsoever that research goals were involved; only 4 percent (three patients) were sure that research was being conducted. Patients tended to assume that anything that happened was part of the treatment; fourteen considered checking questionnaires as helping them gain an understanding of their symptomatology; nine felt that the tape recorder was useful; and two indicated a positive reaction toward a one-way observation window. This evidence suggests that patients are willing and able to interpret almost any feature or activity as part of a therapeutic procedure.

Concern that patients in institutional settings may not be fully aware of the nature of the "treatment" they are receiving has led to a number of suggestions about the procedures to be followed in obtaining consent. These include review of the procedure for obtaining consent that the investigator will use by special local committees considering the situation of the nonfree participant (Levine, 1978b) or by a national committee with the same responsibility (Veatch, 1978, p. 48). It has been suggested that the educated upper-middle class should be used as research participants because they are the "least captive" members of society (Jonas, 1969, p. 237). A pretest of the procedure with surrogate subjects, who are comparable to the intended subjects but who will not participate in the actual research and are not under a physician-investigator's care for a medical problem, may provide an "honest reaction" to the proposed research (Fost, 1975); actual participants are assumed to be compliant when the request comes from their primary physician during an illness. It is considered important to tell the participants why they were chosen (Veatch, 1978, p. 31); this may help them decide how important it is for them to be involved. The proposal could be formulated as a request or invitation rather than a demand (Veatch, 1978, p. 31); assuring participants that they may withdraw at any time may reduce feelings of coercion (Levine, 1978b, pp. 27–30).

A number of suggestions concern the relationship that may develop between the investigator and the participant. Perhaps the most frequent is the already mentioned suggestion that the investigator create an egalitarian relationship with the participant, providing a setting where the participant views the endeavor as a joint adventure in an exploration of the unknown (Mead, 1969). It has also been suggested that the presence of a third, presumably neutral party during the informed consent procedure would minimize possibilities for coercion (Fletcher, 1967a, p. 648). Others suggested that a third party, not directly involved in the research project, should obtain the participant's consent, thus minimizing coercion by an enthusiastic investigator, who may be the participant's physician (Veatch, 1978, p. 32). However, this conflicts with a concern that delegation of responsibility may encourage investigators to be less conscientious about the major ethical issues and the treatment of participants than they would otherwise be. It has been suggested that participants be allowed to consult with others after a request is made and before a decision is reached (Veatch, 1978, p. 31) and that at least a twenty-four-hour period elapse between the request and the decision (Fletcher, 1967, p. 649).

A major concern that has been raised with respect to self-determination is the extent to which the situation of individuals allows them to actually refuse to participate in the project. Examples of such situations include research with prisoners (who may be offered a reduced sentence and better living conditions), medical studies with the poor (who may not be able to afford medical care otherwise), experiments with students (who may be offered a chance for a better grade), and any research with disadvantaged individuals (anthropologists routinely provide food and medical care to those in primitive settings). There is also the exceptional research project in which "the total community may 'engineer' a consent, as when the president, the generals, and the newspapers call with a loud fanfare for a heroic crew of astronautical volunteers to attempt some ultrahazardous exploit" (Cahn, 1961, p. 11).

The general solution suggested for such cases is to ensure that the inducements are not exceptionally attractive in the sense that the general living situation of the individual provides him or her with such basic necessities as food, shelter, and medical care and that the magnitude of the intrinsic benefits is not "extreme." Additional benefits should be considered minor "luxuries" (Freedman, 1975, p. 36). Although it is impossible—and hardly desirable—to avoid the benefit of longer life or better health for individuals who agree to become involved in therapeutic research activity, it is possible to avoid offering substantial reductions in prison terms or substantial contributions to course grades in exchange for research participation. Just how to avoid providing adventurous explorers with overwhelming incentives of fame and recognition is not clear; space exploration, as a research activity, has clearly been conducted with minimum consideration of the incentives for individuals to participate.

Provision of Full Information

No individual can be *fully* informed regarding the procedures and possible effects associated with a research project; if there were full information, there would be no reason to conduct the research—research is only of value when there is ambiguity about a phenomenon. This can lead to the conclusion that the "full information" requirement is unattainable, and to a tendency to reject the entire informed consent procedure as unrealistic (Laforet, 1976). Two other strategies have been used in approaching the problem.

One is to specify all those elements that might be divulged to the participants during the obtaining of consent. Levine (1978b) gives a representative list:

1. Statement of overall purpose of the research.
2. Defining the role of the participants in the project.
3. Explanation of the procedures involved (parties to interact with the participant; location of the research; time when the research is to be conducted; repetition of procedures, if any; and time required of the participant).
4. Description of possible discomforts and risks.
5. Description of possible benefits.
6. Alternative procedures to benefit participants, if any.
7. An offer to answer any questions.
8. Review of what may not be disclosed to the individual.

Presumably, confidence that participants are "fully informed" will be greater as more categories of relevant information are disclosed before a decision is made. But too much information could lead to confusion on the part of the participants, who may not be able to comprehend all the information presented and may respond in unexpected ways.

Such information overload was examined in a study of participants' responses to requests to contribute to a research project on the effects of drugs (Epstein and Lasagna, 1969). Sixty-six individuals, all but two of whom were medical school or hospital employees, were asked to take two tablets of "acetylhydroxybenzoate" or a placebo when they next had a headache. Each subject was told of the study and asked to read and sign one of three versions of written informed consent forms; all contained the same basic information, but more details were given in the longer forms. All the participants who considered themselves in good health—no known problems related to the information provided on the drugs—and who received the short form (thirteen sentences) volunteered to participate. In contrast, only 68 percent of those in good health who read the medium length form (three times longer than the short form) or the long form (five times longer than the short form) agreed to participate.

While the investigators take great satisfaction that the effects described were those of aspirin (as found in a standard text on pharmacology), the fact that the "potential subjects" were almost all associated with the medical enterprise (and may not have trusted physicians), that the individual obtaining consent would not answer any questions calling for value judgments on the safety of the drug, and that probabilities of various effects were deemphasized or stated in general terms (not one quantitative frequency was provided) suggests considerable caution in drawing conclusions based on this study. A demonstration that participants may be confused by too much information would be more convincing if the added information were other than frightening descriptions of remote effects.

The ease with which participants may be overwhelmed with complex information leads to suggestions about the criteria for selecting critical items—the alternative to providing "full information." The problem becomes one of attempting to determine what information may be relevant to confidence that the individual is able to exercise the right of self-determination. One procedure is to let a committee, representative of potential participants, make the judgment, (Veatch, 1978, p. 27; Levine, 1978b), or to use a committee representative of both investigators and participants. Another way is to systematically interview surrogate subjects and allow them to determine what is relevant (Fost, 1975). All procedures emphasize the selection of information required for confidence that a rational person is making an informed decision. As another alternative one could redefine the objective as that of providing "valid consent" rather than "informed consent." This

would require provision of enough information to ensure that
the participant is responsible for his own decision (Freedman,
1975).

Comprehension

Confidence that the participant has provided knowing consent when the research procedure is associated with complex or
subtle risks is one of the most difficult problems to resolve; it is
clear that an elaborate written description, even if it is provided in
"ordinary language," may be difficult to fully comprehend. Often
the investigators themselves do not fully appreciate the phenomena or the possible effects for participants. This is considered a
more significant problem in nontherapeutic research where the
investigator has not accepted responsibility for benefiting the participant in some way.

Various suggestions have been made for ways to increase
confidence that comprehension has occurred, including the use of
highly educated participants (Jonas, 1969, p. 235), who are most
likely to understand the information and its implications; the availability of a consultant to discuss the study with the participant; and
a time delay between the request for participation and the decision
to become involved. A frequent suggestion is to provide an independent measure of comprehension by questioning the subject
(Gray, 1975, p. 244) or by providing the participant with a written
questionnaire that tests knowledge of information (Miller and Willner, 1974; Levine, 1978b; Annas, Glantz, and Katz, 1977). The
most carefully prepared protocol of this procedure envisions a
standard written consent form followed by a written questionnaire
containing open-ended questions; only subjects who responded to
these questions to the satisfaction of the investigator would be allowed to participate, that is, sign the written consent form (Miller
and Willner, 1974). This would place a willing, inarticulate participant in a rather awkward situation—he or she might wish to become involved in the research but be unable to pass the informed
consent test. By contrast, reluctant but discrete participants could
"refuse" to participate by repeatedly failing such a test until the
investigator gave up.

Problems with the Informed Consent Model

There are several problems with the ideal conception of the procedure that "should" be used if individuals are to provide informed consent. They include the limits of individuals (some with limited training and background) to absorb and comprehend information, the difficulty in establishing an egalitarian relationship between investigator and participant, and the intuitive (rather than legal-rational) processes used by many individuals to make such decisions.

There seems to be little question that the limits of most individuals to absorb and comprehend information may quickly be reached in many research projects. There is substantial evidence in social science to suggest that when an individual is required to make a decision regarding ambiguous alternatives he or she will tend to rely on the judgments of others; those perceived as experts or of higher status will have a substantial influence upon such decisions. (This is one of the recurrent findings in research on factors affecting conformity, reviewed in most social psychology texts.)

Individuals may feel comfortable refusing a request from one seen as an equal, such as a colleague, work peer, friend, or relative. But to expect that egalitarian, symmetrical-influence relationships will develop between investigators and participants is relatively naive; there has never been a social system where it has not been possible to measure a differentiation in influence. Since most investigators are better educated, have higher social status, are more informed about the research situation, are considered persons in authority by the research staff, and will be seen as more influential by the participants—it is difficult to determine just how an egalitarian exchange might be created. In fact, the dominance of the investigator is recognized in comments regarding egalitarian relationships, for it is suggested that the investigator should create such an atmosphere. Clearly, individuals with a potential for controlling a social atmosphere have more influence than others.

While it may be possible for investigators to modify their relationship with participants to encourage them to ask questions and to feel that they are being given consideration as persons, the establishment of an egalitarian research partnership between investigator and participant seems an impossible ideal for all but the simplest projects or very special research situations, which would probably involve a small number of participants and a rather intensive relationship (as in experimental heart transplants or extended observation of a small primitive culture).

The third issue is the extent to which individuals follow the legal-rational model—completing cost-benefit analyses—regarding their participation in complex, potentially hazardous activities. Some evidence suggests that such decisions are made instantaneously, without attention to information or careful consideration of possible effects and their probability of occurrence. For example, six of the sixty-six individuals (9 percent) approached about participation in the drug study mentioned earlier (Epstein and Lasagna, 1969) refused to even read the protocol, regardless of its length. In a study of the effects of various informed consent procedures upon participation in a survey interview, it was found that 7 percent of the individuals contacted refused participation before any description of the study or interview was provided (Singer, 1978). Some potential participants are obviously not interested in providing an "informed refusal."

Even more dramatic are the decisions made by donors in kidney transplant operations, who are asked to consent to a procedure with some risk and no direct personal benefits—the surgical removal of a healthy organ. It has been found that the major mode of donor decision making is instantaneous; 77 percent of the 30 donors in one study (Fellner and Marshall, 1970, p. 1247) and 61 percent of the 114 in another (Simmons, Klein, and Simmons, 1977, p. 241) reported that the decison was "immediate," "instantaneous," "split-second," and the like. Frequently they made their decision when they first heard, usually over the telephone, that they were potential donors, long before an extensive series of tests, a full presentation of information, and discussion of consequences by the physicians (in an informed consent meeting) had taken place.

The lack of impact of informed consent procedures is reflected in a study of the recall of information provided to patients in advance of beneficial cardiac surgery (Robinson and Merav, 1976). After two patients denied that a tape-recorded preoperative informed consent interview even occurred, the recollections of twenty patients four and six months following surgery were tested and compared to the tape-recorded informed consent meetings. Even with coaching to assist memory recall, patients could provide only 42 percent of the information accurately. Problems with details, attribution of errors, and fabrication—for example, claiming the physicians made promises that were not made—were common. Further, there was little relationship between self-confidence and accuracy of recall; "the poorest score of all twenty patients interviewed was achieved by a patient who responded authoritatively and expressed no doubts regarding his recollections" (Robinson and Merav, 1976, p. 212).

In summary, there are at least three features of the ideal model of informed consent that are inconsistent with substantial evidence developed within social science—reliance on the judgment of others when confronted with decisions with ambiguous alternatives (increased when the others are experts or of higher social status), the normal development of asymmetrical patterns of influence in social exchange, and the propensity of individuals to make important decisions *without* a rational, careful consideration of all alternatives and possible effects. It is not clear how consideration of these "natural phenomena" will affect confidence that participants have exercised self-determination in making decisions about research. They probably influence other important decisions that individuals make—selection of spouses, purchases of residences, entering careers or occupations—and there is a basic assumption that individuals generally exercise self-determination with respect to these choices. It seems reasonable to think that as long as individual participants are willing to accept partial responsibility for the consequences of their decisions they are exercising self-determination (Freedman, 1975).

Considerations for Implementing Informed Consent

Three factors seem to be fundamental in affecting confidence that the individual rights of participants, particularly the right of self-determination, are being respected—the rights that may be infringed, the nature of the individual's situation, and the characteristics of the procedure used to obtain informed consent.

These factors appear interrelated—changes in any one will affect confidence that appropriate respect has been accorded to individual rights. In a sense, the informed consent procedure is a residual factor. As potential effects on rights and welfare become more serious and as participants become less capable of self-determination, concern over the question of informed consent increases, and a more fully developed procedure is required to provide confidence that participants are willing volunteers.

One way to avoid the need for analysis of each research situation is to insist that a full, formal consent procedure always be utilized. This may be accompanied by the argument that any research endeavor that does not involve all elements of informed consent is unethical. This, however, assumes there are no important objectives other than ensuring that the right of self-determination is respected. If such a right were the only important goal, then the easiest way to prevent its infringement would be to prohibit all research. Because there are other valued objectives, it is necessary to consider how these objectives may be balanced.

For research applications, the basic problem is one of trying to achieve a satisfactory compromise among three desirable objectives—confidence that self-determination is being respected, minimization of costs, and development of scientific knowledge. As in any situation where it is necessary to develop a compromise, it is more difficult when the objectives are seen as dichotomous—if, for example, confidence that self-determination was respected is "present" or "absent," costs are considered "high" or "low," and a contribution to scientific knowledge is considered "possible" or "impossible." This in fact does not seem to represent the current conception of the latter two points. Financial costs, for example, can easily be considered a continuous variable, and the additional costs required to achieve the other objectives can readily be estimated in terms of money. Scientific objectives are frequently viewed in a more flexible manner; only the most rigid scientists argue that projects "do" or "do not" achieve scientific goals. Most projects can be considered in terms of the *extent* to which they contribute to science, that is, affect confidence in statements about phenomena.

But there seems to be substantially less flexibility in the concept of informed consent, which is frequently associated with dichotomous notions of moral "good" and "bad," "right" and "wrong," or "justice" and "injustice." It is not unusual for discussions of informed consent to set forth the characteristics that must be present before informed consent can "really occur" (or before the writer can be confident that self-determination was respected). If there were a greater awareness that (1) informed consent is a procedure designed to solve problems associated with the establishment of "guaranteed individual rights" and that (2) the mechanism is designed to provide observers with confidence that such "guarantees" are respected, there might be a greater willingness to look upon "respect for individual rights" as a continuous variable that reflects the *degree* of respect for individual rights.

A major problem confronted by social science investigators who initiate research at the benign end of the continuum of effects for participants is that some ethical commentators insist that a full informed consent procedure be utilized for *all* research. The principle that participants must be exposed to an elaborate informed consent mechanism is applied without consideration for the issues that led to the development of informed consent procedures or other important objectives associated with research. Considerations related to this problem include the scope of research to which informed consent is applied, costs associated with acquiring informed consent for *all* research, the effect of procedures on acquiring a representative sample of participants, and the incompatibility of the procedure with the study of unbiased representations of phenomena. The first two are administrative in nature, the latter two scientific; all will be reviewed below.

Scope of Application

Problems with the scope of application seem to derive from two tendencies: the bifurcation of research as "ethical" or "unethical" on the basis of whether or not a full informed consent procedure is utilized and an inclination to consider any collection of information related to a scientific issue as research. In many cases a full informed consent procedure is expected, even when there is virtually no possibility of negative effects for the participants and when threats to individual self-determination are absent.

For example, it has seriously been suggested that such products of the human body as blood, sweat, urine, and feces are the property of the individual and that any research involving such material cannot be conducted without the informed consent of the "donor," preferably in written form (Altman, 1974). While this may seem to be a frivolous issue, it has substantial implications for hospitals, where such human products are routinely used for research and training of physicians or technicians. Further, many hospitals keep substantial "product banks," consisting of frozen human products, to allow analysis of past clinical cases when new problems (or new diseases) are identified. In cases where the identity of the donor remains anonymous, a small increase in confidence that individual rights of self-determination are being respected may not be worth the additional administrative costs and the potential complications for achieving scientific objectives.

A direct analogy exists to social science research, which may involve the study of household refuse as an indicator of consumption patterns or the study of organizational refuse by industrial "spies" or investigative journalists. In fact, the practice of shredding sensitive organizational documents may be a tacit acknowledgement that once the refuse has been discarded—to be collected by janitors—it becomes part of the public domain; relinquishing control of refuse may be taken as providing informed consent to its examination by others. Would confidence that the right to self-determination is being respected be increased if informed consent were obtained from the source of refuse before it was examined?

A second type of situation is the study of behavior conducted in public—at meetings, on streets, in restaurants or bars, and so forth. For example, it is not clear how the study of crowd movement or pedestrian traffic will provide a threat to individual self-determination or welfare, even though such study may be research. While there is little question that the study of sexual behavior in private settings should be preceded by full, formal informed consent of the participants, should not individuals who choose to engage in sexual behavior in public locations be viewed as providing "consent" to observation by others. Such behavior has been systematically recorded by social scientists (Humphreys, 1970b) as well as by television newspersons. An example of the latter were the discrete portrayals of prostitutes servicing their clients in cars, doorways, and parking lots in full public view. Filmed covertly, these scenes were presented on national television ("Weekend," September 4, 1976), but presumably the "informed consent" of these professionals and their clients was not obtained. In a similar fashion, undercover observation of a radical group may be considered infringement upon privacy, but the observation of formal religious ceremonies in open or public settings would not seem to be a serious encroachment upon the rights of privacy.

A third, and rather extreme, situation involves the remains of a deceased person; it has been seriously suggested that informed consent be required for all medical research conducted upon products of surgery or autopsies that are sent to a laboratory for pathological examination and later used in research (Holder and Levine, 1976). While surgery products are similar to the bodily products described earlier, the autopsy case is unusual because the individual providing the material, the deceased, does not provide the informed consent. Informed consent is to be provided by the next-of-kin; the justification of this procedure is that it prevents relatives from experiencing unusual grief from knowledge of unnecessary mutilation of the deceased.

A clear analogy exists to social science research with historical artifacts, often acquired from grave sites or burial mounds— the pyramids, for example, are basically large burial mounds. To what extent should research that involves destruction of such locations take into account the religious beliefs of the descendants of the deceased? There have been incidents of American Indians disrupting careful excavations, claiming they demonstrated a disrespect for their religious backgrounds. Such considerations are present in a proposed code of ethics for field archaeology (Smith, 1974).

These have been examples of extreme cases where insistence upon a full, formal informed consent procedure could create administrative problems and interfere with the scientific objectives of a project, while providing only a small increase in confidence that respect for individual rights and welfare have been maintained. A more flexible application of informed consent might be more productive: not only would it avoid complicating innocuous research with procedures that seem to provide little benefit, but it might help to avoid the "trivialization" of ethics (Ingelfinger, 1975)—the blind application of elaborate procedures to all research, obscuring its careful application to those endeavors where it may be an important asset.

Costs of Obtaining Informed Consent

The focus of much discussion of informed consent has been on clinical medical research, where the number of research participants is small (usually in the dozens) and the physician-investigator is in frequent contact with the patient-participant, who may be hospitalized. In such situations a complete informed consent procedure does not add significantly to the burden of completing the research, and it may already be involved in the approval of therapy. But when research involves large numbers of participants—in the thousands—and each is contacted relatively briefly, perhaps for less than an hour, the additional time required to complete an elaborate informed consent procedure may be a considerable financial burden.

It is not unreasonable to expect that in some situations the costs of obtaining informed consent may be greater than those of conducting the research itself. New regulations regarding access to records compiled by government agencies require the consent of the individual involved before information (such as that on measures of intellectual aptitude, delinquency, academic performance, and the like) can be examined by investigators. Similar regulations exist for public schools; both the pupils and their parents must be contacted before the information can be examined by researchers. If a study is to focus upon a small number of individuals with special characteristics, the costs of obtaining the informed consent of a large number of potential participants for use of data in administrative files just to locate a few special characteristics could be prohibitive.

Biased Selection of Participants

Almost no research on individual processes is conducted on an entire population; the usual procedure is to involve a small number—the sample—as participants in the research. A major issue is the extent to which the sample can be considered representative of the population, although the seriousness of this problem may vary considerably with the phenomena under investigation. Some types of phenomena are considered so commonplace and unaffected by individual variation that anyone is assumed to be representative of the whole population, as in studies of many medical problems, biological processes, and even some social science phenomena—studies of learning, sensory perception, and so forth.

But if there is reason to suspect that the phenomenon is significantly affected by individual differences, it is critical to obtain participants in such a way that there is no systematic relationship between individual differences and the phenomenon under investigation. A random selection is the model of an ideal procedure to minimize this problem; such a model assumes that all eligible individuals will have an equal opportunity (or a known probability) of becoming participants. It is well established, however, that most procedures for the selection of participants will not result in a random selection, since systematic biases may be generated by the procedure for obtaining the cooperation of participants. The greater the percentage of participants who refuse to become involved in research or the more unique those who are not included, the less the confidence that the research patterns are representative of the total population and the less the possibility of achieving the scientific objective of increased knowledge of natural events and processes.

The nature of the informed consent procedure may influence the decision of some eligible individuals whether or not to become involved in research, even though the experience may be relatively innocuous or benign. The majority of research on the decision to participate has emphasized the individual characteristics of volunteers for psychological experiments. It is possible to have high confidence that such volunteers are better educated, of higher social status, more intelligent, have a higher need for social approval, and are more sociable than nonvolunteers (Rosenthal and Rosnow, 1975, p. 195). There has also been examination of the situational characteristics associated with the decision to become involved in research. For example, if the individuals are interested in the research topic, expect to be favorably evaluated by the investigator, perceive the investigation as important, feel "guilty" or "competent" at the time of the decision, or receive significant material incentives, they are more likely to become volunteers than they otherwise would be (Rosenthal and Rosnow, 1975, p. 197). If utilization of elaborate and formal consent procedures prevents investigators from making the research topic interesting, from stressing the importance of the research objective, or from offering unusually large material incentives, confidence that the sample is representative of the population may be decreased as the percentage of those who reject an opportunity to participate increases. Further, it is quite likely that a full informed consent procedure— perhaps for an innocuous study—may by its very elaborateness create resistance among the potential participants. They may be scared off by a legalistic ritual that is more complex than justified by the possible effects upon their rights and welfare.

Influence on Phenomena

There is, moreover, clear evidence that the implementation of a full informed consent procedure may in fact defeat the scientific objectives of a research project. This is not a universal phenomenon, for it occurs only in those studies where the participant's knowledge of the research purposes and procedures will have an effect upon the phenomenon under investigation. But the problem does affect a wide range of the phenomena studied by social and biomedical investigators.

Perhaps the most dramatic form of this problem involves an individual's concept of well-being. There is substantial evidence to suggest that when expectations of improvement exist, improvement can be identified, observed, and measured—generally referred to as the "placebo effect." This effect seems to be most prevalent with therapies that involve the use of drugs, where the active therapy can be unambiguously measured, but it may also have an effect in other types of treatment, such as psychotherapy. The problem that develops in the research context is that, when the "real" effect of the therapeutic agent is under investigation, the research solution is to administer the therapy to individuals with the appropriate symptoms and provide a harmless surrogate to a matched group of control subjects. If the full, formal informed consent procedure is utilized, then those who receive the harmless surrogate must be informed of that fact, and it will not be possible to compare their improvement with that of the group receiving the real therapy.

Full disclosure of the purpose and procedures of a research investigation may have substantial effects upon the phenomena in all three major types of social science research—experimental studies, survey research, and field observation. But the effects may be quite different and unpredictable in specific research situations. The greatest overall problem is that many individuals consider social scientists to be "social experts" and often attempt to portray socially desirable, or at least socially acceptable, attitudes and behaviors in their presence, perhaps hoping to receive a positive personal evaluation.

In carefully controlled studies, such as the typical social psychological experiment, a major problem that develops is the apparent desire of participants to be "good subjects," to cooperate with "science" and produce the "right answer," that is, behavior consistent with the research hypotheses. This tendency has been studied at length, and is referred to as the "experimenter effect" (Rosenthal, 1967, 1968; Barber and Silver, 1968). It is not unusual for a participant to ask, at the conclusion of an experiment, "Did I do the right thing?" A less frequent, but observable, response is that of a participant who attempts to sabotage a research study by acting in unexpected ways or who is suspicious and guarded in terms of any response. In all cases, the scientific objectives would be better achieved if the participants were unaware of the true purpose of the research—they might then act naturally with respect to the phenomena of interest. Consideration for the rights and welfare of participants may be assured by alternatives for obtaining informed consent or by a careful, intensive explanation of the research at the conclusion of the study.

One study has estimated the effect of a formal consent procedure upon an experimental study of verbal conditioning, a phenomenon highly susceptible to conscious influence by the participant (Resnick and Schwartz, 1973). In verbal conditioning individuals are rewarded (with a positive verbal response) whenever they produce preselected words and phrases; the dependent variable is the change in the frequency of the "rewarded" words and phrases. Two conditions were involved, an ordinary solicitation for volunteers and a solicitation that included exhaustive discussions of the research objectives and results of past studies. There were two major findings: (1) college students were very reluctant to participate after hearing the exhaustive, complete discussion of the research; and (2) a less significant increase in rewarded words and phrases occurred among participants receiving the exhaustive description, compared to the ordinary solicitation participants. Hence, knowledge of the research objectives and past findings had substantial effects on both willingness to participate—perhaps because no curiosity about the study remained—and on the phenomenon itself.

In survey research, the major problems associated with ensuring a complete and honest response are the "social approval" phenomena and concerns about the material to be covered in the interview. Often it is possible to receive full, honest responses to sensitive questions after respondent and interviewer have developed rapport. Further, the length of interviews may vary, depending upon the responses a participant provides. Hence, it is sometimes possible to acquire information from lengthy interviews dealing with sensitive information that may seem unreasonable if presented out of the context of the interview situation. In fact, *full* disclosure may require completion of the interview, with the caveat that the respondent may refuse to answer questions he considers embarrassing or an invasion of privacy.

A study of the reaction of potential survey respondents to variations in the completeness of a description of research objectives, in the extent to which the responses would be confidential, and in the requests for signatures (to demonstrate that informed consent had been obtained) found that only the requests for signatures had a statistically significant effect upon the rate of involvement (Singer, 1978), reducing the response rate from 71 percent to 64 percent if requests were made before the interview and to 65 percent if made afterwards. While the promise of strict confidentiality tended to be associated with a slight increase in the response rate to sensitive, personal questions (dealing with the use of marijuana and alcohol or sexual behavior), there was no dominant pattern related to the substance of the questions.

It is widely suspected that any type of systematic observation by an outsider—journalist, social scientist, and so forth—may affect behavior in social settings, work locations, political groups, deviant subcultures, and the like. In terms of the rights of individuals, a distinction between public and private social settings may be useful. For example, the study of male homosexual behavior in a public restroom (Humphreys, 1970b) might be considered appropriate as long as one assumes that the participants have given their "informed consent" to be observed by selecting a public location for their activity. In contrast, a study of "swingers" (married couples exchanging spouses for sexual activities) in a private setting where considerable effort is devoted to screening acceptable members raises somewhat different issues (Sorensen, 1977; Symonds, 1970). In either case, concern for the rights and welfare of the participants must be demonstrated in other ways than obtaining informed consent if the investigators are to obtain a "natural" view of the phenomena.

In summary, the dogmatic insistence upon full informed consent procedures for all research—regardless of the impact upon administration, costs, selection of participants, or the phenomenon under study—does not seem to promote an optimal solution to the research dilemma, particularly when the gain in confidence that the rights and welfare of participants are being protected is small and the ability to achieve scientific objectives is substantially impaired. Other mechanisms that may be used to demonstrate consideration for the rights and welfare of participants, some more effective than the utilization of informed consent, will be reviewed in Chapters Five, Six, and Seven.

Limits of Application

The informed consent procedure is considered to be the most general solution to a recurrent problem in modern societies: how to resolve the conflict when actions that might promote the general welfare encroach upon individual rights. Presumably, if all the conditions associated with informed consent—competency, freedom from coercion, full information, and comprehension—are present, observers will have confidence that the rights and welfare of research participants have been given appropriate consideration. There are, however, limits on the extent to which the informed consent procedure can provide such confidence; some are present in all research, and others are related to the major right protected by informed consent—self-determination.

No matter what participants agree to—literally or implicitly—it is assumed that investigators continue to share a major responsibility for their well-being. This may be why the major justification for informed consent is that it reflects respect for self-determination rather than shifting *all* responsibility for effects to the participant(s). If the converse were true, investigators would be encouraged to use elaborate procedures to acquire a legally binding informed consent and to conduct research in ways that might not consider the consequences for participants.

It is generally assumed that, depending upon the research procedure, investigators will demonstrate concern for the participants in a number of ways; for example, treating them in a dignified manner, taking precautions to keep personal data confidential, ensuring that negative effects are quickly detected and promptly minimized, and avoiding denigrating or condescending descriptions of participants or their actions. But there is almost no research situation where informed consent—by itself—is adequate to provide confidence that all these rights of participants will be given full consideration. The use of informed consent may not provide confidence that the participant's self-determination has been respected in those situations where the participants do not expect to make decisions on their own behalf. For example, an investigator who studies the processes within a family, such as interaction between parents and children, may find it necessary to obtain information from all members of the family. If the parents provide consent for the family, it is not clear what consent of the children, even if they are teenagers, would mean in families where everyone accepts the parents' right to make such decisions.

In a similar fashion, the study of individuals in certain societies may result in confusion when informed consent is requested of the participants—they may feel bewilderment when offered an individual choice for the first time. Members may be part of an autocratic political structure, where the "head person" makes all the decisions for the group, or of a consensus political structure, where joint decisions are made by all members of the group. In either case, the individuals are assumed to conform to the decision made for the group, and the notion that they have a right to make their own decisions may be quite disconcerting to them. Offering them an opportunity to make an individual decision and thus introducing them to the idea of self-determination may produce detrimental effects, effects that may outweigh the possible increase in confidence that their rights and welfare are being protected.

There are also those situations where only a portion of an individual's activities are considered self-determined; organizational work may be seen as controlled by administrative supervisors. If the supervisors agree to engage in a project of possible benefit to the organization, they may in fact be providing informed consent for their subordinates. In this case, to ask subordinates for their informed consent may be a meaningless gesture and may endanger their places in the organization rather than show respect for their rights and welfare.

A second category of situations where respect for the rights of individual self-determination may not be demonstrated by the application of informed consent involves those in which the focus of research is a phenomenon that is a property of a social aggregate or social system. Examples might be rumor transmission, emergence and maintenance of influence structures, development of group cohesiveness, decisions in real juries, and the like. In such cases, the direct effects on the rights and welfare of participants may be negligible, and the data may not even be collected from individuals (it may be based on public records, journalistic accounts, physical traces, and so forth). There is some ambiguity about who should provide consent in such research and about the nature of the issues for which consent is actually being provided.

If there are possible effects for both individuals and the social system, perhaps consent should be obtained from both sources. But if there is a minimum of effects for participants, the best source of consent may be those legitimate representatives of the social system, individuals with a responsibility for the continued welfare of the system (political unit or other organization) and its members. It may well be possible to have confidence that the "rights" and welfare of the social system are given appropriate consideration if such representatives provide their consent to the research. However, this may lead to the completion of only that research that will promote the interests of the current authorities rather than of the general public or disadvantaged groups. It has also been suggested that obtaining or honoring informed consent provided by those who are publicly accountable need not be considered necessary or important in all situations (see Chapter Eleven).

By itself, then, informed consent appears inadequate as a source of confidence that the rights and welfare of participants are protected in most research; investigators are assumed to retain responsibility for the participants, regardless of what they sign, and are expected to take precautions to protect their welfare. While informed consent does provide some assurance that there has been consideration of the participant's right to self-determination, there are situations where even this advantage may not be present, such as those where the participants do not consider themselves as having a right to self-determination or where the unit of analysis is the social system.

Summary

All societies with a tradition of respect for the rights and liberties of individuals are confronted with instances in which benefits can be achieved, either for the society or specific individuals, through encroachment upon personal rights and liberties. The most general solution to this problem is to allow the individuals who may be affected to forgo these rights and liberties, presumably in a voluntary, informed way. A problem that confronts observers is determining whether a decision to forgo rights represents the free will of the individual, when the only observable evidence is the actual decision itself.

The dominant solution has been to focus on the context in which the decision is made rather than on the agreement to forgo rights. This attention to the context of the decision reflects the low confidence attached to agreement as evidence of willingness to give up rights and liberties. This is particularly true when there are no obvious personal advantages resulting from the decision, such as participation in research that will contribute to scientific knowledge only.

Considered as a mechanism to provide observers with confidence that the rights and welfare of participants are shown proper consideration, informed consent is often thought of as either "present" or "absent" and is associated with a suspicion that investigators may fail to follow the spirit of the procedure—by not allowing participants to actually refuse involvement in research. This has led to numerous suggestions regarding the conditions necessary to ensure that consent has "really" occurred. One suggestion is to view consent as a continuous variable and then to consider the extent to which various features must be incorporated to ensure that participants will take some responsibility for the effects they may experience. Participants may be willing to accept substantial responsibility for such effects with a less formal or elaborate procedure than is currently envisioned by some commentators, but the degree of willingness probably depends upon the nature of the effects, the consent procedure, and the research activity. (This is clearly an issue open to and suitable for investigation.)

There are several desirable objectives that may be incompatible with the implementation of full informed consent procedures. These include minimization of administrative complications and financial costs, as well as the achievement of scientific objectives. The last may be jeopardized when informed consent procedures produce a bias among those willing to participate in the research and thus lower confidence that the participants are representative of the population of interest or when full information about the purpose and procedures of the research has substantial effects on the phenomena under examination. More useful compromises would occur if there were a greater awareness of (1) these multiple objectives associated with research, (2) the other procedures that may be required to ensure confidence that investigators are responsive to the rights and welfare of participants, and (3) the utility of conceptualizing informed consent on the basis of the degree of confidence it provides observers that participants were informed volunteers.

Despite the importance of informed consent and its value for contributing to confidence that the rights and welfare of participants are being given consideration, there are clear limits on its utility. For almost no research activity will it serve as the only indicator of concern for the participants; investigators are assumed to retain responsibility for the possible negative effects for participants—no matter what they may have signed—and take precautions to minimize their occurrence or severity. Further, there are those instances where the participants themselves do not consider they have a right to self-determination or where the unit of analysis is a social system rather than individual participants. Finally, there has been recent evidence to suggest that an elaborate informed consent procedure that includes descriptions of unlikely, but serious, effects—not uncommon in drug research—may actually lead to the presence of such effects, particularly for individuals who are highly suggestible; full, formal informed consent may actually precipitate negative effects for participants in some situations (Loftus and Fries, 1979).

5

Overt Experiments
and Analysis of
the Research Dilemma

The most straightforward procedure for establishing high confidence in a causal relationship between variables is to create a situation where one or more variables may (or may not) influence the phenomena of interest. But just as experimental procedures provide confidence that the controlled variables influence the dependent variables, they also provide confidence that investigators supervising the research are responsible for effects upon participants, both intended and unintended. In short, the major advantage of experiments for scientific objectives is also the major consideration in terms of the research dilemma: high confidence in responsibility for effects for the human participants (biomedical, psychological, or social).

This chapter will consider two major types of experimental research in social science. The first is that conducted primarily to

116

resolve intellectual issues related to variables controlled for a short period of time—usually less than an hour, occasionally for one or more days, very infrequently for more than a week. It is oriented toward the typical social-psychological experiment, although it may be conducted by an anthropologist, political scientist, psychologist, or sociologist. A second major type of experiment, which involves long-term attempts to modify important aspects of programs affecting an entire community, or social experiments, will also be considered. This kind of experimental research is often initiated to assist in the resolution of important policy questions and is designed to estimate the effects, reaction to, and costs of new government programs or procedures.

Controlled Settings

The scope of research and the range of effects that can occur in controlled settings are without limit; a complete analysis of all alternatives is impossible. The following discussion analyzes the research dilemma issues for three examples—a study of individual reaction to stress, a study of compliance to authority that generates stress for the participants, and a study of role adaption that subjected some participants to humiliation. The following discussion illustrates how the five research dilemma issues—research program effects, research project effects, participant effects, distribution of effects, and consideration of participant rights and welfare—can be used to organize the analysis of research. (These five issues were reviewed in the introduction to Part One.)

Development of Standardized "Stress Situations"

The response of individuals to situations of stress can be of considerable importance: not only are such experiences unpleasant, but the ability to cope with a stressful situation in a rational manner can have substantial consequences for both the individual and others dependent upon him or her. While situations of extreme stress may occur infrequently in the lives of ordinary individuals, they are not unusual for persons in certain occupations—police officers, fire fighters, surgeons, soldiers, airline pilots, and the like. Knowledge that would lead to more appropriate responses in stress situations would probably have benefits measurable in terms of lives saved.

Several strategies are available for research on individual response to stress. One is to study the actions of individuals in stressful situations created by natural events; those who respond "well" can then be compared to those who respond "less well." The problem with such an approach is that both the nature of the stress situations and a "good" response may vary considerably, to say nothing of variations in prior experiences of stress, training, or characteristics of the individuals. There is the further problem of collecting accurate information on the features (context) of the stress situation, the alternative responses available to the individual, and his actual response—the recollection of individuals exposed to stress may not be a reliable source of data.

An alternative is to develop a standard "stress situation," one where the essential characteristics of the situation, as well as the range and quality of responses to the stress, can be established with confidence. If investigators can create such situations when needed, the relationship of personal characteristics, training, or experience to adaptive and maladaptive responses to stress situations may be systematically examined. If the research is successful, there will be high confidence that the mechanisms that affect differential responses to stress situations are understood, and recommendations related to the type of individuals or training associated with good stress responses can be developed.

Critical to the implementation of this strategy is the development of a set of standard stress situations, suitable for systematic study of reactions to stress. This has led to research (Berkun and others, 1962) on the development of such situations, as well as measures of the extent to which responses to stress were adaptive. Because participants seemed to assume that there was a small or nonexistent likelihood of danger in obvious experiments, it was necessary to develop situations defined by the participants as "real" to produce the cognition of stress. To satisfy the requirement that cognitive stress, as opposed to physical stress (hunger, cold, heat, or fatigue), be produced by the situations, three criteria were adopted as indicators that a satisfactory "reproduceable stress situation" had been developed: participants' subjective reports of high stress, changes in task performance, and changes in physiological responses (measured by characteristics of the participants' blood or urine)—all in comparison to participants in control or nonstress situations.

Investigators developed five different types of stress situations and exposed participants to them to determine if any of the situations met the three criteria. All test situations were similar: individuals were asked to participate in a relatively innocuous activity during which an "emergency" occurs. The major research question is the extent to which the "emergency" creates stress for the participants. One was a simulated aircraft malfunction, during which ten participants were engaged in a study of the effects of altitude on psychomotor performance. After an emergency "ditching" into the ocean is announced, they are asked to take a test on knowledge of emergency procedures and to complete a questionnaire (twenty-three items) on disposition of personal items in the case of death. Three studies were identical except for the nature of the "accident"; in all of them, a participant at an isolated outpost (expecting to report the presence of aircraft) is informed that he is threatened by unexpected nuclear radiation, a sudden forest fire, or misdirected artillery shells. He is requested to provide information on his location over a radio to facilitate a helicopter evacuation. The radio becomes inoperative, and the extent to which the participant follows instructions for testing and field repair of the radio is used as a measure of performance. In a fifth situation the participant is led to believe that he (1) caused an explosion critically injuring another and (2) is to relay vital information for obtaining medical treatment over this radio; the radio becomes inoperative (the same radio from previous situations), and adaptive behavior means following the instructions for testing and repair of the radio.

Only three of the five situations met the criteria established for a satisfactory stress situation—the aircraft emergency, the misdirected artillery fire, and the demolition accident. In all three situations the participant was provided with both verbal information regarding an "emergency" and sights and sounds consistent with this information, such as a stopped propellor or a simulated explosion. A significant difference among the responses of inexperienced soldiers (the participants), experienced soldiers, and controls (recruits in similar situations who did not encounter an

emergency) was also found. Further, in all five situations the perceived stress, as measured by adjectives chosen from a subjective
stress scale, was quite high; the mean responses were represented
by the adjectives "unsteady," "nervous," "worried," and "unsafe,"
although the range of responses clearly included participants at the
upper end—"frightened," "terrible," "in agony," and "scared stiff."
Some of the more concerned participants in the isolated outpost
emergencies were not exactly "stiff," for thirteen (21 percent) ran
out of the area without attempting *any* radio repair; eight of these
were confronted with the misdirected artillery shells (33 percent
of those in that situation).

In brief, there seems to be little question that high levels of
stress—measured in three different ways—were experienced by
a substantial proportion of the 105 inexperienced recruits (the total
number of participants in all five conditions). At the same time,
there were no reports of deaths or injuries resulting from these
experiences, which lasted about four hours for each participant.
Further, the participants were under the continuous care and supervision of the sponsoring organization, the U.S. Army; if any
major problems had been encountered following the research, they
could have been identified and responded to with dispatch.

Research Program Effects. The major positive effect of such
research is the potential for increased effectiveness of individuals
placed in roles where they may encounter substantial stress. For
the sponsor, the U.S. Army, this can be measured in terms of a
reduction in deaths and injuries of individuals who might otherwise collapse under stress. The application to the types of stress
situations confronted by policemen, firemen, surgeons, airline pilots, and the like would seem to be obvious. The major negative
effects may be the time and resources required to conduct the research, but this is unlikely to be a major factor considering that the
marginal costs (additional expenditures) are quite small. Most of
the individuals involved in the army experiments were full-time
"employees" and would have been engaged in one military activity
or another anyway.

Research Project Effects. The major positive effect of the project, in terms of the overall objective, was indirect—developing
standardized stress situations that could be systematically used in

later research. While there was some evidence collected on the relative effectiveness of experienced and inexperienced participants (providing knowledge about the influence of experience on responses to stress situations), the focus was on "calibration," that is, developing standardized situations that could be efficiently recreated to produce a known level of stress. This followed completion of the first stage of the research (examination of available data on effective and ineffective individuals in combat situations) and preceded systematic research on the factors (such as personality, training, or experience) associated with variation in responses to stressful situations. The negative effects were the costs—nominal for the military—and the time participants took from other organizational activities. There is the additional possibility that the deception procedure might reduce the participant's confidence in military authority and increase suspicion or distrust of social scientists, but the general ambivalence toward military authority is so well established among enlisted personnel that it seems unlikely that such a study would have a major influence. The resultant attitude toward social scientists might well be related to the explanation and debriefing procedures provided for the participants; a "truthful" explanation appears to have been provided, but it is not described in detail.

Participant Effects. Perhaps the major effect for the participants was removal from the routine of military life for half a day to be provided with a personalized diversion and perhaps knowledge of their own response to a situation of stress—which could be of substantial future benefit. There may also have been some satisfaction from contributing to the development of potentially useful knowledge. The major negative effect was the experience of stress—temporary, though unpleasant. Unfortunately, there is no discussion of the postresearch reaction of the participants.

The balance of the positive and negative effects for the participants is difficult to estimate with precision. The research clearly did not provide any substantial direct positive benefits, but the experience may not have been more severe than the basic training activities missed by the participants, although the negative effects may be of a different character in basic training—physical stress, fatigue, or learning stress, to say nothing of the depersonalized treatment common in the military. The balance of the effects for the participants were probably either neutral or slightly negative; it seems unlikely that they would have been strongly negative for a substantial proportion of the participants.

Distribution of Effects. The major benefactors of the information resulting from this research program would be both those who depend upon individuals to perform effectively in stress situations and the individuals subjected to stress themselves. While society as a whole depends upon the performance of soldiers, physicians, and others who confront stress, these same individuals must, in cases of personal danger, also rely upon their own responses. The social category that was the source of research participants—military recruits—was also the social category that might benefit from research findings that produce more effective responses to personal stress. This does not appear to be an unjust distribution of costs and benefits among social categories of individuals.

Consideration of Participants' Rights and Welfare. It should be emphasized that no specific informed consent was obtained from the participants with regard to these specific "military experiences"; they were selected at random from among military recruits—before, during, and after basic training—and told what they would be expected to do. Participation in the military, however, involves a consent to engage in diverse, dangerous activities that may involve new and untried techniques and procedures.

Perhaps the most important point regarding the participants' rights and welfare is that they were all in the U.S. Army, an organization that accepts considerable responsibility for the well-being of its members, providing complete medical and psychiatric care at no cost to the "patient," especially when the problem is service related. While there is no question that the participants were misled—they were asked to engage in an innocuous activity and were then confronted with an "emergency"—the experience was completed in the context of an organization that accepted responsibility for their total welfare. Further, measured against the ordinary ambiguities, uncertainties, and hazards of military training and service, the "accidents" and subsequent experiences do not seem that dramatic. Since only healthy young males were involved, the possibility of medical problems that could result in unforeseen complications was minimized.

In summary, there seem to be substantial benefits to be gained from increasing knowledge of individual responses to stress situations. Although the negative effects for participants may outweigh the positive, these were not extreme compared to the ordinary activities of military recruits. The rights and welfare of the participants appear to have been given attention, despite the fact they were misled about the nature of the experience they were to encounter. Finally, it does not appear as if one social category of individuals was unjustly "used" to benefit another social category; military recruits were the participants but also major potential beneficiaries of applications of the research findings.

Limits on the Exercise of Authority

A major factor contributing to the luxury of modern life in industrialized countries is the efficiency that accrues when large numbers of people are organized to promote a single objective or a set of related objectives, as in construction, manufacturing, education, and administration of social programs. Such coordinated efforts would be impossible without the ability to implement plans that require the differentiation of activities, themselves integrated in such a way that all contribute to the final objectives. In most cases, the impossibility of including all participants in the planning and decision-making process—if only because that would result in an inefficient use of time—means that many of the participants will be expected to follow instructions or "obey orders." Since routine administration of rather innocuous activities is common in most organizations, a "habit of obedience" may develop among participants and respect for authority may become an important societal norm.

A problem of some interest, if not of substantial practical significance, is determination of the extent to which this "norm of habitual obedience" may persist among ordinary individuals. Stated differently, is it possible to observe the conditions under which individuals will fail to obey instructions from a person in a position of authority? Not only may such knowledge have implications for the administration of organizations (both private and public), but it may also facilitate understanding of how organizations with questionable ends—ends that seem inconsistent with widely shared objectives and values—are able to function. Examples of "ordinary" people acquiescing to the requests of superiors in "legitimate" organizations to facilitate "bad ends" are legion. The most dramatic examples occur in wartime, such as the events that occurred in Vietnam and the Nazi bureaucracy's routine and systematic extermination of over six million individuals (a considerable organizational feat, monstrous as it was).

Such considerations led to the creation of a research procedure that allowed systematic variation of the factors encouraging acquiescence to a person in authority, a person who requested—for seemingly reasonable ends—the commission of acts counter to the norms of everyday life. This is the "obedience to authority" research program that led to an open and extensive discussion of the issues emphasized in this book (Milgram, 1963, 1964, 1965, 1968, 1972, 1974; Baumrind, 1964; Erickson, 1968; Etzioni, 1968; Kaufman, 1967; Orne and Holland, 1968; Patten, 1977a, 1977b; Ring, Wallston, and Corey, 1970). Out of concern for the ability of the Nazi government to develop smoothly functioning "death camps," a research situation was developed to simulate the conflict an ordinary person would encounter in a similar situation—a conflict between the desire to comply with the apparently legitimate requests of a person in authority and an assumed reluctance to inflict pain on an innocent person. (In a sense, this is a version of the dilemma that confronts individuals when service to the state requires acts that are counter to the standards for a moral or good person (see Chapter Two).)

The initial plan was to develop a research situation that would provide for a range of responses beyond that elicited from ordinary individuals, so that the effect of various factors (characteristics of participants, physical setting, experimenter, and the like) on the participants' obedience could be examined. Each of the participants (ordinary individuals, solicited through newspaper ads) would arrive at the research setting and encounter another participant (actually a confederate of the research team). After being told that the project was concerned with learning processes, one was chosen to serve as the "teacher" and the other as the "pupil." A rigged "random" procedure resulted in the confederate's always adopting the role of "pupil."

After signing informed consent forms (both agree to continue the procedure to the end), the "teacher" is asked to read a sequence of four word pairs to the "pupil." Testing of memory retention was based on correctly identifying the second word of each pair after the first word was read to the participant; there were thirty such sets of four word pairs. Each time a mistake was made (and a nonresponse was considered a mistake) the "teacher" was to (1) increase the shock level and (2) administer an electric shock. The range of available shocks was from 15 volts (level 1) to 450 (level 30); at level 20 (300 volts) the label on the equipment warned "Extreme Intensity Shock"; at level 24 (360 volts) it warned "Danger: Severe Shock"; at level 28 (420 volts) the label indicated "XXX"—in red.

The major dependent variable in the research was the refusal of the teacher to follow the instructions of the person in authority, the experimenter, who encouraged him to continue to administer increasingly severe shocks to the "pupil"—who continued to make mistakes or failed to respond. This encouragement took the form of a series of standardized statements: "You must go on," "The experiment requires that you go on," or "I'll take responsibility." Expectations that the "teachers" would refuse to continue were consistent with the judgments of psychiatrists, college students, and middle-class adult males, all of whom predicted that most participants would defy the experimenter before completing one third of the shock scale, a mean shock level of 120 to 150 volts (Milgram, 1974, p. 29).

The actual results were quite different. In most conditions a substantial number of participants were obedient and continued to provide quite painful and dangerous shocks to the "pupil" in compliance with the instructions of the experimenter. The results of nineteen different experimental conditions are summarized in Table 6; from 0.00 to 0.92.5 percent of the participants—in general, ordinary young and middle-aged males—provided the maximum level of shock for the "pupil" under the revised procedure. All those conditions where the majority of the "teachers" refused

Table 6. Summary of Major Results of Experiments in the Obedience to Authority Research Program

Percentage Administering Max. Shock[a]	Mean Shock Level[b]	Exp. No.[c]	Experimental Condition
Original Condition			
30.00	17.88	4	Touch-Proximity (n = 40) "Teacher" must hold "pupil's" hand on metal plate to complete circuit and operate equipment simultaneously
40.00	20.80	3	Proximity (n = 40) "Teacher" and "pupil" in same room
62.50	24.53	2	Voice-Feedback (n = 40) "Teacher" hears "pupil" protest over intercom
65.00	27.0	1	Remote (n = 40) "Teacher" hears only protests by banging on wall
Revised Procedure			
.00	10.00	12	"Pupil" demands to be shocked (n = 20) Experimenter instructs "teacher" not to go on
.00	10.00	14	Experimenter serves as "pupil" (n = 20) Ordinary man instructs "teacher" to go on
.00	10.00	15	Two experimenters give conflicting instructions (n = 20) Ordinary man serves as "pupil"
2.50	5.50	11	"Teacher" chooses shock level (n = 40) "Pupil" protests coordinated to shock level
10.00	16.45	17	Two peers rebel (n = 40) "Teacher" task subdivided into three activities, subject "shocks"

			Ordinary Man Gives Orders (n = 20)
20.00	13	16.25	Experimenter leaves; "ordinary man", an accomplice, suggests increasing shock levels as own idea
20.50	7	18.2	Experimenter absent (n = 40)
			Orders to "teacher" received over telephone
40.00	9	21.40	"Pupil" does not give full informed consent (n = 40)
			Insists on right to terminate at will prior to becoming involved
47.50	10	20.95	Research conducted in commercial building (n = 40)
			All other conditions on campus of major university
50.00	6	22.20	Variation in personnel (n = 40)
			Different experimenter-"pupil" team
65.00	5	24.55	Voice-feedback condition: male subjects (n = 40)
65.00	8	24.73	Voice-feedback condition: female subjects (n = 40)
65.00	16	23.50	Two experimenters (n = 20)
			One served as "pupil"
68.75	13a	24.90	Subject as bystander (n = 16)
			"Ordinary man" assumes right to administer shocks on own initiative
92.50	18	26.65	Peer administers shock (n = 40)
			Subject maintains records on "pupil's" performance

[a] Refers to the percentage that administer shocks at the 450-volt level ("Danger," "Severe Shock," and "XXX" labels on equipment). In all but one condition, Exp. No. 12, this reflects obedience to the instructions of another; in Exp. No. 12, the experimenter instructs the "teacher" to terminate the study; he is always compliant.

[b] Equipment involved 30 levels of shock, labeled from 15 to 450 volts at 15-volt intervals. The shock level, in volts, can be computed by multiplying the level by 15; for example, level 10 was 150 volts.

[c] Indicates the number of the experiment as described in Milgram (1974)

Source: Descriptions based on Milgram (1974). Numbers in parentheses indicate the number of participants in each condition, a total of 636. Except in Exp. No. 8, all participants were male; chosen to represent different ages in the following proportions: 20–29, 20 percent; 30–39, 40 percent; and 40–49, 40 percent. Occupational categories were represented as follows: skilled and unskilled workers, 40 percent; white collar, sales, and business, 40 percent; and professionals, 20 percent.

to administer the maximum shock level included factors that conflicted with the authority of the experimenter: the personal presence or touching of the "pupil"; an experimenter who instructed the "teacher" to stop; an ordinary person (not an experimenter) who provided instructions to shock the "pupil"; conflicting instructions from two experimenters; or a "peer" who refused to cooperate. The tendency to acquiesce to authority and provide the punishment was increased when the "pupil" was in a more remote situation or when the "subject" was acting as an accessory to the activity, doing clerical work and not operating the equipment.

The first major finding from this research, then, is the ease with which ordinary individuals—men and women who are decent citizens—can be encouraged to inflict pain upon another that may result in serious injury. (The "pupil," a rotund man in his fifties, mentions a heart condition and requests that the study be stopped.) There is no question that the contextual features of this situation and the presence of the experimenter had a profound effect upon the responses of these ordinary individuals, all of whom had a strong tendency to obey authority.

The second major finding is the extent to which this experience provided a high level of stress for the "teacher" rather than the pupil, who was never actually shocked.

> Subjects were observed to sweat, tremble, stutter, bite their lips, groan, and dig their fingernails into their flesh. These were characteristic rather than exceptional responses to the experiment.
> One sign of tension was the regular occurrence of nervous laughing fits. Fourteen of the forty subjects showed definite signs of nervous laughter and smiling. The laughter seemed entirely out of place, even bizarre. Full-blown, uncontrollable seizures were observed for three subjects. On one occasion we observed a seizure so violently convulsive that it was necessary to call a halt to the experiment. The subject . . . was seriously embarrassed by his untoward and uncontrollable behavior. In postexperimental interviews subjects took pains to point out that they were not sadistic types and that the laughter did not mean they enjoyed shocking the victim [Milgram, 1963, p. 375].

In short, there was substantial evidence that the stress for the participants, usually those who were obedient and administered the full range of shocks, was extreme. Such stress was acknowledged by both the participants and the investigator associated with the research.

In addition to the stress experienced by the participants in the research, the investigator became concerned over the possibility that these ordinary individuals might realize that they could have contributed to the death of an innocent participant—by providing shocks to someone with a heart condition. Immediately after the typical pattern of behavior became clear (as reflected in Milgram, 1963), measures were taken to ameliorate any negative effects and to determine the extent to which permanent negative effects might have been incurred by the participants. The first was to provide a complete description of the purposes and procedures to all participants immediately following the session (including a friendly encounter with the "pupil") and provision of a written summary to all participants following the completion of each experiment. Procedures to measure the effects included a follow-up questionnaire and a psychiatric interview with a sample of forty participants one year after they were involved in the research.

The responses reported from the questionnaires indicate that both the obedient and defiant participants were strongly supportive of the research (Milgram, 1964, p. 849). Ninety-two percent of the participants returned the questionnaire (nonrespondents tended to be younger), and only 1.3 percent expressed regret at participation; 15 percent were neutral about participation; and 84 percent were glad to have participated (43.5 percent of all participants were "very glad," and 47.8 percent of the obedient participants were "very glad"). Eighty percent "felt that more experiments of this sort should be carried out, and 74 percent indicated they had learned something of personal importance" (p. 849). The report of the psychiatrist who interviewed the forty participants twelve months after the study (Errera, 1972, p. 400) indicates that: "No evidence was found of any traumatic reactions. A few accepted responsibility for their actions and described their distress when faced with their willingness to inflict pain on another human being. They felt that as a result of the experiment they had learned something valuable about themselves."

A reasonable interpretation by a critic of the research (Baumrind, 1964) suggested that the participants would be "overwhelmed" with guilt when they realized what the results might have been had they really administered electric shocks. However, individuals appear to have an unexpected facility for denying responsibility for their actions and thus protecting themselves from a "guilt experience" (Milgram, 1964, 1974). Participants found numerous ways of rejecting their responsibility for their actions—they were only following orders, they were part of a system they could not influence, and so on—or they assumed a position of moral superiority over the authority figure who "caused" their behavior. In short, cognitive or psychic mechanisms prevented the participants from experiencing significant levels of guilt, an important research finding in itself.

Research Program Effects. Substantial benefits would probably accrue from a precise knowledge of the conditions under which individuals will be compliant to those in authority. Not only would such knowledge allow for an understanding of the conditions that lead to efficient and conflict-free operation of organizations, but it would also help predict when substantial noncompliance could be expected and when influences from other sources might have a major effect, leading individuals to be ambivalent about compliance with organizational directives. Given the importance of organizations and persons in positions of authority in advanced societies, thorough knowledge of these phenomena could be quite useful. One aspect of such research would be understanding how authority structures are developed and modified (as features of the social structures in which they operate); complementary research would study the response of individuals in authority structures. The major negative effects might be related to the location of the knowledge rather than to the knowledge itself; it might be considered an instrument of those in positions of influence for manipulation of organizational members, but this goes beyond the question of effects to that of application. It is also possible that the information could be utilized by average individuals to modify the influence of authority structures.

Research Project Effects. This particular project attempted to explore the conditions that produce obedience to, and defiance of, authority by individuals under very special conditions, those where the behavior may result in effects counter to most social norms, such as inflicting pain upon another. While this is not the usual type of situation in which authority is exercised—in most situations

there is consensus among all parties about the goals in question—
it may be considered an important limiting case. If authority can
be successfully exercised in this type of situation, it would suggest
that it will be difficult to find any situation where authority will be
systematically resisted by subordinates. While the experiment had
no obvious positive benefits for the participants, except a possible
increase in self-knowledge, there is a substantial positive benefit to
society—and the participants—if the knowledge gained helps to
ensure that those in positions of authority will be responsive to
major social values and norms.

Participant Effects. There were no systematic, major positive
effects for the six to seven hundred participants in this research
project. There may have been benefits in terms of the cash payment (a relatively modest $4.00 to $4.50), participating in an interesting experience, being involved in a contribution to scientific
knowledge, or increased self-knowledge, but these could not be
considered major benefits. The major negative effects were the
time required to participate, the stress experienced by a substantial
proportion of subjects—extreme in some cases—and the possible
realization of the type of behavior they could have committed under real-life conditions, outside the controlled research setting.
One of the findings, however, was that cognitive mechanisms are
put into operation that tend to prevent full development of self-
blame.

Distribution of Effects. The bulk of the participants in the research project were young to middle aged adult males from the
New Haven, Connecticut area and belonged to the working and
middle class (based on occupational characteristics). The burdens
of the research were not shared by women (except for one study),
younger or older citizens, those with very low or very high social
standing, or those in other parts of the United States. While there
were few direct benefits to the research participants, all these other
social categories may benefit from the general knowledge that resulted from this series of studies. It is clear that the burdens of the
research experience were not equally shared by individuals in all
social categories; it is equally clear that the distribution of burdens
does not appear to have been dramatically unjust, if it was unjust
at all.

Consideration of Participants' Rights and Welfare. This research procedure was one in which there was little or no direct benefit to the participants and in which they were under the illusion that they were inflicting pain upon another individual. The right to full and truthful information was, to some extent, infringed—the participants were initially deceived about the true nature of the research and the objectives of the project, a deception that was, however, fully revealed after the research was completed. The careful attempt to determine the extent to which the participants resented and objected to the treatment they received, the systematic follow-up by a trained psychiatrist of the sample of participants, and the reports of continuous monitoring of the study and termination of the procedure for individuals under extreme stress all suggest a concern for the effects upon the participants and a serious desire to ensure that no permanent effects or extremely severe temporary effects would occur. Evidence from the participant reports indicates that these efforts were successful. The crucial element in reducing the sense of resentment by the participants appears to have been the careful "dehoaxing" or debriefing that followed the procedure; a study on this feature of the "obedience paradigm" indicates that, as long as the participants were informed of the deceptions involved, their evaluation of the experiment was unmistakably positive (Ring, Wallston, and Corey, 1970).

In summary, a research program that increases understanding of the limits and functioning of authority would probably lead to the more effective operation of organizations and increase the ability of individuals to resist "bad orders." The research project under consideration appears to have been a reasonable procedure for measuring a clear indication of acquiescence to authority (pushing a button on the shock panel) and systematically varying important situational features. The effects for the individuals cannot be considered benign: they suffered extreme stress and a possible awareness of their willingness to harm another at the request of a person in authority. But participants appear to have received no lasting negative effects, and some of them think that the research provided important information. The attention shown to the participants by the investigator would suggest that although they were misled about the nature of the research experience, their rights and welfare were given adequate consideration. There is little reason to suggest that the distribution of burdens and benefits among social categories was unjust, with individuals from any one category suffering for benefits provided to other social categories. The value of the project can be judged only on the basis of its contribution to knowledge and possible contributions to the improvement of society.

Role Acquiescence in a Total Institution

Two major phenomena, readily observed in organizations with a custodial goal, are difficult and expensive to examine under highly controlled (standardized) conditions. The first is the socialization process involved when individuals adopt new roles (positions with well-defined social expectations); the second is the speed with which such processes operate. While it is frequently observed that individuals in similar social positions (or statuses) exhibit similar behavior, the extent to which this is due to socialization into the position (learning the expected behavior and attitudes) or to selection of individuals with unique traits or personalities is not well established. The distinctiveness of "position characteristics" is accentuated in special types of situations and particularly in so-called total institutions. These organizations are deliberately designed to provide for two distinct types of social roles—that of the "kept" (patient, prisoner, recruit, student, and the like) and that of the "keepers" (staff, guards, officers, teachers, and the like).

The financial cost of creating a new social organization to explore such issues encourages research strategies that provide a maximum information payoff rather than exploration of all logical alternatives. Such a design (Haney, Banks, and Zimbardo, 1973; Zimbardo, 1973a, 1973b) was developed by planning a simulated prison to be staffed with young males (between ages eighteen and twenty-five) selected from among seventy-five applicants considered to be the most stable (physically and mentally), most mature, and least involved in antisocial behavior. Those selected signed a contract agreeing to play either a "guard" or "prisoner" role for up to two weeks in return for adequate diet, clothing, housing, medical care and fifteen dollars per day; it was made explicit that those assigned to be prisoners should expect to be under surveillance (no privacy) and to have some basic civil rights suspended during "imprisonment," although no physical abuse would be allowed. After all participants had agreed to these terms, eleven were selected at random to be "prisoners" (with two chosen as standbys) and nine as "guards" (with one standby).

The "guards" helped in the final preparation of the "prison" (a basement section of an academic building not used much during the latter part of August), and the "prisoners" were "arrested" by a local police force that volunteered to assist in the study. Once in the jail the prisoners were deindividualized (were allowed no undergarments or showers, wore smocks, shower slippers, and stocking caps, and were addressed by number only) and the guards were "militarized" (given khaki uniforms, whistle, police nightstick, and reflective sunglasses). The guards were told they were to "maintain a reasonable degree of order within the prison necessary for its effective functioning" (Haney, Banks, and Zimbardo, 1973, p. 74); they worked on three eight-hour shifts per day (three "guards" each). The "prisoners" were "prisoners" twenty-four hours per day, as agreed to in the contract. Two aspects of the simulated prison were perhaps not representative of real prisons; the first is the low ratio of "prisoners" to "guards," a maximum of 3.6 to 1, usually less. The second was that neither group of participants had much to do other than "being supervised" or "supervising."

There were two major results from this research procedure. The first was that the behavior of the "prisoners" and "guards" was dramatically differentiated by the end of the procedure. The "prisoners" became very passive, disorganized, and apparently totally subservient and thus exhibited a "learned helplessness syndrome"; the behavior of the "guards" was marked by verbal and physical aggressiveness, arbitrariness, and dehumanization of the "prisoners." "None of these [results] were predictable from the medical, social, or educational histories of the subjects, nor from a battery of personality test scores" (Zimbardo, 1973b, p. 245). In other words, there were marked differences in the behavior and attitudes of the participants in the two roles, which appeared to be primarily related to conformity to commonly shared stereotypes about "guards" and "prisoners"—no explicit role instructions were provided. These "situational forces" were so strong that the research staff, acting as "prison administrators," began to adopt the supervisory mode of orientation.

The second major finding concerns the speed with which the transformations occurred, although the major evidence for this is somewhat obscured by the intensity of the experience for the "prisoners," "guards," and research staff. On the morning of the second day—thirty-six hours after the "prisoners" were "incarcerated"—there was a "rebellion." This was subdued by the "guards" with carbon dioxide fire extinguishers and followed by increased attempts at control and harassment of the "prisoners." On the same day the first "prisoner" was released because of extreme depression, disorganized thinking, uncontrollable crying, and fits of rage; three more were released for similar problems on subsequent days and a fifth when he developed a psychosomatic rash over his body after a "parole board" rejected his "parole appeal." By the sixth day, with no let-up in the aggression and harassment by the guards or in the disorganized passiveness of the prisoners, the entire procedure was terminated. Less than half of the planned time had elapsed.

Following termination of the experiments, "three separate encounter sessions were held, first, for the prisoners, then for the guards, and finally for all participants together. Subjects and staff openly discussed their reactions, and strong feelings were expressed and shared. We analyzed the moral conflicts posed by this experience and used the debriefing sessions to make explicit alternative courses of action that would lead to more moral behavior in future comparable situations. Follow-ups on each subject over the year following termination of the study revealed the negative effects of participation had been temporary, while the personal gain to the subjects endured" (Haney, Banks, and Zimbardo, 1973, p. 88).

Research Program Effects. General advantages would include an increase in knowledge about the socialization or acculturation of individuals, important activities that all persons are associated with at one time or another. A second would be a more precise understanding of the processes within formalized social organizations with asymmetrical power structures, which are quite common in developed societies and are found not only in prisons, but in schools, the military, many hospitals, and to some extent, in commercial organizations. Such information may affect the structural and supervisorial policies of these organizations; it may lead them to be more effective or perhaps more humane. The major negative effects would be the costs involved in this kind of research project and the possibility that the balance of the anticipated effects for the participants would be negative.

Harder to predict than its outcome is the impact of empirical research on a community of scientists or on public policy. It would appear, if the reports of the principal investigator are accurate (Zimbardo, 1973b), that this particular study had a major impact beyond its expected audience (the sponsor, readers of professional journals, and the like). Such impact can be inferred from the approximately 850 (through July 1973) items of correspondence (125 with criminal justice administrators, legislators, and politicians), and from the variety of television specials, feature stories in the mass media, and articles and editorials in over one hundred newspapers that were devoted to this project. Investigators participated in congressional hearings and class action suits (on behalf of prisoners) and gave presentations to numerous lay, social science, and criminal justice professional groups. In sum, the impact of this project has probably been as great as any other social science finding (despite the exploratory nature of the research), perhaps because of the realistic nature of the setting and the dramatic character of the outcome.

Research Project Effects. The major advantage of the simulated prison project was the process for selection of the role occupants, who were assigned at random from a carefully chosen homogeneous population that was considered to be psychologically stable and above average in intelligence and education. This process increased confidence that any major patterns related to the organizational roles would be a result of the features of the situation rather than of individual differences. The major negative effects were the costs and time involved, possible ambivalence about the extent to which a "real prison" had been simulated (this would be a major issue in the absence of *any* differences between "guards" and "prisoners"), and the potential negative balance of the effects for the participants.

An additional issue raised with respect to this specific project is that it may have the negative effect of "subverting the atmosphere of mutual trust and intellectual honesty without which . . . neither education nor free inquiry can flourish" (Savin, 1973a, p. 149). This is made more specific in comments (Savin, 1973b) about the possibility of universities or students coming to regard professors as deceitful and dangerous. But it would be hard to argue that this is a *major* negative effect, if the contract signed by the participants is accurate and there is no permanent damage done to participants.

Participant Effects. For this particular study, effects were sharply differentiated for the two categories of participants. The "guards" experienced little psychic stress, although some guilt was expressed by a few over their treatment of prisoners. They appeared in fact to enjoy the "total" control over other individuals a great deal, to the extent that they worked overtime without pay and were disappointed when the study was terminated in advance (this did cause a loss of pay). It is possible that, upon reflection, the guards felt remorse and personal dissatisfaction over discovering the type of treatment they were capable of displaying toward other human beings, but there is no systematic evidence of this.

The stress and humiliation experienced by the "prisoners" appeared to be quite real, resulting in severe reactions by five of the original eleven. There were anecdotal accounts about "prisoners" who cleaned toilets with their bare hands, memorized meaningless rules, and so forth. Further, after several days those who had not been released for their own welfare appeared willing to take any tack to gain release—forfeiture of all money earned, demands for bail money, and similar acts. Such effects appeared to be temporary in nature, and the "prisoners" reported lasting benefits in a one-year follow-up.

Distribution of Effects. The participants in this study were young males drawn from the more intelligent, better adjusted segments of college students, mostly of middle- and upper-middle-class backgrounds. But major benefactors—in terms of new social policies—would be prison inmates, prison guards, and society in general. Clearly, the social category that experienced the costs was quite different from the social category that might experience the benefits. There have been suggestions that such an uneven distribution of costs and benefits is not unjust, but appropriate (Rawls, 1971).

Consideration of Participants' Rights and Welfare. The major evidence related to this issue is twofold. First, an informed consent form—the contract—was completed by all participants prior to the initiation of the project. This form apparently specified the administrative conditions, the pay, and the anticipated loss of privacy (for both "prisoners" and "guards," while they were at "work"), and included an agreement not to engage in physical abuse. In retrospect, it would appear that the conditions of the contract (as reported in the research articles) were probably not adequate in terms of precision or scope. However, the intensity of the experience was not anticipated, either by the investigator or the institutional review board that approved the project. The second major line of evidence about consideration of the participants' welfare comes from the actions of the investigators during the course of the study; namely, their release of severely distressed "prisoners," their control over the "guards," the early termination of the project, and the post-research group therapy sessions.

In summary, this is a research activity that has pursued two important issues: the extent to which situational characteristics affect performances in complementary, but dramatically different, roles and the speed with which these performances emerge. It appears to have provided a dramatic, convincing demonstration of the extent to which situational demands are more important than individual differences, a conclusion that has substantial potential application to policy decisions related to prison administration. The major gain in general knowledge about these issues is a direct result of the specific research design—the experimental procedure and random assignment of participants to the different roles. Major negative effects were experienced by one half of the participants, but these effects seem to have disappeared after completion of the study. Several actions on the part of the experimenters provide evidence that the rights and welfare of the participants were given serious consideration—an explicit, written informed consent statement; removal of "prisoners" who exhibited the effects of extreme stress; and termination of the entire study soon after it was initiated. Finally, there is evidence that the major burdens were borne by individuals from advantaged social categories and that the major benefactors would be individuals from less advantaged social categories, an uneven distribution of costs and benefits that many nevertheless consider equitable.

Deception in Research: Illusions and Consent

The deception of participants in controlled research settings where the real purpose of the study and—perhaps more important—the nature of the experiences to be expected are concealed from the participant has raised a variety of concerns. The basic problem involves two major issues. First, individuals have a right to be fully informed, in advance, about the nature of any research experience, particularly if there is a strong possibility of severe negative effects, temporary or permanent. Second, it is clear that knowledge of the phenomena under investigation or the experiences to be expected may have substantial effects upon the reactions of the participant—and, hence, influence the phenomena. A considerable percentage of social science research in experimental situations now involves some form of deception. Such widespread deception probably results from both a desire to obtain useful scientific data (the unbiased reactions of the participants) and from knowledge that the negative effects will usually be mild and temporary.

Nevertheless, concern with the rights and welfare of participants has led to discussion of mechanisms that might provide a satisfactory compromise between those rights and scientific requirements. (The total prohibition of all research utilizing deception would clearly not be a compromise; it would merely eliminate a wide range of research procedures long associated with significant contributions to social science.) Three major approaches have been to consider alternatives to research that involves deception, to develop mechanisms for satisfying the requirements of informed consent, and to minimize the effects of deception (after the research has been completed).

The major alternatives to an experimental research design in a controlled setting are generally an experimental research design in natural or field settings, a nonexperimental research design (developing descriptions of observations through surveys or observations), or some form of asking participants to imagine or simulate their actions (usually referred to as role playing). The use of experimental designs in natural settings, where "ordinary events" are systematically created, has an additional set of problems if the participants are "unaware" that research is taking place (see Chapter Seven on covert research); nonexperimental designs encounter the problems associated with attempts to make inferences about causal relationships between variables—the disadvantages that led to the use of experimental procedures in the first place.

The last alternative, role playing, has received serious attention, at least among social psychologists. This alternative involves describing a situation to participants and asking them to describe how they would act, given a choice between different alternatives. While this has the merit of not subjecting the participants to a psychologically real set of stresses and conflicts and prevents them from feeling that they would be responsible for some "bad deed," it has one major disadvantage—substantial research suggests that there is a low relationship between what people say they would do and what they will really do. Further, the more socially sensitive or controversial some of the behavioral alternatives are, the less there is confidence that the individual's stated intentions can be considered a reliable guide to his or her actual behavior.

If the congruence between attitudes and behavior were not problematic, the task of developing a useful body of knowledge related to the actions of individuals would be considerably simplified. Instead of elaborate experiments and complex questionnaires, with attention to subtle nuances of the situation and prior experiences of individuals, any specific intellectual question could be resolved by merely asking a group of people (presumably a random sample) what they would expect to do when confronted with certain information or problems. This has been referred to as psychology by consensus (Freedman, 1969). The most dramatic evidence that this does not provide a satisfactory procedure for the study of individual behavior comes from individual predictions of self-disobedience in the conformity to authority study reviewed above. *No* "self-predictors"—undergraduates, middle-class adults, or psychiatrists—predicted that they would go above the 300-volt level of extreme intensity shock (Milgram, 1974; p. 29); in fact, substantial percentages of comparable individuals faced with the actual research situation administered shocks at the maximum level of 450 volts (see Table 6).

One alternative for ensuring that the rights and welfare of the participants—particulary the right to self-determination—have been given consideration is to acquire surrogate informed consent. In instances where the fully informed consent of the actual participants would jeopardize the purpose of the research, it may be possible to obtain the "reactions" of a group of individuals to the research procedure by providing them with a full and complete description of it. If they find the procedure acceptable, knowing they would have been deceived, the research can then be conducted with a category of comparable individuals, and confidence that the rights of the actual participants have been given appropriate consideration will be increased because of the approval provided by the surrogate participants. Concern that the surrogates may inform the participants about the research can be minimized if the two groups are taken from different geographic areas (different regions of the same city or similar universities in different states). Alternatively, a committee representing the participants could provide the judgment and be "sworn to secrecy" until the actual research was completed. An unresolved issue associated with this procedure is the percentage of surrogates who must approve a project before it is considered suitable for administration to the real participants. Ideally, a project would receive complete approval or disapproval, but usually there will be a mixed reaction. Baumrind (1971) has suggested that 95 percent must approve a project; if the average cooperation rate for surveys (proportion that agrees to the interview) is used as a guide, approval by 85 to 90 percent may be considered acceptable.

Perhaps the most widely employed solution to the problem of deception in research is to provide a debriefing of the participants—a full and complete description of the research and the nature of any deception employed, a general discussion of the results, and procedures to minimize any negative effects for the participants. This has the advantage of being more efficient than other solutions (since it minimizes the preresearch complications of obtaining surrogate consent) and focuses all effort on the individuals who may experience the negative effects—the research participants. The use of extensive and elaborate debriefing or "dehoaxing" is an acknowledgment that the rights and welfare of the participants may have been infringed and that it is the treatment of the participant after the research that is crucial when the procedures involve mild and transitory effects.

Some empirical evidence suggests that such debriefings tend to mitigate the negative effects of deception for the participants. Perhaps the most dramatic such evidence comes from a replication of the obedience to authority research (Ring, Wallston, and Corey, 1970). The same research procedure used by Milgram (1974) was employed, but mock auditory stimuli (administered over headphones) were substituted for mock electric shocks; despite the verbal protests of the "confederate-pupil," 91 percent of the "teachers" (undergraduate females) were fully obedient and administered the most painful level of sound. The real purpose of the study was to determine the response of the participants following different types of debriefing. Using only obedient participants, three post-experimental procedures were followed: an accurate discussion of the procedure and a rationale for obedience, an accurate discussion of the procedure and a rationale for defiance, and a polite "thank you" with no discussion of the true nature of the procedure or the performance of the "teacher." The major findings were that only 3 percent of the debriefed participants (one out of twenty-eight) regretted participation in the project or felt that such research should be prohibited, compared to 43 percent (six out of fourteen) of those not debriefed. Further, 96 percent of those fully debriefed did not resent the deception and did not consider the research unethical. A somewhat larger incidence of "guilt" (35 percent) was found among participants who were interviewed by telephone two to five weeks after the experience than among those who participated in the original compliance to authority research (Errera, 1972), perhaps because the follow-up for the original study occurred a year after the experience. In short, a careful debriefing of participants had a substantial effect in reducing any negative feelings about the use of deception in the research.

A more elaborate study of the effects of debriefing was completed by having undergraduates read descriptions of six different
research procedures and provide evaluations of them (Berscheid
and others, 1973; Schulman and Berman, 1974). Major independent variables included the extent to which the studies might produce stress for the participants and the nature of the descriptions
provided to the participants. The four studies considered stressful
involved:

1. Obedience to authority (the study developed by Milgram).
2. Perception of and attitudes toward a powerless "victim" by subjects after they had ostensibly harmed the "victim" with an electrical shock.
3. Effectiveness of hypnosis on length of time individuals would
   immerse their hands in cold water.
4. Participant's response to a benign situation made to appear
   frightening through the presence of "danger cues."

The two studies considered nonstressful involved:

1. Effects of distraction on attitude change.
2. Extent of cooperation between two subjects in a bargaining
   situation.

Variation in the "consequences" for the participant was unrelated
to the dependent measures; all analysis involved combining participants presented with a request to "judge experiments" with
those asked to "evaluate projects you may be asked to participate
in."

The participants evaluated written descriptions of the six
studies each of which was provided in seven variations; four of
these variations involved more or less complete descriptions of the
research objectives and procedures and three involved the addition
of a debriefing. These seven variations are presented at the top of
Table 7. Each participant read the descriptions in a test booklet
and completed his or her responses on a written questionnaire,
working alone in a quiet room with, but isolated from, other
respondents.

Table 7. Evaluations of Research Procedures with Varying Degrees of Information Provided to Participants

Information Provided	All Conditions	Rationale	Procedure	Desirable Behavioral Expectation	Undesirable Behavioral Expectation	Neutral Debrief	Desirable Debrief	Undesirable Debrief
Purpose and objective of research		X	X	X	X	X	X	X
Description of research procedure			X	X	X	X	X	X
Socially desirable subject responses				X			X	
Socially undesirable subject responses					X			X
Discussion of typical subject response, implications, and nature of any deception						X	X	X
Number of participants	106	19	18	17	22	8	11	11
Results								
"Would you have chosen to participate?" (1 = definitely not; 3 = maybe; 5 = definitely)								
Nonstressful (two studies)	3.9	3.8	3.7	4.2	3.9	4.2	3.6	4.0
Stressful (four studies)	2.9	3.6	2.4	2.8	2.3	3.4	3.0	3.1

Agreeing to participate (percentage with responses of 2, 3, 4, or 5 on above question)

Nonstressful	99%	97%	97%	100%	100%	100%	100%	100%
Stressful	80	97	65	72	68	91	93	84

Personal reaction following experiment (2 = sadder/less satisfied than before; 10 = midpoint; 18 = happier/more satisfied than before)

Nonstressful	11.5	11.9	11.4	12.4	10.0	11.5	10.9	11.1
Stressful	9.2	11.2	8.1	8.8	7.1	10.0	9.9	9.6

Evaluation of Experiment (2 = not worthwhile/not valuable; 10 = midpoint; 18 = worthwhile/valuable)

Nonstressful	13.0	15.0	12.5	12.6	13.9	13.6	11.3	12.0
Stressful	12.2	15.8	10.0	11.2	9.9	13.6	12.1	12.7

Note: The value in the first column is the average of the values in the next seven columns. The values in columns two through eight are the average (across subjects) of each subject's average response to two (nonstressful) or four (stressful) descriptions of experiments.
Source: Tables 1, 2, 3, and 4 and "Method" discussion in Berscheid and others (1973).

The major dependent variables in this study were the reactions of the undergraduates who read these different descriptions in terms of their willingness to participate, possible reaction following participation, and evaluation of the experiment. The major results, presented at the bottom of Table 7, are related to the stress potential of the experiment and the type of written description provided to the participants. There is clearly a substantial difference in the responses to stressful and nonstressful project descriptions, although for some issues this is a rather small difference—one or two intervals on a seventeen-interval scale. Perhaps more important, the differences are substantially less when the debriefing activity is included as part of the experimental description. The differences in tendency to participate on the four-interval (5-point) scale are reduced to less than one interval when the debriefing is included; or, in other words, there is an 11 percent difference in the percentage willing to participate in the project (an average of 89 percent was willing to participate in the stressful studies that included a description of debriefing compared to 100 percent for nonstressful). Just as striking is the rather narrow range of responses; they are clustered around the midpoint of the scales and give little evidence of a strong positive or negative reaction to any of the issues raised by the questionnaire. This may have been due to the situation in which the evaluations were made, a quiet room where each participant calmly completed an evaluation booklet.

Evidence from these two studies suggests that a conscientious, thoughtful debriefing may have substantial ameliorating effects for deceived participants, as well as improving their general attitude toward the research enterprise. Since it is compatible with the advantages to be gained in the study of complex, easily influenced phenomena, it seems likely that debriefing will be a major procedure for ensuring that the rights and welfare of participants are given appropriate consideration. Ambiguous results were obtained, however, in a study of debriefing alternatives for individuals deceived about an aspect of their self-esteem, suggesting that the effectiveness of debriefing may be related to the phenomena affected by the research (Walster and others, 1967).

A final issue, which is raised by those opposed to any research that creates "illusions," is related to the consequences of deception for further research. Once research relies upon the success of an "illusion," so this argument goes, it is often necessary to determine if the illusion was successful—did the participants interpret the situation as intended by the investigators? Occasionally a substantial percentage of participants will either "misinterpret" the situation or begin to doubt that the procedure is "real." This raises the problem of whether those who do not become suspicious are more compliant, less intelligent, and more trusting than others. (Cook and others, 1970). Also, there is concern with the effect of an "illusion" experiment upon reactions to subsequent experiments. Once a person is deceived, he or she may attempt to respond to future research experiences as a truly naive or "inexperienced" participant, as a "good subject" who attempts to discover the "real" hypothesis and respond in ways that are congruent with these expectations, or as a "troublemaker" who resents past treatment and tries to discover the real purpose of the research so that he can spoil the experiment. A final, more subtle concern is the effect upon the population from which many participants for such research are selected; there is a concern that undergraduate college students will develop a general assumption that social psychologists lie and will mistrust all research in controlled settings, creating an unknown and perhaps unknowable bias to the research findings.

The multitude and complexity of the processes that would be involved in organizing this set of problems is far beyond the scope of this book. But it is clear that a major factor is the strength or potency of the phenomena under investigation. If the process is sufficiently robust and of a general nature, such as the Asch conformity effect (the powerful influence of unanimous opinions of similar others on the stated judgments of an individual, increased for ambiguous issues) or the emergence of hierarchies in small interpersonal groups, then no amount of suspicion or mistrust by the participants will be able to "reverse" the effects. In contrast, if the phenomenon is of a temporary nature and easily affected by contemporary influences, then any slight change in the research situation or the nature of the participants may have a substantial effect. It is for those concerned with a precise discussion of research in controlled situations to review this problem. The basic problem that led to the use of illusions in research remains: concern that knowledge of the research objectives may affect the phenomena being studied.

In summary, it would appear that there is no easy solution to the major considerations that have led to the use of deception in research. But several procedures have been developed to provide confidence that the rights and welfare of the participants will be given adequate consideration. Alternatives to research that utilize the participant's behavior as the source of evidence—for example, role playing or simulation of responses—appear inadequate on the basis of substantial evidence to suggest that verbal judgments and actual behavior are frequently inconsistent. It may be possible to provide confidence that participants would have consented to take part in a project by having surrogates make judgments about the entire procedure. Extensive and careful debriefing procedures appear to satisfy most participants who have been deceived, to the extent that they are willing to become involved in future research and do not condemn the conduct of the research. There is no clear solution to the problem that research using illusions may have some effects on participants who take part in later research projects; this is a complicated issue that seems to be related to the strength or robustness or importance of the phenomena under investigation.

Natural Settings (Social Experiments)

Social experiments are distinct from those in controlled settings in that they usually involve long periods of time (months or years), deal with significant aspects of everyday life (financial assistance, medical care, housing, and the like), and require considerable resources and staff to conduct (dozens of staff members and millions of dollars are not unusual). Further, they are usually initiated to provide information about important policy issues, an aim that may or may not be present in research conducted in controlled settings (Rivlin and Timpane, 1975).

While such experiments are often viewed as a group (because all have policy relevance), they can be considered in two categories, which are based upon the nature of the major dependent variables. One category focuses on the response of individuals, and the other emphasizes changes in the characteristics of social systems. Social experiments that emphasize the effect on individual attitudes or behavior are comparable to research in controlled settings, except that fewer aspects of the participant's environment are standardized during the research experience; it is extremely difficult to involve the participants in such extended studies without their knowledge of the research. Social experiments that examine the factors affecting the characteristics of a social system (such as the crime rate) are somewhat more complex, for the research may be initiated without the awareness of the members of the community. Indeed, the presence of such awareness may not be feasible for many of these studies. Concern over the informed consent of the participants may also be raised when a social experiment focuses upon the responses of individuals and indirectly affects other members of the community without their informed consent.

The following discussion reviews two well-known social experiments with different types of dependent variables. The first is an income-maintenance study in which the major dependent variable is the work-force participation of members of a family unit; the second focuses upon the changes in the crime rate of a well-defined neighborhood in a major city. Although the nature of the dependent variable is different in these two situations, the fact that they are true experiments, with deliberate manipulations of important independent variables, places them in the same category as research in controlled settings, and thus effects on the participants are considered the responsibility of the investigator(s).

Income-Maintenance Study

The negative income tax study is typical of social experiments that focus on individual behavior as the dependent variable (Kershaw, 1972; Kershaw and Small, 1972; Rivlin, 1971). This research involved the examination of the effects of different negative income tax plans (direct cash payments) to "guarantee" a predetermined minimum household income; reductions in payments occurred if earned income for the household increased, but not on a dollar-for-dollar basis. The basic question was the effect on labor-force participation of individuals in households with a guaranteed income—would they work less? This study also allows an estimate of the cost of a guaranteed income program if adopted as the major welfare orientation. The study involved 1,400 families in five cities in the New Jersey–Pennsylvania area that were randomly assigned to one of eight plans (negative income tax schedules) or to a control group (families receiving no "guarantee").

Research Program Effects. Collecting data related to this problem would resolve some of the uncertainty about the different policy options available for those concerned with the welfare of citizens with low incomes. The data would provide evidence to determine whether the advantages of a guaranteed income plan—simplicity of administration, equity (no concern with why an income is low), dignity for the recipient, and incentive for income-producing activities (guaranteed income is not reduced on a dollar-for-dollar basis)—are outweighed by the major presumed disadvantage, a tendency to reduce gainful employment if individuals are provided with a guaranteed income. Considering the cost and impact of a change in the current welfare program, which involves millions of recipients, thousands of welfare staff members, and billions of dollars, resolution of this issue would be of some importance, particularly given the high degree of dissatisfaction with the current welfare system, at both federal and state levels.

An additional objective, perhaps as important as contributing to the resolution of a policy problem, would be to increase understanding of the factors associated with the decision of individuals to work. The dominant assumption by economists has been that the major incentive is financial; this view implies that if a level of financial support is guaranteed, then the amount of work-related behavior would decrease. If the level of work maintained by those with and without a guaranteed income is the same, then other factors may be considered of importance in affecting work activity—desire to make a useful contribution, the social satisfactions of pleasant work associations, wanting to escape the household situation, and so forth.

Research Project Effects. The chief reasons for developing a social experiment to resolve the major issue—does guaranteed income reduce work activity?—were related to social policy concerns and the desire to minimize ambiguity over the causal relationship between variables. This latter was important because the sponsor of the research, the federal government, had the ability to actually modify the major independent variable—the nature of the payment procedure used. Since no such guaranteed income scheme had been used previously, it was not possible to observe the effects on the basis of natural events, that is, past experience. There appeared to be no better way to resolve the issue than use of a social experiment.

The major negative effects of the project were the rather massive costs (a full-time staff of three dozen; annual costs of several million dollars per year for the five-year period; complicated and elaborate computer files) and the long time required to resolve the intellectual issues. This initial study lasted five years, but this is now considered too brief (the participants may be reluctant to quit work knowing that the guaranteed income will terminate in a short period of time); some current studies now provide guaranteed income for up to twenty years.

Participant Effects. Involved here were the positive and negative effects for individuals as members of families, for the household was the unit of analysis for this study (if a household dissolved, the payments were continued but divided among the individual members). The negative effects were similar for all participants: they agreed to participate in interviews every three months and report all outside income (for all members of the household) to the project personnel. In brief, the major negative cost was the time required to provide the information and the possible reductions in privacy associated with contributing information. The families in the control group received little in the way of positive benefits; families in the experimental conditions received somewhat different benefits (depending upon which of eight plans they were involved with), but the payments could range up to several thousands of dollars per year per family.

Distribution of Effects. If the guaranteed income plan turns out to have substantial advantages, such as lower cost and increased dignity for the recipients, both the general public and welfare recipients would benefit. The major contributors to the research were representatives of those on welfare, but the general public contributed through financial support of the project. It would be difficult to argue that disadvantaged individuals were being "used" for the benefit of the advantaged in this type of research, since those in disadvantaged situations stood to gain (many of the participants themselves received considerable direct benefits).

Consideration of Participants' Rights and Welfare. Two features of the research procedures reflected consideration of the participants' rights and welfare. First, all families were presented with a contract that specified the nature of the research activity and the procedures to be followed; it included a guarantee of anonymity with respect to the written descriptions of the research. Second, rather elaborate attempts were made during the operation of the project to ensure that confidentiality of the data would be respected, including a pledge of confidentiality signed by all staff members and an emphasis on confidentiality in the operating procedures of the research organization. Further, a number of means were used to resist attempts by local district attorneys, federal agencies, and legislatures to obtain information on specific families. The major strategies were the arguments that it would not be in the best interests of society to divulge such information and thus jeopardize a major research effort and payment to a state welfare agency to compensate for any "overpayment" to families that were both on welfare and involved in the experiment. Unfortunately, the need for repeated measures on the families over time precluded destruction of the identifying information on them.

In summary, the research in question was related to a major policy issue; the project design appears to have been reasonable for providing information useful for the major intellectual concerns; the effects for participants were largely positive (experimental group) or neutral (the control group); the participants were drawn from the same social category that stood to benefit from applying the resultant knowledge; and the actions of the investigator reflected concern for the participants' rights and welfare.

Effects of Variations in Level of Police Patrols

As a means of determining the optimum level of police patrol activities (officers cruising in vehicles), a study of the effects
of variations in the level of police patrol patterns was conducted
in a midwestern city (Kelling and others, 1974). Matched sections
of the city were subjected to three levels of police patrol activity
for a twelve-month period: reduced (responding to calls for service
at 50 to 60 percent of normal level of activity); normal; and increased (250 to 300 percent of normal level of patrolling). The
effect of this change was examined with respect to a number of
factors: rates of crime reported to the police and estimated through
surveys (of individuals and commercial establishments), estimates
of the fear of crime, the perceived level of police presence (by
"criminals" and "straight" residents), and numerous characteristics
of police activities (response time, officers' use of noncommitted
activity, officers' attitudes, and so forth).

Two features of this study are of particular importance to
the present discussion. First, the project had to be initiated and
conducted in secrecy. If the residents of the affected communities
had become aware of the study, it would have been impossible to
have confidence that their judgments on the levels of police presence or fear of crime were related solely to variation in the presence of police patrols. Offenders might also have taken the opportunity to engage in criminal activity in the reduced patrol areas.
Second, the major measures of effectiveness—the rate of crime in
the various experimental communities—are characteristics of social systems rather than characteristics of individuals. In this sense,
it was a true social experiment, for the unit of analysis was a social
unit.

Research Program Effects. Clearly there is substantial interest
in two major objectives entrusted to police departments—the reduction of crime and the efficient use of police equipment and
personnel. While there are many ways to achieve these goals, there
seems little question that a focus on the organization and allocation
of police officers is a major issue. Any actions that will either reduce the cost of meeting these objectives or reduce the occurrence

of crime (with its economic and human costs) would appear to be of some merit. In short, establishing the relationship between the presence of police officers and the occurrence of crime would have both practical and academic benefits if it contributed to an understanding of factors that affect occurrence of crime.

Research Project Effects. The major advantages of an experimental research design for the exploration of these issues are two. First, there would be substantial confidence in the resultant relationship between the level of police patrolling and the various dependent measures, such as levels of crime. Second, if the level of police patrols had a systematic effect on the dependent variables, such an effect could be easily implemented in the form of new administrative policies. Also, the confidence of police administrators in applying the new knowledge might be enhanced by awareness that the project was conducted by regular police departments in typical communities. The major negative effects would be the costs associated with the project in the form of administrative demands and activities and data collection and analysis. There would be no additional costs for the patrol officers, since they were merely shifted from one neighborhood to another.

Participant Effects. For the participants, there were few major direct positive effects other than the possible reduction in crime experienced by those in the intensive patrol areas. They might experience indirect positive effects after completion of the project, but these would be general benefits resulting from more efficient police administration and would be shared with all residents of the city in which the research was conducted, as well as residents of other cities. The participants obviously could not share in the satisfactions and excitement of being part of an interesting research activity during the project, because they were unaware of the project until its completion. They might have some sense of involvement after publication of the results.

If the level of police patrol activity is systematically related to the major dependent variables (rate of crime, victimization, or fear of crime), the participants in the reduced patrol areas might experience substantial negative effects by virtue of their involvement in the study. Further, if crime increased in the communities bordering the intensive patrol areas and outside the experimental "beats," these residents would become unknowing victims of the research activity. In either case, personal and financial costs might be incurred by those affected by the project.

Distribution of Effects. The areas selected for the project were considered to be typical for the city and representative of all income and ethnic categories. Hence, if the major findings suggested that some improvement in the effectiveness of dealing with crime was possible, then the social categories that were the source of the participants might also be the major benefactors of the knowledge. While nonparticipants might benefit from the knowledge developed from the research, they would be differentiated from participants by geographical variation rather than by variation in social categories.

Consideration of Participants' Rights and Welfare. The project was developed by individuals—police officials—who assumed that variations in police patrol patterns would have an effect on the rate of crime experienced and reported to the police. Out of concern that the project might expose participants in the reduced patrol areas to a higher rate of crime than they would normally experience, the following guideline was adopted for the conduct of the study: "The [police] department would commit itself to an eight-month experiment, providing reported crime data did not reach 'unacceptable' limits. [Unacceptable was defined as a statistically significant variation from predicted crime levels, or as based upon the impressions field commanders received from their daily reports.] If no further major problems developed, the project would continue for an additional four months, totaling a twelve-month experiment" (Kelling and others, 1974, p. 29). In short, despite the imposition of a variation in police protection without the consent of the participants, there was definite concern for the effects that participants might experience.

The nature of the study and the need to keep its occurrence confidential precluded the implementation of any type of informed consent procedure. However, it is clear that the police officials who developed and implemented the project felt that they had a responsibility to determine the extent to which patrol strategy was effective in reducing the occurrence of crime. In light of the concern over an apparently rising crime rate and the lack of effectiveness of any of the existing solutions, it might be argued that residents of the city would expect police administrators to experiment with new procedures and that resistance to innovations providing significant new data would be quite small. However, it should be noted that the highest public official to approve the project was appointed (the chief of police) rather than elected.

In summary, a major practical and intellectual issue generated the research project under consideration. The experimental design appeared to have the substantial benefit of providing confidence in policies derived from the results of the study. The low cost, in terms of resources, was achieved through use of existing police personnel to create the independent variable. Direct effects for the participants could have been quite positive (for those in the increased patrol areas) or negative (for those in the reduced patrol areas). The social categories of the participants appeared to be "average"; there was no indication that one category of individuals contributed to knowledge from which they would not benefit. Consideration of the possible negative effects for the residents of the reduced patrol areas led to the decision to terminate the study if a substantial rise in crime became evident, and this suggests that a concern for the rights and welfare of the participants was present. Participants could be considered to have consented to such an experiment by a general expectation that officials would initiate innovative administrative variations to improve the effectiveness and efficiency of police activity; they were not, in fact, informed directly of the research project until its completion. As a final note, it should be mentioned that the variation in police patrol presence had no statistically or substantively significant effect upon any of the major variables—the presence of additional police did not seem to reduce crime or fear of crime, and their absence did not seem to increase crime or fear of crime.

Summary

Experimental strategies reflect the research dilemma in its most explicit form. The same research techniques that provide the greatest confidence that a causal relationship between variables can be established also maximize the investigator's responsibility for the impact on participants and for the same reason—intentional control of variables influencing the participant. The dilemma is minimized when the benefits of the new knowledge are substantial, the negative effects (especially for participants) are minimal, and there is clear evidence of consideration for the rights and welfare of the participants (such as the use of full informed consent procedure and post-research surveillance to determine and correct negative effects).

Three controversial examples of highly controlled experimental research—a program to develop reproducible stress situations, a study of compliance with authority, and role learning in a simulated prison—indicated that despite substantial, temporary negative effects for participants, important intellectual issues were under consideration, and there was substantial evidence of investigators' concern for the rights and welfare of the participants. A major issue with the first two studies was the inability to fully inform the participants in advance of the research and still achieve the scientific objectives (the powerful effects of the simulated prison were unanticipated by the investigators); this problem frequently occurs with studies of social-psychological phenomena. The most viable solution appears to be a combination of careful surveillance during the study (to detect exceptional reactions and terminate the experience) and a full and complete debriefing after the research has been completed; this generally satisfies participants that they were not abused and have been respected as individuals. Compared to the highly controlled experimental research, the two social experiments—a study of the effects of guaranteed income and evaluation of the effects of changes in the density of police patrol patterns—appeared to have greater potential impact upon public policy. Again, there was evidence that the investigators were concerned with the rights and welfare of the participants, even in the study conducted without their knowledge.

The analysis of the experimental research was organized around the research dilemma issues—research program effects, research project effects, participant effects, distribution of effects, and consideration of participants' rights and welfare; these five issues seemed to cover most of the major concerns that might be developed with respect to a scientific project. None of the examples, even the most controversial, was clearly "good" or "bad"; in every case there were important intellectual issues, often with substantial applied implications, under consideration and substantial evidence to suggest that investigators were concerned with the rights and welfare of the participants. In none of the examples was there an indication that individuals from a disadvantaged social category were being "used" for the benefit of some other—more advantaged—social category. In sum, these examples represented reasonable solutions to the research dilemma; as compromises, they cannot be expected to satisfy the complete range of critics.

6

Descriptive Studies and Analysis of the Research Dilemma

A substantial amount of research in social science—perhaps the majority—does not involve deliberate attempts to affect phenomena, as with experiments, but instead focuses on descriptions of natural processes. Since the phenomena themselves are the major cause for positive and negative effects experienced by the participants, the investigator's responsibility for the welfare of the participants is substantially reduced. When participants are aware of the research activity and have the right to withdraw from involvement at any time, the major issue appears to be the indirect effects for the participants.

Descriptions of natural phenomena will be reviewed in two general categories. The first covers those studies that involve large numbers of participants and (generally) standardized measurement techniques (personality tests, attitude scales, and the like).

The second covers those procedures that emphasize the intensive review of specific cases, the study of either a unique individual or a social system. The following discussion will emphasize the general nature of these studies, reviewing the possible effects for participants and procedures that demonstrate concern for their rights and welfare. The remaining issues—effects of research programs, effects of research projects, and distribution of effects—are relevant to specific projects and will not be emphasized; analysis of these issues would be quite similar to that in the discussion of experimental research in Chapter Five.

Descriptions of Aggregates

Two types of research activities typically involve measures of individual characteristics of large numbers of participants. The first are those that emphasize the prediction of individual behavior, attitudes, emotions, and so on, based on information about the individual's past experiences and current mental traits—these are personality trait research projects. The second are the studies of participants in different social situations and social categories, and these are often used in survey research. Although both types of research activities may have similar direct effects for the participants, the indirect effects may be quite different. For this reason, the two types of research projects will be reviewed separately.

Personality Measures

These measures typically involve elaborate pencil-and-paper tests or other procedures, such as structured interviews, for measuring mental or psychic characteristics. A primary goal of such research is to determine the relationship between these mental or psychic attributes (aggressiveness, cognitive complexity, personality "profile," and so forth) and the individual's present or future behavior, attitudes, and emotional states. In some cases these measures will be supplemented with information on the person's background and previous experiences. A typical project will involve the collection of data on a group of participants, who may be chosen because they are convenient, representative of some special population (mental patients, occupational group, and the like), or representative of the general population. Each individual may complete a series of tests used to measure skills and mental traits and may participate in a personal interview, which serves as a source of information on the participant's life activities or social characteristics. Analysis usually involves attempts to relate this information to current or future behavior, attitudes, or emotions. Success is defined as establishing a high relationship between two general measures, not necessarily as making correct predictions about specific individuals.

Participant Effects. The most frequent positive effect for participants may be the involvement in an interesting experience (the systematic study of themselves), as well as the altruistic satisfaction of contributing to a worthwhile endeavor or the pleasure of expressing an opinion or judgment. In some cases there may be a cash payment or special privileges associated with participation, but such direct general rewards are rare. It has been noted that in some instances—perhaps following a personal tragedy (death of a spouse) or a natural disaster (tornado)—responding to a systematic interview or questionnaire may help individuals regain their composure since they must attempt to provide rational responses (Warwick, 1973). Some individuals may be helped to the development of a more satisfying or stable self-image through the completion of personality tests.

Several types of direct negative effects are possible; the most frequent is the time required of the participant. In addition, it is possible that sensitive or embarrassing issues may be raised, such as ones involving sexual behavior, relationships with intimate associates, or troublesome aspects of life experiences. Descriptions of past activities may also recall painful or unpleasant memories. Except for rather special situations, however, the direct negative effects for those who complete personality tests appear to be few and modest. A major form of indirect negative effect would be embarrassment from disclosure of some types of private information. In order for this to occur, the source of a breach of confidentiality would not only need to know the identity of the participants and their responses but would also need to have some knowledge of what the responses meant—to know how to interpret them would require some training or experience with the measures involved. The importance of this issue has long been recognized among psychologists and others who make extensive use of such personality tests, and there is a strong professional norm against unauthorized disclosure or nonprofessional interpretations of such instruments.

A second category of indirect effects involves the utilization of the information created through this type of research program. It may, for example, be used to help individuals with certain problems or unsatisfying emotional states. In most such cases, the applied professional will be dealing with a special type of information related to a unique individual's specific characteristics or situation. This usually involves extensive consultation with the individual affected, and he or she thus has direct influence on the nature of any treatment. In such applied situations, not only is there the possibility of substantial positive benefits for individuals, but their rights of self-determination will be respected through their direct involvement in the application of the knowledge.

Consideration of Participants' Rights and Welfare. It is impossible to pursue personality research without the cooperation of the participants. Thus, unless undue influence is used to gain their "cooperation" in completing the personality measures or interview, it can be assumed that they are exercising their right of self-determination. Further, such research usually involves a series of discrete operations (such as the items on a test or the questions in an interview); participants are generally free to refuse to respond to any item they find embarrassing or unpleasant—and they frequently do refuse. But during the mid 1960s a controversy developed over possible invasions of an individual's "private personality" through the use of personality tests. The concept of a private personality, which individuals might have a right to maintain as confidential, was developed (Ruebhausen and Brim, 1966) at the same time that concern arose over possible coercion of individuals to complete personality tests and thereby disclose aspects of this private personality without their willing consent. However, the major concern was associated with the use of personality tests as part of the employment interviews; observers were not convinced that the disclosure of private information was completely voluntary in those situations. There was, strangely enough, almost no discussion of the use of such materials in research, where the consequences for refusal would be modest (*American Psychologist*, 1965).

Since the major form of negative effects from personality tests is indirect—through disclosure of confidential information obtained from the participants—the major evidence that investigators respect the rights and welfare of the participants may be the care taken to ensure that such information will not be revealed. Aside from strong professional norms, there are a number of techniques for guaranteeing that such disclosures do not occur, and these will be reviewed after the discussion of survey interviews.

Surveys and Interviews

Common in all areas of social science, the survey interview consists of numerous questions related to an individual's background, life experience, social characteristics, attitudes, behaviors, and so forth. Analysis tends to place emphasis upon individuals in different categories, some of which may be socially defined, rather than upon their unique personal characteristics, as with personality research. Further, such research may focus upon individuals in unique social categories—for example, students, minorities, the elderly, and deviant or radical subgroups. Analysis may emphasize both the distinctive individual features of the participants and those of their various social categories. Some analyses may require only a sample of data collected at one point in time; others may involve repeated measures on the same individual to establish how variables at one point in time were related to differences at a later point in time.

As the number of survey projects initiated annually in the United States for scientific and practical purposes may number in the hundreds of thousands, it would be futile to attempt a review of program effects, project effects, and distribution of effects for even a small number of the wide range of projects that use survey procedures and techniques. But some comments can be made on the most general types of participant effects and on procedures that provide confidence that the rights and welfare of the participants are considered.

Participant Effects. In general, direct effects of survey research are similar to those associated with personality research: an interesting experience, an opportunity to talk about one's self, altruistic satisfaction at contributing to science, and—in some studies—cash payments and special privileges. The major direct negative effects are also quite similar: embarrassment or stress associated with responses to certain items, the time required to be involved, and so forth. This category of research is unique because of the nature of the indirect negative effects, and the most critical of these would stem from violation of the confidentiality of the data or the anonymity of the participants. This is perhaps even more important when the data are of a sensitive, contemporary nature (for example, related to income, occupation, political views, or illegal behavior). There are two types of anonymity that may be of importance in such research, namely, anonymity associated with involvement in the project as a participant and anonymity related to the information collected in the interview.

For research on sensitive topics, those identified as participants may risk substantial negative effects. For example, investigators on one project that involved interviews with political radicals discovered that shortly after an interview was completed, the respondent would be retained for questioning by law enforcement officials. Once it was realized that the interviewers were being followed, the study was immediately terminated (confidential personal communication). Another study of draft evaders in a neutral country was never conducted because researchers were unable to convince the potential respondents that anonymity could be ensured (Sagarin, 1973). In some cases investigators, unsure they will be able to convince participants that anonymity can be protected, may resort to covert research and collect data without the knowledge of the participants. But this substantially reduces the range of data that can be obtained.

A project that had a considerable impact upon the development of issues and problems associated with survey research, and particularly on concern for the anonymity of the participants and potential indirect effects, was the American Council of Education (A.C.E.) project on characteristics of college students (Boruch, 1971b; Coburn, 1969; Walsh, 1969a). Designed to provide information on the behavior and attitudes of college undergraduates during and after they completed college, this longitudinal study involved repeated measures on the same individuals and hundreds of thousands of respondents. Controversy over the project was heightened when measures related to political orientation and activism were included in the survey questionnaire. Substantial attention was drawn to the choice of research issues, possible uses of the data, and suspicion that government agencies or school administrators might be able to identify activist students from the questionnaires. The result of the controversy was a discussion of the major issues by an advisory committee, a statement of principles to guide the research, and the creation of a number of techniques for ensuring participant anonymity. While the large majority of such survey projects do not gather sensitive information, the possibility of such disclosure on sensitive issues is clearly recognized by most social scientists; this has resulted in concern for obtaining legal recognition of a privileged status for research data (reviewed in Chapter Ten) and the development of techniques for minimizing the possibility that such data can be associated with specific individuals.

A second and more subtle type of indirect negative effect involves the use of research results for policy decisions that may affect the participants. In personality research, application of findings frequently involves direct interaction between an applied professional and a client; the client is assumed to provide his informed consent to any treatment, even when it is based upon the research findings. In contrast, research based on survey interviews may be utilized by legislatures and government officials in developing policies that apply to social categories of individuals (the elderly, disadvantaged, offenders, and homeowners, to name a few). Whether or not these social categories will benefit from the use of research results to determine government policies is a matter of some controversy. However, if the policy is based only on the results of the research, the individuals affected will not be able to fully exercise their rights of self-determination; they may consider their treatment paternalistic (at best) or autocratic (at worst). Members of this social category (including the potential participants) may perceive that their right to self-determination is not being respected and respond by attacks on the research activity rather than the government decision-making mechanism.

One example of a research project terminated because of unfavorable response from the community involved an examination of the effects on psychological growth of different interactions between a young (three-and-one-half to thirteen-month-old) child and its mother on the one hand and a daycare center staff on the other. A community research review committee felt that no possible outcome would benefit the black community. If the daycare staff produced "better" psychological growth, the committee feared that black mothers could be forced to place their children there; if the home care children reflected "better" psychological growth, it was feared that such results would justify programs to teach black mothers how to raise their children at home (Brody, 1971). It is not clear that the latter is the most likely use of the results for developing public policy, although it is a logical alternative.

Consideration of Participants' Rights and Welfare. The major factor that contributes to confidence that the participants' rights and welfare are respected, as with personality research, is that they must provide their cooperation or survey research could not be completed. The other major action that indicates respect for participants' welfare is the care taken to ensure that the data remain confidential and the participants remain anonymous. Concern for the participants as a social category would be reflected by the attention given to the analysis and interpretation of the data, to minimize totally inaccurate inferences as a basis for policy decisions. However, the inability to predict the issues or concerns that may arise among policy makers or those promoting a specific political interest makes it extremely difficult to anticipate all possible interpretations and misinterpretations associated with a complex set of data.

In summary, there are some obvious direct positive effects associated with the typical survey interview, some minor direct negative effects (time lost, inconvenience), and some indirect negative effects with a potential for substantial impact in a small number of unusual projects. The major evidence that participants' rights and welfare are given serious consideration is the need for their cooperation to complete the research and investigators' concern for maintenance of participant anonymity and confidentiality of information; techniques to achieve this latter objective will be discussed next.

Maintenance of Participant Anonymity

When information is systematically collected on a large number of individuals (through personality measures, survey instruments, interviews, or any other means), ensuring the anonymity of the participants is a major issue (Boruch, 1971c, 1972; Campbell and others, 1975) that itself raises several questions. One is the relationship of participants' confidence that anonymity will be maintained to the type of information they provide. Another is the relation between techniques for maintaining anonymity and different types of data analysis. Different procedures may be utilized when data are collected at one point in time, when repeated interviews are to be conducted with the same individuals (as in longitudinal studies), when those not associated with the original research activity wish to analyze the data, or when data from several different sources are to be combined for analysis.

A recent (Boruch, 1975) review of the empirical literature related to the effects of variation in perceived anonymity on the responses received found several important patterns. The first was that sensitive information was more likely to be provided if a promise of confidentiality was present, understood, and trusted by the respondent. If the respondent did not understand or trust the procedure designed to assure anonymity, his or her responses were less satisfactory. Improved candor was only in evidence for sensitive information—for example, about drug use or abortions—and not for innocuous information provided in any situation. Further, promises of confidentiality, even if believed, were not sufficient to improve responses in and of themselves (other features of the research procedure also had an effect). In sum, for projects that involve sensitive or potentially embarrassing information—often the kind of information that is most highly relevant to important practical or scientific issues—the usefulness of the research data may be seriously affected by the investigator's ability to provide a credible promise of confidentiality.

The most basic data collection procedures involve the construction of questions (or items) to obtain responses from the participants, the preparation of data for analysis, and analysis of the data by the initial project personnel or sometimes by others. (Additional data may be collected from the same respondents at later points in time.) In terms of the design of the questionnaire or interview procedure, the most basic means for protecting the participant is to avoid any sensitive or embarrassing questions or at least to utilize only those that are important to the research question(s). Further, it is less threatening if questions about sensitive issues are as general as possible. "Have you tried marijuana?" is less likely to be a threat than "When, where, and how much marijuana did you consume the last time you used it?" If at all possible, questions should be phrased so that the response appears socially acceptable. In general, the less unique the information, the less threatening to the participant is public disclosure of the research data.

Other procedures are applicable for situations where a large sample size is expected. One involves a "secret" choice between a sensitive issue (Have you ever tried cocaine?) and an innocuous one (Did you vote in the last presidential election?), where the average response of the population to the innocuous question (the percentage that said they voted in the last presidential election) is known (Boruch, 1971a). The participant is asked to choose between the two items, using a random procedure with a known probability of selecting each item (flip of a coin). The participant chooses the item to be answered and responds—only the participant knows, for sure, which item has been answered. This information can then be used to develop estimates of the response to the sensitive item for the sample and, hence, for the population. This is done by "subtracting" the predictable responses to the innocuous item from the total set of responses. The result is an estimate of the responses to the sensitive item. However, a more precise analysis, such as a cross-tabulation with other information on the respondents, is precluded, since it is not possible to determine how specific participants responded to the sensitive item or even if they chose that item to answer.

An alternative to this procedure, if a large sample is obtainable, would be to systematically vary the information sought from the respondents (Boruch, 1971c, pp. 420–421). One half of the respondents, chosen at random, could be asked identifying information and innocuous background information. One quarter of the respondents could be asked for both innocuous background information and sensitive data but guaranteed total anonymity—they could not be linked to their response by anyone, even the investigators. The final quarter of the respondents could be asked for all information—identifying data, sensitive data, and innocuous background information; measures could be taken to disguise their identity. Responses of anonymous participants to sensitive data might provide estimates for the population from which the sample was drawn; information from the third group could be used to estimate the relationship between the sensitive issues and the more innocuous or background variables. The major advantage of this procedure is that it minimizes the number of participants on whom sensitive data are collected—data that can then be related to specific individuals—and reduces the costs associated with the measures required for respondent security. But it also increases the complexity of the statistical analysis and reduces the precision of the analysis that can be completed in relation to the sensitive issues.

Several concerns are relevant while the data are actually being acquired from the participants. One procedure for ensuring anonymity is simply not to acquire the names and other identifiers of the participants. Alternatively, the respondents can be asked to use an alias of their own creation or to transform well-remembered data (their birthday subtracted from their social security number); of course, such methods are only useful if the identifiers are not forgotten before the next interview. Anonymity, actual and perceived, may be enhanced if names and other identifiers are transmitted separately to the investigator and are linked to the questionnaire or responses by a code number.

An additional problem is ensuring that the research staff will not divulge any information. This may be a more substantial problem when the staff is recruited from the same communities as the respondents—often a major concern in those communities where surveys are conducted by volunteers who are apt to be amateurs (Wolf, 1964). Exhortations to maintain confidentiality, a code of ethics for professional staff members, provision for avoiding interviews where staff and respondents may know each other—or have mutual acquaintances—and provisions for participants to return sensitive responses to the data processing center without the intervention of staff members, such as by mail or in locked boxes that are opened at the data processing site—all these methods may be valuable. In some cases it may be possible to bypass human staff completely, as when the information is gathered via a computer terminal.

Similar problems with security may occur when the data are processed—coded and keypunched—before entry into data files for analysis. At this stage information that identifies the respondents may be destroyed, if it is still available, or it may be immediately separated from remaining, sensitive information. Again, it is possible to insist that the staff members maintain confidentiality of any information and perhaps to require a signed agreement. Mark sense instruments, which automatically translate the respondent's written answers into electronically coded data, or the use of computer terminals to provide direct entry from respondents into data records reduce the potential for problems at the data preparation stage.

Once the data have been prepared for analysis, the most basic safeguard of anonymity is again the destruction of all identifying information or its complete separation from the research data. Further safeguards would include prevention of duplication of records, carefully limiting access to authorized project personnel only, or separation of the data base into different subsets, which would have different bases related to different types of information or information gathered at different times. Additional forms of security may be possible, or necessary, if the data are stored and processed at a major computer center with many diverse users. These methods might include passwords to control access, cryptographic coding (scrambling), automatic monitoring of the use of files, or system verification of hardware-software integrity. Further, different users could be given access to different types or amounts of data, with no one user given access to the entire record on any one individual. Numerous procedures have been developed for maintenance of the security of industrial, military, and government records, and these could be adapted to protect social science data.

Analysis of data by outsiders provides additional problems for ensuring the anonymity of the participants. Such analysis may be conducted by other investigators, by government agencies, or—in extreme cases—in response to a subpoena. Unfortunately, it is quite likely that the identity of some participants can be determined for many data sets, even if the identifiers (such as name, address, and social security number) of the participants have been removed. This could occur under the following conditions: (1) routine demographic data (age, sex, marital status, occupation, residence area, and so forth) are maintained in the file and available, with a comparable coding scheme, in public records; (2) the individual participant has a unique set of such characteristics; and (3) significant resources are devoted to comparison of the known data with the characteristics on the research file. For example, if the respondent is a married lawyer with six children who lives in a particular four-block area and has a high income or a distinctive dwelling, he may be easy to identify in a research file.

Awareness of this problem has led to a number of techniques for allowing access to research data but reducing the probability that the identity of the respondents can be determined. These include use of the initial research personnel to complete analyses for the outsiders (charging them the cost of the activity), restriction on the public variables that are provided (such as birth date, social security number, and residence area), providing a randomly selected subsample of the total sample for analysis, or microaggregation (releasing average data on small subsets, $n = 10$, of participants and thus precluding identification related to any specific participant). Perhaps the most drastic of these techniques is to "inoculate" the data by adding a small "error" term to each variable, a "random" error with a known distribution and an average value of zero. While this would not change the average values of variables used in any analysis and would increase the variance only slightly, it has the advantage of precluding precise comparisons that would unambiguously identify respondents. (The information for the lawyer in the previous example could be modified by a slight change in income, size of family, and other data.) For a large sample such modifications would have little appreciable effect on the analysis and would almost guarantee anonymity for the participants.

While information that could be used to identify specific participants can be destroyed to ensure their anonymity, this information must be retained if the research requires repeated measures on the same individuals. For this reason other techniques have been developed to safeguard the anonymity of participants whose identity is retained. The simplest is, of course, to separate the list of participants from the data and keep them in separate locations, with an identifying number used to provide correspondence between the two files. A more sophisticated version of this procedure is to maintain three files, one with the identifying information and its own identification number, one with the data and a data identifying number, and a third file indicating the correspondence between the two numbers (Astin and Boruch, 1970)—this is the so-called link system. The third file may be kept in a separate location, minimizing breaches of security initiated by project personnel. The ability to resist a legal subpoena is enhanced if the linking list is stored in a foreign country, with an agreement that it is not to be released to anyone outside that country.

When the initial data and the list of participants are kept—in separate form—with one research organization and the linking file with another, the matching of additional data with the initial data proceeds as follows. The initial list of respondents is used to collect additional information, which is prepared for analysis and given a new data identification number. The initial linking file contains the initial participant identification number and the initial data identification number; a new linking file is prepared containing the initial participant identification number and the new data identification number. This new linking file is then delivered to the organization responsible for the initial linking file, where the two files are merged to create a master linking file indicating the correspondence between the initial participant identification number and both the initial and new data identification numbers. A file showing the correspondence between the initial and new data identification numbers is then returned to the research organization to allow comparison of the individual initial responses and later responses or merging of the two files. In brief, the entire procedure can be completed without associating specific participants with the initial data at the research organization. Additional follow-up measures can be completed using the same procedures.

Other problems may develop when there is a desire to utilize data from two sources, whether two government agencies, two research projects, or a government agency and a research project. (Such data may have been collected on the same individuals, households, or other unit of analysis.) In most cases, the need is to efficiently merge data from the two sources, without the disclosure of additional information in each file to personnel working on the other set of files. (A typical case might involve the combination of federal tax data with data from a welfare agency.) Procedures that might be utilized to ensure that participant anonymity is maintained include microaggregation (comparing average data on individuals aggregated into small homogeneous groups from two different sources), a synthetic linking by matching (comparing individuals who have similar basic characteristics, not the same unique individuals) or "link-file brokerage." Link-file brokerage involves a neutral organization, perhaps in another country, that merges the files to provide a combined file with the required information, preventing representatives from one organization from having access to the files of the other organization. Additional procedures for guaranteeing anonymity include cryptographic coding of information not required for merging and provision of summary information on groups of participants.

All these techniques to maintain confidentiality are based on the assumption that there is a substantial sample size—thousands are required in some cases—and that the investigators have the financial and computer resources that make such activities possible, since some of these techniques can substantially raise the cost of data analysis. Further, concerns over breaches of security through "snooping" by research staff become almost as important as fears about outsiders when projects are large, but these concerns can be minimized by careful attention to the selection, training, and supervision of research personnel. Most of the techniques also require the destruction of information, a requirement that may preclude various types of analysis or reduce its precision.

As with most research procedures, the investigator must make a judgment as to which combination of techniques best serves the objectives of the project. Techniques that provide anonymity may facilitate the study of phenomena that would otherwise remain obscure, but there are clear disadvantages to using some of these procedures. When investigators fail to take precautions that will ensure anonymity for the participants, the justification for this must be related to the expense involved or the need to complete special types of data analysis. It is not possible to argue that techniques to protect the data are unavailable.

Direct Observation

Observation of unique events or situations, with the full knowledge of the individuals involved, is a common form of research activity that shares several features with other types of descriptive research. One distinctive difference of the descriptions resulting from direct observation is that they tend to be discursive and anecdotal rather than abstract and general. Of the two different types of research activity reviewed below, the first are "clinical" cases or individual examples and the second are descriptions of individuals and communities based on field studies. In the first the investigator typically has a brief, focused contact with the individual participants; in the second the investigator may have more extensive and more intimate involvement with the participants (both as individuals and as part of a social system).

Individual Case Studies

Detailed examination of individual case studies is frequent in many types of applied social science research—for example, in psychiatric, clinical psychology, or counseling investigations—and may also occur in general research activity. In many situations the participant (who may also be a patient or client) is fully informed of the special nature of his or her problem and the innovative nature of a treatment program, as well as the possibility that the results will be published. Similar situations arise when an investigator wishes to illustrate certain points by describing specific incidents or individuals in detail, even though he may have examined a number of persons. In at least one case, an entire monograph was devoted to one day in the life of one individual (Barker and Wright, 1951).

An example of a clinical publication based on a single case and with potentially embarrassing results is the detailed description of an individual who took part in a successful procedure designed to provide a self-control technique for reducing pain (Levendusky and Pankratz, 1975). The article focuses on the program of treatment and success with a single patient, described as a "sixty-five-year-old retired army officer with a history that included significant military achievement, a productive teaching and research career, and numerous social accomplishments" (p. 165). The patient's medical history was reviewed; as a result of his problem, the author noted, his "mood was somewhat depressed, and he was unkempt and had poor personal hygiene. . . . to control pain in social situations with friends, he would often assume awkward or embarrassing postures" (p. 165–166). This information and the location of the treatment institutions, indicated in the article, would considerably enhance the possibility of identifying the individual concerned. Whether the patient would suffer negative effects as a result of these descriptions is not clear. But public knowledge that the patient was successfully deceived about the source of pain control—the innovative feature of the therapy—could be embarrassing for him.

Issues related to the conduct of the actual research are quite similar to those already discussed and need not be reviewed in detail. The patient who receives direct personal benefits from a previously untried therapy has experienced a positive effect; participants in research who receive no direct personal benefits may nevertheless have the altruistic satisfaction of knowing they have contributed to a potentially useful scientific project. The major issue is the extent to which participants (patients or otherwise) may experience indirect negative effects by virtue of disclosure of their identity and thus their association with events or facts that are potentially embarrassing or distressing.

From the perspective of the investigator (or author), written descriptions are a means to provide readers (other social scientists) with information that will assist them in determining, for themselves, how much confidence to have in the techniques or findings reported. This could be crucial in further applications of the research. If an empirical pattern is very general, quite potent, and not unexpected, then a very general statement may suffice—few details about the situation or the participants will be necessary. Conversely, if the reported events are unique and depend upon unexpected relationships among numerous variables, then there may be substantial reason to provide a great number of details, and this could lead to the identification of the participants.

Such an example comes from a study of the decision processes involved in selection of a kidney donor from among the relatives of a kidney recipient. While little stress and conflict were present in the large majority of cases, there were examples that demonstrated some personal ambivalence on the part of a donor. An example of such stress is described in the following (Simmons, Klein, and Simmons, 1977, p. 289): "The case of the most extreme guilt involved a married daughter (Brenda) who had agreed to donate to her mother, but who became extremely anxious and angry the night before the transplant after she was admitted to the hospital and some minor errors were made by the surgical resident. She alternated between indicating at some points that she was too fearful to donate and at other times that she wanted to continue with the donation. The donor doctor decided that she could not donate in her psychological state and gave her a false medical excuse so that the recipient would be unaware of her unwillingness. Her guilt at having backed out was considerable, as documented by relatives who were aware of the true circumstances." In this case, as in many others, the investigator's goal was to prevent other family members from recognizing the participant (potential donor) and the donor from recognizing the other family members; consequently, not only names were changed but also the sexes and the family relationship of the donor to the recipient.

An example of an elaborate description of a carefully disguised family is found in *The Children of Sánchez* (Lewis, 1961). Organized as an autobiographical description of the lives of four siblings and their father (he had four wives, sequentially) in an urban slum area in a developing country (Mexico), the account portrays the wide variety of challenges that must be faced in such situations, including family conflicts, official corruption, and sexual and emotional development, described at times in quite explicit language. Considerable controversy developed in the host country's popular press over this study. One newspaper assigned two reporters the task of discovering the true identity of the family; after twenty-seven days they claimed to have succeeded, although the identity of the family was not made public (Beals, 1969, p. 35).

Perhaps the journalists were concerned about the possible negative effects for these family members, who were thought by many to share with the investigator a responsibility for portraying their society in a bad light.

These three examples—a patient disabled by pain, a potential kidney donor, and a candid description of a working class family—demonstrate the problems associated with maintaining participant anonymity in distinctive situations, where the details associated with the examples are important to understanding the issues they illustrate. Further, these examples involve three different types of potential negative effects, an individual's reputation in his or her community, an individual within his or her immediate family, and an entire family within their neighborhood. It is a well-established tradition that case studies or descriptions of individuals are presented in such a way that the possibility of identifying the participant is minimized. Such efforts not only reduce the potential for harmful indirect effects but reflect consideration for the rights and welfare of the participants.

Field Observation and Community Studies

Direct observation of natural behavior and events is commonly employed by anthropologists, psychologists, sociologists, and others. Overt field observation is distinct from covert field observation in that participants are aware that the investigators are collecting information for a written record of the group or community activity. It is difficult to review the factors associated with the effects of research programs or projects for many field observation studies, since these are often loosely structured exploratory studies without a precise focus or objective. Frequently they are initiated on the assumption that if the investigator(s) are allowed access to the social setting and an opportunity to talk to the participants, they will be able to discover and describe the important cultural and structural features of the group. Often no explicit theory, conceptualization, or testable hypotheses guide the selection of the data to be collected or even, in some cases, the choice of research site. When the results of such studies provide unusual or influential new descriptions of social and human phenomena, this must be attributed to the intellectual skill and flexibility of the investigators or to lucky accidents that occurred during the study.

Participant Effects. Participant observation and community studies can be considered in terms of both direct and indirect effects for the participants, keeping in mind that the impact of indirect effects (occurring after the research is completed) may be substantially greater than that of the direct effects during the data collection.

Direct positive effects experienced by those in the same culture (or an equivalent culture) as the investigator may be the satisfaction of contributing to a research project and discussing events within the social system, as well as their opinions and judgments, with an articulate, knowledgeable individual. But while pleasant interaction with others is a satisfying experience for many and is frequently the basis for friendship, it could be less than completely satisfying when trained investigators are involved. Careful fieldworkers often attempt to be as neutral as possible regarding events that occur within the social system and to avoid any opinions or activity that could be interpreted as signifying allegiance with, or approval of, any clique or subgroup within the community under study. They may, however, express opinions and even help participants in dealing with outside agencies or individuals, thereby increasing the trust received from the participants and improving rapport.

Additional positive benefits may occur when the community is in a more primitive state, with a poorly developed economic, educational, or medical system. In these cases, the investigator may provide medical care, the rudiments of education, economic assistance (usually in the form of food), and, on occasion, may intervene with government authorities on a participant's behalf. While aid of this kind could affect the phenomena, such temporary, small effects usually will not have a significant influence on the major focus of study (such as language structure, cultural norms, or the social structure). Often a very explicit pattern of exchange develops, with the investigator(s) providing goods (or influence with the authorities) in exchange for information.

The major direct negative effects for the participants are probably the time required for participation in discussions with the investigator(s) and possible invasions of privacy. Extreme invasions of privacy seem unlikely without the cooperation of the participants, since most interactions occur in the course of normal social exchanges, although there may be embarrassment or discomfort when some topics are raised in discussions. In a less developed society, the investigators may place a burden on the economic system if they are treated as guests and do not provide food to compensate for their share from the society's stores. The direct positive and negative effects may be the same as those associated with any other form of interaction with strangers—tourists, salesmen, politicians, or government representatives—except that interaction with investigators may have little immediate consequence for the participants.

Indirect effects for the participants may occur upon appearance of published accounts of the fieldwork. These effects, both positive and negative, may include those experienced by the individuals specifically discussed in the published accounts and those associated with the discussion of the community or social unit. For example, a published account may discuss individual participants in a positive and complimentary way, and this may increase their self-esteem and sense of worth. If the identity of the participants is disguised, this positive influence may affect only the individuals who read the accounts and recognize themselves or others in the specific community who can identify the individuals discussed. In the same way, uncomplimentary or embarrassing descriptions of individuals may tend to reduce their self-esteem and provide a substantial negative effect, which again may be restricted to the participants themselves or to associates who can recognize them in written accounts. This type of negative effect is shared with other research procedures but may be exacerbated by reference to specific relationships or events in the social community.

Perhaps more subtle are the effects upon the individual that result from the way in which the social system or community is presented. Most reports of research on social systems within the United States attempt to disguise the identity of the social unit. This attempt has the added benefit of directing attention to the general nature of important empirical patterns and helps to ensure that negative responses toward the social system from those outside the system will be minimized.

It has of course been argued that to disguise the identity of a social organization or community produces more confusion than benefit, since other social scientists may not have confidence in the information used to support the investigator's claims about a "typical" community or group. Instead, it is argued, only knowledge of the specific community will provide the opportunity to review all of the data relevant to generalizations about other communities or groups (Gibbons, 1975). Nonetheless, a serious attempt to disguise locations is tangible evidence of concern for the rights and welfare of the participants, an advantage that seems to justify continuation of the practice. This may also help to protect the investigator himself from "direct effects," such as retaliation from the participants in a study of organized crime or legal retaliation if the study was carelessly or slanderously written. Unfortunately, even a conscientious attempt to be objective and achieve scientific goals may cause the participants to be demeaned. The usual aim of investigators is to show that the patterns in a specific situation reflect a general relationship that can be expected in other similar social systems. Even when this is done in such a way that the participants and their community are treated with respect and dignity, the individuals involved—proud of the uniqueness and special character of their own community—may feel their efforts are belittled when treated as instances of more general patterns (Becker, 1964; attributed to Everett Hughes).

The possibility that participants may feel demeaned is considerably enhanced when the investigator mixes together descriptive data, interpretations, and participants' personal evaluations of one another and the community. The following statements from the monograph on "Springdale" seem to have this mixed character (Vidich and Bensman, 1968):

> In dominating the village government, the businessmen give to it a character of niggardliness which reflects their scarcity psychology and their interest in low taxes [p. 211].
> The prosperous farmers are parvenues [newly arrived upstarts] who have arrived only since the later thirties and especially since the war and postwar prosperity years. They particularly enjoy their success in comparison to the village businessmen, on whom they look down as penny pinchers and small-time operators.

In turn, they are resented by the business group, who see them as profligate in their spending, investments, and borrowing and as not appreciating the value of the dollar [p. 214].

Public meetings serve as ceremonial occasions at which all of the illusions enunciated reflected the public ideology. In light of the tenacity with which the exponents of the public ideology cling to it, it becomes understandable why it is possible to hear day after day and week after week what to outsiders appears to be an endless repetition of high-sounding cliches and sentimental rhetoric [p. 305].

The people of Springdale are unwilling to recognize the defeat of their values, their personal impotence in the face of larger events, and many failures in their way of life. By techniques of self-avoidance and self-deception, they strive to avoid facing issues which, if recognized, would threaten the total fabric of their personal and social existence. Instead of facing the issues, they make compromises and modify their behavior in some cases, and reaffirm their traditional patterns in other cases. They do this, however, without any overt conscious recognition of the basic problem [p. 314].

It is not clear why the authors find that the usefulness of their descriptions, as a contribution to social science, is improved by the condescending and patronizing tone of their narrative, to say nothing of the casual attribution of motives and attitudes to the various members of the community.

The reaction of the participants to the monograph was reflected in a presentation in the annual Fourth of July parade, described as follows in the local newspaper (Whyte, 1958): "The featured float . . . followed an authentic copy of the jacket of the book, *Small Town in Mass Society*, done large scale. . . . Following the book cover came residents of (Springdale) riding masked in cars labeled with the fictitious names given them in the book. But the payoff was the final scene, a manure-spreader filled with very rich barnyard fertilizer, over which was bending an effigy of 'The Author.'" The masked residents were a reference to the "hidden government"—informal influence structure—that was portrayed in the monograph as controlling the politics of "Springdale."

The participants obviously felt they had not been treated with respect and dignity in the monograph that reported the study. Their response also raises the question of the accuracy of the description of the social structure. If participants find a description of their social structure misleading, this will inevitably reduce confidence in the accuracy of the portrayal despite an investigator's claims to have discovered a "latent structure." One commentator has noted that understanding of a social structure was markedly improved and inaccuracies removed when participants reviewed and commented on a draft of a research report (Bell, 1959). Whether this is a viable procedure for all field studies—sometimes the informal structures may be quite subtle—is not clear, but it may serve to minimize resentment from the participants.

Investigators (generally anthropologists) dealing with less developed societies frequently choose not to disguise the identity of the culture or the participants contributing to their field observations. This can lead to embarrassing situations. In one case a leader of a political group in New Guinea (transformed from a primitive religious cult) with a history of humanitarian activities during the Second World War was discussed, by name, in publications during the early 1950s. In the late 1960s the earlier writings received considerable publicity during democratic elections in which the same individual was a key participant (Mead, 1969). The individual won reelection, and while it is not clear that the publicized reports—his political abilities were compared to those of Churchill and Roosevelt—influenced the outcome, it is a possibility. (The investigator expressed concern that the informant could have lost the election, not that a political process may have been affected.)

An example of a monograph that reflects a combination of the four characteristics reviewed above—description of data, theoretical interpretations, review of personal experiences, and presentation of personal opinions—is provided in an account of a small culture (the Ik) located in the mountainous area in eastern Africa where Kenya, Uganda, and Sudan adjoin. The monograph (Turnbull, 1972), produced after eighteen months of field observation, is organized as a chronological record of personal experiences and includes the following comments:

> It is difficult to know how to thank the Ik; perhaps it should be for having treated me as one of themselves, which is about as badly as anyone can be treated [p. 13].
> They were the only people who seemed to share my opinion of their incredible younger brother, Lokwam. . . . It was one

of the few real pleasures I had, listening to his shrieking and yelling when they caught him and did whatever they did (for it was always out of sight behind their stockade) and then watching for him to come flying out of the *odok* holding his head and streaming with tears while Kinimei and Lotuköi laughed with happiness [p. 123].

Luckily the Ik are not numerous—about two thousand—and those two years (of drought) reduced their numbers greatly. So I am hopeful that their isolation will remain as complete as in the past, until they die out completely. I am only sorry that so many individuals will have to die, slowly and painfully, until the end comes to them all. For the individuals one can feel only infinite sorrow for what they have lost; hatred must be reserved for the so-called society they live in, the machines they have constructed to enable them to survive. . . . The only hope now is the unborn or the unweaned, and had they been rounded up and carted off like cattle, they might have grown up as human beings [p. 285].

This latter reference is to the investigator's recommendations to the responsible national government (Uganda) that the Ik culture be destroyed by dispersing the members in ten-person aggregates (mixed in age, village, sex, and family relationships) throughout the entire country. The suggestion was rejected by government administrators, who did not appear to have strong confidence in the investigator's descriptions of the Ik society (pp. 283–284).*

This monograph also identified specific members of the group by name and through photographs as they engaged in illegal activities—spearmaking and abetting cattle stealing—that could lead to retaliation by the government authorities (Barth, 1974; see also response from Turnbull, 1974). At the same time, the remoteness of the Ik villages, the periodic movement of the people, their high mortality rates, and the low probability that the authorities directly responsible for the Ik (the closest police referred to them incorrectly as Teuso) would have access to the monograph all minimize the likelihood of official retaliation. While there seems reason to believe that the Ik society has a rather unusual set of

---

*It is not clear, for example, why Turnbull did not recommend that the government increase the food rationed and closely supervise its distribution to individual Ik rather than to tribal representatives. If this were done, it would both provide a more humane procedure than deliberate genocide for mitigating the fierce interpersonal competition among the Ik and allow investigators to study the effect of a change in situational context on tribal customs.

social customs—babies ejected from their families at age three, the young prying food from the mouths of the enfeebled, the blind and cripped trampled in attempts to get their share of available food, neighbors defecating on one another's doorways, and all stealing food from all—this investigator apparently did not attempt to separate his evaluations from his observations. His attempt to encourage the destruction of the culture may represent an extreme case of possible negative effects for research participants.

These studies of "Springdale" and of the Ik culture show, then, that reports of fieldwork can have significant negative effects for the participants—effects that could be mitigated considerably if the same information were provided in a different form. This would seem to be a low-cost alternative for investigators; all they need do is separate personal evaluations and judgments from objective descriptions. There are a substantial number of ethnographies or community studies that do provide unbiased descriptions.

Distribution of Effects. The major benefactor from observational studies of social systems is generally the society-at-large, although there may be cases where the participants themselves receive some advantage from the knowledge. Knowledge gained through such studies can sometimes be used to the disadvantage of the participants—if the Ugandan government had accepted the recommendations of the researcher, the Ik society would have been destroyed. However, advantages and disadvantages are usually distributed among different social communities rather than different social categories; all categories in a community that has served as a research site may be equally affected by responses to the research.

Consideration of Participants' Rights and Welfare. Here there are two major issues, the extent to which the participants are aware of the nature of the research activities and the extent to which the investigators attempt to minimize any possible negative effects for the participants.

There is considerable reason for doubting that participants in a field study will have an understanding of the indirect effects that may accrue once the written documents are completed. The ability to acquire truly informed consent is likely to be reduced when the purpose and objectives of the research are not well established in advance, a typical situation for field observation. Further, it is unlikely that most participants, even those from advanced cultures, will have an accurate conception of the content and form of a research report based on field observation, aside from a vague notion that it will include a description of their actions and community. The possibility that those from societies without a concept of research or even a written language will comprehend the idea of science and "published monographs" seems quite remote. Investigators may, however, acquire most of their information in the context of normal social relationships. Participants would in effect be providing the information of their own free will, particularly if much of the information is public in nature and comes out at public meetings or in public settings. While the participants may not be fully aware of the possible outcomes of the research, the majority of the information may be considered public in nature and available to any observer, regardless of his or her purpose.

The major source of evidence regarding concern for the rights and welfare of the participants may come from the extent to which the investigator treats the participants with respect and attempts to minimize any negative effects that may accrue from the research. This would be reflected in the efforts taken to preserve the anonymity of the participants and maintain confidentiality of sensitive information, including the identity of the social organization or community. Attempts in the written descriptions to include as few judgments and opinions as possible and to describe the participants and their society with dignity and understanding help to increase confidence that the investigators were concerned with, and respected, the rights and welfare of the participants.

Investigators may have multiple objectives in completing written descriptions of their observations, including:

1. To provide empirical patterns that other social scientists will trust as objective and replicable.
2. To provide interpretations of the causes and conceptualizations of empirical patterns that will be accepted by other social scientists.
3. To describe the personal experiences and problems involved in acquiring the data, often unique and instructive in themselves.
4. To express their opinions and judgments on the participants, cultural features, and other phenomena they may have observed.

It is possible to accommodate all these objectives in a monograph intended for a scientific readership. The body of the work can emphasize the first two objectives, the third can be placed in a "methodological" appendix, and personal opinions and judgments can be reviewed in the preface. Substantial problems seem to develop when there is only a limited attempt to separate the latter objectives from the first two, particularly when the investigator has a negative, critical, and condescending orientation toward the participants.

Summary

This section has reviewed four common types of overt descriptive research: summary descriptions of individuals based on personality measures, summary descriptions of individuals based on survey interviews, case discussions of specific individuals (or families), and descriptions of social systems or communities based on field observation. All four types of research projects may provide useful contributions to a general research program or intellectual objective, and all may require considerable resources and professional time. The direct effects for the participants seem to be minor, with a mixture of positive and negative aspects. The distribution of effects among those who contribute to the research and those who receive benefits does not appear dramatically inequitable. Fairness would depend upon the social category of those providing information in the research involving individuals. For research involving social systems, the distribution of effects may not be uniform, but it often seems related to geographic differences rather than differences in social categories.

The major negative effects for participants will be the indirect effects that could come from disclosure of confidential information developed during the research. When research involves individuals, these effects can be minimized by obscuring their identity in reports of case studies; if the data are highly technical in nature and maintained in computer files, a number of recently developed techniques will maximize and/or guarantee the anonymity of the participants—after the data have been collected and prepared for storage and analysis. Data describing individuals and social systems will minimize potential embarrassment if they show respect and compassion for the participants and their social structures, institutions, and lives; maintenance of the anonymity of the social system helps to assure that the participants will not be identified or embarrassed, personally or for "their" community.

Research involving individuals—administration of questionnaires, interviews, and case descriptions—can probably utilize the informed consent procedures with a minimum of complications. Researchers who study social systems and observe public activity may not be able to obtain informed consent of all participants affected by the research (all the members of the social system). But respectful descriptions of the participants and the social systems will indicate a concern for their rights and welfare.

7

Unknowing Participants and Analysis of the Research Dilemma

◆━◆━◆━◆━◆━◆━◆━◆━◆━◆━◆━◆

There are a number of advantages, when scientific objectives are being pursued, to developing descriptions of natural phenomena without the awareness of the participants who are the source of data. These advantages—access to information that might otherwise be concealed, minimization of effects that might distort the phenomena, or convenience and efficiency—are of differential importance for various covert research methods. Regardless of which method is utilized, failure to inform participants is inconsistent with an important norm that has developed regarding research—the right of the participants to provide their informed consent.

   This chapter will review four types of covert research—surreptitious field experiments, use of "unobtrusive measures," participant observation, and archival research. In exploring the major issues related to the research dilemma, it will emphasize the extent to which participants have experienced negative effects, direct or indirect. All covert procedures share one crucial feature: participants have not provided their informed consent to contribute to the research endeavor. It should be apparent that a dichotomous distinction between overt and covert research procedures is to some extent inappropriate, since no participant is ever fully informed of all aspects of research (Roth, 1962). It is perhaps more appropriate to speak of a continuum of "disclosure," with the research reviewed in this section at the covert end, and other forms of research toward the overt end, of the dimension. (If the activity can be totally overt, it is unlikely to be research.)

One objective of this volume is to explore the extent to which the five issues developed as guides for analysis of research dilemmas are suitable for all types of research, including cross-cultural research. When an investigator from an advanced society engages in field observation in a poorly developed, primitive society—where the participants may not have an accurate concept of scientific knowledge or the motives of their guest (or visitor)—it is not clear that they can provide informed consent. Such research may be considered "quasi-covert," more because of the uncomprehending participants than the investigator's deliberate actions to conceal. While such a distinction may not be appropriate for research that involves investigators from one advanced society studying participants in another advanced society, it seems proper to also review cross-cultural research in this chapter.

Surreptitious Field Experiments

Two research problems have led to the development of surreptitious field experiments. The first stems from the major disadvantage associated with experiments conducted in highly controlled settings: it is not always clear that the same activities will occur when the participants are not under "surveillance." The second is the low frequency with which some interesting phenomena occur in natural settings, making it extremely inefficient to collect data on reactions to such events. The solution to these problems has been the development of studies designed to produce events that could occur as a result of natural processes, thereby providing an opportunity to systematically observe the reactions of ordinary individuals when they confront events they consider everyday occurrences. Further, some of the features of such occurrences and the setting in which they take place can be varied systematically to provide estimates of the influence of different features of such occurrences. In most cases not only are participants unaware of the research activity (planned nature of occurrences and observation of responses), but there may be no way to inform them they have contributed to a research project.

Examples of such studies related to three substantive areas—altruism and helping behavior, responses to social influence, and measures of community norms—are presented in Table 8. Three aspects of each study are reviewed in the table: the intellectual question, the research procedure, and the major findings. Although these are representative projects, they do not reflect the entire range of surreptitious field experiments or the quality of the results. For most of these studies there should be high confidence that the pattern is representative of a "natural response," due to the use of natural situations and unknowing participants, along with the focus upon measures of behavior.

Review of the five major research dilemma issues in relation to this type of research is complicated by the variety of intellectual concerns represented by the studies in Table 8. The following discussion will treat these issues whenever possible, but will deal with specific projects when necessary:

Research Program Effects. Because these studies are related to three different intellectual issues, separate responses are required for this sample of projects. Perhaps the easiest to discuss, because they appear to have developed in response to a unique, dramatic, and unfortunate event, are the studies of altruism and helping (Macaulay and Berkowitz, 1970). It is widely acknowledged that research on such phenomena developed in response to the murder of Catherine Genovese, the young woman who in 1964 was attacked over a thirty-minute period in a high-density central city residential area and finally killed. Her cries for help were heard and struggles observed by thirty-eight residents of the area, but none provided assistance or called the police (Milgram and Hollander, 1964; Latané and Darley, 1970). This "natural experiment"

Table 8. Example of Surreptitious Field Experiments

Intellectual Issue	Research Procedure	Major Results
Altruism and Helping Behavior		
Is it possible to study altruistic behavior in natural settings as a field experiment? What basic parameters influence altruistic behavior (Latané, 1970)?	Research assistants (undergraduate students) ask pedestrians on the street to comply with simple requests: "What time is it?" "Please give me a dime." Rationale provided for needing the dime was varied.	Major variation by nature of the request; 85 percent provided time, 73 percent change for a quarter, 34 percent provided a dime (72 percent if the rationale was a stolen wallet).
Will help extended to a person in trouble be affected by the race of the donor and "victim" (Gaertner and Bickman, 1972)?	A caller, contacting people selected at random, pretends that a wrong number has been reached and that no more change is available to reach a garage concerning a disabled car on a highway. The "participant" is asked to call a garage for assistance and is given a phone number; if called, a confederate takes a message for the "garage."	Approximately 61 percent of the "participants" that heard the appeal (12 percent hung up immediately) made the "helping call," slightly fewer for white "participants" approached by black "victims" (53 percent).
Will the assistance extended to a "victim" be affected by race (white vs. black) and the apparent nature of the problem (sick vs. drunk) (Piliavin, Rodin, and Piliavin, 1969)?	A "passenger" on a subway train collapses; if no one approaches before the next station, he is helped by another "passenger" (actually a confederate).	In 93 percent of the trials the victim was helped by a "participant"; 100 percent of trials when "ill," 82 percent when "drunk." Race of helping passenger was the same as "ill" victim in 58 percent of the trials.

Table 8. Example of Surreptitious Field Experiments (cont'd)

Intellectual Issue	Research Procedure	Major Results
	Altruism and Helping Behavior (cont'd)	
		same as "drunk" in 89 percent. Ninety percent of first helpers were male; 60 percent of passengers in immediate area were male.
Will assistance to an "ill" victim be affected by severity of the problem (blood or no blood) and presence of a nonresponding "social helper" (Piliavin and Piliavin, 1972)?	A "passenger" with a cane collapses in a subway car; "blood" may trickle from his mouth. A helpful "participant" is allowed to assist the "victim" to his feet; if no help occurs, a "social helper" (priest, intern, or ordinary person) helps the "victim" off the train.	Ninety-five percent of "no-blood" victims were helped (median response of ten seconds) and 65 percent of "blood" victims (median response of twenty-two seconds). Effect of a nonresponding "social helper" (priest, intern, or ordinary person) were indeterminant.[a]
Will the "help" provided to another vary systematically with the need for help and the benefits forgone to provide the assistance (cost to the "helper") (Schaps, 1972)?	A female enters an "exclusive" shoe store, either dependent (with a broken heel) or not, during a busy (waiting customers) or slack (fewer customers than salesmen) period. She rejects any shoes shown until the salesman gives up; service to the "customer" is recorded by a male companion.	Greater service is provided to the dependent "customer" when there are no waiting customers (low cost to helper); customers in all other situations are treated to comparable or less service.
How does variation in perceived responsibility and threat of retaliation affect provision of accurate information pro-	A "passenger" takes a seat next to a "participant" in a subway car (in some cases the "passenger" appears "threatening").	When the "lost passenger" asks the "participant" for directions, the incorrect response is corrected 97 percent of the time;

vided to a confused subway passenger (Allen, 1972)?

Another "passenger" approaches the seat and asks the "participant," the "passenger," or both) for directions. The first "passenger" immediately gives an incorrect response and, after a short time, leaves the area.

when he asks the first "passenger" or both individuals, it is corrected 53 percent of the time. When the first "passenger" appears threatening, he is corrected 34 percent of the time; otherwise, 82 percent of the time.

Response to Social Influence

Will individuals who agree to a small ("low-cost") request be more likely to agree to a large ("high-cost") request (Freedman and Fraser, 1966)?

Housewives, selected at random, receive calls requesting responses to a consumer survey, consent to such a survey, or an "informational" presentation about a commercial research organization. Three days later the same women are asked to allow five or six men to enter their home and conduct a complete survey of products in the home.

Fifty percent of those who provide answers to the initial survey agree to the intensive home survey; 33 percent of those who consented to the survey; 28 percent of those receiving the "informational" presentation; and 22 percent who had received no previous contact.

Will individuals insulted by another, attempting to persuade them, shift in the opposite direction? Is there a "boomerang" effect (Abelson and Miller, 1967)?

Individuals sitting on a park bench are asked to engage in a discussion with another on a public affairs topic. The "other" responds with opinions quite different from those of the "participant" and provides insulting remarks in response to the "participant's" comments.

Average change for an "insulting" opponent was approximately 2 points in the opposite direction (on a 30-point attitude scale); neutral persuasive remarks elicited an average change of one point away from the "opponent."

Will invasion of personal space be related to psychophysiological measures of

Men in a three-urinal lavatory urinated with one adjacent confederate ("close"),

Men in the "close" condition took an average of 50 percent longer (8.4 vs. 5.6

Table 8. Example of Surreptitious Field Experiments (cont'd)

Intellectual Issue	Research Procedure	Major Results
	Response to Social Influence (cont'd)	
arousal (Middlemist, Knowles, and Matter, 1976, 1977)?	one confederate one urinal away ("distant"), or "alone." The delay of onset and duration of urination was unobtrusively measured by a male observer who could not see their faces.	seconds) to initiate urination and one half the time to urinate (9.0 vs. 18.5 seconds) than those in the "distant" or "alone" condition.
	Measures of Variation in Community Norms	
Is it possible to obtain a measure of the political orientation of a community on a sensitive issue while maintaining complete anonymity for the residents (Milgram, 1969)?	Stamped letters, containing innocuous messages, addressed to different types of political groups with obvious titles are "lost" in conspicuous locations (for example, under automobile windshield wipers).	Proportion of letters mailed tends to be related to results of elections (held shortly after the letters were "lost") in open (Boston, Mass.) and restricted (Hong Kong) political climates.
Is it possible to develop an unobtrusive measure of social norms regarding abandoned private property and vandalism (Zimbardo, 1969)?	"Used" automobiles are left on the street apparently abandoned (without license plates and with the hood open); one in a center city (Bronx, N.Y.) and one in a suburban area (Palo Alto, Calif.). All contacts with vehicles by "participants" are discretely filmed.	First "part-stripping" contact on central city vehicle in ten minutes; vandalism initiated in nine hours; and in less than three days the previously operable vehicle totally destroyed, mostly as a result of daytime contacts. The hood of the vehicle in the suburban area was lowered by a passerby for protection from the rain.

Are the tendencies to help strangers different in urban areas and small towns (Milgram, 1970)?	"Stranger" comes to the door of a residence, says that the address of a nearby friend has been misplaced, asks to use the phone to call the friend. If admitted to residence, pretends to make a phone call.	In cities, 75 percent of the "participants" fail to open the door on initial contact; 27 percent allow the phone call. In small towns, 25 percent fail to open the door initially; 72 percent allow the phone call.

Note: These studies, except for Piliavin, Rodin, and Piliavin (1969) and Middlemist, Knowles, and Matter (1976, 1977), were originally compiled by Silverman (1975); later commented upon by Baumrind (1977). These summaries are somewhat different from those in the original; they include descriptions of the purpose and findings as well as the procedures.

[a]The procedure was terminated after the second day due to operational problems, including discovery and harassment by subway police, irrational actions on the part of real passengers (attempting to pull the emergency cord), and impending panic during some blood trials.

led to considerable speculation as to why bystanders would not provide assistance to the victim and resulted in a search for conditions under which such assistance would and would not occur. Research on this problem has been conducted in both controlled and natural settings.

While the interest in altruism and helping was generated by an urban tragedy, the major focus of research appears to be upon "understanding"—interpreted as specification of the cognitive processes that are activated in a "passerby"—the mechanisms that lead to helping a victim rather than upon specific recommendations that would lead to a reduction in incidents such as that involving the young woman. It is, after all, difficult to alter the major factors that affect altruism—for example, the density of a crowd, number of observers, familiarity with the physical setting, or the percentage of males among the observers. The major positive social effects may be an expansion of knowledge about human phenomena and a possible increase of helping behavior under special conditions, perhaps due to knowledge of the research findings, rather than the actual manipulation of variables that would increase altruism. (The reduction of incidents requiring help is a different issue.) Major negative effects might be the financial costs of conducting the research and possible negative effects for the participants.

Studies of the social influences upon a variety of individual behaviors and responses are a major emphasis in many areas of social science (socialization, attitude change, compliance with authorities, measures of personal satisfaction and well-being, work behavior, and so forth). Many of these topics or issues have either scientific interest or practical significance (some have both); major issues are, once again, the professional and financial investment required to conduct the research, as well as the possible effects for the participants.

Studies of variation in social norms and attitudes of individuals in different communities can be defended as providing information about the "social world" that may be of some value to those selecting a place to live or unsure about various social norms. It seems unlikely that such studies will lead to any policy actions that will provide a direct change of conditions, but the research may supply a more accurate description of the differences than is provided by media stereotypes or journalistic editorializing. Further, it may give information on the variation in public services that may be required in different settings—if residents are unwilling to assist those in distress, for example, perhaps more public assistance should be made avaiable.

In short, the study of phenomena in all three areas can be justified on the basis of a general expansion of knowledge, and research in specific areas may be justified for applied purposes. There is, however, no clear and obvious set of positive or negative effects associated with an expansion of knowledge related to any of these three phenomena—altruism, attitude change, or community norms.

Research Project Effects. All the projects summarized in Table 8 share several important features. Most involve the controlled creation of "natural events" presented to a representative cross section of ordinary individuals whose reactions are systematically recorded. In most cases the participants are unaware that the "natural event" was carefully controlled and that their reactions were recorded. The major advantage of this procedure, from the perspective of the investigator, is high confidence that the pattern of responses reflects natural behavior, since the participants are assumed to be responding normally. There is the further advantage that the cost of methods for obtaining participants is usually low (a random phone call, a person returning a lost letter, a passenger on a subway train, those using a public restroom, and so forth).

An indirect disadvantage, frequently mentioned (Jung, 1975; Baumrind, 1977) is that such techniques may have the effect of increasing the suspiciousness of ordinary citizens when such events occur normally, reducing their tendency to provide help or assistance. This argument assumes, however, that the number of such studies is large *and* well publicized, the publicity being substantial enough to have a major effect on the ordinary citizen's perception of social reality. Despite the number of such studies, it seems unlikely that the ordinary citizen would be sufficiently aware of their existence to reduce his altruistic behavior as a consequence.

Participant Effects. A striking feature of these research projects is the modest demands made upon the participants. In most cases they are asked to engage in relatively trivial or low-cost behavior—mailing a lost letter, allowing another to make a phone call, helping a passenger to his feet, and the like. In a few cases the effort required of the participants is somewhat greater, such as that of a shoe salesperson who must wait on a hard-to-satisfy "customer" or the energy required to vandalize an "abandoned" automobile, but it rarely exceeds the range of normal activities. There is little reason to expect that the average participant experiences any physical or psychological stress or any permanent effects. Further, the very nature of these research procedures ensures that the participants will remain anonymous, providing high confidence that their behavior will remain confidential and not become a source of embarrassment.

While the potential negative effects for the participants are modest, the direct positive benefits also seem quite minimal—no greater than the benefits of most everyday social interactions. There may be a feeling of well-being or satisfaction from having helped another (unaware that the other did not really need help), or some of the actions may be satisfying in themselves (friendly conversation with a stranger or the emotional release from vandalism of a car). But there appear to be few direct positive or negative effects for participants, particularly if they are not aware that the events were "created."

Distribution of Effects. One advantage of the use of such research procedures is that the unknowing participants represent a cross section of the general public—those who use public transportation, answer telephones, walk the streets, and so forth. Hence, it would appear that the major social category from which participants are "selected" would also be the major benefactor of a general expansion of knowledge. There is little reason to suspect that individuals from a disadvantaged social category are experiencing negative effects for the benefit of those in more advantageous situations.

Consideration of Participants' Rights and Welfare. Perhaps the most important feature here is that all the events are designed to appear similar to those expected in everyday life. (If they did not seem natural, it would lead to speculation that the "participants" had become suspicious and that their reactions were not spontaneous.) Hence, the events created in these studies cannot provide infringements upon the rights and welfare of ordinary individuals greater than those produced by everyday life events. This is particularly important since involvement in the simulated events is largely a decision of the participants—they don't have to mail a lost letter, help a fallen subway passenger, or smash the headlights of an abandoned automobile. In this sense, the participants have provided their informed consent to become involved; they are just unaware that their behavior is being systematically recorded. Further, there is absolutely no attempt made in such studies to determine the identity of the participants, and in many it would be im possible to do so. Hence, the anonymity of the participants and the confidentiality of their actions are assured.

Finally, some research reports indicate an effort on the part of the investigators to ensure that the "participants" do not experience negative effects. In order to reduce the potential for participant guilt, those receiving phone calls from a "stranded motorist" and not-volunteering assistance soon overheard the motorist say, "Here come the police, maybe they can help me" (Gaertner and Bickman, 1972). A pilot study of interpersonal closeness and urination behavior was conducted in a public university restroom with an overt observer equipped with a stopwatch and clipboard; all participants queried (one half of those observed) gave permission to use the data (after it had been collected) and none was concerned about the research (Middlemist, Knowles, and Matter, 1976, 1977; see also Cohen, 1978). In the study of the subway passenger's reactions to a fallen "victim," the "victim" was always helped to his feet (by a confederate) before the next stop if no "participant" came to his aid—providing some evidence that the "victim" was not seriously injured (Piliavin, Rodin, and Piliavin, 1969; Piliavin and Piliavin, 1972). Further, the study using a "bleeding victim" was quickly terminated, partly because of harassment from subway police but also because some reactions were too dramatic and may have endangered the subway passengers (Piliavin and Piliavin, 1972).

In summary, the major advantage of surreptitious field experiments is the strong confidence that the data reflect "natural responses." There seems, on the one hand, to be little in the way of serious negative effects for the participants, since they need not extend themselves beyond a casual social encounter or momentary altruistic gesture. On the other hand, they receive little in the way of direct benefits other than the satisfaction of assisting or interacting with other persons. The participants appear to be drawn from all social categories; there is no evidence of an unjust distribution of effects. The participants who voluntarily become involved in the created events appear to be providing some form of consent to the research; there is little chance they will be identified and lose their anonymity; and there is some evidence that investigators have acted to minimize potential risks and negative effects for the participants.

Participant Observation

The distinction between field observation, as overt research, and participant observation, as covert research, is very imprecise. In addition to the problems associated with providing full understanding of a research activity to the participants (especially difficult when the investigators themselves are not sure of a project's objectives), there are many situations where social scientists have participated in ordinary social groups prior to (or simultaneously with) becoming a social scientist and then have written about their observations and experiences after leaving the group (Dornbusch, 1955; Homans, 1946; Roth, 1959). For this discussion, only "extreme" cases will be considered, those where the investigator has determined, in advance, that he or she will engage in observation of a social group with the expectation of misleading a substantial proportion of participants about his or her true objectives and social role.

A brief review of the intellectual issues, nature of the research methods, and the major findings from several studies that have used covert participant observation are presented in Table 9. The first of these, the study of male homosexual behavior in public restrooms (Humphreys, 1970a, 1970b) is frequently mentioned in discussions of the research dilemma. The following review will cover the major research dilemma issues with reference to this study; enough detail is available to allow for an informed discussion.

Table 9. Examples of Covert Participant Observation

Intellectual Issue	Research Procedure	Major Results
What is the nature of the activities involved as male homosexuals engage in brief, impersonal sexual encounters in public locations (restrooms) and how do the social characteristics of the participants compare with the general population (Humphreys, 1970b)?[a]	The observer adopted the voyeuristic role of "watch queen" (lookout), thus gaining the confidence of the participants and access to their behavior. The license plates of 134 vehicles used by participants (this excluded two "walk-ins") were recorded, and fifty were interviewed in their homes as part of a legitimate social health survey one year later. The participant-observer conducted some interviews in a "disguise."	Homosexual activity in selected (isolated sections of a park yet convenient to roads) public restrooms was a predictable and routinized activity, conducted between apparent strangers in almost total silence. The social characteristics of the participants were not dramatically different from the general population (in terms of marital status, occupation, education, income, number of children, number of friends, or religion), although they tend to express substantially more conservative positions on political and social issues (not related to homosexuality).
To determine the extent to which newcomers to a therapy group who are similar in social characteristics to existing members will be encouraged to become further involved with the group (Lofland and Lejeune, 1960).[b]	Twelve Alcoholic's Anonymous groups (half dominated by upper-middle-class participants, half dominated by working-class participants) were each visited by two research assistants (two visits each); one dressed as an upper-middle-class male, the other as a working-class male. Each observer participated in the meeting and recorded the extent and nature of all interaction initiated by existing members.	Highest levels of interaction and encouragement occurred for observers in working-class clothes visiting an upper-middle-class group; next highest levels for observers visiting working-class groups (observers in upper-middle-class dress receiving slightly greater encouragement); and least encouragement received by observers in upper-middle-class dress in upper-middle-class groups. The results were

Table 9. Example of Covert Participant Observation (cont'd)

Intellectual Issue	Research Procedure	Major Results
To examine the extent to which disconfirmation of a prediction would lead to increased fervor in proselytizing when appropriate conditions occurred: (1) deep conviction, (2) public commitment to a belief system, (3) a relevant prediction that is unequivocal, (4) unambiguous disconfirmation of the prediction, and (5) social support of other "believers" subsequent to the disconfirmation (Festinger, Riecken, and Schachter, 1956).[c]	Following a mass media article on the prediction of a disastrous natural event on specific data (based on messages received from outer space by the group leader) several contacts were made by the senior investigators with the group leader. Subsequently five research assistants (graduate students) joined the small group of "believers" (less than a dozen) over a period of several months. The focus of observation was the belief system of the adherents and their reactions, both in terms of cognitive structures and behavior, before, during, and after disconfirmation of prediction(s).	incongruent with the investigators' initial hypotheses. After disconfirmation of a major prediction, "believers" in a group of supporters engaged in considerable efforts at proselytizing, which decreased only after repeated disconfirmations of further predictions and official pressure to reduce activities (as a public nuisance). "Believers" who confronted the disconfirmation in isolation showed no attempts at proselytizing and easily abandoned the belief system.
Gain insight into the motivation of personnel (in training), as reflected in both their military and social behavior, to reduce disciplinary problems (particularly AWOL), failures in the course of training, poor performance thereafter, and nonreenlistment. Specific concern with	A twenty-six-year-old first lieutenant was disguised (by changes in personal appearance, minor surgery, and a thirty-five pound weight loss) as a nineteen-year-old juvenile delinquent; this involved nine months of training, coaching by a "young airman," and meetings with a skilled field	Questionnaire measures of attitudes reflected an initially high orientation, which was low during basic training, increased immediately thereafter, and experienced a decline during technical training. Observers's reports helped to confirm the interpretation of this pattern (that is, in-

problems confronted by enlistees during basic and technical training (Sullivan, Queen, and Patrick, 1958).[d]

observer. During the four weeks of basic training and three months at a technical training center, the "enlistee" was in periodic contact with the research team and made numerous field notes. At four times during the field study, all enlisted men in the participant-observer's organization completed questionnaires designed to measure their attitudes toward their training and the service.

crease after basic training attributed to relief that the "worst was over") and the extent to which patterned evasion of organizational requirements was a key to successful adaption to military roles (by shifting emphasis to those activities subject to periodic surveillance and ignoring others).

---

[a] Criticism of this study can be found in von Hoffman (1970) and Warwick (1973); a defense is provided by Humphreys (1970b, pp. 167–173) and Horowitz and Rainwater (1970)

[b] Comments on this study can be found in Davis (1961), Lofland (1961), and Roth (1962).

[c] A review of the ethical issues associated with this study can be found in Smith (1957).

[d] A discussion of the ethical issues associated with this study can be found in the exchange among Coser (1959), Roth (1959), Sullivan (1959), and Queen (1959).

Research Program Effects. In the study of male homosexual behavior, the major objective was to increase knowledge of the range of sexually deviant activities engaged in by mature males and the extent to which these individuals were different from the population in general. Regardless of the societal objectives—to repress "amoral" behavior, help the "sick" recuperate, or understand the variety of sexual acts of typical individuals—an increase in the understanding of the procedures and characteristics of the participants could be of substantial help.

Research Project Effects. The major advantage of covert participant observation in the study of male homosexual behavior in public places is furthering the study of phenomena that otherwise might not be observable; an important aspect of such activity is the care with which the members prevent observation by outsiders—that is, by males not accepted as part of the group. Given the social embarrassment and police harassment (at its height in the late 1960s, when the study was conducted) associated with male homosexual activity, it is understandable why observation would be a problem. Because full confidence of the participants was possible only if the observer adopted the role of a lookout (a "watch queen", warning participants of approaching police, teenagers, or "straight" males), the observer was in essence engaged in an illegal act—abetting a crime. The possibility of criminal prosecution was then a major negative effect for both the observer and project itself. Effects associated with the second half of the project, the survey of the participants in their homes, were similar to those in other surveys, except for certain potential negative effects for the participants (discussed below). While covert participant observation is used to gain access to phenomena that may not otherwise be available for research, it is also used to minimize the disruptive effects of the observation itself, an important advantage in other types of covert research procedures as well. Such an effect may be present (or suspected) even when the participants would have no objection to the research activity.

Participant Effects. A unique direct positive effect for the participants in the study of male homosexual activity was the undisturbed completion of satisfying sexual acts because of the observer's willingness to act as a lookout. However, since it seems

likely that such satisfaction would have been obtained for many of
the participants, in the absence of the research project, the observer's assistance may be seen as facilitating rather than assuring
sexual satisfaction. As with all participant-observation studies,
the positive effects normally associated with contributions to
research—novel experience, altruistic satisfaction, and the like—
were not present. Such effects may have been present during the
interviews completed with a subgroup of fifty, but interviews come
under survey research, not participant observation.

     Major potential negative effects were the risk that partici-
pants would be caught committing deviant acts; this could lead to
arrest, public embarrassment, and substantial disruption to their
personal lives (fifty percent were married and had "good" jobs).
The negative effects associated with the survey interviews were the
time taken to complete the survey and possible embarrassment,
although the latter appears unlikely because of the innocuous nature of the survey instrument (no questions about sexual behavior
were included) and the care taken to prevent this from occurring.
A potential negative effect in all participant observation is the embarrassment and chagrin that may occur if the deception is un-
covered; however, this appears to occur infrequently in participant
observation, or at least it is reported infrequently.

     A major form of indirect effects would be the policy or ad-
ministrative decisions that would result from the research, although it is not always possible to stipulate, in advance, the nature
of such effects. The results of research on male homosexual behavior may create a more understanding and sympathetic social
climate, or they may be used to increase repression and reduce
opportunities for "impersonal sex," perhaps by closing public restrooms or increasing surveillance. In most participant observation,
the indirect effects and the extent to which the participants would
be affected by them are difficult to determine.

     Distribution of Effects. A major contribution of participant
observation may be to increase knowledge that benefits the general
population. In those cases where the participants appear to be reasonably representative of the general population, as with male
homosexuals, there does not seem to be an inequitable relation
between costs and benefits. It is conceivable that participant ob-

servation might be conducted with a disadvantaged group to provide benefits for the majority of advantaged categories, but this
does not appear to be a major issue with respect to such research.

    Consideration of Participants' Rights and Welfare. Since covert
participant observation may infringe on the right of participants
to have a full understanding of the role or objectives of those they
accept as associates, it is important to consider the extent to which
the investigator has taken action to minimize infringements on
other rights of the participants. One major issue to consider is the
possible invasion of privacy. The study of male homosexual behavior took place in a public restroom, hardly an obvious candidate
for consideration as a private domain. It is true that sexual activities
were not initiated until the participants were assured that the setting was temporarily "private"—only by adopting the role of a sexual deviant was the investigator able to observe the "private acts."
At the same time, any individual—journalist, police investigator,
and the like—could have gained access to their behavior in this
fashion. Other settings for participant observation—Alcoholics
Anonymous meetings, groups with radical beliefs, or even barracks
discussions in the military—have this character; the credentials for
admission are ambiguous and easily "forged." It is difficult to argue that such settings are private in the same sense as a residential
bedroom or a physician's office.

    Even if an observer has gained access to "confidential" set-
tings, he probably would not be inclined to disclose the identity of
the participants. In fact, in some settings this would be quite difficult (the therapy group is called Alcoholics *Anonymous*). In the
study of male homosexual behavior, it would have been extremely
difficult to determine identities, due to the constantly shifting
group of participants and the minimum of any verbal communication (fifteen utterances in fifty sexual encounters)—names certainly were not used. For this study, confidence that the observer
was concerned with maintaining confidentiality was increased by
his success at obscuring his purpose from the police, even though
he was apprehended outside a restroom and taken into custody for
several hours (Humphreys, 1970b, pp. 93–96).

    Protecting the anonymity of the participants in the second
stage of this study was more complex, for it involved the specific
identification of the participants based upon the license numbers

of their cars. This information and the subsequent interviews provided a risk either that the homosexual activities of the participants would become known (with potential negative effects for the participants) or that the participants would recognize the investigator during an interview and experience stress and embarrassment when they realized that their clandestine sexual activity had been discovered, even if no public disclosure were made. Several actions taken by the investigator provide confidence that the welfare of the participants was a major concern. The rationale provided to the police for obtaining registration information related to the license numbers was inaccurate; the study was described as related to market research (Humphreys, 1970b, p. 38). The interviews were conducted by either the original observer in a new "presentation" (new hair style, clothes, and automobile) or by an associate a year after the observations in the restrooms. The home interview used was developed for another project designed to assess the current health of men in the area; data from this study was used to compare homosexual males with "typical", presumably heterosexual, males. All identifying names were kept under lock and key and destroyed after the completion of the interviews; the master list was maintained in a safety deposit box.

Covert participant observation can provide extremely useful information for a variety of important research objectives. The major disadvantage for participants is the potential invasion of privacy and possible embarrassment if confidential actions or attitudes are made public. At the same time there is substantial evidence to suggest that most investigators are aware of such problems and take substantial steps to minimize any possible negative effects. In many cases the deviant group may actually gain a spokesperson for its interests, for frequently the investigators become sympathetic and concerned for the participants as a unique social or cultural group (Wax, 1971). While there is substantial potential for abuse in the use of covert participant observation, there is little or no evidence to suggest that this has occurred.

Unobtrusive, Nonreactive Measures

Unobtrusive measures involve physical evidence that reflects human or social variables (Webb and others, 1966; Brandt, 1972;

Bouchard, 1976). In most cases, the participants—the source of the data—are unaware of the nature of the measure or that they are contributing to research. The major advantage of such procedures is high confidence that the measure reflects the effect of natural processes, that is, has not been affected by the research activity or a measurement procedure. The major disadvantage is that it is not always clear which natural process is reflected by the measure (it may not be the phenomena of interest). Such measures are distinct from covert participant observation in that the data are not "passed through" an investigator, and no specific response, purposeful or unknowing, is made to the measurement procedure by the participants.

Unobtrusive measures can be classified as related to physical traces (indirect measures of psychological and social processes), simple observation (careful recording of natural activity), and the use of electromechanical devices (to facilitate accurate recording). Examples of these three types of measures (taken from Bouchard, 1976) are presented in Table 10.

The positive and negative effects associated with projects that utilize such measures are similar to those associated with the use of covert participation observation. They may allow a more efficient collection of data (less equipment and resources may be required), and there will be high confidence that the measurement procedure will not affect the phenomenon itself. The major negative effect will be the low confidence that the measure is a reliable indicator of the variable. For this reason, unobtrusive measures are often used in combination with other, more direct measures, frequently such standard measures of an individual's attitude or behavior as questionnaires or interviews. Unobtrusive measures then become one measure of behavior that can be recorded in other ways; confidence in the use of an unobtrusve measure is based, in part, on its known relationship to other measurement procedures.

Participant Effects. A major positive effect for participants is that their normal activities are not disrupted, an advantage shared with other forms of nonreactive research. Major negative effects would be related to possible invasions of privacy, but unless the measures are taken in private settings such as bedrooms this is unlikely to be a major factor. As with other covert measures, the par-

Table 10. Examples of Unobtrusive, Nonreactive Measures

Physical Traces		Simple Observation		Use of Hardware	
Measure	Variable Indicated	Measure	Variable Indicated	Measure	Variable Indicated
Dust on library books, bent corners, dirt on sections	Use, interest patterns in libraries, sections of encyclopedias	Conformity of behavior to official rules	Trust in authority, respect for authority	Photoelectric cells	Movement of people
Trash analysis	Consumption patterns, use of alcohol	Interpersonal contacts in work, social settings	Informal social networks	Transmitters in books	Physical location
Broken glue spots between pages of magazine	Pages read	Distance of speakers from each other	Degree of psychological closeness (affiliation)	Sitting-sensed chairs	Measure duration and frequency of sitting and leaving seat
Locked vs. unlocked cars, homes	Concern with theft	Seating arrangements of different ethnic categories	Index of attitude, measure of integration	Ultrasonic sound speakers	Body movement
Nose prints on glass in front of exhibit	Visitor rate, age (height) of visitors	Time spent in various spaces, territories, or activities	Relative interest in activities or locations	Hodometer	Electronic recording device placed on the floor to measure use of given areas and pathways
Broken windows, state of repair, and so on.	Pride in public buildings, personal property	Eye-blink rate	Emotionality		
Wear of floor material	Pedestrian traffic, interest in area	Pupil size	Level of interest		
		Body posture	Attitude or interest		
		Voice frequency	Level of emotion		

Source: Taken from Bouchard (1976); source provides reference to the original uses of each measure.

Ethical Dilemmas and Social Science Research

ticipants may not gain the advantage of taking part in a novel experience or receiving altruistic satisfaction. Indirect negative effects may occur if the information is sensitive and can be identified as the product of the participant. However, this is unlikely to occur with measures where there is little or no possibility for identifying specific participants. This would be impossible, for example, if one were studying patterns of floor tile wear in a public place.

Consideration of Participants' Rights and Welfare. No single feature of the measures can be used to determine the extent to which the rights and welfare of the participants are being protected. The major right that may be abridged is the right to privacy or anonymity, and its maintenance depends upon the circumstances in which the measures are applied and the acts taken to ensure the anonymity of the participants. In brief, confidence that the rights and welfare of the participants are being considered is—as usual—related to the implementation of these procedures rather than to the techniques themselves. The issues associated with an unobtrusive, nonreactive measurement procedure—hidden microphones—in a well-known research project will be reviewed as an illustration of the small part the research technique plays in the analysis. In this study the individuals providing the data were completely unaware of the research until public controversy arose many months later. This project is not only one of the best known examples of controversial research, but was the basis for legislation prohibiting the use of unobtrusive, nonreactive measures in a particular social setting, regardless of the positive effects associated with the research program or its intellectual objectives.

Study of Jury Deliberations

Decisions in the legal system tend to be delegated to either a judge or a jury. Concern over the appropriateness of the use of juries to resolve legal disputes led to the development of procedures for the study of the mechanism(s) by which juries—composed of lay individuals—reached decisions related to legal issues, as well as of ways for evaluating the product of their deliberations (Amrine and Sanford, 1956; Vaughan, 1967; Katz, 1972). The major source of information on the nature of the decision-making processes utilized by juries was expected to be data on the discussions of a substantial number (several hundred) of mock juries, groups of individuals similar to those who might serve on juries reaching a decision after hearing a tape recording of a standardized civil trial. The use of standardized trials was important in that it allowed careful observation of how deliberations were affected by such factors as the age, sex, and occupation of the mock jurors.

Concerned that the major source of data about such deliberations was based on mock decisions that had no real consequence, the investigators sought evidence that might increase their confidence that the deliberations of the mock juries were similar to those of real juries. Hence, they felt it was important to collect data on a small sample of real juries making decisions about similar cases. To this end, arrangements were completed to make audio tape recordings of the deliberations of five juries, with the knowledge and approval of the attorneys representing both parties to the civil dispute, as well as of the judges supervising the cases, but without the knowledge of the jurors or the plaintiffs and defendants. It was agreed that the tape recordings would not be listened to by anyone until all appeals were exhausted within the legal system and the cases were closed. Further, the transcripts of the deliberations were to be edited to ensure that the anonymity of the participants (parties to the legal dispute, jury members, and judge) was maintained. These restrictions were agreed to, and eventually tape recordings of jury deliberations for five civil trials were obtained.

Research Program Effects. The research program was designed to determine if the current utilization of the jury to resolve legal disputes was producing optimal results. The major effects of a successful completion of the research program would either be confidence that the current use of juries was the best way to arrive at decisions in the legal system or recommendations for changes in the decision-making mechanism to better achieve a major goal of that system—justice. The negative effects would primarily be the cost and professional time required to complete the research. Considering the historical basis for jury decisions and the existing knowledge of influence processes in small interpersonal groups— those with higher status in the external social system tend to have considerable influence upon group decisions—it was not unreasonable to reconsider the use of the jury for complex decisions.

Research Project Effects. The major advantage of this research project was that, in making it possible to compare the deliberations of five actual juries with the discussions of mock juries, it allowed some inferences about the extent to which the mock jury discussions simulated the "real thing." But because of the way in which the juries were selected (all from one judicial district) and the nature of the cases (all civil), it would be difficult to have strong confidence that these patterns extended to juries deliberating criminal cases or to juries in other parts of the country.

An indirect negative effect of the project, which eventually became a crucial issue after the data were collected, was concern that general knowledge that the project existed—that deliberations of selected live juries had been recorded—might reduce the candor and openness of discussions in other juries. While such knowledge could influence the decisions of other juries, the nature of the effect upon their resulting decisions would be hard to predict— it could actually result in a shift in emphasis toward a discussion of the merits of the case presented by each side to the dispute and away from attention to rumor, gossip, stereotypes, and interpersonal conflict among the jurors. The concern over this indirect effect that developed among legislators and members of the legal system became apparent only after the research was completed.

Participant Effects. In this study, there were several types of direct participants. The procedures adopted appear to have minimized any effects for them. The jury members were not aware of the covert recordings until long after they had rendered their decisions; the project staff made every attempt to maintain their anonymity. Since the recordings were not even played until all appeals had been completed, it seems unlikely that there was any effect for the parties to the civil cases being considered. There was a slight inconvenience for the presiding judges, for the tape recorders were placed in their cloak closets—a research assistant unlocked the closets, turned on the machines, and locked the closets for the duration of the jury deliberations. In sum, there seem to have been almost no direct or indirect effects for the participants, either positive or negative. Such minimal effects were due to the care and attention of the research staff rather than to the inherent nature of the technique—abuses are clearly possible.

Distribution of Effects. The major sources of data were the members of the juries; presumably they were selected to be representative of society-at-large. Since the major benefactor of the research would be society-at-large—inasmuch as the result would be an increased confidence in the decisions made within the legal system—the social category from which participants were selected appears to be identical to that which might benefit from the research. Hence, there seems to be little evidence that an inequitable distribution of effects among different social categories occurred, although some geographic maldistribution might have existed (participants from one region provided data that might benefit all regions of the country).

Consideration of Participants' Rights and Welfare. The major indication that the rights of parties involved were given consideration was the care taken to obtain the consent of the presiding judge and attorneys to both sides of the dispute. In fact, the investigators may have felt they had obtained the consent of the legal system, since numerous legal scholars considered the project of major importance; subsequent events would indicate that the investigators had not obtained such consent. The elaborate precautions taken to ensure that the anonymity of the jurors, attorneys, parties to the dispute, and trial judges would be maintained and that the research project would not affect the normal functioning of the legal system suggest considerable concern for the rights and welfare of all participants, however broadly defined.

Controversy over this research, which was made public when one of the cooperating trial judges played a tape at a judicial conference, was considerable. A two-day hearing held by the Internal Security Subcommittee of the U.S. Senate Judiciary Committee and subsequent legislation that defined "jury eavesdropping" of federal juries as a felony offense (similar laws were passed by numerous states) suggest that the consent of society to study jury deliberations, for whatever purpose, was not obtained. This strong reaction appeared to have several bases; for some who objected to such studies the existing jury system seemed to be closely identified with the "American way of life." The following questions, put to Harry Kalvan, Jr., professor of law and an investigator on the project, are instructive in this regard: "Mr. Kalvan, do you believe in the American jury system?" (Katz, 1972, p. 85). "Do you believe that the American jury system is superior to the Soviet court system?" (p. 90). A second basis for the strong reaction was often related to the right to privacy, even though juries—as decision-making mechanisms—have no rights of any kind as a group; the conditions of deliberation are expected to provide a "fair and just" result. In sum, ambiguity over the need to "improve" the jury system and concern that the conduct of such research may affect the deliberations of all juries led to the creation of laws that prevent covert recording of jury deliberations in the United States. Thus, if the conditions that surround jury deliberations are modified, it will probably not be based on empirical evidence related to their decision-making processes.

In sum, the very nature of unobtrusive, nonreactive measures precludes the possibility of any significant direct effect for the participants, positive or negative. The major source of effects would be indirect, related to the use of information obtained in this way or related to the infringement of rights of individuals (such as privacy). The actions taken by investigators to ensure that unobtrusive measures are used only in such a way that the rights and welfare of the participants are protected have thus far prevented any major scandal involving negative effects for participants who have been observed with unobtrusive, nonreactive measures.

Archival Research: Use of Existing
Administrative and Research Records

A final form of covert research in which the individuals who provide the information are unaware of the research activity or analysis—involves the use of information that has already been assembled; that is, the use of existing research data for new analysis (facilitated by the existence of research archives), the use of administrative data for research purposes, or combining new data with either of the sources of information mentioned above. In many cases the existing data are in a form that precludes identification of individual participants (the U.S. Census data are released in this manner), but in others it may be possible to identify individuals quite precisely (as in administrative records of schools, agencies, businesses, and so forth). While it is not possible to comment on the effects related to various research programs or the distribution of effects among different social categories without reference to specific projects, some general statements about the remaining issues are feasible.

Research Project Effects. One major advantage in using existing records for research projects is that the cost of data collection may be lowered. In many cases, moreover, the only data available are archival in nature (such as historical documents or archeological remains). The cost-advantage is not, however, always as great as might be imagined. For example, it may be expensive to separate the desired information from the available records in terms of programming and computer processing costs when data are stored in magnetic tapes or in terms of the human effort required to search and select items from data in written form (biographies, eyewitness accounts, diaries, legal cases, and so forth). Further, the available information, in either form, may not be the "best evidence"—that is, the most satisfactory indicator of the variables of interest. In short, while there are possibilities for substantial economies, these cannot always be realized.

Several additional advantages are associated with certain types of archival data. If the records are of an official nature (birth certificates, articles of incorporation, official tax returns, and the like) there is no question that they represent significant real-life events. Second, if the data are routinely collected in the course of normal activities, there will be confidence that the phenomena were not disturbed in assembling the data (such as marriage license applications). These advantages may be offset by the complications involved in gaining access to the data, which may require confrontation with complicated administrative routines. (The availability of some government records has been facilitated by the 1966 Freedom of Information Act, but access to data on individuals has been complicated by the Privacy Act of 1974; utilization of data within the jurisdiction of both acts may be quite complicated.)

Participant Effects. As with other covert data collection techniques, a major effect for the participants is the minimum of disruption to their lives. They are not required to spend additional time, energy, or attention to provide data; if sensitive or disturbing information is involved, the stress of reviewing such events is avoided. But the direct positive effects of an interesting experience, altruistic satisfaction of making a contribution to science, attention from research personnel, and the like also will not occur.

Several types of indirect effects are of importance. If the information is not kept confidential, there could be public embarrassment or negative social effects for the participants—a major possibility when several sources of data are combined for new analysis. If the research involves social categories, new information about these categories may embarrass individuals who belong to them. A subtle indirect effect may be related to the impact of the research findings on social or organizational policies in that such policies may be changed without the knowledge or consent of the individuals affected. This may be seen as an infringement upon the right of self-determination, although the extent of the infringement would depend upon the opportunity for open, public debate before the new policies were adopted, not on the existence of a research project.

Consideration of Participants' Rights and Welfare. In many cases, it is either impossible or impracticable to obtain the informed consent of participants who provide information for archival records. The identification of the participants may have been destroyed, they may be dead, they may have moved to an unknown location, or the number of participants may be so great as to preclude contact with all of them. There are some cases where the consent of the participants is not relevant because the data may be considered public—as with trial records, birth certificates, and the like. There are some special situations where some form of informed consent may be present, as when administrative or research data are collected with the understanding that they may be used for unspecified analyses in the future. A committee representative of the participants may provide surrogate informed consent for the actual participants (as in approval by elected or administrative public officials). However, in the large number of cases, the obtaining of informed consent cannot be used as the major indication that the rights and welfare of the participant have been given due consideration.

An important exception occurs with respect to the data collected by public schools, colleges, and universities for use by administrators in evaluating, advising, and educating students and making decisions with respect to the organization. A recent federal law has made the consent of the students or their parents to release the data for nonacademic purposes (such as any form of scientific research) mandatory (Title 20 USC 1232g; Russell Sage Foundation, 1970).

The most tangible evidence of consideration of the rights and welfare of the participants can be found in the precautions taken to protect their anonymity, if living, or in the respect shown for those who are identified by name (as with historical research on prominent persons). If the identity of the participants is not available, their anonymity is easy to preserve, but critical issues can arise when several different administrative records are assembled. It may be important, for example, to ensure that different government agencies are not provided access to the individual data assembled by other agencies. The procedures for maintaining anonymity of respondents or confidentiality of information in administrative files reviewed previously are related to this issue.

If the research involves the analysis of characteristics of social categories of individuals (such as minorities, senior citizens, or working women), respect for their rights and welfare may require that possible misinterpretations of the data be minimized as much as possible. If such analysis is politically sensitive, minimization of misinterpretations may be facilitated by having representatives of different political groups review and discuss the research findings in draft form. This could highlight the major interpretations and implications developed by lay individuals and would provide an opportunity for correcting research analyses if errors of interpretation are in fact present.

In summary, the major positive effects for conducting research with existing data are the potential efficiencies, the unique analyses possible when these are the only available sources of data, and the lack of disturbance to the participants. The major negative effects are the costs associated with such research and the possibility that the privacy of the participants may be infringed. The participants may be indirectly affected if the research results are the basis for new attitudes toward social categories of individuals, attitudes that may affect administrative or policy decisions. Evidence that the rights and welfare of the participants were given due consideration would take the form of precautions to protect the anonymity of the participants, discussions of individual (identified or not) participants that reflect respect and compassion, and some reasonable attempt to minimize inappropriate interpretations of research results related to specific social categories of individuals.

Cross-Cultural Research

The previous discussions emphasized research activities where both investigators and participants share the same culture. The five research dilemma issues were developed to provide guidance in the analysis of research activity conducted in the investigator's moral community, assumed to be an economically advanced representative democracy. There is no assurance, however, that these issues will provide an adequate guide for the evaluation of research conducted outside the investigator's society (Beals, 1967, 1969; Tapp and others, 1974).

Several types of cross-cultural research situations can be identified. The first (commensurate societies) would occur when an investigator from one economically advanced representative democracy conducts research in a second economically advanced representative democracy, perhaps in collaboration with investigators from the host society. A second situation (developing societies) would be one in which an investigator from an economically advanced representative democracy conducts research in an economically developing, politically volatile society, one that may or may not have an indigenous cadre of social science investigators. A third situation (the primitive culture) would be represented by research conducted within a self-contained cultural unit in a primitive stage, one that is economically unsophisticated and may not have a political ideology that includes the concept of individual rights. This last case may be complicated by the existence of a "supervisory society," a political unit that has accepted responsibility for the primitive culture.

This discussion will not emphasize different types of research activity. It is assumed that all types of research are commonly found in advanced commensurate societies—experimental, descriptive, and covert. Research in developing societies and primitive cultures is usually descriptive in nature; there are, however, a few examples of experimental research projects conducted in developing and primitive societies.

Research Program Effects. Analysis of the effects or importance attached to a research program may be quite similar among developed societies with commensurate levels of economic and political activity. The host society may have a commitment to the advancement of scientific knowledge (for its own sake) or may be concerned with the development of knowledge for practical applications. This commitment may be reflected in the contributions provided by investigators from the host society and in the financial resources it makes available for the research. Developing societies may have less concern for the advancement of science and the resolution of intellectual issues. However, there may be a recognition of the potential value of the research, and some effort may be expended to facilitate the research activity. Although financial support may not be provided, even when indigenous investigators participate in the project, there may be support from government officials and agencies. In the extreme case of a very primitive society with an oral culture, members may have little understanding of the idea of science or of advancing a scientific body of knowledge—the activity is not relevant to their lives. At the same time, however, a supervisory society responsible for the primitive culture may consider a detailed description of some aspects of the activities and social structure of the primitive cultures of potential value and may encourage and facilitate the research activity.

Research Project Effects. The effects of a specific research project may be analyzed in quite similar ways in commensurate societies: the project may be seen as useful because of its relationship to general research programs (valued as a scientific goal) or as useful in its own right. In developing societies, the major evaluation may be related to the benefits of a research project rather than its relationship to a more general research program; projects that appear to provide specific benefits may be seen as an immediate asset to the administration of the society. Further, any project that facilitates the development of an indigenous cadre of investigators may be supported for its value as a training mechanism, regardless of its research objective. In primitive societies the project objectives may be partially understood (as a study of their customs) but it seems unlikely that these societies would be able to derive any substantial benefits from the results. Governments responsible for primitive societies, however, may see substantial benefits in increasing knowledge of the cultural system, although they may not have a strong commitment to the general development of scientific knowledge.

Participant Effects. Analysis of the effects for participants in all economically advanced representative democracies may be quite similar. The positive effects of altruistic contributions to science and an interesting experience may be of considerable importance to the participants, while the lost time required for a contribution to the project may be of minor consequence. In developing societies, the participants may have less concern for making a contribution to science and more concern for the direct effects—lost time, payments, and the like—that accompany participation. Members of primitive societies may have no concept of science and find only the direct effects of involvements with investigators of consequence. The satisfaction of treating a "stranger-guest" politely or the food and medical care provided by the investigator may be a source of direct benefits; the negative effects for the participants in terms of time taken from their regular activities or the food and housing provided for a "guest" may be a significant burden. Indirect effects for such participants may be substantial if the description of the society is used to modify the policies of administrators responsible for the primitive society; such effects may be either positive or negative, depending upon the situation. Since the participants in such primitive cultures may have little influence on administrative policies or the interpretations of the scientific descriptions, field research may thus contribute to a reduction in their potential for self-determination.

Distribution of Effects. The analysis of the distribution of effects among members of advanced representative democracies may be quite similar in that the expansion of knowledge or solution of practical problems may provide benefits for all citizens and the participants may represent all social categories in the society. One advantage of cross-cultural research among commensurate societies is that the contributions of participants from one society can provide benefits to a much larger number of individuals—citizens of all similar societies. In developing societies, the general expansion of knowledge may benefit the members of the investigator's home society and may also provide some benefits to the host society, particularly if the research program is related to a specific problem or concern in the host society, the results of the research are available to the host society, and there is an indigenous cadre of social scientists to facilitate application of the results. There appears to be little chance that research results will provide benefits to the members of a primitive culture, since scientific knowledge is not relevant to their daily lives and they may have few mechanisms for utilizing the research results for their own problems. However, paternalistic administrations responsible for the primitive society may be influenced by the research.

In short, members of the investigator's society may benefit from any research (through a general expansion of knowledge, valued for itself), but benefits to the members of the host society will depend upon the sophistication of their own knowledge structure and the existence of individuals who can interpret and apply the knowledge. Because of the potential imbalance of effects, numerous mechanisms have been suggested to help reduce the inequitable nature of the distribution of benefits (translation and publication of research in the language of the host society, shared analysis and publication with investigators from the host society, and so forth). However, for the participants themselves, it would appear that the more primitive their society, the more emphasis is to be placed upon the direct exchange at the time of data collection—the major benefits they receive may be those provided by the investigator(s) at the time the research takes place (food, work, clothing, medicine, and the like).

Consideration of Participants' Rights and Welfare. The major source of evidence that concern exists for the rights and welfare of research participants is the extent to which the participants did not suffer negative effects by virtue of their research experience and/or were knowledgeable volunteers. Confidence that informed consent has been obtained is generally based on the extent to which four conditions are met—voluntary decision, competence of individual to make a decision, complete disclosure of all the relevant effects associated with participation, and an understanding of the meaning of these effects (see Chapter Four).

When cross-cultural research involves educated and literate participants from an economically advanced participatory democracy, it is possible to assume that they (1) understand what science and research involve and (2) are accustomed to a respect for self-determination. It hardly seems likely that the participants from a primitive society would have the same type of understanding or response to a request to participate in research. Individuals from developing societies may be seen as having an intermediate status; for the following discussion only the case of a primitive society will be considered as an illustration of the issues.

It may be difficult to have confidence that the conditions associated with informed consent procedures are present when individuals from primitive societies are involved in research. Any request of a person from an advanced society, particularly when it is approved by administrative authorities, may be seen as a "nonnegotiable demand"; it is unlikely that members of the primitive society will have an accurate conception of the idea of research and its possible effects, much less comprehend the significance of either. Perhaps the only condition that may be present is the intellectual and emotional competence to make a decision, but this would be substantially undermined by the lack of knowledge about science and research and the possible lack of familiarity with the idea of a right to self-determination. The situation is somewhat complicated by the fact that while a refusal to become involved can be taken at face value, it is difficult to have confidence that an agreement to participate by a nonliterate person has the same meaning as informed consent of members of advanced societies.

There are two indicators of whether the rights and welfare of the participants have been respected in the absence of informed consent. The first is the nature of the surrogate consent that is involved, initially through the decisions of the investigator as to what research is to be conducted and later through the approval of various committees in the investigator's home country and of government officials responsible for the primitive cultures. At best, however, these are imperfect mechanisms since they may not accurately reflect the perspectives of the members of the primitive society. Further, the responsible government officials may have a vested interest in having an informal "informer" in the primitive culture.

Perhaps the more important evidence that the rights and welfare of the participants have been respected will be the actual treatment accorded them during the research, the nature of the descriptions of the participants, and the extent to which steps are taken to minimize possible negative effects of the research reports. If the participants are not subjected to more than observations by and discussions with the field observers and the observer's presence does not detract from their effectiveness in everyday life, then it is possible to have confidence that they were not misused. This confidence would be heightened if they received tangible direct benefits (pay, food, or medical care) by virtue of participation. If the descriptions of the participants reflect a respect for their values and orientations and are neither patronizing nor denigrating, these would also provide confidence that the investigator respected the participants and their situation. Finally, concern for participants' welfare may also be reflected in attempts to ensure that the descriptions of the research are presented in such a way that any possible policies adopted by administrators responsible for the primitive societies will be in the best interests of the primitive participants, as interpreted by the investigator. While this is a difficult problem for investigators, any effort may be better than none.

Research that involves participants from societies that lie between the extremes—neither a developed modern state nor a primitive society—may reflect consideration of the rights and welfare of the participants in a combination of activities, including attempts to employ informed consent procedures, descriptions that reflect respect for the participants, and concern that the utilization of the research results will not affect the participants in negative ways. The number of possible alternatives is too great for a systematic review here.

This discussion leads to two conclusions. First, the five research dilemma issues provide a useful framework for organizing the relevant considerations. Second, the analysis is substantially

more complicated when two or more moral communities are involved, each with a different level of educational sophistication and
with political ideologies that may be radically different. It is not
clear that members of very primitive societies will receive any benefits from the research other than direct rewards from the investigators or be able to provide their informed consent as envisioned
by the ideal model developed in economically advanced representative democracies. Perhaps the major basis for confidence that
nonliterate individuals will not have their rights abused when confronted directly with research is their ability to avoid involvement,
which may take the form of clever excuses, total disappearance, or
disruptive or inaccurate responses to the research.

Summary

Four types of covert research conducted without the knowledge of the participants and with few direct effects for them have
been reviewed in this chapter. As research techniques, their major
advantage is the minimum of disruption to the phenomena under
investigation, along with a minimum of inconvenience for the participants, particularly in the case of archival research and unobtrusive measures. Surreptitious field experiments and participant observers elicit reactions from the participants, but to events and
activities expected in the normal course of their daily lives; their
responses are assumed to be similar to those expected in everyday
life. In brief, there is little or no chance that the use of covert research methods will provide significant direct effects—positive or
negative—for research participants.

In the absence of major direct effects, the chief problem
with covert research techniques is their potential for infringing
upon the rights of the participants—particularly the rights to privacy and to self-determination. A potential for abuse of these
rights is present, especially with the use of unobtrusive, nonreactive
measures or analysis of certain types of archival records. The issue
is less clear cut with regard to the use of participant observers, for
if the research participants choose to engage in activity in the presence of another (with undisclosed objectives), they are in a sense
providing their consent to the observation of these activities. This

is even truer when the settings for the "confidential events" are such public locations as streets, parks, or civic facilities. Surreptitious field experiments provide little opportunity to record private behavior, since they often are conducted in public or utilize brief exchanges between participants and "strangers."

The emphasis on the individual right of self-determination and the principle of informed consent developed with respect to experimental medical research, usually in a therapeutic setting, reflect an attempt to minimize infringement upon an individual's control of her own welfare—physical, psychological, or social. The major issue would seem to be the extent to which the research provides a risk to an individual's welfare rather than her awareness of the research and consent to contributing to it.

While covert research techniques may be used to gain access to information without the consent of the participants—information that could be embarrassing or lead to substantial social damages—there is little evidence that such negative effects have occurred as a result of social science research. (It is important to note that anybody can use these procedures, social scientist or not). In most cases considerable care has been taken to protect the identities of the participants and to describe their actions and attitudes with respect and consideration. While the inability to utilize informed consent procedures to provide confidence that the participants' rights and welfare have been given appropriate consideration creates problems, the integrity of investigators may be considered as a suitable guarantee that the participants have not been, and will not be, injured.

Part Two

━━◆━━◆━━◆━━◆━━◆━━◆━━◆━━◆━━◆━━◆━━

The ideal model of scientific activity has tended to include substantial autonomy for investigators in the conduct of research. Increasing public support of the scientific enterprise and the expanding scope of research with human participants have been accompanied by more involvement of the public and uncertainty among investigators regarding the resolution of the research dilemma. This leads to the following question: What societal mechanisms or collective guidelines provide assurance to the general public and scientific investigators that the resolution of the research dilemma will be morally acceptable? A review of the advantages of scientific autonomy, as well as the nature of various informal restrictions that bear upon investigators, will help to place the solution in perspective.

Resolving the Research Dilemma: Restrictions on Investigators' Autonomy

━━━━━━━━━━━━━━━━━━━━━━━━━━━━━━━

Why Autonomy?

One of the major norms among the scientific community is that of scientific freedom, sometimes referred to in more general terms as academic freedom. Respect for the intellectual autonomy of the investigator in choice of problems and procedures for resolution appears to have developed and persisted for several reasons.

First, as an intellectual exercise divorced from the mundane, practical concerns of technology, engineering, or medicine, science was for many centuries considered an innocuous, though challenging, hobby of aristocrats and was accorded the same status as painting, music, hunting, travel, wenching, and the like. Because science was an avocation of the wealthy, all resources devoted to the activity—chiefly the time of the aristocrat-scientist—were from

227

private, not public, sources (Bernal, 1965). Moreover, the activity was pursued to satisfy esoteric, private interests with minimal applied value, and there was little systematic research with human or social phenomena—the major focus was on physical phenomena. In those few instances where "research" was conducted with individuals (chiefly related to medical problems), the participants were usually persons considered less worthy than other members of society and not accorded the full range of human rights. Under such conditions, there is ample justification to conduct science as a private affair, with maximum autonomy for the investigator.

A second factor complements this tradition of investigator autonomy (or scientific freedom), namely, recent views on the nature of the process of creating science and the conditions that foster major advances. Current conceptions of the advance or cumulation of scientific knowledge emphasize conceptions shared by members of the scientific community rather than knowledge as Truth, reflecting the "laws of nature." Associated with this perspective is the emphasis upon the development of new orientations, theories, or paradigms—intellectual structures that guide the collection and analysis of data and provide the basis for major new advances (Kuhn, 1962; Lakatos and Musgrave, 1970).

The creation of new conceptualizations or paradigms is a poorly understood but very subtle phenomenon. At an elementary level, the invention of new paradigms may be described as the creation of new concepts and/or new relationships between concepts. In developing new concepts—the most difficult feature of new conceptualizations—a scientist must take existing sensory input (sight, sounds, smells, or tactile sensations) related to a phenomenon, resist the tendency to define these sensory inputs in established ways that may have been acquired during cultural or professional socialization, grope for new ways of organizing these sensory inputs, and produce ways of describing them to other scientists. This last step, description, is made more difficult by the lack of suitable terminology for describing radically new concepts. Once the new concepts are developed, they are organized into statements describing interrelationships, statements that will eventually be compared with empirical descriptions of a particular phenomenon. It is misleading to think of this as a sequence of well-defined steps, for in most cases the creative scientist will be simultaneously engaged in three crucial endeavors: (1) inventing concepts, (2) developing statements, and (3) comparing the statements with empirical data, sometimes obtained from ongoing research projects. Occasionally, the results of these activities lead to the development of new conceptualizations that provide major alternatives to established theories or paradigms.

This perspective allows speculation on the conditions that will facilitate the development of new conceptualizations. Several of the more obvious conditions are enough time to work on the problem, enough resources to engage in research and data analysis, and the training and skills to engage in fruitful scientific activity. Several additional factors are more subtle, such as (1) an atmosphere of playful trial and error, (2) the freedom to pursue hunches, insights, and undefined or poorly explicated lines of inquiry without formalizing the hypotheses guiding the research, and (3) encouragement to consider alternatives to established ideas or patterns of behavior. One common thread in autobiographical accounts of creative individuals (Einstein, Poincaré, Dryden, Mozart, A. E. Housman, Thomas Wolfe, and Gertrude Stein) is that ideas "flow," "bubble up," emerge from "combinatory play," or are "a confus'd Mass of Thoughts, tumbling over one another in the Dark" (Wallach and Kogan, 1965, pp. 13–15). While most of these accounts are from individuals who create in areas where it is easy to try a new idea (literature, music, or mathematics), the freedom to experiment with new ideas, without fear of reprisal, is critical for all areas.

Encouragement to reexamine established ideas and theories, however, is perhaps even more important. Most people are familiar with the objections to radically new theories, such as the one that placed the sun, not the earth, at the center of the solar system, or Darwin's view that natural selection, not divine guidance, had created present-day forms of life. Perhaps less well known is the absence of any research on the human anatomy for over seventeen hundred years, despite a considerable amount of sophisticated work prior to 200 A.D., due to prohibition of dissection of human corpses (Lassek, 1958).

While it is widely assumed that new ideas and theories often meet considerable resistance before gaining acceptance, it is not often realized that the most vociferous opponents are not the lay public, who seldom understand the issues involved, but other scientists, who may find their life's work jeopardized by the new theories (Barber, 1961). Prominent scientists have placed numerous obstacles in the way of new theories, either because the theories challenged their own work and their stature in the scientific community or were inconsistent with existing religious, philosophical, or political dogma. Consequently, many new theories have taken several scientific generations to gain acceptance. Concern with the opportunity to produce new scientific ideas and fear that scientific innovation may be stifled are major reasons that many scientists are so concerned with the protection of scientific freedom—the freedom to pursue and develop any issue that seems of intellectual significance, relying solely on the evaluations of other scientists to determine which new ideas will be accepted as useful *after* they have been fully developed and compared with data from research.

A third factor consistent with the others, the historical tradition of scientific freedom and the concern for furthering science, involves the personal characteristics of scientists. Major motivations for those who choose a scientific career are the satisfaction of curiosity about the world in general and the reward of solving challenging intellectual puzzles. Both goals are likely to be realized more fully if the individual has the autonomy to select the phenomena for study and exploration or the intellectual puzzles to be solved (or attempted). In some cases these choices may be considered idiosyncratic or irrelevant, but it is clear this forms a major motivation for many investigators.

Restrictions on Autonomy: Resources and Objectives

Restrictions on the absolute autonomy of investigators have always been present. They are most obvious with respect to the first two research dilemma issues: the development of research programs or intellectual issues and the development of research projects designed to contribute to the resolution of intellectual issues. There have always been limits on the funds and facilities available for the conduct of research, but the restrictions become more apparent when the investigator must place substantial reliance upon public support or public facilities.

In addition to restrictions on resources, restrictions on the cognitive flexibility and scope of issues to be examined also develop among investigators; a reduction of intellectual range is a major feature of the socialization processes involved in scientific training. While the overt, formal attempts to limit the scope of research are generally resisted or even condemned, the implicit restrictions may be just as influential. Such restrictions may take the form of subjective judgments among scientists about what are important issues or appropriate approaches, judgments reflected in decisions about publication, the focus of conferences, hiring and promotions, or support for research.

While it is obvious that some phenomena must be studied in settings that minimize damage to ordinary citizens—deserts, for example, must be used for the study of atomic or nuclear fusion—there have been recent attempts to restrict the scope of fundamental genetic research out of concern for the effects if an uncontrollable form of life were developed. This situation is unusual in that it is the first modern example of restrictions upon scientific research that were initially proposed and supported by scientific investigators. However, some of the same individuals who proposed the original restrictions are now concerned that they may have been "too conservative," and that the small potential risks may not justify the effects of the restriction upon research activity (Berg and others, 1974; Budrys, 1977; Watson, 1977).

In general, there have always been restrictions upon investigator autonomy resulting from the resources available for research, the scientific socialization of investigators, and the adoption of certain perspectives on phenomena and theorizing. There have also been instances of restriction based on concern for uncontrollable negative effects of research. However, there is little question that the community of scientists exerts a minimum of direct influence over the activities of individual investigators. Most influence is in the form of rewards for those contributions considered to be significant, and these rewards are based upon evaluations after the research has been completed.

Restrictions on Autonomy:
Informal Factors

In an ideal sense, investigators should have complete freedom to pursue any research procedure or technique that will help
resolve important intellectual questions and thus will contribute to
a research program. Even assuming that sufficient financial resources are available, however, there are clear limits on what would
be considered acceptable when the research involves human participants, particularly if they derive no direct, personal benefits
from the experience. A number of informal factors affect the judgments of investigators regarding these limits, most of which result
from their participation in society as ordinary citizens.

The most obvious of these limits are those imposed by the
ordinary course of social conditioning and professional socialization of investigators. This conscience-creating process can exert a
considerable influence since most scientists have received rather
extensive formal education and are usually individuals with considerable insight into the effects of their actions and research procedures. As such, it can be expected that they will have a greater
awareness of the important moral and ethical issues associated with
research activities than will the ordinary citizen. These will be reinforced by collegial evaluations of the effects and implications of
research. Indeed, many of the most influential observations on the
moral propriety of research activities are provided by colleagues.
These two factors, one informal and unconscious, the other explicit
and overt, can have a substantial effect upon the research techniques implemented by investigators.

Equally important, there are some activities that participants
themselves may resist, particularly if they are conducted in such
a way that those taking part feel abused, degraded, or bored (the
last may be the most significant). While there seem to be few limits
on the amount of effort that will be expended by some willing volunteers, more extreme activities may be accepted only if accompanied by a full explanation, a respect for the participants' dignity,
and a demonstration of concern for their rights and welfare. This
form of resistance, from the phenomenon itself, may in particular

serve to restrict the autonomy of investigators who attempt to explore sensitive issues

In general, then, a major problem associated with allowing investigators substantial autonomy is low public confidence that they will resolve the research dilemma issues in ways consistent with existing societal norms. There is nevertheless general respect for the expertise of scientific investigators and belief in the importance of their judgment in determining crucial scientific issues and appropriate methods of study. The remaining chapters in Part Two review three procedures that have been developed to provide confidence that investigators will not abuse human participants involved in research and to maximize investigator autonomy: standards of professional associations (Chapter Eight), administrative mechanisms (Chapter Nine), and the legal system (Chapter Ten).

8

Professional Associations and Standards for Research

Since social science associations often act as intermediaries between their members and society, this chapter will focus on the procedures adopted to provide confidence that members will conduct research in ways consistent with the norms and values of society. The first section considers the general strategy that has been adopted by professional associations and the reasons for its distinctive feature, peer review. The second section will consider the nature of the codes of ethics that have been adopted by associations representing social scientists. Consideration of the extent to which the applied professional model is appropriate for the situations confronted by investigators and of the extent to which it provides the desired results is the focus of the third section.

Professional Associations as Intermediaries

In functioning as intermediaries between their constituencies and society, professional associations attempt to demonstrate convincingly that their members can provide valued services for the general public (such as medical care, legal advice, or the development of new knowledge) and to give assurance that all members in good standing will be able to provide such services. Procedures to standardize the quality of such services must achieve two disparate objectives: they must be considered fair and equitable by the members, so that they will support and cooperate with the procedures of the association, and they must provide members of society with confidence that the inept, irresponsible, or unethical are not engaged in professional practice. A number of actions may be taken to provide such quality control, including evaluation and accreditation of educational programs, licensing procedures, the development of principles (codes of ethics) to serve as standards for the practice of the profession, procedures for investigating possible instances of substandard or inappropriate professional work, and penalties that can be implemented to encourage compliance with standards. Confidence that the interests of society have been given appropriate consideration should be increased when the review committees or supervisory boards of professional organizations include "typical" citizens as well as practitioners.

While professionals generally feel more comfortable when their activities are evaluated by colleagues, this is frequently interpreted as protection of their own interests; the substantive basis for such a preference is often not discussed. But the preference may actually be based on the need for the applied professionals to make decisions in situations where there is considerable ambiguity about the consequences of their actions. Such decisions may involve matters of judgment, perhaps even a best guess about which factors are important, rather than the unambiguous application of explicit rules or procedures; indeed, the latter are frequently delegated to paraprofessionals or technicians (Scott, 1966).

In these complex, ambiguous situations the applied professionals may feel, perhaps correctly, that they can only make what seems to be the best possible decision and then take action on the client's behalf. If the client's problem is solved, or at least not aggravated, then there is no basis for complaint. However, if the client's problem is not solved or becomes more serious, it is often impossible to determine whether the applied professional was (1) "unprofessional" by virtue of incompetent, careless, or unethical behavior; or (2) a diligent, conscientious individual unable to control the outcome. In both cases the client has suffered, but it is difficult to determine the degree to which the applied professional was responsible for the outcome.

Professionals prefer that evaluations be based on the circumstances of the situation and the actions taken on behalf of the client—which they are able to control—rather than the outcome, which they may not be able to influence. If evaluations are to be made on the basis of the situation and the decision, the only individuals competent to evaluate the decision maker's judgment are other professionals, since only they will understand the problems and issues in making complex decisions under conditions of uncertainty. This results in procedures, emphasized by the associations representing applied professionals, that involve the evaluation of professionals by one another.

A number of features of such regulatory mechanisms reflect this emphasis upon professional evaluation and at the same time encourage members to support the procedure:

• Standards are developed and administered by professionals in a manner that is, in large part, applicable to the day-to-day conduct of professional affairs.
• Professional training includes exposure to the standards of practice, both in formal exposure to the content of an explicit code and informally in the context of specific cases.
• There are review committees, composed of other professionals, charged with the responsibility of receiving and evaluating complaints and determining if some member of the profession has acted incompetently, carelessly, or to achieve personal gain at the expense of the client's welfare.
• The privilege of practicing the profession may be withdrawn

from those who are not willing or able to meet the minimum standards. (In some cases this has the sanction of the legal system.)

While there is some question about the success of such a procedure for providing confidence to members of society that acceptable standards of quality control are maintained, there is no question that it is the mechanism preferred by applied professionals, for it has been universally adopted. There is also little question that it has been the model adopted by associations representing social scientists in their role as investigators.

Control of Investigators

A major response—the only explicit reaction of social science associations—to the research dilemma has been the adoption of one aspect of the applied professional model, namely, development of sets of standards. Such imitation has several causes. First, formalizing standards is the only operating model in existence and seems suitable for imitation, since both applied professionals and investigators deal with specialized knowledge not well understood outside their collegial group. Many ambiguous and uncontrollable factors are involved in the conduct of both activities, factors that are not easily comprehended by nonprofessionals.

Second, many scientific investigators are also applied professionals, as in the case of physicians or clinical psychologists, and tend to use the same professional associations to promote these two different activities. In the social sciences, the only discipline with a substantial number of national codes of ethics is psychology, and the major emphasis in these is on the conduct of practitioners as they apply their knowledge to practical problems. Third, many of the issues related to the research dilemma have been confronted by medical scientists and partially resolved through the development of codes of ethics that are assumed to guide all research with human participants; the Nuremberg Code (Appendix 2) and the Declaration of Helsinki (Appendix 3) are the best-known examples.

As part of their responsibility as applied professionals specializing in healing, physicians have adopted the view that they should also promote medical knowledge and adhere to ethical principles in performance of their dual role.

A review of the nature of the existing procedures was the focus of a UNESCO-sponsored, worldwide survey of all national associations representing social scientists (Reynolds, 1975a, 1975b). Lists of national associations representing anthropologists, econonmists, political scientists, psychiatrists, psychologists, and sociologists were used to dispatch slightly over three hundred letters of solicitation in late 1973 and early 1974. Replies were received from ninety national associations and codes of ethics from twenty-four. Virtually all had adopted the format of developing a set of standards for the conduct of research, some accompanied by procedures for evaluation of complaints and sanctions for noncompliance. Because all associations had adopted a similar orientation and dealing with all twenty-four codes was awkward, they were combined into a single composite code, which required translation of fourteen codes into English and standardization of terminology. Each unique statement from each code was identified and organized into a format that provided a cogent overview. The composite code of seventy-eight statements is provided in Appendix 4.

It should be noted that the degree of congruence among these statements was real—no two statements were obviously inconsistent. However, emphasis clearly varied among codes. For example, a code would have a statement such as "deception is allowed in research" in the middle of a discussion that clearly reflected a concern for the welfare and rights of human participants. In contrast, another code would suggest that deception is allowable only under certain conditions, such as the absence of an alternative procedure suitable for resolving the intellectual issue and the use of additional precautions to protect the rights of the participants. Since no unambiguous, general criteria for combining principles with different emphases could be developed, all discretely different principles were included. Inconsistencies of omission were of course present. No one principle or statement was found in every code of ethics. Some omissions may have reflected variation in the types of problems or issues that preceded the development of the codes and thus have been unintentional. Other omissions may have been intentional, serving to minimize conflict over the desirability of such principles. The omission of any principle related to informed consent in the code of the American Sociological Association—which represents a substantial number of researchers engaged in unobtrusive, participant, or field observation—may reflect such a problem.

More elaborate analysis of the conditions (type of professional association, country of origin, and so forth) related to different types of principles is precluded by several factors. First, the preponderance of codes adopted by psychologists and representing clinical psychology (sixteen of twenty-four unique codes) minimizes the variation in the content and emphasis of the codes, making any analysis of variation difficult. Second, in codes that emphasize clinical psychology, it is difficult to determine with precision the extent to which principles are considered applicable to research with human participants rather than to assistance to clients. It is not unusual for the introduction of this kind of code to state that the principles apply to both clients and research participants, but the actual organization of the code and expression of principles leave some doubt as to the degree to which those producing the code were actually considering research situations when they created the principles. Finally, as can be seen from the number of times that each principle was present in a code, there are very few cases where any statement is found with considerable frequency (66 percent of the statements are located in one or two codes; 16 percent in three, four, or five codes; 16 percent in from six to ten codes; and 2 percent in fourteen or fifteen codes).

Despite the presumed importance of the issues, very few codes incorporate much in the way of penalties for noncompliance. Only 50 percent (excluding those related to psychiatry) provide for any penalty (expulsion from the association); 28 percent are explicitly presented as advisory; and none specifies any benefits to the investigator for compliance (other than continuation of membership in the association). Some codes make reference to legal sanctions for failure to maintain confidentiality, but only in relation to activities pursued as applied professionals (clinical psychologists), not as scientific investigators.

Clearly, the most significant empirical data were the low percentage (approximately 7 percent) of over three hundred national associations responding with any type of explicit code. (Frankel, 1976, reports the same pattern from a survey of political science associations.) Assuming that all those with any type of code were willing to contribute a copy of the code for analysis, this low percentage of replies must reflect an absence of codes of ethics related to the use of human subjects in research or any other aspect of professional activity. When the quality of the professional talent and the effort required to produce a code of ethics acceptable to a diverse membership are considered, it is understandable why so few codes of ethics were available. Further, the advantages to applied professionals of having an explicit code of ethics, which can form a base for developing professional autonomy within the society, explain why the majority of the codes are associated with the applied work of psychologists.

Adequacy of Procedures

Concern with the adequacy of the procedures adopted by the social science associations leads to three types of analysis: examination of the extent to which the applied professional model is appropriate for scientific investigators, the extent to which it assists investigators in resolving dilemmas, and the extent to which it would provide ordinary citizens with confidence that it was an effective mechanism for assuring minimum or even uniform standards of performance.

The success of the applied professionals' model of quality control seems to be based on the nature of their occupational life—applying a well-accepted body of knowledge to the problems of clients—that is notable for the following features:

• Financial support is usually provided by a clientele, or an organization representing a clientele, and the loss or gain of one client is not a significant financial issue.

- The problems of the client are approached with a well-developed body of knowledge that can, in many cases, be routinely applied to a well-defined set of problems.
- Societal legitimation may have developed to the point where an exclusive right to utilize a body of knowledge in solving certain types of problems is provided to the profession; nonprofessionals may be legally restrained from offering to solve such problems.
- The client's interests are assumed to take priority at all times, and the major issues are related to alternatives for promoting the client's interests.
- Responsibility for decisions is clear; they are made by the professional and applied with the consent of the client.
- The applied professional may deal with a number of clients every day, and the autonomy to make immediate and timely decisions reduces the administrative costs of providing assistance.

These important features suggest that the development of a set of principles regarding ethical conduct of applied professionals would be a relatively straightforward task, since there is little ambiguity over the role that the professional must play. The only major problem is that the body of knowledge available to the professional is a changing one, but this is usually resolved by assuming that the professional will use currently accepted standards.

The occupational life of the scientific investigator, who is concerned with the development of empirically based knowledge, has a somewhat different set of characteristics.

- Financial support is usually provided by an organization in which scientific activity may or may not be the major focus. Maintenance of the organizational position becomes a major issue.
- No clients, as such, exist; an analogous role is occupied by the organization or society.
- Individuals, as participants in research, may be research material rather than clients who are expected to benefit in some direct fashion (there are, of course, exceptions in applied research).
- The basic focus of research activity is on exploration of the un-

known; potential risk to participants in research can only be estimated and never eliminated.
- Responsibility for decisions is not always clear, since financial
  support and encouragement from others may accompany an investigator's decision to conduct a research project.
- The problem of attempting to balance the rights and welfare of
  human subjects with the potential benefits from conducting the
  research is a recurrent and difficult issue.

Several major differences would suggest that it may be inappropriate to use the applied professional procedure as a model
for the control procedure for scientific investigators. First, there
is the difference between the position of the client, for whom the
applied professional is assumed to be working, and the research
participant, who may be participating in a study without receiving
direct, personal benefits. Second, the major benefactor of the applied professional's work is considered to be the client, who pays
the applied professional for his or her services. In contrast, the
major benefactor from the investigator-participant relationship is
likely to be society (which benefits from the increase in knowledge)
or the investigator (whose career may be advanced). Third, the
status of the scientific/technical knowledge utilized in each situation
varies considerably; it is well defined and widely shared in the case
of the applied professional, poorly defined and ambiguous in the
case of scientific research. Finally, attribution of responsibility is
unambiguous in the case of applied professionals. Their responsibility for their analysis and activity is limited only by their ability
to control phenomena. In the case of the scientific investigator,
responsibility may be shared by the investigator, the sponsoring
agency, the host institution, and the participants (if they provide
their informed consent to become involved in the research). .

Hence, there are substantial reasons to be skeptical that a
procedure for providing standardized or minimally adequate performance among applied professionals is applicable to scientific
investigators. The nature of the knowledge, types of problems,
sources of financial support, and basis for evaluation may be quite
different in the two types of activities. All they seem to share is a
highly technical knowledge.

Perhaps more serious than a lack of congruence between the roles of applied professionals and scientific investigators is the limited extent to which a "code-review of infractions" procedure provides assistance to investigators. It is difficult to see how the current mechanisms can assist investigators with a complex, sensitive research dilemma where there is a clear contrast between desirable intellectual objectives and potential negative effects for participants. The list of principles gives some help to those conducting routine or nonthreatening research, but no guidance on how to resolve difficult predicaments.

Even more problematic is the status of an investigator who follows the principles, completes research, and then finds that a dissatisfied participant has brought legal action against him. While it is possible that the investigator's defense may be strengthened if his procedure was consistent with a code of ethics, there is no formal commitment by the associations to assist the investigator in his defense with either legal counsel or an offer to cover legal expenses, although this has been done voluntarily (Carroll, 1973). Investigators may be better served by a mechanism that allows them to seek competent advice when faced with complex and ambiguous research dilemma issues, that is, a mechanism that allows them to share the responsibility for the decision and possibly even the burden of costs for legal fees or damages to participants. While such a procedure may not be used often, its existence would provide recognition of the complexities and ambiguities associated with research and the contribution that major advances make to the profession and its public image, as well as indicate respect for research on significant, sensitive problems. It is unlikely that the cost of such a guarantee would be very high; as the review in Chapter Three suggests, the rate of actual damage to participants is very low. However, a demonstration of support for investigators and tangible evidence of concern for participants could encourage investigators to work on important, sensitive problems rather than avoid them out of concern for unanticipated legal actions.

As a demonstration of concern for participants and to provide assistance to investigators conducting research that is either routine or does not pose major threats, professional associations could sponsor the cataloguing and evaluation of the common research procedures utilized by their members, identifying the conditions under which each procedure poses little or no threat to the rights and welfare of participants. Investigators could then select and implement appropriate procedures with confidence that the participants would not experience negative effects. Such an approach would be more useful for investigators concerned with routine research than would ethical guidelines that might be ambiguous in application and inconsistent with specific scientific objectives. Further, such an approach would demonstrate an interest in the actual effects for participants rather than in the creation of a pious ritual to improve a public image.

Even if the current procedure of code and evaluation of infractions is adopted in good faith, it does not seem to provide an investigator with much assistance in resolving the research dilemma. Moreover, it may be used simply as a basis for criticism of adventurous investigators who fail to adhere to "sacred principles," formalized without consideration of the context in which the controversial research was conducted. A critic may then invoke the authority of the code, making it extremely difficult for the investigator to demonstrate that his efforts were directed toward providing substantial benefits or reflected an honest attempt at resolving the research dilemma. Suspicions about career aspirations or personal interest always cloud interpretations of an investigator's motives. It would not be a surprise to discover that such codes of ethics received their strongest support from those not involved in innovative, potentially dangerous research activity.

The code of ethics/sanction violators procedure seems to have even less promise for providing confidence to the ordinary citizen that the rights and welfare of participants will be given serious consideration. High confidence would probably require a procedure that included systematic monitoring of research activity to discover problems, advantages to the participants for utilizing the complaint procedure, meaningful penalties for investigators who violate the principles or ignore review procedures, and substantial advantages for investigators who comply with the system. At present, none of these features appears to be present. There is no systematic monitoring of social science research activity by any association; there is no advantage for any individual (participant or not) to bring possible infractions before an association (most cases are initiated by other members, usually after the research has been completed); finally, there are no meaningful punishments for noncompliance and no substantial advantages for the members who do comply with the procedures.

The lack of sanctions and rewards is perhaps the most important, for it indicates that the procedure is not taken seriously. The major problem that confronts professional associations, particularly in the United States, is that it is quite possible for a social scientist to have a productive, respectable career without participation in any professional association. As a result, the threat of expulsion has little or no real meaning for investigators, although it may provide some degree of embarrassment. Further, the lack of apparent advantages for complying with either the statements of principles or the review procedures—all associations emphasize the full responsibility attributed to the investigator—suggests that these are meaningless gestures for an individual coping with a "dangerous" research problem. If associations were to provide some form of insurance for those who complied with their procedures or accept an obligation to assist investigators conducting approved projects, it would demonstrate support for investigator-members who choose to deal with sensitive and crucial issues and would provide an advantage for those complying with the standards or review procedures. As it is, there is no reason for an outside observer to think that the members have received any encouragement to comply with the standards.

In short, the procedures of developing standards of conduct and review of infractions adopted by social scientists' associations appear to provide few advantages for scientific investigators, regardless of their acceptance and viability for applied professionals. They do not provide guidance for the resolution of difficult research dilemma issues, nor do they have those features that would lead the public to have confidence that the rights and welfare of participants are being protected. Perhaps the most positive aspect is that the procedures set up an explicit standard for "ordinary" research, even if only by implication. This may help define those situations that require additional precautions.

If the procedures developed by the professional associations were seen as useful mechanisms for resolving research dilemma issues, there would be substantial evidence that they are being used for that purpose. At present, there is not much evidence of that kind. If the general public had little confidence that these mechanisms provided adequate protection for participants, the development of other procedures to provide such confidence could be expected, and this has in fact happened. Those developed and implemented by federal agencies that support or supervise research will be reviewed in the following chapter. At the same time, however, associations representing social science investigators need not consider this evidence of their own inadequacies, for the same federal mechanisms also apply to biomedical investigators, indicating a lack of confidence in the control mechanisms developed and implemented by such wealthy and influential professional associations as the American Medical Association.

9

Federal Guidelines for Research with Individual Participants

Mechanisms for reviewing research that involves human participants are relatively new phenomena, first appearing in 1966 (Frankel, 1975); procedures for resolving problems of the level and nature of financial support and standards for the use of animals in research were well established long before this date (Department of Health, Education, and Welfare, 1968). Concern over the treatment of participants by biomedical and social science investigators appears to be the basis for legislation creating standards for research with human beings, national commissions to consider the issues, and administrative actions taken at the initiative of government officials.

There are three major aspects to the development of organizational guidelines, almost exclusively related to standards and procedures of federal government agencies—the Department of

Health, Education, and Welfare (DHEW) and the Food and Drug
Administration (FDA) have taken the lead in this regard. The first
is the scope of application of these guidelines; that is, the research,
investigators, and participants covered by the principles. Second
are the standards developed for the application of informed consent. The third involves the establishment of committees to review
and evaluate research proposals; committee procedures are complicated by an emphasis on incommensurate objectives.

   While this chapter is organized around these three organizational issues, the latter two provide clear examples of the major
philosophical solutions to important societal issues. The emphasis
upon informed consent reflects concern for the rights of the individual, particularly the right of self-determination. A major focus of committee review of research activity is the application of
a risk- or cost-benefit analysis to proposed research activities; they
represent society in applying a utilitarian analysis as a strategy for
solving the second major societal dilemma—criteria for evaluation
of programs that affect society as a whole. However, this emphasis
in the committees is frequently confounded by two other objectives: to incorporate a variety of technical expertise and thus provide protection for the participants and to act as a source of surrogate informed consent, making decisions on behalf of participants
who are unable to comprehend the research activity or who cannot
be fully informed for technical (scientific) reasons.

Scope of Administrative Guidelines

   Organizational resolution of the research dilemma takes the
form of administrative guidelines and procedures. But unlike legal
standards, which often have universal application, such guidelines
usually cover a limited scope of activity. It is possible to consider
the range of application of federal guidelines in three categories
(Curran, 1969; Frankel, 1975; Quimby, McKenzie, and Chapman,
1975): (1) research conducted outside federal agencies but supported by federal funds, (2) research conducted outside federal
agencies and supported by nonfederal sources, and (3) research
conducted within federal agencies. Mechanisms used to exercise
control under the second category are very imprecise, allowing

much research to be conducted without application of any federal guidelines.

Standards for External Research Supported by Federal Funds

For most social scientists, particularly those outside the government, the most important source of influence over research involving human participants has been the procedures adopted by the Department of Health, Education, and Welfare (DHEW) for all biomedical or social science research supported, in whole or in part, by the DHEW. While there has been clearance of questionnaires used in research supported by the Office of Education since the mid 1960s (Conrad, 1967), the emphasis in this discussion will be upon the general standards now applied to all research by DHEW. The details associated with these standards have been under continous modification, although the basic structure of the rules has not changed since their introduction in 1966.

Considered to apply to all DHEW "grants and contracts supporting research, development, and related activities in which human subjects are involved," the guidelines have two major features (Title 45 CFR 46.101 [a]). The first is a set of standards or criteria to be used in evaluating all proposed research projects; the second is the requirement that the standards must be applied by the institutions or organizations in which the research is conducted, using procedures specified by DHEW. The latter requirement ensures that (Title 45 CFR 46.102 [e]): "No grant or contract involving human subjects at risk shall be made to an individual unless he is affiliated with or sponsored by an institution which can and does assume responsibility for the subjects." This requirement makes it highly unlikely that an investigator, acting alone, can expect to receive funds for research from DHEW.

If a research project involves a "subject at risk," it is liable to review by a special set of criteria. The key definition is as follows (Title 45 CFR 46.103 [b]): "'Subject at risk' means any individual who may be exposed to the possibility of injury, including physical, psychological, or social injury, as a consequence of participation as a subject in any research, development, or related activity which departs from the application of those established and accepted methods necessary to meet his needs, or which increases the ordinary risks of daily life, including the recognized risks inherent in a chosen occupation or field of service." This statement is carefully phrased to exclude activities that are therapeutic in nature and not "experimental"—established and accepted methods necessary to meet participants' needs—or part of their ordinary activities. A recent interpretation of "subject at risk" by the secretary of DHEW (*Federal Register*, 41 [125] : 26,572) excluded from this category those individuals involved in studies of procedural alternatives to administrative programs, such as certain social experiments. The courts have not always agreed with this distinction (*Crane* v. *Mathews*, 1976).

If a research procedure is considered not to involve "subjects at risk" (that is, no individuals are subjected to risks greater than they would experience in their ordinary life or in established therapeutic procedures) it should not, presumably, be subjected to further review. In practice, not only is *all* research supported by DHEW funds that involves contact with human participants to be reviewed, but all such research conducted at an institution, regardless of sponsorship, has to meet DHEW standards.

"Responsible institutions" are expected to honor several obligations imposed upon them by the DHEW. They are (Title 45 CFR 46.102 [b]):

1. To determine whether or not the potential benefits justify the risks to the subjects;
2. To review the means taken to protect the rights and welfare of the subjects at risk;
3. To ensure that legally effective informed consent will be obtained from the subjects at risk; and
4. To conduct a timely review (that is, at least annually) of the project to ensure that it is conducted appropriately.

In general, such decisions are made by an institutional review board (IRB) to be established under appropriate guidelines at the "responsible institution." However, several exceptions are worthy of note—specification of informed consent and utilization of special categories of subjects—and these will be reviewed in the following sections.

Research Privately Supported but Regulated by Federal Agencies

There are two major examples of federal agencies regulating research supported from private sources. The first is the expansion of the scope of the DHEW procedure from all projects it funds to all projects conducted at an institution (or entity) that receives any funds from DHEW for projects. The second is the control of drug research with human beings by the Food and Drug Administration (FDA). While other agencies are associated with research conducted outside the federal government, it appears that this involves a limited number of projects and participants (National Commission for the Protection of Human Subjects of Biomedical and Behavioral Research, 1978f).

The extension of DHEW guidelines and procedures to all research involving human participants at an entity engaged in any research with human subjects supported by DHEW funding is based on a new section (474[a]) of the National Research Act (Public Law 93–348) enacted on July 12, 1974 (*Federal Register, 40* [50] : 11,854): "The secretary [of DHEW] shall . . . require . . . each entity which applies for a grant or contract . . . [to] submit . . . assurances . . . that it has established a board to review biomedical and behavioral research involving human subjects conducted at or sponsored by such entity in order to protect the rights of human subjects of such research." Although the applicable regulations (Title 45 CFR 46) do not explicitly state that application shall be made to all projects conducted at an entity where projects are supported by DHEW, the interpretation sent to all entities from the Office for Protection from Research Risks makes this requirement clear (Chalkley, 1975).

In effect, this requires that *all* research conducted at an entity where *any* research with human subjects is supported by DHEW be subjected to the reviews and guidelines required for projects supported by DHEW. While the scope of this application may be restricted by the careful distinction of "classroom, laboratory, or field exercises" and "demonstrations and other service activities" from actual research, it does include a substantial amount of research activities. To the extent that these standards are more strict than the ones that would otherwise be applied to research, investigators not supported by the DHEW could claim that their right to self-determination is infringed by virtue of institutional acceptance of DHEW support for other investigators.

The basic responsibility of the Food and Drug Administration (FDA) since the enactment of the Food, Drug, and Cosmetics Act in 1938 has been to ensure that the public is not offered the opportunity to purchase food, cosmetics, or drugs—complex products frequently having subtle effects—that pose hazards to their health or well-being (Curran, 1969; Schmidt, 1975). The FDA's responsibilities were expanded in 1962 to include an additional responsibility with respect to drugs; the agency must ensure that drugs provide some benefit, as well as be safe. Since empirical evidence for the safety and effectiveness of drugs is provided by commercial drug manufacturers to support a request to offer a drug for sale, the FDA has the responsibility of supervising the conduct of research with human participants for investigational new drugs (INDs) prior to submission of a new drug application (NDA).

For purposes of FDA approval, research related to drugs is divided into four categories; the three that involve human participants are given official designations. They are as follows (Title 21 CFR 312.1 [a] [2] [10]):

- *Initial Phase:* only animal and in vitro (for example, in test tubes) data are available.
- *Phase one* starts when the new drug is first introduced in man . . . with the purpose of determining human toxicity, metabolism, absorption, elimination, and other pharmacological action, preferred route of administration, and safe dosage range.
- *Phase two* covers the initial trials on a limited number of patients for specific disease control or prophylaxis purposes.
- *Phase three* [involves] assessment of the drug's safety and effectiveness and optimum dosage schedule in the diagnosis, treatment, or prophylaxis of groups of subjects involved in a given disease or condition.

Phases one and two are frequenty referred to as the clinical pharmacology phases and phase three as the clinical trial. The total amount of evidence from such research submitted as part of an

NDA may be summarized in from two to fifteen *volumes*, supported by ten to as many as four hundred *volumes* of raw data (Schmidt, 1975).

The regulation of the conduct of research with human subjects has been complicated by the increased tendency to conduct such research in other countries, a shift facilitated by the international character of most major drug companies. The FDA will accept data collected abroad as satisfactory for phases one and two of the research; phase three data from abroad may be used to supplement phase three data collected in the United States. Perhaps in response to suggestions that phase one and two studies were being conducted abroad to avoid FDA regulations regarding the use of human subjects (Ragolia, 1975; *Federal Register, 42* [10] : 3,076), regulations for such research outside the United States were adopted effective May 9, 1975 (Title 21 CFR 312.20). These require investigators to follow the principles of the Declaration of Helsinki (Appendix 3) or the regulations of the host country, whichever provide more protection for the research participant. Some of the requirements related to use of informed consent and review committees are less stringent than might be required in the United States, but the general emphasis is similar (*Federal Register, 40* [69] : 16,053).

Internal Research Supported by Federal Funds

Research with human participants is an important part of the activities conducted by numerous government agencies, both state and federal. At the present, there is considerable regulation of the procedures to be used within such government agencies when human participants are involved in research. These include the regulations of DHEW, the Public Health Service (PHS), the National Aeronautics and Space Administration (NASA), the Veterans Administration (VA), and the Department of Defense (DOD), as well as the air force, army, and navy. While there may be comparable rules associated with research conducted within and financed by various individual states, it is beyond the scope of this work to review them here.

The regulations related to research conducted within DHEW are quite unambiguous (Title 45 CRF 46.301); they require the application of the procedures and guidelines for external research to "all research, development, and related activities conducted by employees of the [department]." The procedures to be followed within the PHS are quite similar, with an emphasis on a prior committee review of all research not intended to provide benefits to the participant (Quimby, McKenzie, and Chapman, 1975). The alternative of "no review" when there is no "subject at risk" does not appear to be available. Procedures for investigators within the VA require that research meet the standards of the VA, DHEW, and, when investigation involves the study of the effects of drugs, the FDA. In general, the procedures are similar to those adopted by DHEW, including the requirement of a prior committee review and compliance with the procedures for obtaining informed consent (Quimby, McKenzie, and Chapman, 1975, pp. 153–155).

Several government agencies are involved in activities that require individuals to subject themselves to considerable risk as part of their normal job activities. One of these, NASA, has a set of carefully specified regulations, similar to those of DHEW, but not to be applied to "a specially trained adult who knowingly follows a specialized calling or occupation generally recognized as hazardous, and for whom the test, experiment, or evaluation procedure forms an integral part of his calling or occupational performance" (Quimby, McKenzie, and Chapman, 1975, p. 146). If the research does not form an "integral part of his calling," the individual is to be treated as a typical research participant. Research proposals are to be reviewed by "authorized NASA officials" who are expected to consider, among other things, "whether the subject or his representative will be compensated, by reason of insurance, workman's compensation, or the like, in the event the subject suffers loss, injury, illness, disease, or death as a result of the human research" (1975, p. 149). This emphasis appears to be unique among procedures related to reviews of projects involving human subjects in research (1975, pp. 144–152).

The regulations provided for in the Department of Defense (DOD), including the air force, army, and navy, are quite similar to those of other agencies. But a distinctive feature of the regulations of the military is that research is treated in different categories. The DOD has issued two directives, one related to clinical investigations and the other to research with drugs. Both the army and the navy have separate sets of regulations concerning these activities; the air force has two sets of regulations affecting medical research in general, including both drug and clinical investigations, and a third for nonmedical investigations. In all three services, it is explicit that any research involving drugs must be within the guidelines set by the FDA. Although the army has a special category of drugs that meet FDA criteria but are not approved for use in the general population, they are considered relevant to the special needs of the army (such as biochemical warfare).

All three services have special regulations pertaining to "all other" research (that is, research not involving drugs or clinical investigations) that may benefit the participant. In general, the regulations specify the conditions under which informed consent is required, how it is to be obtained, and the administrative mechanisms—use of review committees—necessary for approval of research. Both the army and the navy regulations state unequivocally that prisoners of war will not be used under any circumstances. Special precautions are provided for the use of nonmilitary personnel, including an army legal interpretation that volunteers cannot be utilized but that nonmilitary individuals can be paid for participation (the military can even provide funds for the civilians to purchase insurance coverage). As in the NASA standards, regulations related to "other research" are usually carefully worded to exclude those hazardous duties that are part of the normal responsibilities of some military personnel (handling explosives, flight duty, underwater tasks, and so forth)

A review of the federal standards adopted by major agencies that conduct research with human subjects as part of their ordinary work suggests that there is no unrestricted "license to investigate" for scientists employed in federal agencies. If the rules are adhered to, it would appear that the situation is comparable to that in nonfederal organizations when research is sponsored by federal funds. There is a similarity in the procedures and philosophies among the various sets of standards created by the DHEW, and, to some extent, by the FDA, and these were, in turn, heavily influenced by the Nuremberg Code, the first major statement on these issues. (These conclusions are consistent with the recent review of federal agency policies and procedures, prepared by the staff of the Na-

tional Commission for the Protection of Human Subjects of
Biomedical and Behavioral Research, 1978c).

Standards for Informed Consent

Expecting that participants will provide informed consent
is the most widely used procedure for ensuring that individuals
retain control of their own rights and liberties. For social science
investigators, the organizational guidelines for informed consent
that may have the most effect on their research are those of
DHEW, specified as follows (Title 45 CFR 46.103, [c]:

> "Informed consent" means the knowing consent of an in-
> dividual or his legally authorized representative, so situated as to
> be able to exercise free power of choice without undue inducement
> or any element of force, fraud, deceit, duress, or other form of
> constraint or coercion. The basic elements of information neces-
> sary to such consent include:
>   1. A fair explanation of the procedures to be followed, and
> their purposes, including identification of any procedures which
> are experimental;
>   2. A description of any attendant discomforts and risks
> reasonably to be expected;
>   3. A description of any benefits reasonably to be expected;
>   4. A disclosure of any appropriate alternative procedures
> that might be advantageous for the subject;
>   5. An offer to answer any inquiries concerning the pro-
> cedures;
>   6. An instruction that the person is free to withdraw his
> consent and to discontinue participation in the project at any time
> without prejudice to the subject; and
>   7. With respect to biomedical or behavioral research which
> may result in physical injury, an explanation as to whether com-
> pensation and medical treatment is available if physical injury oc-
> curs and, if so, what it consists of or where further information
> may be obtained. This subparagraph will apply to research con-
> ducted abroad in collaboration with foreign governments or inter-
> national organizations absent the explicit nonconcurrence of those
> governments or organizations.

The last clause was added as an interim regulation, late in 1978
(*Federal Register, 43* [214]: 51,559), and involves only physical injury.

A number of other agencies have also developed guidelines for the application of informed consent. A summary of the major features of these guidelines is provided in Table 11, ranked in order of their frequency of occurrence. But this list is misleading in several regards. First, it represents a mixture of standards for different kinds of research, some related to drugs, some related to clinical medical studies, and some related to general (nontherapeutic) research. Second, there is some overlap in jurisdictions. The VA and all three military services, for example, require all drug research to meet the standards of the FDA; hence, their own regulations are based on the assumption that the FDA standards will be adhered to. Nevertheless, the most frequently cited features of the procedure—explanation of discomforts and risks, voluntary decision, legal capacity to consent, description of research objectives and procedures—are those considered important since they were first explicated in the Nuremberg Code (Appendix 2).

A major problem in many types of research develops when the participant's detailed knowledge of the research purpose and design interferes with achieving the scientific objectives of the project. It has been well established that when individuals receive medical treatment, including drugs, that they expect to be effective, they will show both psychological and physical indications of improvement; this is referred to as the "placebo effect" (Barber, 1967; Bok, 1974; Honigfeld, 1964). The typical research solution—when the "real" effectiveness of the drug is under examination—is to provide the test drug (of unknown effectiveness) to individuals with a specific problem while others, with comparable problems, are provided with a harmless substance (a placebo) or a drug with known effectiveness. The effectiveness of the test drug is then estimated by comparing the reactions of those receiving the test drug with the reactions of those who received the placebo or the drug with known effectiveness. However, if *all* participants are provided with complete information regarding the research, including the fact that some received a placebo, the potential for establishing any positive benefit from use of the new drugs, aside from a "perception" of improvement, is lost.

Similar problems develop in some areas of social science research, where knowledge of the process under investigation, such

Table 11. Characteristics Included in Various Administrative Standards for Informed Consent

Characteristic	Total Mentions	DHEW[a]	FDA	PHS	NASA	VA	Army, Clinical	Army, Drugs	Army, General	AF, Medical	AF, General	Navy, Clinical	Navy, Drugs	Navy, General
Explain discomforts and risks, known and unknown	11	X	X	X	X	X	X		X	X	X		X	X
Must be voluntary decision	10	X	X	X	X		X		X	X	X		X	X
Legal capacity to consent, participant or guardian	10	X	X		X	X	X		X	X	X		X	X
Explain purpose and objectives	10	X	X	X	X	?	X		X	X	X		X	X
Explain procedure and techniques	10	X		X	X	X	X		X	X	X		X	X
Make right to withdraw clear, or limitations on right once study initiated	8	X	X	X	X		X		1	X	X			
Possible to withhold information from participant if knowledge would bias study	7	X	X				X	1	1	X	1			X
Offer to answer all questions	6	X					1	1	1	1	1			

Use of language understandable to the participant	5
Describe direct benefits to the participant	4
Describe alternative therapies	4
Information may be withheld to protect the participant/patient	3
Inform participant if he may be used as a control	2
Participant should understand implications of research for self	1
FORM OF CONSENT:	
Implied	1
Orally	3
Orally, with witness	1
Written	6
Written, with witness	4

Note: X indicates *explicit,* I indicates *implied in discussion,* and ? indicates *ambiguous as discussed in rules.*

[a] 45 CFR 46 (1976), especially 46. 103(c) and 46. 110.

Source: Quimby, McKenzie, and Chapman, 1975, for all columns except DHEW.

as response to pressures to conform, perception of others, reaction to different leadership styles, and attitude change, may have a substantial effect on the individual's response and, hence, on the phenomena under investigation. This has led to a change in guidelines regarding fully informed consent, frequently in the form of stating the conditions under which less than fully informed consent is allowed.

The regulations of DHEW specify that the informed consent procedure may be "modified" when three conditions are met (Title 45 CFR 46.110): (1) the risk to the subject is minimal; (2) it would interfere with the objects of the research; and (3) any alternative means for obtaining the research objectives would be "less advantageous to the subjects," that is, provide for greater infringement upon their rights and welfare. The FDA guidelines are less precise, stating that (Title 21 CFR 310.102 [h]): "Consent means that the person involved . . . is provided with a fair explanation of pertinent information concerning the investigational drug, and/or his possible use as a control, as to enable him to make a decision on his willingness to receive said investigational drug." In other words, the information need not be complete but should be detailed enough to allow a decision by the potential participant, who must be informed if he *might* receive the experimental drug or a placebo or even a drug with known, and possibly less potent, effectiveness.

Other organizations have specified as follows the conditions when "full disclosure" is not necessary:

> An explanation so detailed as to bias [the subject's] response or otherwise to invalidate findings is not necessary in those procedures that involve no risk of physical harm to the subject [Quimby, McKenzie, and Chapman, 1975, pp. 94–95].
>
> [The volunteer] must have sufficient understanding . . . so far as such knowledge does not compromise the experiment. He will be told as much . . . as will not invalidate the results [p. 177].
>
> The provisions of this regulation do not apply to the human engineering portions of a research project when they involve only hazards involved in normal training or other normal military duties and when disclosure of the research conditions would defeat the purpose of the investigation [p. 187].
>
> He [the volunteer] will be told [details of the study] . . . in such a way as not to invalidate the results [p. 198].

In short, exceptions to the policy of providing complete information are not uncommon, where the research objectives cannot be achieved otherwise and when the risks to the participants are small.

There is also substantial variation in the actual mechanism to be used for obtaining and documenting informed consent. For example, all three military services require that the consent procedure for general research be completed in the presence of an individual not involved in the research and that a written statement be signed by the volunteer, the witness, and the person obtaining consent. But, at the opposite extreme, the army allows—at the discretion of the investigator—implied consent for phase four drug studies (use of investigational drugs which, although not FDA approved, are essential to the mission of the army and which, after testing, are considered by experts to be safe and effective). This is consistent with the standards of the FDA, which vary with the stage of research (21 CFR 310.102 [h]). Phase one or two research requires the full informed consent of the participants in writing. In phase three studies, which frequently utilize the services of physicians in ordinary practice, "it is the responsibility of the investigators, taking into consideration the physical and mental state of the patient, to decide when it is necessary or preferable to obtain consent in other than written form. When such written consent is not obtained, the investigator must obtain oral consent and record that fact in the medical record of the person receiving the drug" (21 CFR 310.102 [h]).

Except for those studies where the primary procedure for obtaining informed consent "would surely invalidate objects of considerable immediate importance," the DHEW guidelines require either the subject's signature on a detailed written consent form or the subject's signature on a "short form" after receiving an oral presentation of relevant information; if the "short form" is used, a witness must attest that the oral presentation occurred (Title 45 CFR 46.110).

A major recent change in the DHEW regulations has been the addition of elaborate new standards for informed consent for special categories of subjects. The first such standards to be officially adopted were for activities that involve "women who could become pregnant" or "women who are in fact pregnant." These regulations are quite complex (Title 45 CFR 46 [B]) and include reviews not only of research by committees or responsible institutions but also of the DHEW criteria designed to protect the rights of the fetus as well as of the mother. Additional standards for the use of prisoners have been adopted (*Federal Register, 43* [222] : 53, 652), and standards for children and institutionalized mental patients have been proposed (*Federal Register, 43* [141]: 31,786; *43* [223]: 53,950).

A final issue is the extent to which the guidelines suggested for informed consent by various federal agencies are consistent with those that are legally required (see discussion earlier in this chapter). Most of the recommendations will meet the legal requirement for informed consent for therapy that is designed to benefit the patient-participant—legal competence to give consent, freedom from coercion, and full disclosure. However, only the navy's guidelines for general research emphasize the fourth criterion required for nontherapeutic research—comprehension of the possible effects. Most striking is the failure of the DHEW criteria to be consistent with legal standards—"knowing consent" does not place a clear stress on comprehension—and this suggests that the DHEW criteria were developed with clinical research as the model of scientific investigation involving human participants since legal standards for that kind of research do not emphasize comprehension.

Prior Review of Research

Those responsible for research, such as administrators in federal agencies, would like to ensure that all projects will result in major intellectual achievements, bestow substantial benefits on society, and provide only benefits—no risks—for the research participants. Since it is almost impossible to achieve all these results for any project, several subsidiary issues are usually considered for resolution: (1) assurance that the threat to the rights and welfare of the participants is minimized; (2) a judgment that risks to the participants are justified by potential benefits; and (3) confidence that informed consent procedures will be applied in an appropriate fashion, particularly when "full information" cannot be provided without affecting research objectives.

There are two important characteristics of these issues and their relationship to the goal of having confidence, in advance, that a project will be administratively satisfactory. First, there is no obvious "correct" solution; no unambiguous criteria exist for determining beforehand the appropriate decision on a project. This is particularly true of research in new areas, where there is little experience with the phenomena or the research techniques to be employed. As a result, confidence in the decisions regarding a project will depend on the nature of the procedure used to arrive at a judgment rather than the specific resolution. The characteristics of the individuals involved and the procedures they follow will be of primary importance in affecting confidence in the "correctness" of the output. This is quite similar to the decisions produced by the legal process (Levine, 1978a), where justice may be considered the product of a decision mechanism rather than a characteristic of the "answer."

Second, different mechanisms for creating decisions will engender high confidence for different types of issues. Confidence in judgments about procedural safeguards for protecting participants and the nature of risks and scientific benefits may be highest if made by specialists—scientists and applied professionals—who are technical peers of the investigators. In contrast, confidence in judgments about the rights and liberties of the participants and the relative "value" of risks and scientific (or practical) benefits may be highest if made by informed citizens—social peers of the investigator(s) and participant(s). This will be of particular importance when participants cannot be "fully informed" without affecting the scientific objectives of the project and prior review of the project is expected to provide surrogate informed consent. In brief, two types of judgments about the use of human participants provide administrators with confidence that projects should be supported, one related to the technical adequacy of the procedure for protecting the welfare of participants and the significance of the research issue and the other related to the extent to which societal values and individual rights are affected or respected by a specific project.

Organizations that are responsible for decisions about predictable, recurrent issues often establish sets of guidelines or standards to be followed by those making the decisions. One example would be the standards developed for informed consent (reviewed above). But the inability to predict objectives or procedures to be developed by scientists precludes the imposition of specific standards. An alternative is to review the research prior to its initiation and/or provision of financial support (Frankel, 1975).

Two types of prior review procedures have been adopted by federal agencies responsible for research activity. One is to have the research approved by an organizational official, usually after consultation with either a committee responsible for a review of the research or staff experts in the organization (legal, medical, and the like). This procedure, or a variation, is to be followed in evaluation of research conducted within the three military services (air force, army, and navy), the VA, NASA, and the PHA (Quimby, McKenzie, and Chapman, 1975). A variation is provided for nonfederally supported research supervised by the FDA; review committees are required only for projects where the participants are institutionalized and the institution takes responsibility for the participants' welfare (as in the case of prisoners). In such instances a committee is to review all projects, and the administrators may approve, modify, or disapprove only those projects sanctioned by the committee—administrators may not approve projects rejected by the committee (21 CFR 312.1 [2] [10] [c]). The FDA-initiated committees are designed to ensure that the rights and liberties of incarcerated participants are not abused, but the value of conducting the research and the use of nonincarcerated participants are not subject to committee review (aside from the judgment of the FDA on the entire drug research program).

A second, perhaps unique, procedure is utilized by the DHEW. It allows the final decision on ethical criteria to be made within "responsible institutions" for ordinary research, as long as the DHEW guidelines for establishing and conducting a decision mechanism are followed. "Responsible institutions" are expected to provide DHEW with a "general assurance"—a description of the procedures used to implement the review conducted at the institution and applied to all activities that involve human subjects. This general assurance should include: a statement of the institutional principles guiding the evaluation of projects (the statement will not supersede DHEW policy), the size of the institutional review board (at least five members), the heterogeneity of the members' backgrounds (not all from one professional group), the attendance required to conduct business at a meeting (at least a majority), the relationship of board members to projects reviewed (none is allowed), the institutional affiliations of the members (at least one must not be affiliated with the responsible institution), the frequency with which ongoing projects must be reviewed (annually), and the actions to be taken if a problem is found in an ongoing project (Title 45 CFR 46.106). Further, the "responsible institution," after adhering to the guidelines specified by DHEW for reviewing projects supported by federal funds dispersed by the DHEW, must specify its willingness to accept responsibility for performance of the research and "have available the facilities and professional attention required for subjects who may suffer physical, psychological, or other injury as a result of participation in an activity" (Chalkley, 1975, p. 2). It is not clear who is expected to pay the costs for "attention required for subjects."

There is no question that the DHEW regulations have had a major impact upon the review of projects within research-oriented institutions, especially universities and hospitals. Prior to the initiation of the procedure by the PHS in 1966, there was very little evidence of any type of review of projects. For example, a 1961 survey of every university department of medicine (Welt, 1961) regarding the existence of ethical review procedures found that 24 had or favored a review committee (8 had procedural documents). A 1962 survey of 86 departments of medicine produced 52 responses; 9 institutions had procedural documents relating to research (only 2 were applicable to all clinical research), and only 16 had standardized consent forms (Curran, 1969; Frankel, 1975). It seems reasonable to assume that there were no reviews related to social or behavioral science research. Thirteen years later, in 1975, there were at least 113 medical schools with review committees, and at least 424 universities, research institutions and organizations, excluding VA hospitals, with institutional review boards (Institute for Social Research, 1976c, p. 224).

Characteristics of Review Boards

Because of the importance of institutional review boards (IRBs) as organizational mechanisms for resolving major dilemmas associated with research, a description of their major features will be presented. It will be based upon a survey of IRBs completed for the National Commission for the Protection of Human Subjects of Biomedical and Behavioral Research (Institute for Social Research, 1976c; Gray, Cooke, and Tannenbaum, 1978). Descriptions of experiences with specific IRBs are provided by Cowan (1975) and Melmon, Grossman, and Morris (1970).

There are several ways to consider the composition of IRBs. One is to consider the background of the members. A sample of 760 members whose training could be identified (it could not for 77) were distributed as follows (Institute for Social Research, 1976c, p. 64): medical/dental, 39 percent; biological sciences, 13 percent; social science, 17 percent; law, 7 percent; and other, 23 percent. This provides a description of the aggregate of board members included in the sample, not of any particular review board. It is also possible to consider the composition of the IRBs by focusing upon the extent to which individuals with different backgrounds are represented. It would appear that although those who have done biomedical and behavioral research are found on IRBs in all types of institutions (89 percent of all IRBs), IRBs usually have members with legal (69 percent), administrative (88 percent), and "outside-the-institution" affiliations (94 percent).

In terms of the scope of projects to be reviewed, a substantial number of IRBs reported reviewing many types of research in addition to that funded by DHEW (Institute for Social Research, 1976c, p. 78), including research not funded by DHEW (92 percent of all IRBs), unfunded research (87 percent), no-risk research (86 percent), graduate or medical student research (97 percent), undergraduate student research (80 percent), and some previously reviewed research (61 percent). The proportion of IRBs within universities that review these various types of projects is slightly lower, particularly for no-risk research (61 percent) or undergraduate student research (51 percent). To complement this process of inclusion, most IRBs have developed procedures for screening proposals brought to its attention to eliminate those not justifying a careful review (p. 86); 62 percent of all IRBs (34 percent in universities, 86 percent in medical schools) have some type of screening criteria, generally excluding projects not using human subjects (35 percent of all IRBs), projects involving routine clinical procedures (8 percent), or projects outside the jurisdiction of the committee (8 percent). Routine screening to preclude IRB review of low- or no-risk projects occurs in only 4 percent of all IRBs, and all of those are in universities (9 percent) and medical schools (7 percent).

Once a proposal reaches a board, it is assigned to an individual for preliminary review for one half of the boards and to a subcommittee for approximately one fourth; presumably proposals are considered by the entire committee in the remaining one fourth (Institute for Social Research, 1976c, pp. 15–16). In 20 percent of the boards where subcommittees review a proposal, they are expected to make the final decision on the project (these may be the institutions with a large number of proposals to review); in the remainder of the cases the subcommittee reviews the proposal and makes a recommendation to the full board (p. 88). Two thirds of the boards make their decisions by majority vote; unanimity is expected in one fourth, and a consensus is obtained without a vote in 10 percent (pp. 84, 85).

The attitudes toward the proposals by the committee members seem to reflect the multiple purposes of the committee reviews. When asked to choose between two alternatives for describing the committee purposes, the 693 members were almost equally divided between the "protection of human subjects" and "to balance the need for protecting human subjects with the need to develop new knowledge," whether their training was in biomedical science, social science, or "other" (Institute for Social Research, 1976c, p. 74). When asked which type of emphasis was placed upon review of proposals, more than nine out of ten emphasized the two major issues: the balance of risks and benefits and the procedures used to obtain informed consent. The agreement among IRB members with differing backgrounds is very high, suggesting that the heterogeneity of committee members does not provide dramatically different strategies of evaluation, although this similarity of attitudes may be due to the socialization of the individuals while at work on the committee; they may develop group standards that are unique in relation to their loyalties outside the review committee.

While the typical IRB judgment is to approve a project without modification (Institute for Social Research, 1976c, p. 98), this occurred for less than one half of the 781 proposals studied (it varied from 37 to 49 percent, depending on the nature of the institution). Thirty to 45 percent of all projects were modified by the IRB (highest for hospitals, lowest for universities); 4 to 7 percent were informally modified, and for 3 to 16 percent of the projects (highest for universities) additional information was sought (which may result in modification of the project). Once a board has made a decision, it tends to have substantial impact, for decisions are subject to further review for only 25 percent of the IRBs (p. 90), primarily in institutions with hierarchical structures (hospitals and mental institutions, for example) rather than those with a collegial structure (9 percent for universities and 5 percent for medical schools). Proposals rejected by the IRBs are given a further review in 13 percent of all cases (p. 92) and an investigator may appeal a decision of 37 to 62 percent of the boards—58 percent in universities and 38 percent in medical schools (p. 93).

The key individuals who responded with regard to the activities of the boards considered their major problems to be administrative in nature (Institute for Social Research, 1976c, p. 99), rating as "very" or "somewhat" serious the problems of getting members together for a meeting (38 percent of key informants), coping with the high volume of work (25 percent), need for rapid action due to agency deadlines (20 percent), and the lack of precise DHEW guidelines regarding procedures or standards (19 percent). Disagreements between the review committee and investigators over the purpose of the committee were seen as a "minor" or "negligible" problem by 91 percent of the key informants, as was antagonism of the investigators toward the committee (85 percent), disagreements among committee members about their purpose (88 percent), or frequency of changes in DHEW policy (91 percent). By and large the same pattern of evaluation is present when the committee members comment on the problems confronting the IRBs (p. 180). One additional "serious" or "somewhat serious" problem identified by one fourth of the members is the amount of time spent reviewing research proposals with essentially no risk.

The attitudes of the research investigators who had submitted proposals to the review boards and of the review board members themselves toward the review committee and its procedures suggest general agreement that the committee makes a positive contribution—it protects subjects, improves research, and is reasonably efficient—although investigators are more concerned than committee members over unwarranted intrusions into autonomy, the scope of issues that committees consider, qualifications for judgments, and the extent to which the committees may impede research. Social science investigators are the least positive toward the committee, perhaps because they consider their research to have adequate scientific justification and low risk for participants. They may also be concerned that the committee will block any supposedly controversial projects.

One of the unresolved problems associated with the current review committee procedure relates to its dual role of evaluating the technical judgements of the investigators with respect to the conduct of research (including the nature of risks and benefits) and representing society and the participants in determining if the research justifies completion and provides appropriate consideration for the participants' right to self-determination. Evidence of organizational ambivalence on this point is present in several proposed changes in the DHEW regulations for the review procedure. For example, one set of proposed regulations (*Federal Register, 38* [221]: 31,738–31,749) for research involving children required each DHEW agency to establish a review committee; these committees would evaluate projects approved by the "primary review committees"—which would focus on scientific merit and design—in relation to ethical issues and societal acceptability. No more than one third of the members would be actively engaged in research, development, or demonstration activities involving human subjects (*Federal Register, 38* [221]: 31,741). Further, for research with children and prisoners, it was recommended that a separate "protection committee" be established to represent their interests with respect to *each* project (*Federal Register, 38* [221]: 31,741–2, 31,744). Neither procedure was adopted or incorporated into the DHEW regulations.

Despite numerous comments regarding the dual function of the review committees (Levine, 1978a; Reynolds, 1972; Veatch, 1975), the current DHEW solution is to utilize only one committee, but to insist that at least one member be from outside the research institution. As an "improvement" on this solution, Barber and others (1973) have suggested that individuals be trained to become "professional outsiders," although their capacity to represent the "outside" (that is, society) may lessen as they come to adopt the norms and values that emerge within the committee.

Evaluation of Effects of Review Boards

There are two different strategies for evaluating the use of committees to review research prior to its inception. The first strategy is to examine the products of deliberation—the decisions of the IRBs—and their effect upon the scientific enterprise and society. The second is to consider the extent to which the establishment of a review process provides a satisfactory "buffer" between the scientific enterprise and society. This latter approach amounts to determining the extent to which elected representatives of society consider the prior review approach to be a satisfactory device for resolving the major issues that continually recur in scientific research with human participants. The first type of evaluation will be reviewed in this section, the second in the concluding section.

The initiation of a systematic prior review of all research might lead to changes in:

- Physical, psychological, or other effects upon participants;
- Infringement of participants' rights and liberties;
- Cost of conducting scientific research (administrative costs; that is, shifts in proportion of scientific talent devoted to administrative tasks, reduction in research funds available for research projects, and so forth);
- Development of scientific knowledge or occurrence of scientific advances;
- Benefits that may accrue to society; and
- Orientations and attitudes of scientists, participants, lay public, elected officials, and the like toward scientific research.

If a systematic attempt to provide reliable measures of these effects had been made over the past several decades (since the 1950s), the

evaluation of the effects of prior review of research would be simplified. Since no such data appear to be available, other strategies
for evaluation must be considered.

The major tactics for assembling "objective" data on the effects of the prior committee review procedure have been of two
types. The first is to examine the nature of decisions about proposals; this method seems to reflect both the types of standards
utilized by the committees and the nature of the research proposals
that are submitted for review. The second tactic tries to estimate
effects by systematically measuring the judgments of review board
members, investigators, and so forth regarding the effects of the
committee. An example of the first tactic—use of administrative
records (involving data collected from the National Advisory
Councils and Committees of the Public Health Service)—indicates
that the proportion of proposals that raised ethical problems
dropped from 7.4 percent of all proposals in June of 1966 to 3.2
percent in June of 1967 (just after the prior review procedure was
initiated) and to 2.4 percent in June of 1970; the percentage of
"problem" proposals that were disapproved at the national level
was constant at about 53 percent (Nejelski and Lerman, 1971, p.
1100).

Similar statistics were collected in the fall of 1969 from a
national survey of institutions engaged in biomedical research. Key
respondents (that is, committee chairpersons) from 293 institutions
provided information indicating that 32 percent of the committees
had rejected one or more proposals, 3 percent of the committees
had had at least one proposal withdrawn, 31 percent had required
revision, and 34 percent had never rejected or required revision
of a proposal (Barber and others, 1973, p. 159). The national sample of institutional review boards completed in 1976 found more
evidence of "intervention." Analysis of projects revealed that 40
percent were modified either formally or informally, more information was sought for 10 percent of the projects, and 44 percent
were not modified in any way; there was no evidence of outright
rejection (Institute for Social Research, 1976c, p. 98). Evidence
from the last two studies suggests that the outright rejection of a
proposal by an institutional review board is a rare event, perhaps

because the review board members provide suggestions to the investigator on modifications to meet the objections of the committee.

This type of data is often taken to mean that very few proposals with serious ethical problems are presented to the committee, that committees provide a conscientious review, thus preventing proposals with ethical problems from being initiated, and that this represents an improvement over the situation existing prior to the development of committee review. But confidence in such inferences related to all research would be higher if (1) all research were subjected to a prior committee review; (2) committees in different institutions utilized the same, or comparable, standards for evaluation of the proposals; and (3) a substantial amount of "ethically questionable" research had been conducted prior to the inception of committee review—specifically, if a substantial number of participants had been abused. As there are reasons to believe that none of these assumptions about the review process or the prior state of affairs is correct, it is difficult to determine how much confidence to have in the interpretations noted earlier.

In the absence of data for any objective measures of research that has been conducted at institutions or at least of proposals submitted for financial support, one alternative is to ask knowledgeable individuals associated with the social science enterprise their judgment on the effects of the prior review; this is the second tactic for attempting to evaluate the effect of this procedure. It should be no surprise to discover that 76 percent of the "key" individuals involved in these committees indicate that the committees have been "very effective in protecting participants" in biomedical research (Barber and others, 1973, p. 162). In a similar fashion, interviews of committee members find that 99 percent agree that the review procedure has helped to protect subjects and 75 percent agree that it has improved the quality of research (Institute for Social Research, 1976c, p. 179). Unfortunately, the phrase "quality of research" is somewhat ambiguous and cannot always be interpreted as referring to scientific advances; it could refer to elegant verification of widely accepted hypotheses. This is particularly important in relation to the comments of 26 percent of the review board members—one in four—who agree that the procedure has "impeded the progress of research" (Institute for Social Research, 1976c, p. 179).

A second major category of informants is composed of the investigators at the various institutions. One survey of key review committee members asked them how well the procedure had been accepted by investigators; 52 percent reported that the review committee work was "very well received"; 37 percent "fairly well received, no opposition"; 11 percent reported "some opposition"; and none reported strong opposition (Barber and others, 1973, pp. 163–164). In a study of investigators who had submitted proposals to the committees, the actual pattern is somewhat mixed. While 98 percent agree that the review procedure has protected subjects, only 67 percent agree that the prior review procedure has improved the "quality of scientific research" and 45 percent—approximately one half—agree that the procedure has "impeded the progress of research" (Institute for Social Research, 1976c, p. 179). These responses represent the judgments of investigators who cooperated with the committee and submitted proposals for review; there are no data from these two studies on investigators who avoided committee review, either intentionally or because it was not required by their institution's procedures.

Interviews conducted with a random sample of 100 investigators (response rate of 95 percent) who had submitted proposals to a health science subcommittee of an Institutional Review Board (IRB) at a large midwestern university focused upon experiences with their most recent proposal (Glynn, 1978). One quarter reported that the IRB located a problem in their research that they had not considered. Major impacts of the review were on consent forms (50 percent of the projects), subject selection (12 percent), or method of obtaining consent (5 percent). Ten percent of the investigators felt that responsibility for participants would be shared by the IRB; 15 percent had shifted research emphasis (away from sensitive areas or human participants) because of the review procedures, usually to avoid delays—occasionally fatal to a project—and the administrative complications involved; 25 percent reported bypassing the review board for changes in projects or new projects, but this was usually for research that involved secondary data analysis or pilot studies. In general, the major effects of the review procedures were multifaceted, with both desirable and undesirable reactions reported by the principal investigators.

Two important types of effects of prior committee review have not received careful, detailed study—the effects upon the development of science (and associated benefits for society) and the effects upon participants. The first type of effect is one of the most difficult phenomena to measure and generally requires attention to changes over substantial time periods (decades). But measures of effects for participants are far less complex and well within the scope of techniques in biomedical and social science, and it is control of these effects that is considered to be the basic justification for the prior committee review procedure. Although some data exist on the types of effects experienced by participants in certain types of research (reviewed in Chapter Three), there is no systematic evidence reflecting the general impact of research on members of society.

In summary, available evidence on the effects of the prior committee review suggests that a substantial percentage of proposals raises questions during the review but that very few are rejected by the review commmittee; projects instead are usually modified to meet the objections of the committee. Committee members appear to think that their contributions protect participants and improve the quality of research. Cooperating investigators agree that participants are being protected; they are less positive about the effects on research. No direct evidence exists as to the effect of the procedure on the development of scientific knowledge or on research participants. The lack of reliable information on the effects of review committees may be related to other justifications for the procedure; evaluations are often based on the acceptability of review committees to society as a means for resolving the research dilemma rather than the actual results of their proceedings.

Acceptability of the Prior Review Procedure

Several factors suggest that the acceptability of this procedure as an organizational innovation to solve the problems of administrators may be unrelated to *any* empirical data about its effects on the research enterprise, society, or participants. First, the alternatives for administrators are limited to complete prohibition of research, unrestricted or unfettered research, or some form of control. Since there are well-established reasons for avoiding either of the extreme solutions—complete prohibition or unrestricted research—some type of control will probably be expected as a condition of societal support (both financial and legal) for research. Second, because of the universal introduction of the prior committee review procedures (preventing comparison with any scientific activity in the United States not subject to this form of control), the lack of useful objective data (particularly for historical comparisons), and the problems of measuring the effects of prior committee review, it may be impossible to provide a convincing empirical estimate of its impact.

But a third factor may be the most important: confidence in the correctness of the procedure may be unrelated to the product, that is, the judgments regarding research projects and subsequent effects. There is substantial precedent in the legal system for allowing a "committee" (jury or multijudge court) to resolve an ambiguous situation, with confidence in the decision based upon the fact that (1) a judgment is required and (2) the "committee" is a mechanism that will receive the greatest degree of acceptance by diverse interests. Unless a procedure that will receive greater approval for providing judgments about research activity can be developed, it seems unlikely there will be any fundamental modifications in the prior review procedure.

The emphasis upon committee review has resulted in a national level of review for types of research considered extremely sensitive. The federal regulations require DHEW to establish two ethical advisory boards, one to counsel the Public Health Service and its components and the other to counsel all other agencies and components within DHEW. While these boards, which are similar to institutional boards but represent national interests, are to provide advice on ethical issues, they may also require certain categories of research to be approved by the ethical advisory boards; current federal regulations require that only research involving "human *in vitro* fertilization" (artificial creation of human life) be so approved (Title 45 CFR 46.204). The ethical advisory boards may, however, ultimately serve as a national court of last resort for other types of controversial research.

Thus, even though the effects of the prior review procedure are unknown or ambiguous, its acceptance by institutions and investigators, the nature of the issues to be resolved, and the orientation toward a decision-making process by administrators suggest that there is no basis for expecting major changes in the current procedure and certainly not its total abandonment. It seems more reasonable to expect modifications of the existing mechanism.

Summary and Future Developments

Those responsible for federal agencies, both elected officials and administrators, have initiated numerous organizational procedures to solve the basic dilemma associated with research involving human subjects—how to balance concern for the participants with the development of scientific knowledge. There are three aspects to the organizational solution. The first is expansion of organizational (federal agency) control; this is particularly important for social scientists in relation to the DHEW for its guidelines must be applied to all research conducted at an institution that accepts DHEW funding for any research. The second is an emphasis upon procedures for obtaining informed consent—an attempt to ensure that no individual will be denied the opportunity to control his or her own rights and liberties. The third is a quasi-legal review procedure for evaluating the potential utility of specific research projects and the extent to which they will promote societal values (and be consistent with community standards); such review is completed prior to the initiation of a project and, in most cases, equal emphasis is given to all projects regardless of the potential risk to the participants.

The implementation of the current control system appears to have been due to a combination of factors: lack of systematic, reliable data on the experiences of participants in research, wide publicization of several dramatic examples of research that raised questions about the treatment of participants, information suggesting that physicians who conducted research were not always fully cognizant of a responsibility toward their patient-partici-pants, dramatic examples of social science research that demon-strated its potency, and a general suspicion that investigators could not be trusted to make decisions affecting participants. The cur-rent system, including the prior review procedure, seems to have been accepted by both administrators and investigators; it is un-likely there will be major changes, such as total abolition of current procedures and standards or total prohibition of all research. What is more likely, and has been developing, are modifications in the details of present practices.

It is difficult to see how the scope of the system could be increased, since all research using human participants and related to federal agencies—whether conducted within such agencies, re-lated to drugs that must receive federal approval, supported by federal funds, or conducted at institutions receiving federal funds for research—is expected to be consistent with various standards, all quite similar. If there is a change, it may well be toward stan-dardization of the criteria for informed consent and of the pro-cedures for review of research; the DHEW guidelines are most likely to serve as the basic principles, with variations adopted for specific situations.

It is possible that some research conducted at academic in-stitutions, in private organizations, or on a consulting basis may involve no "responsible institution," and, hence, it will not be sub-jected to federal scrutiny, directly or by proxy through an insti-tutional review board (IRB). But this would be a small fraction of all research; if oriented toward scientific objectives, it is likely to be completed on a modest budget. Perhaps the major area of social science research not formally covered by the federal guidelines is that completed for administrative or policy purposes within state (nonfederal) government units; this often involves surveys but may also include social experiments. It is not clear how or if this re-search will be explicitly covered by federal (DHEW) guidelines, although there may be a tendency for state and local agencies to adopt the DHEW standards in evaluating projects, if any review is initiated.

Up to the present time, elaboration of the guidelines has focused upon the procedures for obtaining informed consent and the use of special (social) categories of participants in research. In addition to the new regulations for research with fetuses, pregnant women, *in vitro* fertilization (*Federal Register, 40* [154]: 33,526; *40* [170]: 40,163; *40* [215]: 51,638; *42* [9]: 2,792; *43* [7]: 1,758), and prisoners (*Federal Register, 43* [222]: 53,652), new policies have been proposed for the use of children (*Federal Register, 43* [141]: 31,786) and those institutionalized as mentally infirm (*Federal Register, 43* [223]: 53,950). All these changes were initiated in response to the reports compiled by the National Commission for the Protection of Human Subjects of Biomedical and Behavioral Research (1975, 1976, 1977c, 1978a). In most cases the recommendations have been very conservative, suggesting severe limits on nontherapeutic research where there is even modest risk to the participants, being extremely cautious about infringement upon the rights and welfare of participants, and calling for virtual prohibition of some types of nontherapeutic research, regardless of potential societal value, the desires of the participants themselves, or lack of evidence of negative effects (National Commission for the Protection of Human Subjects . . ., 1976).

　　　　In terms of the prior committee review procedure, the most reasonable development would be an elaboration of the quasi-judicial nature of the procedure, with further attention to the processing mechanism as the basis for confidence in the resulting decisions rather than to the nature of the decisions or effects upon participants and the scientific enterprise. The review of research in sensitive areas may eventually be divided between two committees, one to make decisions regarding technical aspects of research projects and the other to judge projects solely in relation to societal values; the ethical advisory boards of DHEW emphasize social more than technical questions. Some attempts to standardize the considerations included in risk-benefit analysis could develop; the current procedure allows each of the hundreds of IRBs to complete this evaluation in their own way, and the evaluations may change as the composition of the committees change.

10

Legal Developments
Affecting Investigators'
and Participants' Rights

The final resolution of issues regarding the allocation of public funds and facilities for research rests with the political and legislative processes at federal, state, and local levels. The final resolution of issues regarding the treatment of individuals by investigators, applied professionals, and government agencies, rests with the legal system. Resolutions that develop within the legal system tend to be less precise than those produced by professional associations, legislation, or administrative procedures but are considerably more influential in defining the boundaries for the treatment of research participants, as they have universal application and violation may lead to substantial personal sanctions, including financial loss and incarceration.

In the sense that the research dilemma reflects incongruence between solutions to two major societal issues—justification for a political state (leading to an emphasis on individual rights) and criteria for societal actions (leading to an emphasis on benefits to the aggregate)—it is another instance of a basic problem present in a multitude of issues in modern democratic societies.

Resolving such problems has been a major activity within the legislative and legal systems, and two mechanisms appear to have developed. The first is the enactment of legislation and the establishment of administrative guidelines; such statements represent the end product of one resolution process. The second are judicial decisions that involve reinterpretations of existing laws, administrative procedures, and—of considerable importance in the United States—the constitution (Black, 1963; Brest, 1975; Emerson, Haber, and Dorsen, 1967; Lockhart, Kamisar, and Choper, 1975; Mason and Beaney, 1972).

This chapter will review the major issues and patterns of legal developments related to social science research (more attention has been given to biomedical research; Katz, 1972). It reflects several recent attempts to distinguish trends in this area (Breger, 1976; Capron, 1975; Nejelski and Peyser, 1975; Tropp, 1978), as well as speculation on events that may occur (Annas, Glantz, and Katz, 1977; Mulford, 1967; Nash, 1975; Nejelski and Lerman, 1971; Nejelski and Finsterbusch, 1973; Ruebhausen and Brim, 1966; Silverman, 1975; "Social Research and . . .," 1970). There is considerable ambiguity about the legal status of many social science research activities; it has been suggested that ("Legal Implications of . . .," 1960, p. 265) "the environment in which . . . [psychological] human experimentation is pursued may be aptly termed extralegal in that the legal bounds have not been delineated by judicial or legislative pronouncements." This is partly because many of the issues have been raised only recently and partly because those affected by the social science enterprise have only recently begun to seek redress through the courts or control through legislative action. At any rate, understanding the emphasis of the legal system and the resolutions that define the "legal bounds" requires attention to a number of issues.

Organization of Legal System Resolutions

Legal standards regarding the social science research enterprise—legislation and judicial decisions—emphasize the rights (or liberties) of parties (individuals, organizations, or the state) and the relationships (cooperative, competitive, or conflicting) between parties. The conception of rights utilized in legal discourse is somewhat more complex than the notion reviewed earlier in Chapter Two. Aside from the notion of right as "justice, ethical correctness, or consonance with . . . the principles of morals," three specific features of an individual's rights are associated with legal usage (Black, 1968, p. 1486): (1) a power, privilege, faculty, or demand, inherent in one person and incident upon another; (2) powers of free action; and (3) a capacity residing in one man of controlling, with the assent and assistance of the state, the actions of others. The important aspects of this view of rights include the privilege of acting autonomously and securing the assistance of the state to influence others to provide certain rights, such as the right of an accused to the power of compulsory processes to ensure that witnesses will provide testimony to facilitate a speedy and just trial. Individual responsibilities and obligations often are defined in terms of the rights of others, those affected by the exercise of such duties. A basic strategy for developing a convincing legal justification for any course of action is to show how it promotes the rights of individuals or parties affected by the action.

Since the "rights of parties" are emphasized in legal principles, it is useful to have a clear specification of the parties that may be considered to have rights, and this is presented in Table 12. Neither the list of affected parties nor the list of rights is exhaustive, and new entries are constantly being created. Specific individuals may have rights or liberties associated with several different categories (or roles). Research participants have received the most attention in discussions related to research, although the largest number of individuals have probably been affected—even if only in a small way—as members of the public-at-large or of future generations.

Table 12. Rights Associated with Various Parties-at-Interest Involved with the Research Enterprise

Party-at-Interest	Rights
Public-at-Large	General expansion of knowledge
	Development and maintenance of knowledge useful for solving social problems
	Evaluation of the conduct and success of publicly supported programs
	Assurance that scientific research is in accord with accepted moral standards
Participants	Self-determination (choice, liberty)
	Life (personal security, freedom from physical abuse or mental stress)
	Privacy
	Dignity and respect
	Freedom of thought
	Freedom of travel
	Property
	Freedom from deception
	Due process (in all government activities)
	Equality of treatment (by government actions)
Investigators (Individuals)	Ordinary rights of citizens (see above)
	Privacy
	Recognition for contributions
	Claimed, not recognized:
	Privilege of maintaining sources and content of data confidential
Investigator (State)	Collect descriptive data useful for public goals
	Develop effective administrative programs
	Develop efficient administrative programs
Future Generations	(Ambiguous at this time)

The source of the legal standards that define the appropriate relationship between parties and specific rights under consideration may have a substantial effect upon the types of actions that are taken to control the observance of rights. Such action may take the form of (1) protecting or benefiting the party whose rights were not observed or (2) affecting the parties seen as responsible for the violation. The latter might take the form of requiring offenders to make restitution to the injured parties, preventing them from continuing the actions that invade the other's rights, or actual punishment (such as a fine or incarceration).

For example, the invocation of constitutional law* may involve public policy developed by states for a particular issue, and the results of the court's deliberation may be the continuance or prohibition of a policy that is thought to affect the rights of individuals or groups. If individuals can show that they have sustained damages from participation in a research project, they may be able to achieve some direct recompense through the invocation of tort law† or, depending upon the interpretation of the informed consent procedure, through laws related to contracts.** If the investigator also has a helping professional relationship with the research participant, the individual may be able to claim negligence in the exercise of fiduciary (trustee) responsibilities. (Such a shift has recently occurred in medical malpractice; see Annas, Glantz, and Katz, 1977.) In the latter two cases, the investigator or the

*"That branch of public law of a state which treats the organization and frame of government, the organs and powers of sovereignty, the distribution of political and governmental authorities and functions, the fundamental principles which are to regulate the relations of government and subject, and which prescribes generally the plan and method according to which the public affairs of the state are to be administered" (Black, 1968, p. 385).

†"A private or civil wrong or injury . . . independent of a contract. . . . A violation of a duty imposed by general law or otherwise upon all persons occupying the relation to each other which is involved in a transaction" (Black, 1968 p. 1660). Recovery under tort law appears to require proof of damage (Nash, 1975), using evidence of damage that will satisfy the courts.

**"A promissory agreement between two or more persons that creates, modifies, or destroys a legal relation. . . . An agreement, upon sufficient consideration, to do or not to do a particular thing" (Black, 1968, p. 394).

sponsor of the research (host institution, funding source) may be liable for the financial costs or damages sustained by the participant(s). In extreme situations, the actions of an investigator supervising a research project may be seen as in violation of criminal statutes (an offense against the state), in which case incarceration could result—punishment is emphasized to discourage offenses against the state.

Presentations in the following sections will emphasize each "party"—or role related to the research enterprise—in isolation, without reference to other parties or roles. The major mechanisms for resolution, through the courts or legislation, are activated by disagreements between parties with distinct, conflicting rights or liberties. But these mechanisms sometimes ignore the fact that specific individuals may occupy different roles simultaneously. For example, all individuals, whether research participants or investigators, are members of the public-at-large.

The problem of analysis becomes even more complex if more than two parties are involved. When it is a question of the potential interests of the state (all the citizens) in transactions between participant and investigator, some activities may be against the best interests, or rights, of all the citizens. When all potential parties, rights, types of legal relationships, and multiple-party situations are considered, it is clear that the number of specific problems exceeds the capacity of the legal system to provide solutions. Resolution in the legal system tends to develop in response to specific problems, problems brought to the attention of the courts by legal action or by the political process. Since problems related to the social science enterprise have only recently become apparent, there is considerable uncertainty about their legal resolution. In much of the following discussion, it will be possible only to speculate on the types of rights that might be considered important; many issues have yet to be resolved by the courts and legislatures.

As a final contribution to ambiguity, solutions to problems in the legal system do not reflect, and are not expected to reflect, the *right* answer. For many of the objectives assigned to the legal system (such as justice), the correct answer is largely a subjective judgment; there is no objective procedure known that will produce a "correct" solution—one universally accepted as appropriate.

Hence the emphasis in the legal system on procedures to provide decisions: an appropriate procedure is one that is generally accepted as an equitable mechanism for arriving at a decision. The result has been the elaboration of decision-making procedures that are designed to minimize or standardize those factors expected to provide an unreasonable advantage to one party-at-interest. In brief, the legal system is organized to provide an acceptable decision procedure, not correct decisions.

Rights of the Public-at-Large

The rights of the public-at-large—the public interest—should be the basis for any activity that utilizes public resources and provides special privileges for those conducting the activity. Although the Constitution mentions no specific right to conduct or participate in research (Annas, Glantz, and Katz, 1977, p. 54), several important public benefits or rights are recognized through legislation, including:

- Right to a general expansion of knowledge.
- Right to the development and maintenance of a body of knowledge useful for societal problems.
- Right to a public accounting of the conduct of programs designed to promote public objectives.
- Right to assurance that scientific programs are conducted within accepted moral and ethical standards.

Legislative recognition of a public right to an expansion of knowledge is reflected in the first function assigned to the National Science Foundation (Title 42 USCA 1862): "To initiate and support basic scientific research and programs to strengthen scientific research potential and science education programs at all levels in the mathematical, physical, medical, biological, engineering, social, and other sciences, by making contracts or other arrangements . . . to support such scientific and educational activities and to appraise the impact of research upon industrial development and upon the general welfare." There follows a description of six other functions that specify activities designed to promote this general goal, clearly an acknowledgment of a public interest served by the promotion of basic research. (It would appear reasonable to consider basic research as that without a direct, immediate application to practical problems.)

An even broader acknowledgment of the public value of an expansion of knowledge is recognized in a privilege extended .to other federal agencies (Title 42 USCS 1891): "The head of each agency of the federal government . . . is hereby authorized, where it is deemed to the furtherance of the objectives of the agency, to make grants to . . . institutions or organizations for the support of basic scientific research." But since most agencies have immediate practical purposes, it is not clear that "basic scientific research" was meant to cover the same activities supported by the National Science Foundation.

Recognition of a right of the public to benefit from the development of scientific knowledge is present in the mission of the National Science Foundation—that is, to appraise the impact of research on industrial development and on the general welfare—as well as in other legislation. For example, the Public Health Service is expected to (Title 42 USCA 241): "conduct in the service, and encourage, cooperate with, and render assistance to other appropriate public authorities, scientific institutions, and scientists in the conduct of, and promote the coordination of, research, investigations, experiments, demonstrations, and studies relating to the causes, diagnosis, treatment, control, and prevention of physical and mental diseases and impairments of man, including water purification, sewage treatment, and pollution of lakes and streams." Other government agencies, such as the military and the Food and Drug Administration, systematically support and conduct research and development for objectives considered to be in the public interest.

The right of the public to be confident that public funds are promoting their intended purposes is well established. Elaborate mechanisms are designed to ensure that public funds are not misappropriated, including systematic audits of the uses of such funds. Ensuring that the programs themselves achieve the purposes established by legislatures is more complex. For programs with specific objectives it may be possible to gauge progress, but when the objective is to "strengthen scientific potential," it is far more difficult to make evaluations. Both of these forms of evaluation are recognized by legislatures in the auditing activities of the government and in the studies of government programs, frequently conducted by the General Accounting Office.

Recent legislation suggests recognition of the public's right to have confidence that research involving human participants is conducted within appropriate guidelines, particularly if supported by public funds. The creation of a National Commission for the Protection of Human Subjects of Biomedical and Behavioral Research and its basic charge (Public Law 93–348 [202]) to "conduct a comprehensive investigation and study to identify the basic ethical principles which should underly the conduct of biomedical and behavioral research involving human subjects" reflect such a public right. In a sense, this is part of a general right to assurance that special privileges extended to various professional groups are justified by the resulting benefits.

The absence of constitutional status for a right to engage in research would indicate that it must be justified on other grounds, either by showing that it provides other benefits (realizing basic rights) for the public-at-large or by establishing research as a new right through additional legislation. Both strategies are reflected in recent developments. Public concern about the rights affected by research—this is the basic research dilemma—is reflected in attention to the relationship between the expansion of knowledge and its effects on other rights.

Participants' Rights

The legal standards that may be used to determine the rights of participants are affected by the nature of the research activity and the research participant (individual or organizational entity). The most general class of participants is composed of those directly involved in traditional research activities—experimental, survey, or observational—where a private "party" (individual, group, or organization) develops and completes a research project, collecting data from individuals to resolve scientific or policy questions. When research to resolve policy issues is initiated by the state, participation may not be voluntary; the rights of those affected are somewhat different and will be discussed separately. Different issues are also involved when those indirectly affected by research are considered; these issues again will be reviewed separately. Finally, attention has been given, in one special case, to the status of research "participants" who are not individuals but part of a social system subjected to investigation.

Individual Participants Directly Affected by Research

For individual participants, two major issues are paramount. First, the nature of the rights that may be affected by involvement in a research project and, second, the conditions under which participants may agree to relinquish—at least to some extent—such rights. A discussion of these rights—freedom of choice (self-determination), life (security of the person), privacy, dignity, respect, property and so forth—will be emphasized in the following paragraphs. Factors associated with informed consent and associated legal principles will be reviewed later in this chapter.

Private Research, Participation Voluntary. The basic right to self-determination or freedom of choice is the focus of the concept of liberty. It involves the privilege of determining for one's self the nature of activities that will be pursued—work, play, marriage, and many others. It is, for example, the basic right associated with the prohibition of slavery. This right, which has clear applications for those consciously participating in research, is related to an important philosophical issue, "When is a person acting on the basis of his own free will?" While this problem is minimized for an autonomous adult engaged in the normal activities of everyday life, it becomes much harder to resolve the "free will" issue when the individual is in an institutional setting (whether school, mental hospital, or prison) or is highly dependent upon influential persons who urge involvement in particular activities (parents, physicians, employers, teachers, or counselors).

The individual right of self-determination has been extended to include the right to choose whether to become involved in research activities. But it is unclear whether it now includes *all* research activities. Some research projects involve the collection and analysis of data from activities in public settings (such as pedestrian traffic flow in a shopping center) or for legitimate administrative or political activities (such as the U.S. Census or voting patterns), to say nothing of government programs initiated on an "experimental" basis. If any individual can observe or have access to public information, it would seem that the purpose (research, commercial, journalistic, political, or personal curiosity) would be irrelevant. Hence, the right of self-determination regarding involvement in research projects has its most obvious application for those situations where individuals are (1) asked to subject themselves to special experiences or (2) asked to produce information not divulged as part of their normal, ordinary activities in society.

The right to life (or security of the person) is accorded primary importance in most political systems. While it can be extended to cover all types of rights (Black, 1968, p. 1074), for this discussion it will be restricted to two main factors—freedom from physical abuse and freedom from mental suffering. Providing freedom from physical abuse is one basic justification for the formation of a political state; the obligation of the state to prevent such abuse is reflected in the presence of criminal codes. While the possibility of criminal assault—an intentional, unlawful offer of corporal injury—is slight for most research activities, the possibility of battery—unlawful touching (without consent) of a person by another—is less remote. Courts have determined that it is battery for physicians to conduct surgical procedures without the consent—expressed or implied—of the patient. The recent trend in these cases, however, has been to argue that the physician was negligent in responsibilities to the patient as trustee of his physical care (Annas, Glantz, and Katz, 1977) rather than guilty of criminal assault. In social science research, either type of physical abuse would seem to be quite rare, but those projects that involve direct recording of physiological states with instruments that touch the person (for example, to record galvanic skin response) involve the possibility of legal battery if the participants do not give their consent.

Mental anguish may be experienced by participants in social science research; it is legally defined as (Black, 1968, p. 1137): "mental suffering resulting from the excitation of the more poignant and painful emotions, such as grief, severe disappointment, indignation, wounded pride, shame, public humiliation, despair, and so forth." Any project that involved emotional distress beyond that anticipated by the participant could be viewed as infringing upon the right to personal security. However, while the right to be free from unanticipated emotional distress may be well established, determination of the magnitude of the infringement appears to be a problem for the courts. Establishing damages (in financial terms) for mental anguish is difficult unless there are such clear physical symptoms as ulcers, nervousness, or headaches (Nash, 1975; Breger, 1976).

Some types of social science research involve the deliberate creation of negative states. Obvious examples would be research on stress and pain (Sternbach, 1968). Further, some types of behavior modification programs are designed to modify the orientations and behavioral predispositions of such "asocial" persons as sex offenders through the use of various types of reinforcements (both positive and negative). Mild electric shock or drugs that create unpleasant sensations may be used as "negative reinforcement" to discourage certain types of behavior (United States Senate, 1974). In other research, stress and anxiety may accompany the phenomena of major interest, and it is difficult to conduct any kind of research that does not produce some nervous participants.

The right to privacy, which may be the individual right most frequently affected by social science research, was only recently (1965) established as an explicit constitutional right in the United States. In reviewing a state law that defined the use of contraceptives as a criminal offense, the Supreme Court ruled the law unconstitutional because it violated a "right to privacy" considered to be implicit in the First, Third, and Fifth amendments, as well as in common law preceding the constitution (*Griswold* v. *Connecticut*, 1964). This judgment gave the right to privacy legal status equal to other rights mentioned in the Constitution. In response to the concerns of citizens, new federal regulations regarding access to administrative records in federal agencies and public schools have been created to ensure that data collected from or about individuals for administrative purposes will not be divulged to others and that the individuals concerned may check them for accuracy (Title 5 USCS 552a; Title 20 USC 1232g).

Privacy as related to social science has been defined as (Ruebhausen and Brim, 1966, p. 426) "no more, and certainly not less, than the freedom of the individual to pick and choose for himself the time and circumstances under which, and most importantly, the extent to which, his attitudes, beliefs, and behavior and opinions are to be shared with or withheld from others." While there is wide agreement on how to define private physical space and some types of private acts, such as written correspondence, the definition of a private personality that should be insulated from either covert or overt examination raises considerable problems. Ambiguity exists over the extent to which an individual is aware of the nature or content of "private material" that may be part of his or her personality—suppression or ignorance of subconscious thoughts is a well-accepted feature of the human mind. This leads to substantial problems in establishing how the individual can specify "private material" that is to remain "unexamined."

The right to be treated with dignity and respect has a more ambiguous status than some of the previous rights. While there are obvious cases, derived from common law considerations, where a person is entitled to recompense for damages to his dignity—for example, those created by practical jokes (Nash, 1975)—it is less clear how this would be determined in relation to research. One writer has suggested that some forms of deception may affect the dignity of the individual by reducing the sense of being in control of one's life (Breger, 1976).

Attention to the right to be treated with dignity and respect is, in part, generated by a concern over the use of deceptive presentations in social science research. This concern arises when researchers do not present the nature of the project accurately (disguise the fact of the research itself), create illusions to ensure that the reactions of the participants will be "natural," or actually create events in natural settings (such as simulated medical emergencies to facilitate observation of bystander response) that would not have existed except for the research interests. While in most legal cases deceit is related either to practical jokes (Nash, 1975) or attempts to defraud another for personal financial gain (Silverman, 1975; Nash, 1975), the use of deceit to advance scientific goals provides a new situation with few legal precedents. It would be difficult to estimate the "damage" when the deceiver receives no financial gain and the deceived suffers no financial loss and perhaps only minimal "mental distress."

The applications of the right to private property (or the right not to be deprived of private property without consent or due process) to participants in research in the United States are not clearly established. In some other cultures, however, information about individuals or social systems may be considered "property" (Beals, 1967). If confined to research in the United States, the use of parts of a person's body (for transplantation) or its products (blood, urine, and the like) for research is usually encompassed by standards related to the security of the person or the right to privacy. It may, however, be possible to consider an individual's time (time absorbed by participation in a research project) as a personal resource or as "property."

There has been speculation that the right to freedom of thought may be infringed by various techniques designed to influence the thoughts or orientations of individuals. It is argued that individuals are autonomous only when they are able to determine their own justifications for adopting certain perspectives or values and that any technique of behavior or thought control tends to replace an individual's judgments with those of the investigators (who decide what is appropriate). Hence, any procedure designed to affect personal thoughts—even, for example a reduction in the gratification associated with fantasies involving sexual acts with children—reduces the individual's capacity to organize his own thoughts and justifications for them. If the Constitution is interpreted as reflecting a respect for the right to self-determination in all areas of thought and behavior, then any type of behavior modification may infringe upon that right (Dworkin, 1976).

Most of the rights described above are considered to be "alienable," that is, they may be relinquished by the individual under certain conditions. While this is not true of all rights—one cannot consent to be murdered—it is the case for most rights affected by biomedical or social science research. Major issues center on determining the conditions that ensure that the right is legally forgone. This question will be pursued in more detail later in this chapter, following discussions of the rights of others (the state and individuals as investigators) associated with the social science enterprise.

Public Research, Participation Required (Social Experiments). While governments have always tried innovative and novel solutions to societal problems, only recently has the intellectual machinery of scientific research been systematically employed for assessing the effects of new programs. Such programs, often referred to as social experiments, include the following examples (the first and third were reviewed in more detail in Chapter Five):

- Negative Income Tax Experiment. In order to determine the effects of direct cash payments to low-income families on work behavior of employable adult family members, a sample of families was chosen for such transfers (which were systematically reduced as the earned income increased) and the effects on earned income compared with similar families in the same communities (Kershaw, 1972).
- Housing Assistance Supply Experiment. In an attempt to determine the effect of providing low-income households with a cash subsidy, specific to housing, on the choice of housing and the changes in the supply of housing (an alternative to providing government-sponsored housing developments), all eligible low income families in two communities were provided with vouchers that could be used to supplement their expenses for housing (rental or mortgage payments) (Rand Corporation, 1976).
- Density of Police Patrol Patterns. Concern with the effects of variations in police surveillance upon the occurrence of crime and community perceptions of police led to systematic variation of police patrol patterns among comparable neighborhoods in a major city (Kelling and others, 1974).

The critical feature of these programs for this discussion is the minimal choice regarding participation for the residents of the communities selected as research sites.

From a legal perspective, such research programs can be considered government activities and are thereby related to the rights of any citizen with regard to all government actions, specifically the right to due process and equal treatment (Breger, 1976; Capron, 1975). The basic justification for the procedural criteria of due process and equal treatment is to ensure that the judiciary and elected officials, responsible for administering society, do not take capricious and irresponsible actions that will infringe upon the fundamental rights of the citizens or that such infringements take place only when there is ample justification. In a sense, this is a recognition that contributions to public well-being may require infringement of individual rights. But it also calls for careful attention to all critical elements and a mechanism that will allow for the implementation of decisions based on a utilitarian analysis. As with the basis justification for rights themselves, due process and equal treatment are seen as additional protections of the citizens against unjustified abuse by public officials.

Due process was included in the Constitution to ensure that major individual rights—life, liberty, property, and movement—would not be restricted without the "regular course of administration through courts of justice" (Fifth Amendment to the Constitution). Legitimate infringement upon these rights takes the form of penalties for a violation of criminal law (that is, a serious infringement upon the rights of others). This concept has since been expanded to mean that "law shall not be unreasonable, arbitrary, or capricious, and that means selected shall have real and substantial relation to object (or goals)" (Black, 1968, p. 590). In other words, due process is now applied to a wide variety of government programs, many of which are not directly related to trials of those accused of criminal acts.

The due process feature of the Fifth and Fourteenth Amendments to the Constitution can be interpreted as encompassing two important features of government programs: (1) the relationship of a project to the goals of legislation and (2) the means by which a project will help to achieve those goals. For the most part, the courts have not questioned the ends of legislation in the recent past; the fact that legitimately elected public officials have approved the legislation has been considered sufficient justification (*Aguayo* v. *Richardson*, 1973; *California Welfare Rights Or-*

ganization v. *Richardson,* 1972). If the contribution of a research project to legitimate public programs is clear and explicit (preferably in the original legislation), it appears that courts will assume that initiation of the research project is appropriate (its actual design and conduct are a different matter). For some programs, the statutory requirements (program goals) may be temporarily suspended for "demonstration projects" (Title 42 USCS 1315). In short, the courts assume that, when citizens elect public officials, who in turn adopt legislative goals and approve research programs designed to contribute to the achievement of these goals, that the citizens' rights to due process are not infringed.

The problem of means, in relation to due process, refers to the nature of the procedures or programs designed to achieve the goals of legitimate legislation, for some of the alternatives may infringe upon fundamental rights. The current status with respect to the courts is summarized in a recent review (Capron, 1975, p. 154): "When a fundamental interest is at issue, due process requires that the state's purposes, if found to be compelling, be sought by the least drastic means. If the knowledge needed to improve the laws 'is impossible to obtain in any other way,' and the experiment has been designed to minimize its adverse impact upon the subjects' fundamental interests, systematic experimentation is possible. The problem for those charged with reviewing social experiments will be to determine how seriously to regard the incidental invasions of privacy caused by such experiments." In brief, the conduct of social experiments is not likely to be challenged by the courts on the basis of failure to observe due process if they are designed to achieve important state objectives and minimize infringements upon individual rights.

The second constraint, equal treatment, has been legally defined in this way (Black, 1968, p. 631): "Equal protection and security shall be given to all under like circumstances in his life, liberty, and his property, and in the pursuit of happiness, and in the exemption from any greater burdens and charges than are equally imposed upon all others under like circumstances." In essence, there should be very strong justification for treating individuals unequally, and courts have given "strict scrutiny" if differentiation is made on the basis of sex, race, or religion or if fundamental rights are involved—privacy, association, voting, and travel (Breger, 1976, p. 28).

The problem that develops for the implementation of societal experiments is that the major benefits from such research are based upon providing individuals with different experiences, or "unequal treatments," so that the effects of such "inequality" can be systematically measured and related to the variation in treatment. Unequal research treatment has been divided into three types: (1) selection of a problem for study (and associated target population), (2) selection of a particular location, and (3) selection of individual participants to receive variation in treatment (Capron, 1975, p. 156). There appear to be no fundamental rights associated with emphasis upon different problems; legislatures and administrators are not obligated to give equal treatment to all "problems." The major issues are related to decisions regarding other forms of potentially unequal treatment.

The first court case to deal specifically with the issue of equality of treatment regarding the selection of geographical locations for an experimental program involved a study of the effects of requiring employable welfare recipients to accept job training or suitable jobs. The program was initiated in 25 percent of the regions of a state selected, in part, on a random basis. The court held that (*Aguayo* v. *Richardson*, 1973) "the Equal Protection Clause does not place a state in a vise where its only choices in dealing with the problems of welfare are to do nothing or plunge into statewide action." There are a number of justifiable reasons for introducing new programs gradually. As long as the process of introduction is relevant to the goals set by the legislature, it is not likely that a challenge would be sustained by the courts.

The right of equal treatment involves special considerations in the actual selection of individuals to participate in a research program. Three factors appear to be critical: the individual characteristics used as the basis for selection, the nature of the selection procedure, and the type of effects the individuals would be expected to experience. Characteristics related to race, sex, or religious affiliation are considered to be of special importance; any procedure selecting research participants that places special emphasis upon them is likely to receive close scrutiny by the courts. The nature of the effects to be experienced by the participants is generally related to what they might experience in the absence of a research program; few participants in a research program would have reason to object if they received greater benefits than they might normally expect. But burdens that might be greater than would ordinarily be expected—for example, a longer prison sentence (Norris, 1966)—may cause substantial problems; it is unlikely they would be permitted by the courts. In essence, this places a restriction upon the effects (or treatments) associated with societal experiments—the participants can never be subjected to burdens greater than they would normally encounter in the absence of the research program.

The final issue for consideration is the random assignment of individuals to different treatments or research experiences. Since citizens (and participants) have a right to expect that rational criteria will be used for matching participants and research experiences, the issue is whether random assignment is rationally related to the purposes of the project. This appears to be the case for most projects, as any other basis would involve personal judgments that could reduce confidence in the inferences based upon the results of the research endeavor. Therefore, as long as random assignment is the most rational way of achieving the objectives of the research endeavor, it will probably be considered appropriate by the courts (see Capron, 1975, for a possible exception).

In general, if a societal experiment is to receive judicial approval after court challenge, it should have the following characteristics:

1. The objectives of the program, to which the research activity is related, should have been approved (legitimated) by elected public officials.
2. The purposes of the research activity should be reasonably related to legitimate objectives of a public (social) program.
3. The design of the research, that is, the actual research procedures, should provide an appropriate means for achieving the research objectives.

4. The design of the research should provide a means for achieving the research objectives that minimizes the burdens and discomforts of the participants, compared to alternative research designs.
5. No participant should be expected to experience burdens or costs associated with the research that would be greater than those expected in the normal course of events (in the absence of the research).
6. Procedures for discrimination among participants should be related to the research objectives and should not be capricious or simply based upon the subjective judgments of administrators; random assignment may be considered an appropriate procedure for some research goals.

Note that these criteria apply to projects imposed upon the participants; if participants are voluntarily involved, many of these features may not be considered crucial.

The fundamental basis for allowing social experiments to proceed—and requiring citizens to participate—is the "consent of the governed," represented by approval of elected officials. The elected officials provide surrogate informed consent for all the members of society. The more details of the research procedures and techniques approved by the elected officials, the greater the possibility that the courts will approve the conduct of the research program. Social scientists involved in the design of legislation for societal experiments should give serious consideration to this tendency of the courts.

Individual Participants Indirectly Affected by Research

The rights of individuals not directly involved in a research project—but affected indirectly—are more ambiguous and more a matter of speculation than the rights of those directly affected. Potential problems could be reviewed in relation to individuals who experience indirect effects of societal experiments, to individuals affected by changes in an intimate associate involved in a research project, and to categories of individuals who may be affected by the application of knowledge developed from research projects.

Examples of potential effects on those not directly involved as participants in social experiments include the following (taken from Tropp, 1978):

- If police patrol patterns are systematically varied to explore the effects upon the crime rate, does this infringe upon the rights of those individuals who become victims of crimes that might not have occurred if the research had not been conducted?
- If a study of the housing choices selected by those with housing vouchers to "spend" increases the housing costs for all residents in a community, does this infringe upon the rights of those not provided with vouchers and paying more for housing?
- If a study of income maintenance raises the wages expected by a substantial number of workers and, in turn, the labor costs of the local industries, does this infringe upon the rights of local entrepreneurs who may experience reduced profits, as they compete with others in communities where wage rates are not affected?
- If a study of health services requested by individuals with different (more or less liberal) health insurance programs raises the cost of health care in a community, does this infringe on the right to security of person of those not involved in the study but who may pay higher medical costs or receive fewer services as a result?

There is, as yet, no resolution to such problems, either in terms of moral philosophy or legal precedent; such issues have not yet been brought to the attention of the courts.

Participants directly and indirectly affected by societal experiments share one characteristic: neither category has any choice about the effects it may experience. Hence, the interpretations of due process and equal treatment as they apply to participants directly affected also apply to those indirectly affected. The major new complication for any litigation would be demonstrating that the research activity was a major cause of the effects on the participants indirectly affected—experience with crime, increased housing costs, change in quality or cost of medical care, and so forth.

A more speculative issue is raised by research involving characteristics that are used (by others) to place individuals in social categories or to stereotype them. For example, research on high-density central city neighborhoods may find that young residents— who perhaps come from households with modest incomes and little emphasis on intellectual goals—do not do well in academic settings. If the members of one racial group dominate in such a community, it may lead unsophisticated observers to interpret the results as meaning that "*all* _____ s do poorly in school." The result is that policies or actions related to the academic opportunities available to _____s may be affected. Since the effects may be experienced by all _____s, not just those involved in the research activity, the nonparticipating _____s have been indirectly affected by the results of the research project.

In summary, the rights of those not directly affected by a research activity have not been legally established, although there has been speculation on the issue. Except for rather special situations—nonparticipants residing in a community involved in societal experiments—it is not clear that legally recognizable rights could be established for nonparticipants.

Social Systems as Research Participants

A substantial amount of research, particularly in social science, is conducted with organizations or parts of social systems. In such cases, the participant is no longer a single indivdiual, although the rights of individual participants may be involved. One example, discussed earlier in a somewhat different context, involved the deliberations of juries. Despite the informed consent of attorneys for plaintiffs and defendants, as well as of the presiding judges, audiotape recordings of the deliberations of six juries in civil cases (analysis was not initiated until all appeals were exhausted) created enough controversy to bring about the enactment of federal and state statutes prohibiting any type of research that would reveal the deliberations of any jury in any way. The jury appears to have been considered an inviolate aspect of the legal system and not to be subjected to external influences of any type, regardless of the goals of the research.* Aside from this one example, there has been little systematic attention paid to the rights of organizational entities or social systems as they are affected by research activity. This is probably due to the association of rights with individuals rather than with collections or aggregates.

Investigators' Rights

A number of rights are connected with the design and conduct of scientific research; those that have received serious attention from legal scholars are the ones affected by the nature of the research and the participant's relationship to the project. The most general case is that of individual scientists (or groups, institutions, and organizations) acting as investigators. More complex is the right of the state when it initiates research to gather information for policy issues or to meet legal requirements.

Individual as Investigator

Individual investigators are assumed to have a number of rights that are available to all citizens, although they may take a slightly different form when scientific research is involved. While there is no specific First Amendment "right to research," one analysis suggests that if a case arose such a right would be recognized by the Supreme Court (Robertson, 1978); since the publication and reading of a scientific article cannot be prohibited, it would be anomalous to prevent the research leading to its publication. There is, however, one special right—the legal privilege of keeping the source and content of data confidential—that many social science investigators would like to have but that currently does not exist.

Existing Rights. Freedom of inquiry and thought, freedom to communicate and discuss ideas—these rights are available to scientific investigators as they are to all citizens, and they are relatively

*It is possible to interpret this controversy as related to an individual's right to a trial by jury; although it would appear that the fundamental right is to "justice," many clearly assume that a jury decision automatically provides justice. It is no longer possible to collect empirical evidence related to this last question in the United States.

noncontroversial. As long as the rights of others (such as research participants) are given proper consideration, there is little legal restriction on exercising the right or freedom to pursue any research topic. However, the freedom to pursue research does not include the right to the resources to conduct research; freedom to conduct research may mean little if such resources are not available.

Two additional general rights have received special attention as they relate to a general right of the public-at-large (as sponsors of research): (1) the right of investigators to privacy and to recognition and benefits associated with the development of new scientific ideas, and (2) the right of the public-at-large, as sponsors of research, to have full access to descriptions of any research supported with public funds (barring unusual circumstances, such as concern for national security). These rights are affected by the review and selection process used by the government agencies providing financial support for research.

There is no controversy over the practice of making public the research proposals that have been selected for government support as publicly supported projects, they are in the public domain. Concern arises over the possibility that the proposals and evaluations may be made public during the review process—that, in other words, proposals submitted for review and anonymous evaluations provided by other investigators not associated with those submitting the proposals may become public information. From the perspective of the investigators, there is concern that wide, uncontrolled dissemination may allow other investigators to have access to scientific ideas (and perhaps conduct related research) before the originator is able to explore the issues fully and receive recognition for his or her contribution. Making the idea public has the effect of allowing competing investigators access to still-tentative ideas that are in a sense "private thoughts." The premature disclosure of a proposal could be considered an invasion of privacy and a threat to an investigator's right to receive credit for intellectual contributions.

A request for disclosure of research proposals being reviewed by an agency of the federal government under the Freedom of Information Act was supported by a judicial decision (*Washington Research Project* v. *Department of Health, Education, and*

Welfare and others, 1973). The court found that the "noncommercial scientist's research design is not literally a trade secret or item of commercial information" (excluded from disclosure by the Freedom of Information Act). Factual information developed in evaluation of the proposals—for example, during site visits—was also to be disclosed upon request. This ruling allows commercial firms to request copies of proposals and research designs prepared by noncommercial scientists as part of research proposals and the privilege of using this material without compensation to, or perhaps even acknowledgment of, the scientist's contribution.

The matter of anonymity of outside reviewers who comment on research proposals involves other issues. Since the number of indivdiuals specializing in many areas of science is small and these individuals frequently have multiple interrelations, it is often difficult for individuals to provide an objective, unbiased judgment on a research proposal if they expect to be identified with their comments. For this reason, a system of obtaining anonymous reviews on proposals and thus maintaining the privacy of discussions among review panels (whose membership is public) has been developed. This allows individual scientists the freedom to provide frank comments on research proposals, a freedom that should increase the benefits received (in terms of knowledge gained) from the expenditure of public funds. In one relevant court case it was found that a consultant's evaluations of projects (site-visit reports) were privileged partly because all factual material was disclosed by the agency. (*Washington Research Project* v. *Department of Health, Education, and Welfare and others,* 1975).

From the perspective of the public, as research sponsors, this "procedural confidentiality" may be seen as an opportunity for a special group to control the disbursement of public funds without the scrutiny of the general public or the elected officials who represent it. But a recent study of this system in the National Science Foundation found little evidence that a closed, confidential review of projects led to allocation of research funds on other than scientific merit (Cole, Rubin, and Cole, 1977). Further, examination of the problem by the National Commission for the Protection of Human Subjects of Biomedical and Behavioral Research (1977b) led to a recommendation of strict confidentiality of all projects and review procedures (written evaluations and meetings of advisory committees) until the funds are awarded, finding no basis for assuming that public disclosure of research applications or their evaluations would protect the rights and welfare of human participants. The eventual resolution may not satisfy all individuals involved, but it is a case where the proprietary rights of investigators to their intellectual products obviously may be affected. Further legislation on this issue, modifying the Freedom of Information Act (Title 5 USCS 552), may occur in the near future.

    "Investigator's Privilege": Legal Immunity for Research Data. From the perspective of most investigators, research involves assembling data from individuals and social units to facilitate the production of new knowledge that either will be used directly for social benefits or will contribute to the general advancement of science. Since most of the information obtained is relatively innocuous (even though of a private nature), involves major societal problems (such as poverty or crime), or possesses an ambivalent legal status (such as data on drug abuse), there seems to be little reason to delay granting immunity to researchers to prevent public disclosure of such information. Rumors and actual examples of infringements upon this investigator's "right," knowledge that physicians and lawyers have such a privilege, and the well-publicized cases involving newspersons (who appear to be gaining support for a "newsperson's shield")—all have encouraged social science investigators to think that such a right is justified (Carroll, 1973; Carroll and Knerr, 1976a, 1977; Feuillan, 1976; Hendel and Bard, 1973; Kershaw and Small, 1972; Nejelski and Lerman, 1971; Nejelski and Finsterbusch, 1973; Shah, 1969; "Social Research and . . .," 1970). Given this perspective toward empirical research and its potential for contributing to society, it is not unreasonable to expect that social scientists would be concerned—and often indignant—to discover that research data and sources are not immune from the subpoena process, even when cooperating respondents are promised confidentiality and anonymity.

    Current legal standards for confidentiality are based on the assumption that all citizens have a duty to provide information to assist the legal and legislative systems in executing their responsibilities; these standards encompass criminal trials, grand juries, legislative bodies, civil litigants, and administrative agencies. It is assumed that the interest of all citizens—the public interest—is best served when such disclosures can be expected as a major obligation and duty. The power to require individuals to produce relevant information—in the form of either personal accounts or written records—encourages individuals to discharge this "duty." The special case of criminal trials is mentioned in the Sixth Amendment to the Constitution, which states: "In all criminal prosecutions, the accused shall enjoy the right . . . to have the compulsory process for obtaining witnesses in his favor."

Contrary to the basic legal assumptions about the testimony of individuals, which emphasize the duty of the citizen to the state, many individuals assume that private information shared with friends can be kept confidential. Although agreements of honor between "gentlemen" to maintain a confidence were recognized as privileged in the seventeenth and early eighteenth centuries in England (Wigmore, 1961, pp. 530 531), communications between friends have no special status—they cannot be legally withheld from disclosure if subpoenaed.

One type of "friendship relation" that has a privileged status, or immunity from the compulsory process, is that of marriage, relating to all communications (verbally, in writing, by gesture, personal presence, and so forth) between spouses. This privilege is, however, carefully defined and does not extend to information exchanged before or after marriage, communications overheard by a third party, civil cases in federal courts, legal action related to the marital relationship, or criminal proceedings affecting the interests of the other spouse or the family, such as child abuse (Gard, 1972, p. 748). In short, while a general privilege exists (if one spouse is told of a crime committed by the other, he or she cannot be forced to testify to this knowledge), it is carefully circumscribed and does not relate to all aspects of any communication between two individuals who were married at one time.

Many social scientists feel that the type of privilege extended to communications between physicians or attorneys and their patients or clients, as well as to newspersons (the "newsperson's shield") provide a precedent for a "researcher's shield." All these cases are, however, somewhat different from that of an investigator conducting research. A discussion of these differences will help to demonstrate how precisely (or narrowly, depending upon the point of view) such privileges are defined.

　　The attorney-client privilege originally evolved from common law, perhaps as a result of the complexity of the legal system and the inability of a nonlawyer to fully understand the system and how all rights might be exercised; it is almost universally established by statute at the present time. This privilege does not extend to knowledge about future intentions to commit crime, and advice on acts to minimize the illegality of future activity is considered to involve an attorney as an accomplice. The physician-patient privilege has been established only by legislative statute; it is not recognized in English common law, and generally extends to civil actions only, not to criminal cases. In addition, physicians may be required to divulge information to the proper authorities with regard to a number of conditions observed in a patient, such as a contagious disease, gunshot or knife wounds, or suspected cases of child abuse. Thus, in both legal and medical situations there are clear and explicit limits on what information may remain confidential; it must be related to a specific problem and involve a professional relationship—casual statements or those made in the context of a friendship relation are not privileged (Gard, 1972). Similar privileges have been extended to priest-penitent or accountant-client relationships in some states, always by legislative statute (Schroeter, 1969).

　　Perhaps the professional-client relationship closest to that of social scientists and respondent-subjects is the relationship between psychologists and clients. A review of applicable state laws completed in 1969 (Shah) found that thirty-three states have laws that provide a privilege of confidentiality for psychologists in a consulting relationship with clients. The laws vary considerably by state, and in many cases the specific conditions under which the privilege does not hold (some types of criminal trials, for example) are clearly specified. A recent incident has modified the legally specified obligations of clinical psychologists somewhat. When the parents of a young woman murdered by a clinical psychologists's patient sued for damages on the grounds that the psychologist had advance knowledge of the intent to harm the victim and failed to warn the victim or her parents, the court determined that the psychologist did have a "duty to warn" (Annas, 1976).

Perhaps the most important aspect of the "professional" privileges already established by statute is that information is controlled by the patient, client, or penitent. This privilege is thus not a professional privilege at all, for it allows the client/patient/penitent to control information retained by the professional; if a person in one of these categories agrees to disclose the information, it must be done, regardless of the consequences for the professional (Gard, 1972).

The analogy between newspersons and social science investigators appears more direct than it actually is. First, the justification for the privilege of confidentiality is much different. In the case of newspersons it is argued that the free flow of information—"freedom of the press" provided for in the First Amendment to the Constitution—would be hindered if news sources could not remain confidential, and there is substantial evidence to suggest that this would indeed be the case (Blasi, 1971).

Second, and equally important, a newsperson's privilege does not exist with respect to federal laws, although by 1973 at least twenty-five states had adopted legislation related to privileges for newspersons (Cook, 1973). Newspersons currently are required to seek federal immunity on a case-by-case basis—after a subpoena has been issued—and the current standards were set by the Supreme Court in *Brazenburg* v. *Hayes* in 1972 (Nejelski and Finsterbusch, 1973). While the court refused, by a five-to-four vote, to grant newsmen a First Amendment testimonial privilege (before a grand jury in a criminal case) that other citizens do not enjoy, several factors were associated with this opinion that affect the status of court-determined privileges for newspersons. To begin with, the majority decision referred to a "paramount" or "compelling" state interest in overriding the First Amendment privilege. It was also noted that newspersons should be required to testify only on matters directly relevant to the investigation at hand, not in relation to their general information-gathering activities. Finally, Justice Powell suggested that the merits of each case should be considered separately. Since Powell voted with the majority, this suggested that his judgment might have been different if the facts of the situation had been different. Subsequent to this decision, newspersons have been successful in retaining the First Amendment privilege in civil cases but continue to be required to identify sources in criminal cases—or suffer the penalties.

Application of the "newsperson's shield" criteria was involved in a recent case concerning an investigator and his research materials (Culliton, 1976). A civil suit between a public utility and a supplier resulted in a subpoena to an investigator who was studying management decision processes at the time that the equipment, provided by the supplier, was selected and ordered. The subpoena requested information on the identities of the executives involved in the decision to purchase the equipment as well as on the substance of their deliberations. The attorneys retained by the university employing the investigator argued that (1) journalists had been granted immunity in all civil cases in the recent past, (2) the information could be obtained from the witnesses (the executives) on direct questioning, and (3) a violation of confidentiality in this case would have very detrimental effects on future research. This latter point was substantiated by affidavits from twelve leading scholars. The decision in favor of the investigator was based on the court's discretion over what is to be admitted as evidence, not on interpretations of the First Amendment related to "freedom of research." Given all aspects of this case, it seems unlikely that it provides much additional legal support for a "researcher's privilege," if only because subpoenas arising from civil litigation are not a major threat to the integrity of research data.

While the status of a privilege for newspersons is currently less than clear cut, the relation of an investigator's status to the First Amendment privilege of freedom of the press is even more ambiguous. Although much descriptive social science is similar to the activities of newspersons—it has been referred to as "slow journalism"—a great deal of social science research is distinctly different, particularly in those instances when natural events are affected by the investigator (as in experiments), when special data collection techniques are used (such as projective tests, measures of physiological response, sophisticated questionnaires, and the like), or when special analysis is conducted to determine patterns and relationships not obvious on initial examination. Attempts to provide protection for social science investigators through analogy to news-persons would, at best, only cover a portion of social science research activities.

Realizing that the most direct route for developing a legal privilege for investigators is through legislative statute—there is universal agreement that such privileges will not come from judicial recognition through case law—two model statutes have been proposed. Boness and Cordes (1973 p. 258) developed a statute that includes: "Except as provided in Section 3, a researcher shall not be compelled in any proceeding to disclose the identity of a research subject, facts from which the identity of the research subject might be inferred, or information furnished by an individual research subject to the researcher." The exception occurs when the "action which is the subject of the legal proceeding is murder, sabotage, espionage, treason, or a specific threat to human life" (Boness and Cordes, 1973, p. 259). The privilege is the investigator's, for the investigator has the right to divulge the information.

Another model statute is somewhat stronger (Nejelski and Peyser, 1975, pp. 8–9); the critical Section 2 reads as follows: No person shall be compelled pursuant to a subpoena or other legal process issued under the jurisdiction of the United States or any state during the course of any judicial, administrative, or legislative investigation or adjudicative proceeding to give testimony or to produce any information storage device, object, or thing that would (1) reveal any subject or impair any subject relationship by revealing the identity of the subject or the content of information . . ., whether or not any explicit or implicit promise of confidentiality had been made . . . or (2) reveal the contents of any information received, developed, or maintained by a researcher in the course of [analysis and publication]. As proposed, there are no exceptions to this privilege except when waived by both the researcher and the participant; if the identity of the participant is not known to the researcher, the researcher alone controls the information. This would provide a much more general, unambiguous privilege than extended to any other category of individuals in the United States.

While there is no current privileged relationship extended to social scientists as a special type of occupational or professional group, there are precedents for extending privileged relationships to certain types of data collection or research projects conducted or sponsored by the federal government. The oldest is the protection provided for U.S. Census data, derived from its status in the Constitution. The data collected by the Social Security Administration is also immune from forced disclosure. More relevant to general research is the privileged status granted to approved projects related to alcohol and drug abuse or sponsored by the Law Enforcement Assistance Administration (LEAA).

The decennial U.S. Census is in fact a social science research activity mandated by the Constitution that takes on the enumeration of citizens for the purpose of apportionment of representation. While the Secretary of Health, Education, and Welfare is allowed to provide reports and summaries of the census data, it is stated that "in no case shall information furnished . . . be used to the detriment of the persons to whom such information relates" (Title 13, USC 8[C]). Further, only sworn officers and employees are allowed to examine individual reports, and no data may be furnished in any form that would allow identification of any establishment or individual. Finally, copies of any reports prepared for the Census Bureau but retained by responding organizations are immune from subpoena (Title 13 USC 8–9).

While the regulations for the records maintained on individuals by the Social Security Administration emphasize the preservation of confidentiality, a number of administrative activities, such as settling claims for benefits, require that information be made available (Title 20 CFR 401). Consequently, nineteen different purposes are described as justifying disclosure. Most of these deal with administrative activities; several are related to the investigation and prosecution of persons who provide services to individuals covered by Social Security programs and become involved in charges of fraud (such as physicians); only one deals with potential criminal prosecution of individuals described by the Social Security data and that is restricted to "the commission or threatened commission of an act of espionage or sabotage or other similar act inimical to the national security" (Title 20 CFR 401.3 [i] [4]). However, the most recent address of an individual may be provided to a court in cases where a person is not providing satisfactory child support.

The Drug Abuse Prevention and Control Act of 1970, which emphasized the benefits of research on the impact of drug use, allows the Secretary of Health, Education, and Welfare to grant authority to "protect the privacy of patients" (that is, research subjects) by withholding "names or other identifying characteristics" from anyone not connected with the program. "Persons so authorized may not be compelled in any federal, state, or local civil, criminal, administrative, legislative or other proceedings" to identify research subjects. The Drug Abuse Office and Treatment Act of 1972 sets forth a wider range of functions (drug abuse prevention programs) and allows disclosure of confidential information if authorized by a court of competent jurisdiction—the immunity from disclosure is not absolute. A similar provision is contained in the Comprehensive Alcohol and Alcoholism Prevention Treatment and Rehabilitation Act of 1970.

The guarantees of the 1970 federal drug law were the key issue when a witness to a murder testified that she saw the offender run into a drug treatment clinic where she had been a patient; she also thought that she had seen the individual in a waiting room on a previous visit. Photographs of all research participants with characteristics similar to those of the suspect were subpoenaed; the director of the project refused to provide the information and was cited for contempt. The ruling was narrowly (four to three) overturned by the U.S. Court of Appeals on the grounds that the federal statute was unambiguous and that all proper procedures had been followed to acquire authorization for immunity from subpoena; several federal agencies filed briefs on behalf of the investigator (*People* v. *Newman*, 1973).

Investigators holding a grant or contract with the Law Enforcement Assistance Administration are covered by the following clause (Title 42 USC 3771a): "Except as provided by federal law or other than this chapter, no officer or employee of the federal government, nor any recipient of assistance under the provisions of this chapter shall use or reveal any research or statistical information furnished under this chapter by any person and identifiable to any specific private person for any purpose other than the purpose for which it was obtained in accordance with this chapter. Copies of such information shall be immune from legal process, and shall not, without the consent of the person furnishing such information, be admitted as evidence or used for any purpose in any action, suit, or other judicial or administrative proceedings." It has been observed (Carroll and Knerr, 1977) that this has the advantage of automatically conferring immunity from subpoena upon investigators but that such immunity extends only to written records (not personal observations), does not include immunity from legislative subpoenas, does not extend to knowledge of future crimes, and is limited in that local authorities may determine that local, rather than federal, law may prevail. Further, one instance where investigators were not able to use this regulation as protection from local subpoena substantially reduces the protection provided (Carroll and Knerr, 1977, p. 3).

It has been argued (Kershaw and Small, 1972) that certain types of projects, those designed to resolve policy or administrative issues, might be granted immunity from the subpoena process on the basis that such immunity is an executive privilege. Although this argument might apply to those projects that are specifically developed to resolve immediate concerns of government administrators, it might not apply to projects designed to explore problem areas without a direct and timely application to policy and that would include most scientific research. Hence, it could provide justification for a privileged status for data collected during a social experiment that was designed to contribute to the resolution of particular policy issues, but probably not for general research activity with a scientific focus.

It would appear that the activities of social science investigators are not comparable to those of applied professionals and that the extension of the "newsperson's shield" to social science investigators would not encompass many types of research activities. Justification of a privilege for social science investigators would require evidence to support three major points (Breger, 1976):

1. That there is substantial evidence that the legal and administrative system has used "compulsory processes" to publicly disclose information and identities of participants assembled in confidence during a research activity.

2. That the effects of these disruptions have been detrimental to the conduct of social science research.
3. That the value of the product of "unhindered" social science research—to society, the public interest—outweighs the value—to society—of being able to require disclosure of information.

Note that the third issue discusses the relative advantages gained by society from two different activities—the benefits of social science research versus the benefits of facilitating specific legal or administrative proceedings through compulsory disclosure. In this sense the arguments in support of an investigator's privilege are analogous to those supporting newspersons rather than applied professionals. In the latter case, the benefits are for the clients.

Evidence related to the first issue—attempts to disclose research data acquired in confidence through legal processes—can be gathered in two ways. One is to marshall all relevant public judicial decisions—this is the typical strategy of a legal scholar. The alternative is to examine all threats or attempts to issue subpoenas, the outcomes of which may or may not be resolved in public, judicial decisions. Without the protection of a privileged relationship, the threat of a subpoena, the resulting complications, and potential sanctions (such as incarceration) may encourage an investigator to release information on an informal basis, particularly if legal assistance is not readily available or affordable.

There are a few examples of situations where subpoenas have been issued to investigators for information based on research data. These include:

• A U.S. Senate investigation committee issued two subpoenas for access to data collected (via questionnaire and observation) of street gangs in an urban area; after a verbal assurance of confidentiality, the Senate investigator was given access to the data (which identified specific individuals); returned material "inadvertently taken from the project office"; and subject matter from the project was subsequently published in newspaper accounts of the Senate investigation (Walsh, 1969b).

- Data from the files of an income-maintenance experiment were subpoenaed by a local county prosecutor in an investigation of welfare fraud (families receiving funds from both state and project sources in excess of state limits); the matter was resolved when the federally financed project reimbursed the state for "estimated" overpayments in the amount of twenty thousand dollars (Kershaw and Small, 1972).
- Three scholars were subpoenaed because of their possible knowledge concerning the private publication of the "Pentagon Papers," which related the history of American involvement in Southeast Asia. In all three cases the courts denied the social scientists the right to withhold information acquired with a promise of confidentiality; one social scientist (Samuel Popkin) served eight days in jail, until the grand jury was discharged (Carroll, 1973; Nejelski and Peyser, 1975).

These examples suggest that the threat of subpoena is real and that investigators have no general basis for protection that will be recognized by the courts. The two incidents where investigators were able to resist subpoenas reviewed earlier, the civil suit involving the public utility (Culliton, 1976) and the murder case where a suspect might have been participating in a drug treatment program (*People* v. *Newman*, 1973), were special situations and the bases for the court decisions were clearly not relevant to scientific research in general.

Investigators who conduct research on illegal activities or on the criminal justice system are especially open to requests for information from authorities. Using information gathered through informal networks, Carroll and Knerr (1977) found five different incidents in which investigators were subpoenaed to testify with regard to criminal actions. Investigators on one project complied with four subpoenas; one investigator complied after being jailed, and one complied voluntarily. An informal resistance was successful in one case, and in the fifth the investigator claimed that, since he had observed illegal acts, he would be subject to prosecution for failure to report such acts if he provided any testimony related to his observations. This Fifth Amendment claim (the right not to provide self-incriminating evidence) was accepted, and he was not required to produce any information. The same problems have occurred in other countries; for example, several researchers in Germany were required to testify in open court about criminal activities that occurred while they were engaged in participant-observation research (Nejelski, 1973).

Evidence of informal demands to divulge confidential information is more difficult to obtain, since there is no systematic public record comparable to that for legal decisions. But there are several well-known examples: attempts by the FBI and the State Department to gain access to research files describing sexual behavior of specific individuals who took part in the Kinsey studies (Hendel and Bard, 1973, p. 399); attempts to obtain evidence related to organized crime in public testimony from a knowledgeable criminologist (Nejelski and Lerman, 1971, p. 1092); and a request of a Senate committee to review files on individual families in an income-maintenance experiment because the committee "did not believe the way in which the numbers were turning out and wanted to 'add them up themselves'" (Kershaw and Small, 1972, p. 271).

An attempt to locate examples of pressure, formal and informal, to disclose research data received wide publicity. Under sponsorship that included all major national social science associations, the project compiled documentation on specific instances brought to its attention. Although 245 instances where confidentiality was a problem were identified, only 55 involved attempts to obtain access to confidential information, and the threat of a subpoena was present in only a few dozen instances. Many of the efforts to obtain information were in fact initiated by sponsors, clients, or employers (Carroll and Knerr, 1976b).

One of the more dramatic cases in which an investigator lost control of confidential information involved a research project—sponsored by federal agencies—that focused on the performance of organizations engaged in federally funded research. A university professor, on leave to a nonprofit research organization, acted as principal investigator, promising the research organizations that all information would be confidential. Once the project was completed, a federal research administrator demanded to know the identity of the organizations that had provided confidential information. Despite considerable efforts on the part of the principal investigator, the nonprofit research organization eventually provided the identities to the federal administrator. This case is unusual because the "respondents" were not individuals, but research organizations, and the federal administrator wanted the information for its value in assessing the quality of the work completed by the organizations; seriously detrimental effects for the "respondents" were a clear possibility. The case is still being disputed and is now under review by the Committee on Scientific Freedom and Responsibility of the American Association for the Advancement of Science (source confidential).

      Perhaps even more unusual are the interagency disputes within the federal government. The General Accounting Office (GAO) is charged with determining if federal funds are being used as expected by Congress. Its audits usually involve contracts for equipment or services, where a precise count of goods or activities is possible; different problems develop with respect to research projects. While data are sometimes simply reanalyzed by the GAO staff, in some cases it has requested the names and addresses of respondents in social experiments so that interviews can be verified or even repeated. In one such instance, the same respondents had been promised complete confidentiality by the investigators. Moreover, the normal changes that occur over time would be expected to create somewhat different responses to any replication of an interview, particularly if the experimental variables were having the intended effect. No universally satisfactory resolution to these problems has been developed, although compromises—including having a GAO audit team present during the course of the research—have been tried (Baratz and Marvin, 1978).

      The extent to which there have been legal attempts to require disclosure of information and identification of sources is difficult to establish with certainty. But there clearly have been attempts to gain access to information gathered in confidence and some of them have been successful. The situation confronted by newspersons can be considered as a basis for comparison. A recent survey of 1,470 newspersons and editors (a representative, though not random, sample) found that 20 percent of those who returned the questionnaire (975) and answered the question (869) reported being served with a subpoena at some time; 54 percent of those subpoenaed indicated that they had eventually provided the information, even though some had resisted (Blasi, 1971). This is substantially greater than the 8 percent of 314 social scientists who indicated that they had "a confidentiality problem" in their recent research, based on a national survey late in 1975 and early 1976 (Carroll and Knerr, 1976a); very few of the "confidentiality problems" involved subpoenas.

In summary, it would appear that while a few dozen subpoenas—less than ten have been clearly identified—may have been issued to social science investigators, hundreds have been issued to newspersons. In any news organization there are probably several individuals who have had to confront a subpoena that required disclosure of information or—more critical for reporters—the source of the information. In contrast, it is unusual for a social scientist to know any investigator who has been served with a subpoena. Experience with subpoenas for the two groups is thus substantially different.

Evidence on the effects of the legal subpoena, or of failure to be able to guarantee confidentiality, on the success of research is more difficult to develop. There are, however, several specific case examples, some relevant evidence in the literature related to survey research, and, as a basis for comparison, judgments of newspersons on the influence of subpoenas on their data-gathering potential. The most dramatic example of research disrupted as the result of a subpoena involved a Senate committee's disclosure of data acquired from the study of urban youth gangs (King, 1971). The project was terminated immediately after these data were made public; the investigators had experienced difficulty establishing rapport with the gang members, and the public disclosure was thought to have destroyed the already fragile relationship (Walsh, 1969b). In the study of researchers who encountered problems of confidentiality, only four additional incidents of disrupted research could be located after a national, multidisciplinary search (Carroll and Knerr, 1976b). In sum, the number of research projects that have actually been terminated because of public disclosure of data is very small, although there may be others that were not initiated over concern for lack of protection.

There are a number of examples of problems, complications, and additional expenses generated by threats to the integrity of data. They include: the need to cope with subpoenas in an income-maintenance experiment (Kershaw and Small, 1972); the scholars who were entangled in the legal system over subpoenas issued to determine the source of the publication of the "Pentagon Papers" (Nejelski and Peyser, 1975); the creation of substantially more complicated record-keeping systems—with some files maintained outside the country—to minimize the potential for public .disclosure through subpoena (Walsh, 1969a; Boruch, 1971b); and the modification of files to prevent the identification of specific individuals, thereby reducing the precision of analysis that is possible (Campbell and others, 1975). While research can proceed under a threat of subpoena, defense against the legal system requires resources and ingenuity that could better be devoted to scientific research.

A survey of the literature related to the effects of variations in "promised confidentiality" on the information provided by research participants—emphasizing respondents in survey research—found that participants' responses appear to be unaffected if they consider the information innocuous; credible promises of confidentiality do not affect the responses (Boruch, 1975). But if the procedures are considered likely to provide anonymity, more information is obtained from respondents about sensitive issues (such as abortions or drug use). Hence, the respondents' confidence in the ability of investigators to assure anonymity through immunity from legal subpoena could have an effect on the candor with which they provide sensitive information. A national sample of 314 social science researchers indicated that 73 percent agreed "strongly" or "somewhat" that "legal protection is necessary to ensure subject cooperation;" 48 percent agreed "strongly" or "somewhat" that "legal protection is necessary to reduce my own inhibitions" (Carroll and Knerr, 1976a, p. 417).

The threat of subpoena is very real for newspersons, one of five having been served with a subpoena. In interviews with newspersons and editors Blasi (1971) found that the threat of subpoena resulted in instances of refusals to provide information about stories and a reduction in the rapport between reporters and their sources (a reduced willingness of both parties to tolerate tape recorders). There were also instances of improved relationships between sources and journalists who specialized in militant and radical groups (when newspersons were jailed). In a questionnaire survey, 80 percent of the respondents stated that they felt that the threat of the subpoena had *not* affected their ability to cover a story "in the last 18 months"; 10 percent said there was a detrimental effect, and 10 percent "didn't know." The "subpoena threat" is seen as more of a problem for those covering trials or radical and militant groups than for other newspersons.

   This section has reviewed the current status of a special privilege for social science investigators regarding the content and identification of sources of their research data. Current legal standards are based on the assumption that the obligation to facilitate accurate and informed decisions in judicial and administrative proceedings should take precedence over any promises of confidentiality to participants or possible effects upon future data collection activities. The analogy to the privilege for applied professionals is weakened by the lack of benefit to the research participants, whereas the major benefactor of the privilege for applied professionals is the client-patient. While the analogy to newspersons is somewhat more direct, if only because the major benefactor of both unhindered scientific research and journalistic investigation is society in general, only a portion of social science research would be encompassed by an extended "newsperson's shield," since the majority of such research involves more than observation and recording of everyday events. Several model statutes have been proposed to cover social science investigators; these tend to be comparable to, or more extreme than, those extended to other professional groups.

   Although a general privilege for researchers has not been incorporated into the legal system, there are examples of privileges extended to data associated with particular projects. The most obvious of these involve the U.S. Census and the Social Security Administration, but special federal legislation has also provided immunity for records related to approved drug research, regardless of sponsorship, and any research supported by the Law Enforcement Assistance Administration (generally related to crime or the criminal justice system). While data collected from research oriented toward resolution of policy issues do not have privileged status, it has been argued that data of this kind might be covered under the concept of executive privilege.

A convincing argument that special legislation is needed to establish an investigator's privilege would require documentation for three points: (1) that the number of subpoenas initiated for social science data or sources has been considerable, (2) that this has had a clearly detrimental effect on the products of social science research, and (3) that the benefits from the imposition of "compulsory process" are less than the benefits from unhindered social science research. When the situation of social science investigators is compared to that of newspersons, the number of subpoenas issued to investigators appears to be quite modest—perhaps less than a dozen in comparison to the hundreds that have been issued to newspersons. Further, few effects of the subpoena process seem to be in evidence; the effects as perceived by newspersons appear to be modest and idiosyncratic. Justification of the benefits of social science research to society is a major issue associated with all problems discussed in this book.

It seems reasonable to conclude that, aside from the special case of those doing research on crime and the criminal justice system, there is little evidence that the subpoena threat is a major problem for social science research. The question may really be one of morale or recognition; the subpoena threat is clear evidence that the value of the social science enterprise is not recognized by current legal standards. A legally sanctioned researcher's (or scholar's) privilege would be tantamount to recognition that the work of social scientists is important, at least as important as the activities promoted by "compulsory process." However, this appears to be an ineffective rationale for the passage of legislation; it seems unlikely that elected officials (many with legal training) would adopt a privileged status for a professional group just to provide it with a "status symbol."

An alternative would be to expand the current procedure for providing immunity for specific projects or activities. While only special types of projects are now granted immunity from subpoena, each specified by legislative statute or the constitution, this could be expanded to allow any project to be approved in advance of its inception, regardless of subject matter, purpose, or source of financial support. A review could be completed and immunity granted within the U.S. attorney general's office. This would have

the advantage of allowing immunity to be given for specific projects, without the need for special legislation related to a specific
area of research. Further, it would not involve extending a special
privilege to a poorly controlled mass of professionals with diverse
political and intellectual orientations. The major disadvantage is
that confidential data collected outside the context of a specific
approved project would not be covered; it is this type of confidential data that led to the subpoenas issued to scholars in the investigation of the "Pentagon Papers."

State (Government Agencies) as Investigator

Many activities developed, initiated, and executed by government legislative or administrative agencies can be considered
research. In such cases the investigator is not an individual or research organization but an agency that represents the people. Two
rights—entrusted to these agencies by society—have been suggested as justifying such research: the right to develop useful
knowledge about social problems or social conditions (so that appropriate actions to ameliorate a problem or undesirable condition
can be taken) and the right to vary programs in attempting to determine the most efficient or effective course of action (Capron,
1975).

The right to collect descriptive data related to a specific social problem or condition is usually established through legislation
adopted by elected officials. This presumably reflects the judgments of citizens about the needs of society. Such social approval
not only provides the legitimation (or authority) for such activity
but directs the focus of research efforts to those problems considered most pressing. The right to engage in systematic experimentation to improve the effectiveness or efficiency of social programs
has been adopted as a statute applying to at least one agency. The
Social Security Act specifies (Title 42 USCS 1315): "In the case of
any experimental, pilot, or demonstration project which, in the
judgment of the Secretary [of HEW], is likely to assist in promoting
the objectives of [specific references to various objectives], in a state
or states . . . the Secretary [of HEW] may waive compliance with
any of the requirements of [references to specific requirements],
as the case may be, to the extent and for the period he finds nec-

essary to enable such state or states to carry out such project." In short, subject to some restrictions, various program alternatives or trial projects may be conducted.

In several cases the courts have upheld the exercise of this right afforded the Secretary of HEW. A study of the effects of requiring welfare recipients to pay a nominal cost (a maximum of three dollars per month) to determine the effect on the utilization of health care resources (consultations with physicians, drug purchases, and the like) was found to be within the scope of authorized demonstration projects; all of the arguments for terminating the project related to the interpretation of statutes regarding equal and just treatment for welfare recipients (*California Welfare Rights Organization* v. *Richardson,* 1972). Again, an attempt was made to determine the impact of requiring employable members of families receiving assistance to register for training and employment in selected social service districts of a single state. This project was also found to be within the scope of the privilege, even though representatives of the welfare recipients claimed they were denied equal protection and due process (*Aguayo* v. *Richardson,* 1973).

It is clear that individual administrators must represent public interests in the design and supervision of research. It has been argued that experimental programs that compare the effects of two treatments on individuals are justified only when the administrators are genuinely uncertain or ambivalent about which treatment may best serve the participants. If the administrators have arrived at the conclusion that one course of action is actually superior—based upon whatever subjective evidence and personal impressions are considered relevant—then conducting the research merely to develop "scientific evidence" may not be justified. This argument, seriously entertained by those with legal training, makes the varying standards and criteria for developing confidence in knowledge quite apparent (Breger, 1976, p. 31; Fried, 1974, pp. 157–165).

In sum, it would appear that administrators representing the state have a right—almost a duty—to engage in certain types of research, and in some cases there is a clear legislative mandate to collect descriptive data. Administrators have systematically tried to develop better, or more efficient, programs ever since there have been administrators, but only recently have the intellectual and methodological techniques of science been incorporated into such activities. As long as the programs provide proper recognition of the individual rights of liberty, self-determination, equality of treatment, and due process—a complex problem in itself—there seems little evidence that the courts will interfere with such endeavors.

Relinquishing Rights

The ultimate legal justification for guaranteed rights or liberties is that they provide a restraint on the use of influence or power by government leaders responsible for the administration of the state. (Alternative interpretations are provided by Brown, 1975, and Veatch, 1978.) However, one of the rights provided to individuals is the right of self-determination, which implies that they should be able to forgo certain rights if they so wish. In order to ensure that individuals are not deprived of basic rights unjustly, the circumstances under which they may forgo rights are carefully circumscribed. Certain rights may be relinquished by two categories of individuals associated with the social science enterprise—research participants and investigators.

Research Participants and Informed Consent

In general, most individual rights are considered to be transferable—not "inalienable"—and an individual may forgo such rights if he or she wishes. However, this is not true for all rights, such as the right to life, freedom from mayhem, or actions that would constitute a public nuisance (violating the rights of others). Based on the notion that the king (representing the state) was entitled to healthy, productive citizens (who could engage in work and combat), it was illegal in earlier times for the individual to forgo the right to life (agree to self-murder or suicide) or to freedom from mayhem (an action that disables, disfigures, or renders a body useless). The modern justification for a nontransferable right to life and avoidance of mayhem is the assumption that all individuals should be capable of making productive contributions to society; to consent to mayhem could lead to becoming a ward of the state (Annas, Glantz, and Katz, 1977, pp. 50–53). This is the major rationale for prohibiting or regulating activities such as dangerous sports that may maim or cripple willing participants and for encouraging individuals to take "reasonable" safety precautions, using seat belts in cars and wearing safety helmets when riding motorcycles.

Except for these special rights, individuals are allowed the privilege of relinquishing almost any other rights they may have. The legal action (one recognized by the courts) that transfers these rights is the giving of consent. A concise history of the development of the legal notion of consent, and its increasing importance, is provided by Capron (1975, p. 137): "In the thirteenth century the criminal law against forcible injuries was extended to civil action for trespass. The interferences encompassed by the early law were so direct, severe, and even violent that the absence of consent could be assumed; as the scope for action for trespass increased, the absence of consent became an element of the cause of action. Some offenses might be illegal if committed without consent, but permissible with it or if consent were implied from the context. The rule that absence of consent is an element of action for assault and battery applied in medical treatment, as elsewhere." In short, if a person is modified or changed in substantial ways without his consent, that may be considered a trespass upon, or battery (unlawful touching) of, the person.

There is little question that the first authoritative application of consent to research with human participants was formalized by the Nuremberg tribunal during the trial of Nazi medical researchers. Emphasizing existing practices in medical research, the first statement of the Nuremberg Code (see Appendix 2) focuses upon informed consent, interpreted as having four important characteristics (Annas, Glantz, and Katz, 1977, pp. 6–7):

1. The individual must be legally competent to give consent.
2. The consent must be voluntary (free from force, fraud, duress, coercion, and the like).
3. The individual should have sufficient knowledge to make an enlightened decision.

4. The individual should understand, or comprehend, the elements of the subject matter (should know the possible outcomes and risks associated with each).

A review of judicial decisions related to medical research suggests that only the first three elements are required for therapeutic situations (where a patient is expected to receive direct benefits from the new procedure), but all four are considered necessary for any nontherapeutic research (Annas, Glantz, and Katz, 1977, p. 54).

Because of the importance of informed consent in the ordinary conduct of medical practice—it is involved whenever a physician obtains the cooperation of a patient for any therapeutic program—there has been substantial attention to this issue by the courts (Annas, Glantz, and Katz, 1977; Capron, 1975). Two points are of major relevance to this discussion. First, the criteria for "sufficient" knowledge has shifted from the "standard in the profession" to the following (*Halushka* v. *University of Saskatchewan*, 1965): "The subject of medical experimentation is entitled to a full and frank disclosure of all the facts, probabilities, and opinions which a reasonable man might be expected to consider before giving his consent." In short, the standard is to be set by judicial judgments of what a "reasonable" person would want to know rather than the practitioner's conception of what is relevant, perhaps based on what other practitioners are doing.

Second, a review of the court decisions regarding physicians engaged in medical practice (not research) suggests that (Annas, Glantz, and Katz, 1977, p. 58) "while many physicians complained bitterly about the informed consent doctrine, it is, in fact, almost impossible for a patient to win a suit founded on failure to obtain informed consent in the absence of independent negligence in the treatment by the physician." In short, even though informed consent is considered necessary in situations where a physician "trespasses" upon the person of the patient, its absence alone has been only an additional factor in cases where the patient charges that professional negligence or error has caused personal damage. By analogy, it would seem that failure to obtain technically correct informed consent, by itself, would not lead to a court-supported action involving a research project. Only if some other type of wrong could be demonstrated—invasion of privacy, extreme stress, or permanent injury—would lack of appropriate informed consent become a critical issue.

Substantial problems are encountered with special categories of research subjects—fetuses, children, prisoners, and the institutionalized mentally infirmed. Suggested standards specific to research on fetuses have recently been produced by the National Commission for the Protection of Human Subjects of Biomedical and Behavioral Research (1975). They are quite complex and take into consideration the stage of fetal development, whether or not abortion is anticipated, the informed consent of the mother, the wishes of the father, the extent to which the fetus is considered viable, whether or not the research has therapeutic value and for which party (mother or fetus). Research that involves the fetus is generally allowed to proceed but under very carefully prescribed conditions; the legal status of these recommendations has yet to be determined. Research with the fetus, however, is not likely to be a major concern among social science investigators.

Parents (or legal guardians) are generally allowed to provide consent for children when the child may receive direct benefits (such as in therapeutic research), but the consent of the child is also required for nontherapeutic research. The issue of determining when a child can provide informed consent has yet to be resolved; the recommended solutions tend to emphasize the criteria of age (ages ranging from six to fourteen have been suggested). It is possible that the investigator could be held responsible for determining if the child has the intelligence and maturity to understand the consequences involved. If a child cannot give personal consent, it may not be legal to involve him in any nontherapeutic research with a substantial risk of negative effects (Annas, Glantz, and Katz, 1977, pp. 94–96).

Individuals who are institutionalized—in prisons or mental institutions—raise special issues regarding consent to involvement in research. The problem has been especially acute for medical research with drugs as well as for some forms of psychotherapy (psychosurgery and electroshock therapy). The legal issues have become of greater concern as various types of behavior modification techniques—token economies (good behavior results in tokens that can be exchanged for luxuries or privileges), systematic desensitization (unrealistic fears are unlearned through confrontation in nonthreatening situations), and aversive conditioning (asocial or deviant desires are suppressed through association with unpleasant experiences, such as a mild electric shock)—have been adapted for use with institutionalized persons. The legal literature on behavior modification as applied to institutionalized populations is considerable; it stresses applications as therapeutic procedures (rather than scientific research), and associated issues concerning the right of the individual to accept or refuse treatment, and the extent to which behavior modification procedures violate the basic rights of the inmates, including the right to autonomy of thought ("Behavior Modification and . . .," 1975; Ayllon, 1975; Friedman, 1975; Kassirer, 1974; Levick and Wapner, 1975; Spece, 1972; Wexler, 1973; "The Nascent Right to . . .," 1967). Less attention is given to develop useful therapeutic techniques, such as ones that involve behavior modification, which is difficult to do without research opportunities. A recent development is the establishment of a "right to treatment" for mental patients involuntarily confined on the basis of a civil hearing. Involuntary confinement is assumed to imply that an effective treatment procedure is available, and this in turn implies that research with treatment procedures has and will be carried out ("*Wyatt* v. *Stickney* and . . .," 1973). (A comparable "right to rehabilitation" has been discussed for criminals, which might involve some behavior modification techniques, but it has no legal status.)

While it is reasonable to assume that most prisoners are capable of understanding what would be involved in a research program and the consequences to themselves, a question arises about the extent to which their decisions are voluntary—free from coercion or excessive persuasion. If the conditions in a prison are so bad that the only escape is to participate in research studies (some of which involve special living quarters), there might be doubt whether the individual's decision is completely voluntary, that is, whether anyone could reasonably refuse the offer. Standards for such participation have been changing; if research participation provides rewards equivalent to other forms of prison "employment" and if no individuals in positions of authority (guards or wardens) are involved in the request for participation, the prisoner's decision may be considered voluntary. It has been suggested that prisoners should have at least twenty-four hours to make a decision (rather than respond at the time a request is made) and access to a counselor who can advise the prisoner without having a vested interest in the outcome (Annas, Glantz, and Katz, 1977, pp. 132–134).

Involvement of institutionalized mental patients in research has raised questions of voluntariness, although the major focus in legal discussions has been upon their competency to provide legally valid consent. There is a clear trend for the courts to make a distinction between a person's institutionalized status and legal competency; in most states the determination of legal competence is distinct from the procedures that lead to institutionalization. The recent trend is to assume that any legally competent institutionalized individual has the right to provide consent for therapeutic research; consent for minors and those legally incompetent can be provided by their guardians. If the research activity provides no direct benefits for the participants (institutionalized mental patients), they must provide personal consent; this would imply that such research could not be conducted with legally incompetent patients. However, standards related to this mixture of research focus and the legal mental competence of participants are not well established; it may be that benign nontherapeutic research (low risk to the participants) may be conducted with the guardian's consent. It is possible that in the future courts will make a distinction between legal competence and the intellectual sophistication required to understand the possible effects of research experiences (Annas, Glantz, and Katz, 1977, pp. 182–183).

While the Nuremberg Code is an appropriate standard for evaluating much research completed with human subjects, there are two major problems associated with its criteria when applied to social science research. The first is related to the participant's knowledge of the purposes and effects of the research project; this provides difficulties in instances where knowledge of the phenomenon under study would affect the phenomenon itself, a problem also found in many types of drug research (the "placebo effect" has already been discussed). The second problem lies in the assumption that informed consent should be required for all individuals participating in any type of research, even if it involves data collection related to public activities (such as a study of traffic patterns after a sports event) or secondary analysis of data collected for administrative purposes (such as the decennial U.S. Census data). Neither of these problems appears to have been given much attention by the legal system, perhaps because there have been no cases of "damage" associated with such research, whether informed consent existed or not.

From the perspective of the investigator, who is considered responsible for all effects of research, the proper implementation of informed consent is the major demonstration that the rights of the research participants received recognition and that the participant understood that some rights might be relinquished during participation in research. The greater the potential for risk— serious negative consequences—the greater the importance of utilizing a detailed informed consent procedure, on both moral and legal grounds. There are, as noted above, some research situations where it is not possible to achieve the scientific objectives and at the same time satisfy all the major features of informed consent—legally competent, voluntary, knowledgeable, and comprehending agreement from the participant. Some techniques for resolving this problem, developed within social science, were reviewed in Chapter Five; there is, at present, no evidence bearing on the legal status of these other procedures that demonstrate consideration for the rights and welfare of participants.

Investigators and Public Involvement in Research

A number of rights associated with the conduct of scientific activity (creating and testing of ideas) are based upon the assumption that the individual investigator is engaged in a private endeavor. As long as the research is the personal, private activity of the investigator, he or she can be assumed to have all the rights accorded an ordinary citizen. However, once the enterprise ceases to be a private, individual activity and involves either other individuals or the expenditure of public funds, the rights of other citizens become involved and the investigator may have to relinquish personal rights, often without "informed consent," that is, without full knowledge of what has been forgone.

All individuals are accorded the freedom of thought that is usually referred to as academic or scientific freedom when extended to investigators. The scope of human imagination is the only limit on the development of intellectual structures (theories) or scientific hypotheses. However, not all issues are available for exploration when the research involves other individuals; unrestricted freedom of thought does not imply unrestricted freedom to conduct research that may infringe upon the rights of others. As noted earlier in this chapter, a greater infringement upon the rights of participants is justified when the purposes of the research are in the public interest but under no conditions is an unrestricted right to engage in research justified.

For example, two important rights for most investigators— the right to privacy and the right to be recognized for intellectual contributions—appear to be affected by recent decisions regarding the confidential status of research proposals submitted for federal financial support. It is now clear that such research proposals are to be considered public documents, and this means that others may "borrow" and develop a scientific issue without acknowledgment of, or assistance from, the originator. Most scientific investigators would probably prefer not to waive these rights when applying for public support of research activity, and it would not necessarily be in the public interest for them to do so. This problem was not explicitly considered by the originators of the Freedom of Information Act, although it may be within the spirit of their intention, which was to make government decisions more open and accountable to the public.

Except for the rights of investigators to privacy and recognition for contributions, there has been very little attention given to the rights of individual investigators, although some has been shown to the rights of public officials to engage in research related to policy issues or public programs. This lack of attention to the rights of investigators involved in scientific research may result from a general bias in favor of the underdog, usually considered to be the research participant.

Rights of Future Generations

Current political and moral philosophies—and the legal system based upon these orientations—are organized around the rights, obligations, or interests of existing participants in the society. The major issues are those of control of resources and individual actions in the present or immediate future, and hence the emphasis upon the rights of existing individuals and the conditions under which these may be waived. Legal analysis traditionally focuses on review of past decisions as a source of solutions for current problems. There is, however, no question that future generations comprise a major category of individuals affected by current research, just as the current generations are the major benefactors of research conducted in the past. For some types of research, future generations may be more affected than any existing individuals. (The advances in child health care that have led to dramatic decreases in infant mortality and increased longevity led to benefits experienced by millions of individuals who were born after the knowledge was developed.) Further, the effects of failure to conduct research or of attempts to retard its development may be difficult to determine, for the absence of benefits—benefits forgone—may be impossible to estimate for any particular project.

In relation to current legal standards, future generations have several unique characteristics. First, and perhaps foremost, it is impossible to obtain their informed consent. It is possible only to speculate on what is in their best interests or the actions to which they might voluntarily consent. This is a major problem with research involving fetuses; it is not possible to obtain the informed consent of a potential member of a future generation. The same problem has been mentioned in discussions of clonal research, which involves the potential for production of biologically identical individuals. One argument was based, in part, on the "terrible consequences" for an individual to be identical to another, reflecting an interpretation of the personal accounts of identical twins; Kass, (1972).

A second important characteristic of future generations is that they are not consciously involved in the legal system, which is organized to resolve conflicts between parties that can be represented by counsel or political groups before the courts or legislatures (see Chapter Two for another solution suggested by Rawls, 1971). As a result, the interests and rights of future generations, which cannot retain attorneys or appear on their own behalf, are likely to be slighted in favor of those who can provide direct input into judicial and legislative decisions. The interests of future generations are frequently raised by those whose present interests coincide with those attributed to future generations—for example, by environmentalists promoting the maintenance of a scenic natural feature or investigators speculating on potential benefits for future generations. This may result in suspicions that unbiased representation of the future generation's interests is not being given. In brief, since the legal system is not organized to incorporate the interests of future generations in any systematic way, there may be little attention given to benefits they might receive from present activities, including scientific research.

In addition, the future benefits of any specific research project or program of activity are likely to be ambiguous, for it is widely recognized that many, although certainly not all, benefits from scientific research were not foreseen at the time the research was conducted. If a resolution of conflicting rights related to a specific project were in progress, and the potential benefits to the future generations were ambiguous, it would be no surprise to discover that the conflicting interests of present parties were given more emphasis; the effects on existing individuals would simply be more certain and easier to measure.

There are many examples of past research that involved some cost—often major in terms of contemporary standards, modest in terms of the standards of the time—that provided major benefits to present-day society. However, the current legal system does not encourage systematic attention to the rights of future generations; the informed consent of these generations cannot be obtained, and the effects of research projects on their welfare are ambiguous and difficult to estimate. It would appear that they are expected to make the best of the situation they will confront—the status of the physical environment, society, and scientific knowledge—when they arrive.

Conclusion

The major purpose of this chapter was to review the legal resolutions of a major dilemma that has developed with respect to social science research and the extent to which unambiguous legal standards are present. Obviously, a great deal of uncertainty remains; the number of possible conflicts exceeds the capacity of the legal and political systems to provide resolutions. However, the really critical question may be the extent to which important issues have been legally resolved. There seem to be four issues that are crucial—the rights of ordinary citizens (as participants), the issues associated with the waiver of these rights (standards for informed consent), the legal status of societal experiments (where individuals have no choice about participation), and the current status of a privileged relationship (immunity from the subpoena process) for research sources and information. Few other conflicts over rights, regardless of their challenging complexity or apparent importance, appear to have received substantial attention from legal scholars, the courts, or legislators.

The rights afforded ordinary citizens in the conduct of their everyday lives—the right to life, self-determination, privacy, freedom of thought, association, religion, and so forth—are the major factors governing the relationships between research participants and investigators. The legal standards that govern such relationships in the context of research projects are neither more nor less ambiguous than those governing ordinary social intercourse. Of importance to social science research is the lack of precision of standards for the right to be treated with dignity and self-respect. There is also little legal precedent for a right *not* to be deceived, and it is difficult for the courts to estimate the damages (costs) associated with the infringement of such rights. In brief, the relationships between investigators and participants are ultimately regulated by the legal standards governing the relationships between any two citizens.

Considerable attention has been given to the procedures to be followed for the waiver of rights—the criteria required for legally valid informed consent. Based upon the explication of the Nuremberg tribunal, informed consent includes four elements: legal capacity to consent, freedom from coercion or duress, knowledge of all relevant consequences, and comprehension of these consequences. The legal adequacy of the procedure is likely to be viewed from the perspective of a "rational participant" by the courts. Two additional rights are involved when there is no choice about involvement in the research (that is, when the research is supervised by government agencies): the research activity itself must meet the standards of due process (related to legitimate public objectives and conducted in a fashion that will minimize burdens to participants) and equality of treatment (participants are not to be selected for special treatment without justification, and the selection procedure should not discriminate against special categories of citizens).

The right of citizens to engage in research is not mentioned in the U.S. Constitution, although it is legally recognized as (perhaps) one aspect of freedom of thought. Research must be conducted within the constraints necessary for respecting the rights of all citizens. The right of the state to engage in research to further legitimate state ends—solutions for new problems, more effective or efficient programs, general expansion of knowledge—is also recognized. As long as the criteria of due process and equality of treatment are followed, the state may engage in research without the informed consent of the participants. Since the elected officials are providing surrogate informed consent for the citizen-participants involved in societal experiments, the more features and aspects of the research that are included in legislation rather than simply based upon the judgments of administrators, the more likely it is that the courts will support the research programs.

One legal privilege of major concern to social science investigators—legal immunity from compulsory disclosure through the subpoena process—is clearly not afforded to *any* professional group engaged in nontherapeutic research (the case of physicians who use new procedures for a patient's benefit is a different one). Despite considerable discussion and controversy over this issue, it is clear that the situation of investigators engaged in research is quite different from that of applied professionals and newspersons. If such a privilege were established, it would probably be based upon legislative action; it is unlikely that the courts would recognize such a privilege, since all existing legal privileges have been established by legislative statute.

A review of available evidence suggests that it might be difficult to argue convincingly that a special privilege for social science research data is justified. There is only modest evidence to suggest that the potential disclosure of data through legal subpoena is a major threat to the general conduct of social science research. However, for specific types of projects, such as those related to the criminal justice system and illegal activity, the threat of a subpoena is more imminent and potentially disruptive than for others. A legitimate social benefit may be obtained if legal immunity is provided for special projects, a step that is now possible. Since precedents for such "project immunity"—rather than immunity for a professional group—are now present, it may be possible to extend this review process to allow any project to be considered for immunity, regardless of its sponsorship or purposes. This may provide adequate protection from disclosure for specific, bounded research activities; it may not be adequate for social scientists who engage in systematic collection of sensitive material outside the context of a formally recognized project.

A review of the writings of legal scholars and judicial decisions reveals that there is a substantial bias in the legal system in the resolution of problems toward elaborate, complicated, and technically complex applications of the social compact philosophy. Such decisions and judgments attempt to explicate the conflicting rights of all parties to the dispute, speculating on the appropriate allocation of the rights between citizens and the state and, among citizens within the state. Serious consideration of an alternative analysis—a utilitarian emphasis on the costs and benefits associated with various alternative actions—occurs only in special cases, where the potential benefits to existing individuals are direct and substantial or where no basic rights are threatened. Such analyses may be more prevalent in reviews of alternatives by legislatures than in judicial decisions. The legal emphasis on rights tends to reduce attention to the effects on those most likely to benefit from the conduct of research or to suffer negative effects from its absence (in the form of benefits forgone).

One thing is clear: regardless of the analyses, judgments, or weight of judgments amassed by scientific investigators, the courts have the final say. If there are substantial problems or dissatisfactions with the current legal system or the decisions and precedents it generates, scientific investigators—including social scientists—will not find remedies in their own resources, professional associations, organizational affiliations, and the like. It may be necessary to retain competent legal counsel to advise on the conduct of scientific activities to avoid legal conflicts. Failing this, the only reasonable course is to attempt to change the law through legislation adopted by elected officials. However, since a substantial majority of elected officials are attorneys or emphasize legal analyses, it will be necessary to formulate arguments and positions in the terminology of the legal system or risk misunderstanding and failure. The most drastic alternative, revolution and a new social order, hardly seems reasonable.

Part Three

Perhaps the most fundamental issue to be resolved by social scientists is the relationship between their professional activities and their role in society as citizen-intellectuals. In other words, what orientations help to minimize complications associated with incongruencies between scientific obligations and the responsibilities of citizenship? The attempts to resolve this problem are reflected in the different philosophies and strategies regarding the appropriate orientations for scientists. Several of these strategies and the extent to which they provide satisfactory resolutions are reviewed in Chapter Eleven.

Decision makers of most modern, complex societies have determined—with varying degrees of enthusiasm—that the benefits of a permanent scientific community outweigh the costs. But individuals who choose a scientific career may find themselves con-

338

The Social Scientist's Relationship with Society

fronted with several conflicts, such as the research dilemma associated with the study of social and human phenomena. Further, any scientist, regardless of the focus of his or her research, may confront the application of knowledge dilemma: What responses are available to scientists when scientific knowledge may be utilized to achieve goals inconsistent with their personal values? The conditions under which scientists can take effective action when the product of the scientific enterprise—useful knowledge—is used for objectives that they feel, as moral persons, would not be good for society or mankind are the focus of Chapter Twelve. A review of the major conclusions developed within this volume, speculation on selected future developments related to the research dilemma, and strategies for maintaining societal support of the social science enterprise are treated in the concluding chapter.

11

Variations
in Professional
Philosophies

Investigators are most likely to devote their full attention to professional work when they see little discrepancy between their scientific orientations and the values they hold as citizen-intellectuals. If they are satisfied (or unconcerned) with the current social, economic, or political structures of society, their full energies can be devoted to the controversies and challenges associated with the development of science—creating theories, gathering data, discussing the relative merits of various explanations, and so forth. Few scientists, however, find themselves in such idyllic situations, where they feel comfortable devoting themselves entirely to science without concern for the interrelationship between the scientific enterprise and society or, in other words, for the incongruencies that can develop between scientific obligations and the responsibilities of citizenship. Several strategies may be adopted to resolve this dilemma. One is to focus upon the dilemma itself, as implied by the exhortation to practice "reflective sociology" (Gouldner, 1970), but most scientists seem to have chosen an approach that will lead to the active promotion of scientific or personal values.

One solution is to accept the current political, social, and economic aspects of society as satisfactory (or the best available) and to emphasize the development of scientific knowledge—the mode of the autonomous investigator. This is usually accompanied by the assumption that the ultimate product of the scientific enterprise will contribute to the welfare of society. An alternative is to accept the existing political processes in society and to emphasize the usefulness of science in solving social problems; applied scientists may be interested in both scientific advancement and the improvement of society; accepting influence from nonscientists distinguishes them from autonomous investigators.

Other strategies center on the promotion of citizen-intellectual values; these reflect a turning away from strictly scientific objectives. A societal mentor might use scientific theory, data, and research (often selectively) to counsel society and promote desired changes. A more extreme form of this approach would be to engage in social activism to promote specific political values or advance the interests of special groups in society, perhaps by conducting research to justify a predetermined position or to provide a political advantage for selected individuals.

This chapter will discuss these strategies in relation to three categories of issues. The first is based upon the assumption that, regardless of which strategy or orientation is adopted, social scientists select problems for attention and work to develop satisfactory solutions. This leads to contemplation of the source of the problem selected for attention, the criteria for an acceptable solution, the source of such criteria, the nature of the individuals who determine the extent to which the problem has been solved, and the characteristics of social scientists who may be attracted to such a strategy. A second set of issues involves the types of relationships that individuals with various strategies or orientations might develop within society, including the nature and extent of interdependencies (between the scientific enterprise and societal decision makers), the potential influence of different strategies on societal or practical affairs, the conditions under which societal acceptance of such strategies might be expected, and the extent to which social scientists will be seen as credible independent experts. A third issue—perhaps the most important for this discussion—is the success of each strategy as a solution not only to the potential moral dilemmas encountered when a researcher adopts a complex role in society but also to the research dilemma and the application of knowledge dilemma.

No matter which orientation is emphasized by social scientists, some degree of interdependence with the rest of society will be present. A satisfactory relationship (reflecting such interdependence) between the scientific community and the individuals that represent society—societal decision makers—would be enhanced by an atmosphere of mutual trust and respect. The extent and nature of the interdependence implied by these orientations and the degree of trust in social scientists that can be anticipated from societal decision makers will be the topic of the last section.

The Autonomous Investigator

Perhaps the most widely acknowledged orientation among scientists is the single-minded pursuit of knowledge with minimal concern for relevance to practical applications. Issues selected for attention are generally developed within the scientific community or reflect the curiosity of the individual scientist. The strategies for defining and approaching intellectual problems and determining whether they have been or should be solved are those of the scientific community, itself a special subculture that emphasizes complex, esoteric technical activities and develops unique and abstruse criteria for incorporating new contributions into the body of shared scientific knowledge. Such incorporation usually depends on the extent to which the new contribution provides an explicit solution to a significant intellectual issue and is consistent with available data.

The autonomy of the individual scientist is related, first of all, to the independence of the professional community of scientists

from society; such independence develops because of the focus and
special features of their activities—difficult, if not impossible, for
nonscientists to understand and evaluate. Secondly, there is the
independence that the individual scientist is accorded in relation
to other members of the scientific community. Adherence to the
norm of scientific freedom provides considerable autonomy for
each investigator, since the worth of his or her efforts is not evaluated until presented to the scientific community for review.

While the actual completion of scientific work may be quite
complex and detailed, the strategy of "total immersion" into scientific norms and values is an uncomplicated philosophical position that minimizes confrontation with moral dilemmas. It may be
appealing to those individuals, often forming the nucleus of a scientific community, who are challenged, fascinated, and motivated
by complex intellectual puzzles. The elaborate guidelines and procedures for determining if scientific puzzles have been solved may
reflect a desire to have unambiguous criteria for accepting solutions as well as a conservative orientation toward new knowledge,
that is, a cautiousness in accepting new ideas until one is convinced
they are scientifically useful. Investigators, deeply committed to the
scientific enterprise, may assume that it is independent of any particular social system, although they may entertain some concern
for the contributions of science to mankind as a whole. Such independence is easier to defend if the phenomena studied are not
directly related to practical applications or individual members of
society (as in the case with a great deal of physical science) or require little or no societal support in the form of resources or privileges. Although almost all scientists require support for personal
subsistence, not all require extensive resources to conduct
investigations.

Emphasis upon autonomy is reflected in suggestions regarding special rights for scientists (Sieghart, 1972; Sieghart and
others, 1973; United Nations Economic, Social, and Cultural Organization, 1975). Adopting the position that the promotion of science is in the best interests of mankind and concerned over abuses
experienced by some scientists (imprisonment, removal from scientific occupations, persecution, and so forth), various groups have

developed lists of "scientists' rights." (Council for Science and Society, 1977, pp. 32–49). These usually include:

- right to scientific education
- right to work as scientists
- protection of scientific freedom
- freedom of expression and opinion
- freedom of movement and residence (within a country)
- freedom of entry (into another country)
- freedom of assembly and association

Most of these rights are similar to those set forth for all human beings in the United Nations Declaration of Human Rights (Appendix 1), but they are somewhat more specific: the right to a *scientific* education rather than the right to a public education, the right to work *as scientists* rather than the general right to work, and—perhaps the most controversial—freedom of entry into any country, which might conflict with the right of those in a given country to select their own visitors or citizens.

The justification for scientists' rights is distinct from that for ordinary rights. The major rationale for ordinary rights is that they provide guarantees that typical individuals will not be abused by those controlling society (effects for individuals not accepted without a just reason and due process). Rights for scientists are justified on the basis that they will promote the ability of scientists to (1) make a contribution to knowledge that may, in turn, benefit mankind, and (2) fulfill a major obligation to society by ensuring that all interested parties will be informed regarding the consequences and implications of the application of new knowledge. This argument assumes that scientists are a unique and valuable resource for mankind and that maximum value will be obtained from this resource only if proper conditions—those specified by the list of rights—are met. For those who disagree that scientists are a valuable public resource, the justification for these special rights may thus not be persuasive.

There are, of course, some problems associated with the implementation of these rights. Perhaps most crucial is determining those individuals who should be considered scientists and accorded special privileges. Further, there has been minimal attention to the restrictions or obligations accepted by scientists to justify such privileges—professionals with unique legal privileges usually accept special obligations or restrictions. Given the special nature of some scientific rights and the controversy over the value of the scientific enterprise in many societies (Samoilovich, 1975), it seems unlikely that these rights will soon acquire legal status.

The adoption of the role of an autonomous scientist, participating in a scientific community independent of the greater society and emphasizing the development of new knowledge and open dissemination of such knowledge to all interested parties, is a straightforward solution to the dilemma of the relationship between professional and citizen-intellectual values. The two activities are viewed as separate and distinct; because citizen-intellectual values are seen as unrelated to professional scientific concerns, this has been referred to as the "value free" conception of science. It is probably a more successful resolution for those studying physical rather than social phenomena, for concentrated attention to physical phenomena may not bring them into contact with unpleasant aspects of society. Those who study human and social phenomena and find various aspects of society inconsistent with their citizen-intellectual values may promote other solutions to this dilemma. It is not uncommon to describe the inadequacies of the autonomous investigator (value free) perspective as a justification for the adoption of an alternative (Foss, 1977); several are described in the following sections.

The Applied Scientist

A slightly different orientation emphasizes the application of scientific knowledge to the solution of practical problems, either those confronted by individuals or those associated with structures or processes within society. While the selection or specification of such problems may be influenced by scientists, the final acceptance may depend upon the judgments of nonscientists: legislators, executives, administrators, counselors, applied professionals, and so forth. Similarly, the criteria for a suitable solution will be those emphasized by nonscientists—elimination of the problem or reduction to an acceptable level—and will generally require close attention to economic factors. For some scientists—those who wish to have an influence upon the practical affairs of society and are less attracted than others to the elegant solution of esoteric intellectual puzzles—applied science might represent a satisfying combination of the two activities. As an orientation toward scientific work, however, the application of science to practical problems may be the most complex of all alternatives. Not only are the individuals who contribute to the specification of important issues diverse and difficult to identify, but the criteria utilized for the development of problems and for determining if they have been solved are likely to be implicit, ambiguous, and varied. Particularly complex is the inclusion of economic considerations in applied analyses—seldom emphasized in "pure" research—for these require attention to the relative advantages gained in relation to additional expenditures for each alternative solution. In other words, they require completion of a utilitarian analysis in its classical, cost-benefit form.

To be successful, this orientation requires that scientists accept a position of substantial interdependence with society. Not only are ordinary citizens involved in the development of problems and of criteria for determining if the problems have been solved, but the implementation of solutions requires the willing cooperation of others. In most cases, scientists are in an advisory capacity, and final decisions regarding application rest with nonscientists. While there is the problem of obtaining the cooperation of typical citizens to implement programs, there are advantages to a position of interdependence when funds are sought for the completion of research and pilot programs.

Successful implementation of this strategy, which emphasizes the mutual interdependence between scientists and societal decision makers, requires that an atmosphere of mutual trust be maintained. Hence, the credibility of scientists as unbiased technical specialists can be a critical element. An objective perspective may not be difficult to sustain when research or development programs are designed to benefit individuals; the wide agreement on the nature of personal benefits (health, positive outlook, and the like) makes it easy for scientists to separate professional objectives

and personal values. Such a distinction may be of greater importance and more difficult to maintain if it is a question of multifar-
ious societal or organizational problems. If attempts at separation
are not successful, the societal decision makers may be suspicious
of the scientist's professional judgments and concerned that their
personal political values may have influenced their professional
analysis, whether consciously or unconsciously.

Investigators or scientists who adopt this perspective may
find themselves in the most difficult of all situations, for the major
moral dilemmas may be more salient and their resolution more
complex with more alternatives to consider. Recurrent confrontation with both the values and standards of the scientific community and the societal norms associated with practical applications
may heighten awareness of numerous incongruencies. Association
with projects that have important practical applications may lead
to more frequent confrontation with the basic research dilemma,
as important features of participants' rights and welfare undergo
examination and possible modification. At the same time, research
with important phenomena that has clear applied value may justify
research with a greater potential for infringement upon participants' rights and welfare than if the only benefits were of a scientific nature (with uncertain practical applications). Social scientists involved in the application of knowledge may be more aware
of potential effects that might be inconsistent with their personal
values but may also be in a position to have greater access to—and
influence upon—nonscientists responsible for the final decisions
regarding application. In sum, investigators who attempt to further the interrelation between the scientific enterprise and practical applications may find themselves confronted with moral dilemmas more often than is the autonomous scientist. But they may
also find that their ability to influence the resolution of such dilemmas in a satisfying manner is enhanced.

Societal Mentor

When a social scientist encounters a condition or activity in
society, either through personal knowledge, research, or informed
speculation, that is inconsistent with her values as a citizen-intel-

lectual, this may prompt a social commentary or critical essay. Acting as a societal mentor—providing critical evaluations and suggestions regarding the structure and institutions of society—has a long, valued history in political science, sociology, and other disciplines emphasizing social philosophy.

A critical issue regarding the development of such social commentaries is the standard or value to be promoted. One strategy is to adopt those values that are considered universally acceptable within society. A societal mentor might, for instance, bring public attention to serious lapses of human rights (incidents of malnutrition, physical abuse, salary inequities, and so forth). A slightly more abstract value would be "freedom of choice" (Kelman, 1965); here the mentor might promote programs or activities that increase the perceived autonomy of the individual, either by creating more actual alternatives for individuals (such as more occupational choices) or by increasing the scope of perceived alternatives (through consciousness raising, psychological growth, reduction of inhibitions, and so forth).

A societal mentor might also examine the relevance of the professional activities of social scientists for promoting the survival and evolution of society, a belief perhaps based on the assumption that continued evolution of a social system will lead to a more perfect society, a better fit with the physical and sociopolitical environment (Foss, 1977). Unfortunately, such general standards do not lead to unambiguous directives regarding professional activities. For example, the research of an autonomous investigator may be thought to provide knowledge that will eventually facilitate the survival, evolution, and "perfection" of society and, hence, to be consistent with these criteria.

The attempt to provide an objective examination of critical features of the social order is comparable to the work of an autonomous scientist in its emphasis upon an aloofness from the structures or processes of society. While empirical data may be included in the discussion, the strategy is distinctive because the commentator's personal values are obviously emphasized in the evaluation. Those concerned with the nature of social systems and seeking to encourage their improvement, but not responsible for the structures or processes in society, may be attracted to this orientation.

The degree of interdependence between a societal mentor and society may be quite low. Except for personal sustenance and access to libraries or public data, few resources are required to pursue social criticism. While some adherents to this approach may engage in data analysis, there is seldom a need for special privileges or substantial resources to conduct extensive investigations. Nevertheless, it is not clear that a societal mentor is seen as an integral part of the social order—the direct relevance of broad analyses to the immediate problems of organizing and administering a society may be slight. The credibility of societal mentors as sources of independent judgments on the nature of phenomena or technical issues may not be a major concern; they are seldom sought for such information. In a sense, the effects of such analyses may be quite similar to those of mass media editorialists, philosophers, concerned citizens, and others who express an interest in the creation of an ideal (or at least better) society and—in turn—affect the normal political processes.

As a resolution to the general moral dilemma, the societal mentor's perspective is antithetical to that of the autonomous scientist. The activities of the mentor are explicitly designed to further personal or political values, in the sense of achieving an ideal society; concern for scientific principles or the advancement of knowledge is generally secondary. Potential dilemmas are avoided by reducing the emphasis on scientific objectives and emphasizing the obligations of a citizen-intellectual. The relevance of this stance to the research dilemma is less clear, since the types of issues approached by a societal mentor may not be amenable to research except in the form of assembling descriptive information, often of a public nature. The societal mentor probably will not confront the research dilemma very often. The lack of systematic involvement in activities designed to develop scientific knowledge of the basic features of social and human phenomena makes it unlikely that a full-time societal mentor will be the first to be aware of potential applications of new knowledge that can lead to detrimental effects for society, although once such problems are identified, a societal mentor may contribute to identification of possible consequences, positive or negative.

In sum, this strategy provides a clear solution to the possible incongruencies that can develop between obligations as a scientist and obligations as a citizen by total emphasis on the latter. It may lead to a minimal interdependence upon society and infrequent confrontation with the research dilemma or the application of knowledge dilemma. As a consequence, adoption of this perspective can minimize confrontation with some moral predicaments associated with the scientific enterprise.

Social Activist

Social activism (direct attempts to change the mechanisms, processes, structures, or institutions of society) is distinct from the approach of social mentors, who may restrict themselves to persuasive arguments (verbal and written) by the emphasis on changing specific programs, procedures, or even—in some cases—occupants of societal positions. While this strategy solves the general moral dilemma by emphasizing personal political values to the exclusion of scientific principles, it may be associated with more immoderate stances, including the modification or misuse of scientific procedures or techniques to achieve personal political objectives.

Full development of the rationale for a social activist strategy reflects a specific set of assumptions about the nature of society and the development of social science (Lundman and McArlane, 1976; Christie, 1976):

1. There is a true state of nature that can be determined through the use of proper investigational techniques.
2. Most individuals in society distort the true state of affairs, perhaps unconsciously, in attempts to persuade, influence, or control other individuals or resources.
3. As all segments of society are involved in competition for resources and influence, no segment of society has an undistorted view of the true state of affairs.
4. The role of the social scientist is to take a position, aloof from intrasocietal conflicts, that will allow determination of the true state of affairs.
5. Those currently in control of resources and information are in a position to systematically distort the true state of affairs (since they control the information) and they do so to serve their own interests—maintenance of influence and control.

6. Given the opportunity, those in control of resources and information will prohibit or discourage any activity that leads to the
   presentation of information or descriptions that are inconsistent
   with those they create or any activity that may compromise their
   ability to maintain influence and control.

This reasoning provides the basis for suspicion and distrust
of those in legitimate positions of authority when they try to influence a research project. It is assumed that social scientists have two
alternatives. They may either (1) accept support and resources
from those in control of the society, and with it control over their
investigations; or (2) attempt to be independent, objective investigators, pursuing sensitive topics without the controls and assistance provided by traditional forms of support (such as the federal
government or large foundations). The study of many human and
social phenomena, such as perception, attitude change, influence
structures in small groups, and so forth offers few challenges to
those in positions of influence; such research may be seen as politically neutral. However, the study of other phenomena (such as
government organizations or agencies) or the way the research on
the phenomena is designed may be seen as a political action, fa-
voring either the advantaged (in positions of influence) or the disadvantaged (in positions of dependence).

This position is presented as a contrast to the dominant alternative, a perspective that assumes agreement or consensus in
society regarding societal goals and the rights and privileges extended to various groups, that is, the "consensus methodology" (as
reflected in the orientations of autonomous or applied scientists).
The alternative, emphasizing the social scientist's identification
with one of several competing political groups, is referred to as
"conflict methodology," based on the assumption that all activity
of social scientists is political in nature and related to competition
(conflict) for political influence. The assumption that all research
reflects a political bias on the part of the investigator can then be
used as justification for denying or ignoring the rights or welfare
of particular participants when expedient for political objectives,
regardless of scientific issues or ordinary concepts of human rights.

For example, investigators involved in the study of public
organizations or agencies are encouraged to publicly disclose

"wrongdoing" on the part of responsible public officials. Even promises of confidentiality, it is argued, need not be honored if disclosure would serve to discourage further public "wrongdoing" (Galliher, 1973, 1974; Warwick, 1974). Investigators are urged to shift to a social activism orientation when confronted with occurrences that are, in their opinion, inappropriate; it is unclear what mechanisms would ensure that respondents are not subjected to unjust or unsubstantiated public criticism. This obligation goes somewhat beyond that accepted by lawyers, who are expected to report only anticipated crimes (legally defined) to the appropriate authorities, not the past misdeeds (by their own judgments) of their clients. The practice of withholding the ordinary rights of citizenship from any group of citizens based on a social category (such as their occupational responsibilities) is a dangerous precedent; it is the same practice that led to the persecution of Jewish German citizens by the Nazi government.

The source of problems emphasized by social activists may be related to their personal experiences or to contact with disadvantaged individuals. The criteria for whether or not a problem has been solved may be based upon the judgments of the social activist or the disadvantaged individuals, not necessarily on those standards adopted by the scientific enterprise, the intellectual community, or society as a whole. Social scientists with a tendency to identify with the disadvantaged, with considerable confidence in their own judgments, and with a conviction that social systems should be responsive to suggestions for improvement—and without delay—would probably be attracted to this perspective.

While there is no necessary relationship between the professional orientation of social scientists and the research methods they use, most individuals who emphasize social activism engage in research that requires few societal resources—participant or field observation, for example—or attempt to minimize their dependence upon the normal (public or "establishment") sources of research support. The extent to which the findings and observations of social activists are systematically incorporated into the decision-making processes in a democratic society is difficult to determine. While they may affect public discussions, they are a source of influence on political or societal values and objectives rather than on objective technical or scientific judgments. There is little reason to expect that the credibility of a social activist as a source of unbiased scientific or professional judgment will be very great. But as long as those pursuing a social activist strategy are honest and straightforward about their objectives and means and avoid attempts to deceive or manipulate either society or research participants, it seems unlikely there will be a systematic attempt to prevent them from pursuing their objectives; such pursuits, after all, are guaranteed by the right to free speech.

Social activism provides an unambiguous resolution of the general moral dilemma in its overriding emphasis upon political and personal values at the expense of scientific principles and standards, which it may in fact distort to achieve personal political objectives. Those who adopt this position will confront few moral dilemmas; this strategy may even bring about "resolution" of the research dilemma by allowing differential treatment of individuals based on the activist's judgment of their worth and value as members of society, regardless of their status as determined by the normal (or legal) procedures or standards. As with societal mentors, the lack of attention that social activists give to the development of new scientific knowledge may preclude awareness of the effects of applying new knowledge, although activists may recognize possible negative effects once the applications are publicized, especially if they affect a social category or subculture that the activist favors or identifies with. In brief, the adoption of the social activist perspective in its extreme form provides an easy solution to the moral dilemmas: it simply avoids any recognition of potential conflicts between rights and does this by giving single-minded attention to the promotion of a social cause, regardless of the implications for the development of scientific knowledge, treatment of particular research participants, or the relationship between the social science enterprise and society, its major source of support and encouragement.

Scientists and Society:
Interdependence and Mutual Trust

No matter which philosophy is adopted by a social scientist, either for a specific project or as a career orientation, there is some degree of dependence upon society, if only for sustenance (except

for those rare individuals who are independently wealthy). Look-
ing at the current social role of scientists, it becomes apparent that
control over the obligations and prerogatives associated with
professional positions in the scientific enterprise is the responsibility of society, represented by societal leaders (legislators, administrators, executives, and so forth), although such control is subject
to negotiation with the scientific community. Based on the assumptions that most scientists are at least minimally dependent
upon society and that the final decision regarding the social role
of scientists will be made by societal representatives, it is possible
to consider the effect of the various research perspectives on the
judgments of societal decision makers. Responses can be considered in terms of the extent and nature of autonomy thought appropriate for social scientists, the degree to which they are considered important societal resources, and the willingness to provide
societal support for the pursuit of activities reflecting each
orientation.

Because of the very loose relationship between the perspectives of scientists and the interpretations made by societal decision
makers of the dominant orientations within the scientific community, the following discussion must be speculative. Several events
may alter this relationship. First of all, a particular social scientist
may choose to adopt a combination of several perspectives, shifting
between orientations for different projects or at different stages
of his career; perhaps few social scientists can be permanently
identified with a given philosophical perspective. Secondly, even
if a given perspective can be identified with a particular scientist,
the philosophies dominant within an aggregate of social scientists
may be quite different. Finally, even if one perspective did dominate among social scientists, or some clearly identifiable group of
social scientists, there is no assurance that it would be accurately
perceived or interpreted by societal decision makers, who may not
have access to a representative sample of scientists or their
perspectives.

Nevertheless, the perspective adopted by an individual social scientist may have some effect on the orientations attributed
to the social science enterprise as a whole by societal decision makers. Two criteria will probably dominate their evaluations of these

orientations. First, to what extent will the special privileges and social resources provided for the enterprise produce benefits for the entire society? This is clearly an application of a utilitarian analysis and involves concern with numerous subsidiary issues, including the certainty of benefits, the range of costs, and the distribution of both among various segments or social categories of society. Second, to what extent will societal decision makers trust scientists who adopt each perspective to provide benefits to the entire society rather than use the resources and privileges to further the interests of special groups chosen by the investigator?

The major societal benefits that may be expected from implementing the autonomous scientist's perspective will be an increase in knowledge—or increased confidence in existing knowledge—and the eventual possibility of practical applications; specific, immediate benefits are likely to be few. Major societal costs will include the support of the scientists, the cost of research and facilities, the possible special benefits provided for investigators (that may in turn allow infringement of the rights and welfare of research participants), and the contributions forgone when intelligent, well-educated professionals do not concentrate on the immediate problems of society. The distribution of such effects will not be uniform, for the major benefactor from an increase in knowledge will be the scientific-intellectual community, although an increase in the societal "store of knowledge" may be considered a general benefit, facilitating future positive benefits for society. However, all of society will experience the major costs noted above. The special treatment of research participants may be distributed in any number of ways, among the disadvantaged, the advantaged, or all categories of society, depending upon the actual research activity.

Whatever the analysis of the potential costs and benefits to society of the autonomous scientist strategy, it seems unlikely to lead to the conclusion that a particular political perspective is being favored at the expense of another, unless the advancement of knowledge is seen as a fundamental feature of a political orientation. Those pursuing an autonomous scientist orientation will be expected to provided information and advice for the deliberations of decision makers; an unbiased, competent response should contribute to their acceptance as a politically neutral societal resource.

The impact of the applied scientist's strategy should be quite similar. The major difference may be the attention given by the applied scientist to more immediate practical benefits, in addition to contributions to knowledge and possible long-term positive effects. The major costs will be the resources required for personal sustenance and research activities, as well as the special privileges developed for relationships with research participants. The resources and privileges will be provided by society as a whole. The contributions forgone may be less of an issue than with the autonomous scientist, however, since the applied scientist is attempting to contribute to specific, immediate problems. By and large, costs associated with this kind of research will be supported by the entire society. As long as societal decision makers have an influence on the issues and strategies pursued in research, it can be assumed that the benefits will be considered relevant to the entire society. If certain categories of citizens receive greater benefits than others but societal decision makers have approved this uneven distribution, the result can be seen as acceptable to society. The political or social values that are reflected by such decisions can be assumed to represent all major segments of society—or at least as much as any political decision can be expected to do so.

Responses to those pursuing the societal mentor strategy may be somewhat different, for the costs to society will be quite low, involving little more than the personal support of the individual. Further, this support may be provided through the performance of other, more practical activities—typically academic in nature—and usually no special privileges are required beyond those associated with the normal exercise of free speech. Societal benefits that will accrue from implementation of the societal mentor strategy may be of a very general nature and may be seen as part of the normal process of identifying and ameliorating problems or injustices within society. The distribution of the costs and benefits associated with this strategy will probably not be considered controversial, for they will have been evenly distributed among all segments of society. While there is no reason to expect social criticism to be politically neutral, explicit and straightforward attempts to influence the structure and processes of society through acceptable channels are unlikely to raise concerns about subterfuge or deception.

Social activism may be the most controversial strategy of all, but not because of concerns about the distribution of resources. As long as the resources required for social activist research are modest or come from private sources, there will be little complaint regarding their use. A more problematic analysis involves the special privileges associated with social science investigators, for the social activist may try to use the research activity to support predetermined conclusions about needed changes for society. In such cases, the decisions of social activists do not represent a concern for advancing knowledge or resolving a specific problem for the best interests of society, but their own personal preferences. Given this perspective, societal decision makers may be reluctant to encourage individuals who pursue a social activist strategy in the guise of scientific research, since it may be seen as an attempt to further narrow political interests. Social activism—honestly presented as such—may be considered a legitimate exercise of the right to free speech and to influence the political process; social activism disguised as scientific research may create some degree of distrust among societal decision makers, resulting in a reduction of resources provided for research and a restriction of special privileges—to say nothing of bringing about a cautious approach in interpreting any research results presented as relevant to a societal decision.

In summary, it would appear that the philosophy of the autonomous scientist or of the applied scientist is least likely to meet with distrust or suspicion from societal decision makers, although they may not agree with scientists regarding the issues for study or the strategies for resolution. As long as the decision makers are involved in these two critical decisions, they should have confidence that the public interest is being given appropriate consideration—as much as in any other societal activity. The more pronounced the immediate practical benefits, the greater the support and enthusiastic backing to be expected of decision makers. The pursuit of the social mentor orientation is unlikely to be considered a problem, for it involves an exercise of the right to free speech and will have low societal costs. The social activist approach could meet with some resistance, particularly if public resources or special privileges accorded social scientists are seen as being used to further personal political objectives rather than objectives that either serve the entire society or have been adopted by the normal political or administrative mechanisms. Societal decision makers may not approve of attempts to usurp their responsibilities—the essence of covert societal activism—and respond by reducing the support and autonomy provided for such activities. As long as only a small number of social scientists or of social science projects reflect a social activist perspective, this strategy will probably not have a major effect on the way societal decision makers view the social science enterprise. But if activists were to dominate the social science community, providing an elitist challenge to the political process, this challenge might be met with resistance in the form of reduced financial support or autonomy for the entire social science enterprise.

Conclusion

The most general moral dilemma that confronts scientific investigators takes the form of potential incongruencies between their obligations as scientists and their responsibilities as citizens. Alternative perspectives for resolving this problem may be considered in terms of the extent to which they provide a solution to this general moral dilemma, as well as to the other dilemmas associated with scientific work. Of course, the reactions that might be anticipated from societal decision makers, who control the resources and special privileges for the scientific enterprise, must also be weighed.

Based on these criteria, the most complex perspective may be that of the applied scientist, whose role involves dealing with important practical problems and attempting to resolve them through the application of scientific knowledge and procedures. While this perspective may exacerbate the dilemmas, it may also provide scientists with considerable public support for their resolution. Although the problem of separating political or personal values from scientific judgments may be greater for those involved in applied than in theoretical problems, the support of societal leaders for the conduct of research may also be substantially greater.

The perspectives of both the autonomous scientist and the societal mentor represent much simpler orientations toward the general research dilemma. The first emphasizes scientific objectives and attempts to insulate them from obligations of citizenship, thus reducing the potential for awareness of a dilemma. The second focuses upon personal political values, with acknowledgment of the usefulness of unbiased scientific research in the achievement of these objectives. The research dilemma (use of participants to achieve beneficial objectives) and concerns about the application of knowledge may impinge on the work of the autonomous scientist; they are unlikely to be as salient for those pursuing a societal mentor strategy. An explicit attempt to separate scientific judgments from personal values by those pursuing either orientation may lead to respect and cooperation from societal decision makers; attempts to manipulate or deceive others as to the nature of research or intellectual activity are likely to elicit suspicion and resentment among both the general public and decision makers.

The most precarious strategy may be that of social activism. While its resolution to the general research dilemma is unequivocal—total emphasis upon political values and societal change—it may produce concern that the scientific role is being misused to promote personal values. There may be suspicion that the privileges and resources associated with the scientific enterprise, provided to advance general societal objectives, are being subverted to advance narrow political orientations, thus usurping a legitimate function of societal decision makers as they attempt to identify pressing social problems and determine how they might be approached.

In sum, there are advantages and disadvantages associated with each professional orientation; in the course of selecting strategies that are personally satisfying, social scientists might consider the possible effects of given orientations upon their relationships with societal decision makers and the resultant impact upon other scientists. Many social scientists may have to choose between a strat-

egy that is personally satisfying and one that promotes trust between the scientific enterprise and society. Regardless of which
perspective is adopted, a trusting relationship with those who support or tolerate (depending upon their perspective) the social science enterprise is likely to be facilitated by an open and honest
portrayal of objectives and interests. Any strategy or philosophy
that leads to attempts to misguide or manipulate others—which
may accompany any of the orientations reviewed above—is likely
to result in suspicion and loss of support.

12

Dilemmas in the Application of Knowledge

Conflicts between a proposed application of knowledge and desirable social objectives can become intensely emotional moral issues when investigators are highly committed to certain principles, including acceptance of major responsibility for effects on the lives of others. Analysis of such situations involves several interrelated issues. The first section of this chapter will review the different types of effects associated with scientific knowledge; the second the individual's responsibility for such effects; and mechanisms that have been developed to control and minimize negative effects will be discussed in the third section. There appear to be two major ways investigators can control the practical applications of scientific knowledge, the potential for influencing the knowledge to be developed is the focus of the fourth section and the ability to influence the application of existing knowledge is emphasized in the

361

fifth. The first section of this chapter will review the different types of effects associated with scientific knowledge and the second the individual's responsibility for such effects. Mechanisms that have been developed to control and minimize negative effects will be discussed in the third section.

Types of Negative Effects

A negative effect can be defined as the difference between the actual state of affairs (regarding existing applications of knowledge) and the ideal state of affairs that would come about if new knowledge were fully incorporated into existing administrative and applied professional practices (to promote objectives with universal approval). With such a conception, there are four ways in which the potential benefits from scientific knowledge may fail to be realized.* First, there can be failure to adopt new practices and procedures with proven value for providing major benefits. Second, procedures and principles with proven utility *and* widely accepted as appropriate by applied professionals may be improperly implemented. Third, scientific knowledge can be used for the advantage of special interests rather than mankind in general, or it can be used to the general detriment of all. While these forms of "abuse" can occur with respect to any type of scientific knowledge, research with human participants is related to a fourth problem—use of data collected for scientific purposes to "harm" individual research participants or aggregates of individuals.

     *There is some ambiguity over whether it is moral for applied professionals to accept compensation for the implementation of techniques or devices that have little or no demonstrable benefit (a positive effect demonstrated through empirical research). Such activities, often associated with applied social scientists—administrators, group therapists, counselors, clinical psychologists, and psychotherapists (Eysenck, 1961)— do not directly involve the activities of social science investigators unless they are involved in the development and application of such techniques. Because techniques with questionable effectiveness may not have developed from a program of scientific research and have little or no relationship to the work of scientific investigators, this type of misuse of knowledge is not specifically covered here. See Bermant, Kelman, and Warwick (1978) for a monograph devoted to this problem.

Failure to Utilize New Knowledge

When new knowledge has been developed and has proven its value for providing benefits, it is often some time before the application of this knowledge is generally accepted. The benefits forgone in the interim between establishment of the value of the new application and its general adoption can in fact be considerable.

Dramatic examples of such "benefits forgone," have occurred in medicine. In two separate settings, techniques to prevent the transmission of disease were resisted, despite substantial evidence supporting their effectiveness in reducing mortality among hospital patients. In 1847 Ignaz Semmelweis, a Hungarian physician working in maternity wards, discovered that if physicians sterilized their hands between examinations of patients, the mortality rate was reduced by an average factor of five; greater reductions occurred when other strict precautions were taken (De Kruif, 1927). A similar reduction in mortality rates was achieved by the British surgeon Lister, who discovered that if postoperative care was conducted in such a way that infections from airborne microbes were minimized (by covering wounds with bandages to maintain a sterile environment), mortality rates among surgical patients dropped from 30 to 1 percent (Farmer, 1962). It was several decades before the procedures developed by either Semmelweis or Lister were adopted as standard practice by other physicians.

In both of these cases, the number of individuals who died because of the reluctance of physicians and surgeons to adopt a technique with proven value must number in the tens of thousands—a clear example of benefits forgone. This type of problem has been a recurrent one in the history of industrial medicine and public health, including recent examples of reluctance to develop standards for exposure to various chemicals, toxic substances, and carcinogens. Some scientists and technicians employed by industrial firms have been unwilling to publicize known dangers, especially when the remedy could be embarrassing or expensive for the industry that employs them (Edsall, 1975b).

A similar situation may be developing in relation to advances in genetics (Etzioni, 1973). The ability to detect the genetic makeup of fetuses, early in a pregnancy, and to predict major physical and mental deformities in time for a legal and safe abortion suggests that the birth of many unfortunates can be avoided. These techniques may provide the possibility for minimizing the number of full-term births that result in subnormal offspring requiring a lifetime of special care—a clear benefit to the parents and society. Resistance might be based on concern that this procedure would encourage the identification of multiple characteristics of a fetus and lead to the abortion of those who are normal but not socially "ideal"—from the parents' perspective—with the "wrong" sex, height, hair color, and the like. Determining socially acceptable guidelines for the application of these procedures may require some time; it remains to be seen how much the delay will "cost."

In many areas of modern life there are individuals in positions to affect social and human phenomena—for example, teachers, administrators in government and commerce, lawyers, members of the service professions, and so forth. These individuals influence the lives of others in a multitude of significant ways, but there seems to be no systematic procedure for incorporating new social science advances into the knowledge base that affects the judgments and decisions of these individuals. In some cases, regression may have occurred, as demonstrated by the following example.

One of the major successes of psychology has been the development of tests to detect those schoolchildren who have either more or less than the normal capacity to learn. Such tests are far more reliable than the intuitive judgments of teachers and administrators and have been successfully used, since their inception seventy years ago, to make distinctions that allow these children to receive special attention, either of a remedial nature or in accelerated classes. Unfortunately, the current emphasis in the United States on equality has included pressures, mainly from parents, for equal treatment of all schoolchildren and, in many cases, outright hostility toward any procedure based on the assumption that children have differences in ability—the use of intelligence tests has recently been abolished or curtailed in several school systems. The cost of this decision to both the less-than-average student *and* the bright student could be considerable. This is seen in the personal story of Thomas Soewell (1973), a black economist whose education remained at a standstill until he was identified as an exceptionally bright child by an intelligence test and moved into an accelerated academic program from the class for slow learners where he had been placed by the school staff.

Improper Application of Existing Knowledge

Once abstract scientific knowledge becomes embodied in devices and techniques suitable for applied problems (in engineering, medicine, and so forth), there is always the possibility that it may be misused. This is true even when the new knowledge can have beneficial effects and is widely accepted by applied profes sionals. Whether it results from misunderstanding or incompetence, failure to properly utilize such techniques represents a benefit forgone, usually to the client.

Such misuse is found in the widescale administration of polygraph tests to employees in the hope of detecting those that have appropriated property or funds from a company or might do so. It has been observed that if a "lie-detector procedure" is 90 percent accurate and 5 percent of one thousand employees in a firm are or may be thieves, then the procedure will identify forty-five out of fifty potential thieves as "thieves," but ninety-five of the honest will be identified as "thieves." Thus, 68 percent of those identified as "thieves" will actually be honest (Lykken, 1974, 1975a, 1975b; Abrams, 1975). Even if polygraph procedures were 95 percent accurate—and 90 percent accuracy may already be a liberal figure—50 percent of those identified as "thieves" in the example would be honest. Since there may be no other evidence to provide a basis for judgment, particularly if a polygraph is used in job screening, this may be an infringement on the right of individuals to be considered "innocent until proven guilty."

The widespread use of this technique in industry appears to have resulted in part from the promotional activities of professional polygraphers, whose confidence is based mainly on experience in criminal proceedings, where individual confessions and court decisions may provide validating evidence. But it also stems from the concern of executives in industry over economic loss due to employee theft, a concern that leads to receptiveness to an easy solution to the problem, and from the naive assumption that individuals can be classified as honest or dishonest without reference to their situational context (Burton, 1976). It seems appropriate to consider this a misuse of a well-developed procedure with some potential value (in criminal proceedings, where the proportion of innocent examined is reduced—thereby substantially reducing the probability of falsely identifying the innocent as guilty—and the final decision is left to the judicial procedure).

Concern over potential misuse of new techniques is widespread in the applied professions that involve the use of abstract scientific knowledge (engineering, medicine, and clinical psychology) as well as those involving other systems of knowledge (law and accounting). Almost all codes of ethics adopted by groups of applied professionals include an emphasis on proper training, awareness of limits of knowledge, and concern for the welfare of the client. Due to the widespread recognition of this problem, examples from the application of physical, medical, or biological sciences would be superfluous.

The failure of those in positions to modify human and social phenomena by using social science knowledge is well known. Despite a significant amount of well-established and empirically supported knowledge, there continues to be an unwillingness or inability to utilize this knowledge, a situation that may result from the lack of organization among those individuals who deal with social and human phenomena (exceptions are counseling services, psychiatry, and clinical psychology). Other reasons may be the failure to understand how scientific knowledge can be applied to routine problems or the incongruence between advanced social science knowledge and the dogmas currently accepted in the profession. In summary, improper application of existing knowledge is a well-recognized problem among the professionals who utilize physical, biological, and medical science to solve practical problems; it is less well recognized among those who influence human and social phenomena.

Misuse of New Knowledge

This refers to the negative consequences that result from the conscious application of newly developed scientific knowledge. These effects are ones that are inconsistent with the personal values of the investigator. Problems of this kind may be confronted by physical, biomedical, or social scientists. A most dramatic example of potential misuse of new knowledge comes from physical science—the development of atomic and nuclear weapons. These new weapons required thousands of man-years of effort by physical scientists, engineers, and technicians; despite some possible benefits, the potential of harm of these weapons to mankind is infinite—they present one of the few realistic possibilities for the elimination of human civilization. Similar problems are related to work in biological and bacteriological warfare, and the history of science and technology provides many other examples of weapons (such as the crossbow and gunpowder) with great destructive potential.

Infrequent, but dramatic, examples of such misapplication of medical and social science technology involve its use in the torture or interrogation of political prisoners. Social science techniques may be used to mislead prisoners into revealing information they wish to keep secret (Vasquez and Resczczynski, 1976). Medical procedures may be applied to increase the discomfort of political prisoners or return them to a "preinterrogation" condition; this could facilitate the effectiveness of additional interrogation or help to disguise the techniques that had been used (Gellhorn, 1978; Sagan and Jonsen, 1976). It is not clear whether therapeutic treatment in such cases is serving the interests of the "patient-prisoner" or of the interrogators. Concern over the misuse of medical knowledge and the moral status of cooperating physicians has led to the adoption of an explicit policy on torture by the World Medical Association ("Declaration of Tokyo. . .," 1976).

Other, perhaps less heinous, examples of possible misuse of knowledge related to social or human phenomena include behavior modification techniques. Behavioral modification refers to a series of techniques for modifying the behavior of individuals through provision of systematic, explicit rewards following desired behavior and, in some cases, the imposition of punishment following undesirable behavior (Krasner and Ullman, 1965). While most successful applications have occurred in situations where the "modifying agent" has complete control over the life of the individual undergoing modification, as in mental institutions, the army, or educational settings, some success has occurred where only partial control over the individual was possible. (There are even cases where individuals reward and punish themselves.)

Now that these techniques are associated with a history of success, those who help refine them are often concerned that they will be used for purposes other than the best interests of the individuals being modified. Others have been worried that the ability to affect the autonomous nature of the individual—who may not be able to distinguish between voluntary actions and actions taken, perhaps unconsciously, to achieve rewards provided by a behavior modification treatment—will be misused. The controversy is somewhat complicated by ambiguity over the nature of "legitimate" rewards (grades, job promotions, or pay raises) and punishments (fines or jail sentences) versus those rewards (candies, prison pay, or inmate privileges) or punishments (denials of privileges, mild electric shock, or noxious buzzers) utilized in behavior modification procedures and considered by some to be "illicit" or "unnatural."

"Project Camelot," designed to explore the pattern of events associated with revolutionary movements in societies, is considered by many social scientists to be *the* example of a project that could generate knowledge that might, in the wrong hands, provide a *potential* for dramatic misuse. Envisioned as a massive cross-societal project and sponsored by the U.S. Department of Defense, the project, if successful, would have resulted in a systematic description of the events that preceded, occurred during, and followed a change in government, whether by peaceful or violent means. Because of the source of financial support, there was substantial suspicion that the knowledge developed from this project would be used to help *prevent* changes of government by providing ways of identifying variables that would assume distinctive values before a revolutionary movement could become a major threat to an existing government. While the actual purpose of the project and the intended use of the knowledge were never clearly specified, these suspicions created enough political controversy and international hostility to cause termination of the project (Beals, 1969, pp. 4–10; Horowitz, 1965).

The third example of potential misuse of scientific techniques involves attempts to influence the decisions of juries through social science survey and attitude measurement procedures (Schulman and others, 1973). The population from which a jury is to be chosen is surveyed to determine the relationship between the personal characteristics (age, sex, occupation, ethnicity, and so forth) of eligible jurors and the major issues associated with a jury trial. This information is then used to influence the composition of the jury in the hope that the majority will be sympathetic to one side of the case. Despite the lack of systematic evidence on the effectiveness of such procedures in influencing jury decisions, they are being utilized more and more frequently in the United States for trials involving ambiguous and complex issues (civil disobedience to promote political causes, corporate price-fixing, or political misdeeds) and with participants who have substantial resources (either in money or volunteer human labor). This "new" procedure represents a refinement on a common practice among trial lawyers—attempting to select jurors favorable to their side of the dispute.

In general, the misuse of scientific knowledge, in the form of techniques and devices to control or predict natural phenomena, may dramatically reflect the dilemma between an investigator's scientific and citizen-intellectual values. This is particularly true when the application of scientific knowledge is controlled by individuals who do not share the same values as the scientist. The major potential for such misuse is probably found in physical science, with some potential developing in relation to social science phenomena. (The application of medical science is generally controlled by physicians, who usually act in the best interests of their patient-clients.)

Misuse of New Descriptive Data

This problem, unique to research involving human participants, turns on the use of sensitive and controversial data about specific individuals. Such data may be collected from individuals, organizations, societies, families, and so forth to facilitate the development of an abstract body of knowledge. But since the data are related to specific individuals or social units, it may be utilized in such a fashion that embarrassment or "damage" results for those described in the data. Thus, data on a specific individual can be utilized to his or her detriment or data about a social category of individuals, such as the residents of a certain area or those with the same ethnic identification, can be interpreted to the disadvantage of the entire social category. There is little evidence that participants have experienced negative effects through the release of social science research data (see the review in Chapter Three), but this does not mean that such effects could not be substantial. Concern for the confidentiality of data and anonymity of participants is an important and widely respected norm among social science investigators. A major unresolved problem is the inability of investigators to provide effective resistance to a legal subpoena, a problem review in Chapter Ten. However, there are only a dozen or so cases where legal proceedings have created serious problems; this problem appears to have been avoided by most social science investigators, except those studying phenomena in criminology.

A different form of this problem evolved from a study designed to establish the relationship between chromosome patterns in adolescent boys and violent delinquent behavior. The research would have involved the examination of six thousand youth incarcerated in juvenile jails and seventy-five hundred from underprivileged families that used a free medical program. Controversy developed when it was made public that the research data on the incarcerated youth would be provided to the staff of the juvenile correctional agencies, a fact not mentioned in the informed consent agreement provided to the parents of the incarcerated youth. This would constitute a provision of confidential information on research subjects regarding characteristics that were not, and are not, considered to be reliably related to delinquent and criminal behavior (the XYY chromosome pattern). Public controversy over the way the project was handled, even after changes in the informed consent form and procedures for handling the data on individuals, was sufficient to cause cancellation of the project (Katz, 1972, pp. 342–346).

The second variation of this problem—data related to aggregates or social categories—occurs when a social scientist publishes data that is given unexpected and unintended interpretations to the disadvantage of the research participants. Because such problems frequently involve minorities, deviants, or other social categories of individuals not in positions of influence, the impression is often given that social scientists are abusing powerless members of society.

One such example, reported by the social scientists involved (Rainwater and Pittman, 1967), turns on interpretations of the use of contraceptives among lower-class women (before the introduction of birth control pills and intrauterine devices). The original report emphasized that such women could not sustain the habits required to practice contraception effectively. This was later interpreted, by those who opposed the establishment of family-planning services, as evidence that such women did not want to limit their families. But this conclusion was inconsistent with the true state of affairs, since these women did want fewer children. Another example is the tendency to misinterpret findings about the intellectual potential (IQ) of those with different ethnic identification in terms of the worth of the individuals involved. Despite the constant emphasis on the small magnitude of such differences by social scientists and the fact that numerous other individual characteristics, both cognitive and personality, are of considerable importance, many concerned with the well-being of disadvantaged minorities continue to interpret findings related to measures of intelligence as a reflection of—or attempts to determine—the overall worth of the individuals.

Forgoing benefits by failure to apply new knowledge is a subtle problem. Losing benefits by improper application of existing knowledge is a well-recognized problem, but its frequency may have been reduced in modern times. When it occurs, use of scientific knowledge to produce effects inconsistent with the citizen-intellectual values of the originating scientists can be quite disconcerting. While data collected in research involving human participants may cause harm if misused, harm to individual participants from breachs of confidentiality is a very rare occurrence; harm to aggregates represented by research data is both infrequent, unpredictable, and difficult to establish.

Responsibility for Effects

Those considered responsible for the negative effects associated with the application, or failure of application, of new knowledge may vary with the nature of the effects. The discussion below focuses upon responsibility attributed to scientific investigators rather than emphasizing all the agents who contribute to such effects.

Failure to Utilize New Knowledge

Attribution of responsibility for benefits forgone from failure to utilize new knowledge involves examination of two different types of individuals, the originating investigators and those dealing with specific problems, usually applied professionals. If the originating individuals (scientists, technicians, administrators, or societal decision makers) withhold information that may have benefits, then it seems reasonable that the entire responsibility should rest with them for any benefits forgone. Further, if originating scientists encourage the adoption of new techniques or procedures before completing adequate research on the possible effects for individuals or society, it is reasonable to consider the originating individuals as responsible for negative effects; the applied professionals could not be expected to foresee these effects. An example of the latter was the attribution of responsibility for the deformed children of mothers who used the sedative thalidomide during pregnancy to the originating source—the firms that developed and sold the drug—rather than to the physicians who prescribed it (Nader, 1973).

In many situations, there is relatively complete examination of a new technique or device before it is presented as a solution to practical problems. The regulations of the Food and Drug Administration represent a recognition of the responsibility of originating scientists to evaluate complex new products thoroughly before they are presented for routine therapeutic use by applied professionals. The failure to employ thoroughly tested new knowledge is considered a failure of the applied professionals, not the originating scientists.

Improper Application of Existing Knowledge

This situation relates to the mistakes made in the application of well-established knowledge. Since the very conception of the benefits forgone in this situation assumes that the knowledge is well accepted by both the scientific community and the relevant applied professionals, the entire responsibility for failures to apply the knowledge appropriately is currently attributed to the applied professional, with the proviso that in some cases unknown factors may affect the results and that the applied professional can be held responsible only for phenomena that are known to be controllable.

Misuse of New Knowledge

Attribution of responsibility for misuse of new knowledge— "misuse" in the sense that the applications produce effects inconsistent with the values of the scientist as a citizen-intellectual—involves a number of interrelated issues. In an attempt to treat these as objectively as possible, a simple example of attribution of responsibility for an everyday occurrence will be presented, followed by an examination of attribution of responsibility when new knowledge is developed and used to create new effects.

In ordinary life, an individual is usually considered responsible for his actions when he achieves a predictable effect through utilization of a technique or device that is familiar to members of the society. For example:

• Person A would like to produce effect E in person B.
• Most members of A's and B's society consider that device X can be relied upon to produce effect E.
• Person A operates device X to produce effect E in person B.

In this situation, person A would probably be considered responsible for producing effect E in person B, whether device X produces a positive effect (a new medical treatment that helps B recover from illness) or a negative effect (a weapon is used to terminate the life of B).

This situation has the following important features:

1. The individual producing the effect is aware of the relationship between his personal actions and the specific effect produced.
2. The individual has control over the variables that determine the specific effect.

3. The crucial variables have a major impact on the specific influence; there is no substantial influence related to uncontrolled or random factors.
4. The relationship between the individual's actions and the specific effect is considered to be relatively direct.
5. From the actions of the individual and knowledge about the efficiency of the device, it is reasonable to infer an *intent* to produce the effect.

Scientific knowledge—in the form of a physical device (such as a weapon) or a procedure (such as a new medical treatment)—is usually not considered primarily responsible for the effects that result from application, nor are those who created the knowledge.

Some devices or techniques for producing certain effects may not be available to all members of a social system. In some cases, only a few individuals have taken the trouble to acquire the knowledge and ability necessary for successful applications, such as the repair of television sets. In other cases, the techniques and devices are considered complex, unpredictable, and with serious consequences if not used with skill and caution; as with the prescription of certain drugs, control may be restricted to a group of trained professionals. In either case, the attribution of responsibility is not affected—the individual who skillfully utilizes a device or technique to create a predictable effect is considered responsible for the results. This conceptualization can be applied to the attribution of responsibility for the creation of new knowledge or techniques, which may then be utilized to achieve specific effects. The relationship between abstract scientific knowledge and specific effects may come about in one of two ways (for simplicity's sake, the combination of the two ways will not be discussed). First, the desire to produce a specific effect generates attempts to develop new devices, which may, in turn, encourage the development of new scientific knowledge. Second, the development of new scientific knowledge may be associated with new devices or techniques that can produce specific effects in a predictable fashion.

The first situation, the emphasis on research and development to produce a specific effect, is probably the less complicated with respect to attributing responsibility. Once the desired effect is specified, three types of individuals are usually involved in the development of the new device or procedure: *originating scientists*, who develop a suitable conceptualization or theoretical framework to guide development of the new technique or device, either by modifying preexisting ideas or creating new ones; *applied professionals,* who work on the actual development of the specific technique or device, often in consultation with the originating scientists; and *societal decision makers*, who control the resources, whether public or private, necessary for the development of the new techniques or devices.

If these individuals, as a group, are successful in producing a device or technique to create the desired effect, they will probably be considered responsible for the new technique or device, since:

1. They were aware of their specific actions and the results they wanted to achieve, that is, they intended to produce the device or technique.
2. They controlled the variables that led to the creation of the new device or technique.
3. It is unlikely that the creation of the device or technique will be attributed to unintended or random effects, although unexpected or serendipitous events may facilitate development.
4. As a group, they have a direct relationship to the development of the new technique or device.
5. It is reasonable to infer that they intended to produce the technique or device and that their efforts were directed toward an explicit goal.

At the same time, if the new technique or device produces some additional effects, unexpected and unintended, attribution of responsibility for these additional effects is not likely to occur, since they were not the result of conscious attempts on the part of the development group.

Confidence in attributing responsibility to the development group (originating scientists, applied professionals, and societal decision makers) for intended effects is likely to be high; there will be little question that the group is responsible for the results. Determining the degree of responsibility to be attributed to any specific individual or group of individuals (such as the originating scientists) is more problematic. Perhaps one guide that might be employed is the degree to which an important contribution of a specific individual (or group of individuals) is unique and distinctive. However, this is likely to be a very rare occurrence, as suggested by research on simultaneous discoveries in science (Merton, 1963). (There is the example of atomic scientists in at least three different countries describing the possibility of atomic weapons at almost the same time; see Cuny, 1961; Zuckerman, 1966). It is probably more reasonable to attribute a share of the responsibility to a *group* of professionals, such as scientists with a particular specialty, but this approach may be unsatisfying to some, since it does not make specific individuals responsible for the effects.

A second type of relationship between abstract scientific knowledge and devices or techniques for applied purposes may be less direct and more unpredictable. A scientist may develop a conceptual framework or theory out of curiosity about a particular phenomenon. Upon reflection, it may appear to him or her that the new knowledge has applications that were not foreseen when it was being developed. Potential applications may be suggested by the originating scientist, other scientists, or applied professionals familiar with the new scientific knowledge and unresolved practical problems. Unlike the previous example where a development group works to create a device or technique that will produce a specific effect, the responsibility for the creation of practical devices or techniques seems more diffuse here, since the application was not foreseen. Even if the originator of the new knowledge provides a unique contribution, it is hard to assign a major responsibility for the new device or technique to the originating scientist, since the practical application was not anticipated. In either of these situations, deliberate creation of new knowledge to facilitate development of new techniques or unexpected application of new knowledge for similar purposes, the attribution of responsibility is related to the development of the new device or technique, *not to its utilization in a specific situation*.

The effects produced in specific situations are usually considered the responsibility of the individuals who apply or control devices or techniques to produce intended results with full intent and full knowledge of their actions. In many cases, particularly

regarding the use of new military weapons, this has been the responsibility of societal decision makers. In other instances the same
individuals who participated in the development of new devices or
techniques have been involved in important applications, particularly in medicine and engineering, where the roles of applied
professionals and scientific investigator may be combined. These
individuals are usually considered responsible for the effects in a
specific situation, although some responsibility may be attributed
to other members of the development group, particularly if the
device is new, unique, or produces some type of dramatic effect.

The most important conclusion to emerge from this analysis
is: It is inconsistent with the ordinary uses of the concept of *responsibility* to attribute major responsibility for the development of
new devices and techniques to originating scientists, much less responsibility for application in specific situations. As long as the
term "responsibility" is associated with the notion of intent, as well
as with the ability to control outcomes through personal actions,
it is inappropriate to apply it to the originating scientists—individuals who focus on the solution of interesting and challenging intellectual problems.

Unfortunately, several features of new knowledge and its
relation to the originating scientists seem to encourage the attribution of responsibility to them. First, there is a tendency to identify new knowledge with specific scientists and assume that these
individuals have provided a unique contribution. Second, the complexity of the knowledge may give the impression that only a few
experts can understand, and control, the use of the knowledge.
Third, the tendency of originating scientists to identify closely with
"their" new ideas encourages the notion that they are responsible
for these ideas in the way that a parent is for a child. Since all these
factors may be involved when scientists accept credit, honor, and
rewards associated with providing benefits, it is not surprising that
they might also be blamed for producing negative effects.

Perhaps the key to this is the uniqueness of the effects produced by new knowledge. There has obviously been a substantial
change in the unique effects produced by scientists. In earlier
times, many of the effects produced by certain devices or techniques were widely known and developed in many different situations. Scientists may have developed theories that helped to un-

derstand or improve these devices or techniques but were not basically involved in their introduction. Since the "easy" ideas have already been explored, additional improvements are possible only with a thorough understanding of the phenomenon, requiring years of training and, perhaps, an elaborate research program. In such cases, it is unlikely that the new effects would have occurred without the input from scientific specialists. But this line of reasoning only holds true for attribution of effects to the scientific enterprise, not to specific individual investigators.

One major question involved here is a general tendency, particularly in Western cultures, to consider human beings as the major cause of most events. The previous analysis should make it clear that many of the effects of research are related to the system that integrates practical problems and new scientific knowledge; it is sometimes impossible to predict the eventual outcomes or effects of such endeavors. This interpretation suggests that a major share of the responsibility should not be attributed to any one person (or group of persons), because each person is acting rationally within the context of the system. It is the way the individuals are interrelated that produces outcomes that do not serve the best interests of all members of the system.

In summary, it would appear reasonable for those participating in the development of a new device or technique—originating scientists, applied professionals, and societal decision-makers—to *share* the responsibility for a new device or technique, with a greater share of the responsibility to be attributed to those who provide unique contributions. In contrast, the application of any device or technique to deliberately achieve certain effects is usually considered the responsibility of those who directly influence utilization of the device or technique—applied professionals, societal decision makers, administrators, and the like.

Misuse of New Descriptive Data

Attribution of responsibility for this type of benefit forgone is related to specific misuses, which can be substantially different in their effects. The first situation involves the use of information about a specific individual for purposes unrelated to the scientific activity that involved collection of the data. Data collected on employees in organizations, political views of ordinary citizens, evidence of deviant or illegal behavior, or even certain types of medical information may be misused by administrators and decision makers to influence the lives and careers of the individuals involved. If such data are collected by a scientific investigator with the understanding that the information will be used only for scientific purposes, it is generally assumed that the investigator is responsible for any abuses that may occur.

A more difficult situation arises when investigators are subjected to pressure, outside their control, to provide data for nonresearch purposes—by a legal subpoena of information for judicial or administrative proceedings, for example. While it is clear that the investigator shares a major responsibility for any negative effects, the conditions under which responsibility may shift to the source of the subpoenas and possible sanctions (threats of fines or incarceration) are not clear. The examples of journalists and investigators who accept incarceration rather than divulge information suggest that at least some individuals are willing to accept complete responsibility; in other instances those subpoenaed have divulged information (see the review in Chapter Ten).

The second type of data misuse—inappropriate interpretations of data related to an aggregate or group of individuals—is also a subtle and difficult problem, perhaps because it is hard to establish *who* will make such misinterpretations. If the mistake is made by persons with professional or scientific training, they would be expected to be acquainted with the problems and techniques of data interpretation and, if the original presentation meets the normal standards of the scientific community, would be considered responsible for any gross errors. In this case, the originating scientist would not be held responsible.

If the interpretations are completed by ordinary citizens or others without the training required to interpret such data (for instance, journalists), the attribution of responsibility is more ambiguous. On the one hand, it is argued that the originating scientist is responsible for ensuring that the appropriate interpretations are clearly described and the reasons for avoiding inappropriate interpretations made clear; on the other hand, it is impossible to anticipate *all* inappropriate interpretations. If the originating scientist has made an honest attempt to describe the data and the reasons for any interpretation, he or she may not be considered responsible for any errors of interpretation if the party in error appears anxious to "see" the data as consistent with a predetermined view.

Summary

Using the ordinary conception of responsibility, it seems unreasonable to consider originating scientists as responsible for the benefits forgone or harm created under the following situations:

1. The benefits forgone are due to the reluctance of applied professionals or others to adopt new techniques or devices.
2. Benefits are forgone or harm is created by inappropriate use of devices or techniques that have well-established beneficial effects if properly employed.
3. Control or use of a device or technique is the legitimate responsibility of an applied professional or societal decision maker.
4. Misuse of data about individuals is attributable to agencies or influences outside the control of the scientist, and such misuse could not be anticipated.
5. Misinterpretations of data on aggregates of individuals occurring after the originating scientist has made an honest attempt to provide reasonable interpretations and their supporting rationale.

Originating scientists could, however, be considered responsible for the benefits forgone or harm associated with scientific knowledge under the following conditions:

1. They participate in attempts to keep new information secret, preventing its use to benefit mankind.
2. They participate in the decision to employ a new device or technique, that may involve substantial harm, to achieve a specific effect.
3. They fail to inform societal decision makers of known negative consequences that may accompany the application of a new technique or device.
4. They fail to maintain the confidentiality of information collected from human subjects for research purposes and used to harm the subjects.

5. They fail to provide appropriate interpretations related to data describing aggregates or groups of specific individuals.

Control of Negative Effects

Now that the nature of negative effects (benefits forgone and harm) and the parties responsible for them have been identified, the mechanisms that might be utilized to control or minimize such effects should be examined. One approach is to review mechanisms that have been, or might be, implemented to minimize the possibility of negative effects. The second is to consider the actions that might be taken by investigators to control the occurrence of negative effects. The following discussion will emphasize the possibilities for control available to scientific investigators, either individually or in the aggregate; it is organized around the types of effects discussed in the previous sections.

Minimization of Failures to Utilize New Knowledge

The loss of benefits involved here, which is usually not attributed to the originating scientist, is difficult to control. Most of the processes that affect the adoption of new knowledge or of related techniques and devices cannot be influenced by the originating scientist(s). Historically, one of the major factors that has encouraged the adoption, and frequently the development, of new knowledge in the physical sciences has been the pressure of competition, either in economic systems or through warfare (Bernal, 1939, 1965).

Adoption of new knowledge related to medical and social science phenomena seems to be influenced by prevailing beliefs and values among scientists, applied professionals, and members of society. Perhaps because they are often inconsistent with existing ideas, many new techniques with potential for providing substantial benefits are only gradually adopted. The slow adoption of techniques to reduce disease transmitted between patients in hospitals was probably due to lack of confidence in the theory behind the new procedure. It seems unlikely that there will be any simple procedure for controlling this type of resistance, especially since it would be expected to occur among most conscientious professionals, conservative about changing accepted procedures.

This problem has not gone unrecognized in the applied professions. It has been clear for some time that certain types of engineers, particularly electrical and aeronautical, find it difficult to keep current with the development of knowledge after completing their formal education. In medicine, concern that physicians might not keep abreast of new techniques has led to the suggestion that they be required to receive periodic recertification to maintain the right to practice medicine (Lyons, 1974). This would encourage individual physicians to engage in continuous education and minimize the benefits forgone by patients. But except for such suggestions, there seem to be few systematic mechanisms that have developed to minimize this type of benefit forgone, although most applied professionals appear to be willing to consider new devices or techniques and to adopt those that may provide benefits. As long as scientists continue to publicize advances and their potential application, they will probably have little influence over utilization of the knowledge or over the magnitude of the benefits that will be forgone.

Improper Application of Existing Knowledge

Almost all applied professionals, as individuals and through their associations, are critical of mistakes that "damage" the client, and they consistently support mechanisms to discourage such errors. When a procedure, technique, or device is thought to provide substantial benefits when properly utilized, applied professionals and the general public naturally prefer to minimize the frequency of improper applications. Control mechanisms for discouraging such mistakes are well developed in most professional groups. In some extreme cases, a legal mechanism has been developed to provide societal sanctions. While the right to practice may be withdrawn from some professionals who make serious mistakes, a procedure now recommended by the American Medical Association would remove a physician from practice *before* a mistake could be made. Thus, the Disabled Physicians Act describes the circumstances, such as mental or other illness, that may constitute evidence that a physician is unable to practice "with reasonable skill and safety to patients" (Cope, 1974, p. 1A).

In the social sciences, the best-organized group involved with applied problems are clinical psychologists, who have developed relatively specific standards for the practice of clinical psychology, complete with accreditation of graduate schools, licensing, and committees that review and sanction those who violate the standards. Of the seventeen codes of ethics adopted by national associations of psychologists, the major emphasis of sixteen codes is on the application of psychology to clients' problems (Reynolds, 1975a, 1975b). These codes usually center on clinical psychology, but frequently other applied areas are treated as well (industrial psychology or counseling). In general, the blame for improper application of scientific knowledge is recognized and accepted as a responsibility of applied professionals. Use of such knowledge by individuals who are not in a professional status, either because professionalism has not developed in a given area or because they are outside a well-defined occupational group, is free from any control mechanism. Fortunately, much of the most potent scientific knowledge is utilized by applied professionals.

Misuse of New Knowledge

Responsibility for the use of knowledge is usually attributed to those attempting to produce certain effects, either applied professionals trying to solve a specific problem or decision makers modifying the process or structures in organizations or society. The desire of investigators to control the utilization of new scientific or technical knowledge to promote objectives consistent with their personal and political values produces one of the more complex and salient quandaries, perhaps the prototype of the application of knowledge moral dilemma.

Four options are available to scientists wishing to have an impact upon the utilization of new scientific or technical knowledge. If neither the abstract conceptualizations necessary to guide the development of devices and techniques nor the devices and techniques themselves exist, investigators may be able to influence the application of new knowledge in two ways: (1) they can refuse to participate in the development of new knowledge or techniques when applications are expected to be inconsistent with their personal or political values; or (2) they can participate with the understanding that applications will be under the control of the contributing investigators or others approved by the investigators. If the abstract knowledge and devices have been developed and may be utilized to achieve applied effects at any time, two additional alternatives have been suggested: (3) Investigators can attempt to inform the societal decision makers and the general public of the consequences of various applications and recommend policies or procedures that may minimize negative effects; or (4) scientists can encourage the development of supranational organizations to control the use of new devices or techniques in such a way that the interests of the entire world rather than a specific country are given consideration (Auger, 1956).

The second and fourth of these options do not appear to be viable solutions. The second alternative, allowing investigators to control applications or the selection of those who will, leads to two complications. First, the source of resources and facilities to develop devices and techniques is usually considered to have the right to control applications, and it is unlikely that the source would relinquish this right. Second, although the structure of most democratic societies allows scientists, as citizens, to have an influence on those who control public decisions about applications of new devices or techniques, it seems unrealistic to expect that their influence on such choices will be increased. The fourth alternative— that scientists organize a world government that will control the application of new scientific knowledge—does not appear to warrant serious consideration; existing international governments seem to have limited influence upon the member nations, and it is unlikely that that one organized by scientists would be more effective, even if it could come into existence.

Hence, there are only two basic options available to scientific investigators for controlling the application of knowledge—through decisions to contribute to basic research or development and through attempts to persuade or influence the individuals who in fact control applications. These have the advantage of allowing some action to be taken by investigators and may also provide a means of discharging moral obligations, but the analysis of their potential effectiveness, situations where there is a consensus that such actions are appropriate, and the consequences for adopting such alternatives is relatively involved. These will be reviewed in some detail later in this chapter.

Misuse of New Descriptive Data

This problem takes two forms, the misuse of specific information that affects individual research participants and misinterpretations that may adversely affect the interests of an aggregate of individuals similar to the research participants.

No norm related to the conduct of research with human subjects is as well established as the norm of maintaining confidentiality of information about individual research participants. Almost any code of ethics related to the use of human subjects includes this principle, even if it is the only principle contained in the code (see Appendix 4). Furthermore, a number of techniques for handling data in such a way to prevent the association of a specific respondent with information about the individual are well-established (see Chapter Six).

A major threat to the confidentiality of data and anonymity of participants continues to be the legal subpoena, although there is no universal agreement that this constitutes a misuse of research information. From the perspectives of many lawyers and politicians, it is not inappropriate to use any available information to achieve legitimate administrative or judicial objectives (such as a fair, speedy trial). The reasons why this "threat" may not soon be removed was reviewed in Chapter Ten. Basically, there have been very few instances where projects have been threatened, too few to justify a universal legal privilege.

Misinterpretation of data representing aggregates of individuals is a difficult form of misuse to control, since there is no way to anticipate which individuals will make the misinterpretation or the nature of the erroneous inferences. Such misinterpretations may occur among professionals, societal decision makers, the public, or journalists. Frequently these misinterpretations are associated with a desire to locate empirical support for previously accepted beliefs and values, as with the "interpretation" of failure to use birth control procedures as a lack of desire to limit children— when it was related to a confusing home situation and relatively complicated birth control techniques (Rainwater and Pittman, 1967).

Since preventing the results of research from becoming public is inconsistent with a major value held by almost all scientists (open dissemination of knowledge), the only viable "control" device appears to be the careful presentation of data and all appropriate interpretations of them. It has been suggested that social scientists should attempt to foresee all possible misinterpretations and make clear why they would be inappropriate, thereby preventing gross abuses of the data. While this suggestion may sound reasonable, it allows the originating scientist to be blamed for all misinterpretations on the grounds that they should have been foreseen. If one assumes that it is impossible to foresee all possible misinterpretations, then this is an unreasonable position, since the originating scientist could be blamed for unpredictable and, hence, uncontrollable events.

The ability of scientists to influence the benefits forgone or harm created because of failures to utilize new knowledge or the misapplication of existing techniques is thus quite limited, primarily because the responsibility for such activities lies with those dealing with practical problems, usually applied professionals, administrators, or legislators. It is easier for investigators to affect the misuse of descriptive data related to either specific individuals or social categories, particularly when they are in direct control of the information involved. They are usually in a position to prevent the disclosure of information on individuals—and a strong norm exists among investigators to do so—and they may minimize possible misinterpretations of descriptive data by careful and complete presentations. However, it is never possible to anticipate all possible interpretations, reasonable or not, so that responsibility cannot be assigned to investigators for all instances of abuse.

Influence on Development of Knowledge

When techniques or devices for practical applications have not yet been developed, scientific investigators may have a substantial influence on the initiation and direction of research. The success of this alternative is somewhat restricted, however, primarily because of the investigator's inability to clearly anticipate the potential applications of knowledge before the relevant research has been conducted. There are only a very small number of situations where all possible effects of applications of "pure" scientific knowledge are predictable, along with the extent to which the applications will be "good" or "bad." The more usual research situation may be that where the basic conceptual framework (or theory) has been developed but where substantial work is required before an operational mechanism will become available. It is when operational mechanisms are created to achieve certain effects—often through a developmental program—that predictable outcomes may contribute to confidence regarding the desirability of implementation.

Nevertheless, scientists are employed at both stages—"pure" research with unpredictable consequences and operational development with relatively precise objectives—and may be able to influence the utilization of knowledge to achieve various outcomes. This influence can be considered from the perspective of the community of scientists (as they affect the decisions regarding various research programs or specific projects) or from the perspective of individual investigators who must determine their involvement with a particular program or project.

Scientists and Societal Allocation of Resources

One of the major influences on the development of scientific knowledge is the allocation of societal resources (from either public or private sources) to pursue intellectual or scientific issues. Federal allocations have taken two forms: allocation of support to specific programs with explicit objectives, usually related to practical problems, and allocation of resources to different scientific disciplines for "pure" research, without concern for immediate practical applications. Scientific investigators often have a major influence on such decisions, providing advice as individual experts, as representatives of their professional specialty, or as administrators working in government agencies or private organizations. Investigators may have an effect on the allocation of funds among various programs or disciplinary groups and, in the case of review committees and some administrators (such as National Science Foundation program directors), a significant impact upon selecting projects to receive financial support.

While these procedures provide a mechanism for incorporating the advice of investigators into the decisions about directions that new research will take, there are several disadvantages from the perspective of the typical investigator concerned with the application of scientific knowledge to practical problems. First, only "selected" investigators have a personal impact on the allocation of resources to research; it is not an opportunity available to all investigators. Second, while the incorporation of investigators from different specialties assures representation of a variety of perspectives, it does not guarantee that the wide range of citizen-intellectual or political values of scientists will be represented. The scientists who have this influence are seldom chosen to represent their professional community; they are usually chosen on the basis of technical competence and—to some extent—personal connections.

In short, some investigators have a substantial effect on the directions of new research, but they are not necessarily representative of the vast majority of scientists. For an individual investigator, the potential for direct influence on government policy regarding scientific research is not very great. The major issue that confronts most individual scientists is related to their personal involvement with a specific project or program of research.

Investigators and Single-Program/Project Decisions

Scientists are frequently faced with the decision of whether or not to contribute to a particular program or project, which may be either the scientist's own creation or one developed by others. Two characteristics of such activities can be considered: the scientific merit of the project and the estimated potential for improvement of the human condition (in ways consistent with the citizen-intellectual values of the scientist). If each characteristic is seen as dichotomous, the result is a simple typology with four categories of projects:

1. High scientific value; high potential benefits to mankind.
2. Low scientific value; high potential benefits to mankind.
3. High scientific value; low potential benefits to mankind.
4. Low scientific value; low potential benefits to mankind.

These two dimensions correspond to the major motivations for scientists—intellectual interest and desire to benefit mankind.

Activities in two of the categories, the first and the last, will probably not present major dilemmas. The potential merit of both characteristics is equal in each project—high scientific value and high potential human benefits, low scientific value and low potential human benefits. Projects low on both characteristics are unlikely to elicit much interest among scientists if they have other options.

Some scientists are fortunate enough to become involved in projects that not only involve interesting scientific problems and potential benefits to mankind but substantial resources and close relations with applied professionals willing to utilize any new knowledge in practical applications. Scientists in such situations would probably be highly motivated and committed to their research and might become so involved as to neglect all other aspects of their lives. This appears to have been the case among the atomic scientists in the United States at the beginning of the Second World War. Threatened by the prospect of Nazi Germany's developing an atomic weapon and possessed of virtually unlimited financial support, they worked diligently to solve interesting scientific issues that would lead to the development of the atomic bomb (Groueff, 1967). As the threat from Nazi Germany gradually diminished and was eventually eliminated, the perceived nature of the project changed for many of the atomic scientists and they came to see it as one of scientific interest but negative potential for benefiting mankind. Perhaps this is the most difficult predicament that could occur for a scientist—involvement with a project during a change in its perceived nature.

Reactions to the other two types of projects will probably depend upon the individual scientist. A substantial number of scientists are involved in research that has some scientific merit but appears to have little immediate value for improving mankind— the stereotype of "pure" research. Contributions to such projects may be accompanied by two related and widely circulated beliefs: that any increase in knowledge will eventually benefit mankind and that the potential benefits or effects for mankind are difficult to predict but could be substantial. Those scientists who find a personal satisfaction in solving challenging intellectual puzzles may well decide to contribute to this type of project. In the same way, many investigators—particularly in the social sciences—elect a scientific career with the hope of improving the human condition. Such persons may reject the opportunity to work on a project with scientific merit and little applied value but enthusiastically contribute to a project with exactly the opposite characteristics.

There has been an awareness that social science investigators may be confronted with moral or ethical conflicts in dealing with the sponsors of research projects. Five associations (representing anthropologists, political scientists, and sociologists in the United States, sociologists in the United Kingdom, and cross-cultural psychologists) have attempted to provide guidance or standards for social scientists who accept responsibility for a project that is conducted to meet the objectives of a sponsor. Relevant statements were obtained during a survey of codes of ethics regarding use of human participants in research (Reynolds, 1975a, 1975b); a composite of these principles is presented in Appendix 5. Two observations can be made about this set of statements. First, they tend to assume that the investigator has alternatives available and that his need for personal support is not an issue. Hence, there is a great stress on the autonomy and independence of the scientific investigator. Second, only one statement treats options in the event that the research is "misinterpreted" or, perhaps, "misused"; a public statement that corrects the "misinterpretation" is recommended.

One type of situation is not covered in these statements, that of deception on the part of the source of financial support; it is assumed that the investigator will have full and complete knowledge of the sponsor and the sponsor's intentions. There have been examples of such deceit, and this can be a major problem if the source of financial support attempts to influence the design of the project or the analysis of data or to use the research to gain access to information that would otherwise remain confidential. Although this now seems to occur less often, some social scientists feel they have been used when supported by "foundations" sponsored covertly by agencies such as the Central Intelligence Agency, even when no attempts to misuse the research activity or results were present (Stephenson, 1978; Liell, 1978; Schulman, 1978). It would probably be best for democratic societies if the government were straightforward in its support of research activities.

While this analysis helps to illustrate how the relationship between the characteristics of projects and the interests of scientists may affect decisions to contribute to different endeavors, it is actually misleading to analyze the decisions of modern scientists within such a framework. First, the issue of the alternatives available to the scientist has been ignored—they may have *no* alternatives or a multitude of attractive options. Second, major decisions are usually related to career options, involving different types of organizations or research programs (a series of related projects) rather than one specific project.

Modern Scientists and Career Decisions

One stereotype about scientists that continues to survive is the conception of investigators as autonomous free spirits, capable of contributing or withholding their talents as they wish. While this was certainly true of some scientists in the past, since they were often independently wealthy and dabbled in science as a hobby, it is equally clear that many were not blessed with this luxury and were forced to live on incomes from the services that they provided as technicians, teachers, or applied professionals (Bernal, 1965). In modern times, most scientists committed to the development of empirically based knowledge are faced with two types of financial problems: resources to cover personal expenses and resources to support research. Only those with a guaranteed source of support for both needs are completely autonomous, and this would be a *very small* percentage of scientists in today's world. While some scientists have been fortunate enough to resolve the problem of personal expenses, almost none of them is able to conduct research without external financial support, except those who work with intellectual problems that do not require substantial empirical research.

Scientists who have solved the problem of personal expenses have usually done so in one of two ways, although a third solution may now and then occur. First, scientists who pursue careers as applied professionals (physicians, clinical psychologists, and the like) are able to develop a clientele that provides a stable income and, thus, are relatively autonomous with respect to any particular client or alternative source of support. Second, the achievement of a relatively secure position (tenure) as an academic faculty member, where the service of teaching is exchanged for financial support provides the freedom to develop or choose research projects congruent with the scientific interests or citizen-intellectual values of the investigator. Finally, a few scientists are independently wealthy.

Those scientists who do not have a dependable source of income to cover their personal expenses generally become involved with organizations, either independent research units, divisions within commercial enterprises, or government agencies. While the exact percentages vary with discipline and country, the numbers are large enough to be considered significant. What is important is that the personal expenses of these scientists are covered only as long as they are willing, or able, to contribute to organizational objectives. This makes it very difficult for them to act with "complete" autonomy with respect to any particular research project, since they may not have any alternative sources of income for personal expenses and the organization may have no other needs they can fulfill.

Alternatives available to scientists with and without a stable livelihood who do not wish to contribute to a given project are reviewed in Table 13. While the number of alternatives is only slightly larger for those with a stable personal income, the potential for complete withdrawal from the project may make it easier for these scientists to have an influence on the nature of the project and the way the knowledge will be used or to generate projects more congruent with their personal values as scientists or citizen-intellectuals.

In contrast, the scientists with a less secure organizational affiliation and fewer options may be forced to make compromises between scientific interests and values as citizen-intellectuals or to make changes in how they perceive their occupational role. If the type of projects for which a scientist is sought and the interests or values of the scientist are so divergent that the scientist finds no project acceptable, then there is almost no way the scientist can

Table 13. Alternatives Available to Scientists for Resolving Incongruence Between Characteristics of Research Projects and Citizen-Intellectual Values: By Need for Support for Personal Expenses

Financial Support		Alternatives
Personal Expense Guaranteed	Need for Support for Personal Expenses and Research — Need for Research Support	
		Changes Related to Scientific Contributions
Yes	No	a) Initiate another project that does not require resources
Yes	Perhaps	b) Initiate a new project that requires resources through personal action
Perhaps	Perhaps	c) Change to a new project within the organization
Perhaps	Perhaps	d) Change projects conducted by the organization
		Change in Perception of Dilemma
Yes	Yes	e) Change personal citizen–intellectual values
Yes	Yes	f) Insulate scientific-occupational values from citizen–intellectual values
Yes	Yes	g) Emphasize ultimate "good" of knowledge, despite potential effects of immediate research project
		Changes Related to Project
Yes	Yes	h) Change the purpose or research plan of the project

Table 13. Alternatives Available to Scientists for Resolving Incongruence Between Characteristics of Research Projects and Citizen-Intellectual Values: By Need for Support for Personal Expenses (Cont'd)

Financial Support		Alternatives
Yes	i)	Change the way the results may be utilized for application in specific situations
		Organizational Change
Not necessary	j)	Quit and join another organization
		Occupational Change
Yes	k)	Leave scientific work entirely and enter nonscientific position

expect to find support for research expenses, regardless of stability of personal income. This is a major unresolved problem for all investigators committed to developing scientific knowledge congruent with their personal values.

The conditions under which individual scientists may resolve the research dilemma through personal control of the development of scientific knowledge (either in pure form or as part of a developmental activity) are quite restrictive, consisting of (1) the ability to predict negative effects that may result from the application and (2) a limited number of qualified scientists willing to contribute to the necessary projects. (If there are a large number of willing, qualified scientists, it is hard for any one investigator to prevent development of the knowledge.) These two conditions are unlikely to occur often. Investigators selected from the scientific community may have an impact upon the resources and facilities devoted to research, but this is seldom the case for the typical scientist.

The ability to resolve the moral dilemma with the option that may be the most personally satisfying—withdrawal from research or developmental activities that are expected to further undesirable effects—may be limited for many scientists. If such withdrawal is tantamount to withdrawal from a scientific career, it may create substantial ambivalence. Only a few investigators have the "total freedom" to pursue a scientific career while working on projects of their own selection, although those with secure positions in academic institutions and applied professionals with a diverse clientele or with personal wealth clearly have more options than investigators dependent upon private organizations or public agencies.

This predicament of trying to satisfy a personal moral imperative inconsistent with the objectives of an externally imposed task is also of some importance in relation to the second major option, attempting to influence those with the responsibility for implementation of new techniques and devices. Because this "action alternative"—persuasion—is applicable to a wide range of situations (virtually any application of scientific knowledge), interest in it may be prevalent among all scientists, physical, biomedical, and social.

Influence on Utilization of Knowledge

The action most often taken by scientists, individually or in groups, to resolve a felt responsibility associated with application of scientific knowledge is the attempt to persuade others, either societal decision makers or the general public. Numerous factors may contribute to the frequent occurrence of this approach, such as the greater predictability of potential negative effects once an operational procedure for utilization is fully developed. Further, as potential applications become more widely known, they may attract the attention of scientists concerned with the possible effects but not participating in projects leading to the final application. Hence, two categories of scientists must be considered: those who were intimately involved with the development of the scientific knowledge or its operational form (and may feel responsible because of their personal contributions) and those not directly involved in development but who feel an obligation to use their expertise to assess the potential effects and ensure that major disadvantages are taken into account before a final decision regarding application.

Scientists' Public Statements and Maintenance of Credibility

While it is clearly appropriate for scientists, as citizens, to make public statements on public issues, they are also considered a major source of scientific and technical information. Scientific issues, often involving highly specialized, esoteric topics, are frequently combinations of technical interpretations and professional judgments. To lay individuals, who frequently are not aware of those aspects considered objective facts as distinct from those considered subjective judgments, an entire analysis may appear to be a personal evaluation. There tends to be a general suspicion of any judgments—even those presumed to be unbiased—if the individual expressing them has a personal commitment to a particular alternative, either for pecuniary or moral reasons. The extent to which a scientist's personal values or political orientations may influence his or her subjective judgments regarding technical issues can substantially affect the credibility of any scientific statement.

Strategies for dealing with the relationship between scientific judgments and personal political or moral values include:

1. Confining all public judgments to scientific and technical issues and making no public statement regarding citizen-intellectual values.
2. Making public statements on both types of issues and maintaining a clear distinction between the two types of judgments and the rationales on which they are based.
3. Providing public statements that combine judgments on the two types of issues without providing any distinction between the rationales supporting each type of opinion.
4. Completely subordinating scientific judgments to values as a citizen-intellectual and thus using "science" in a deliberately biased way.

If scientists have a substantial body of abstract knowledge to support their judgments, so that they are correct most of the time, the first strategy—confining public statements to technical or scientific issues—is likely to give them a reputation for providing accurate, objective information useful for practical applications. However, the recent trend among scientists toward involvement in public affairs would suggest that this strategy will not be embraced by all scientists. Further, there have been suggestions from nonscientific public commentators that scientists have an obligation to openly discuss the implications of scientific and technical issues for citizen-intellectual values and that to do otherwise puts the public at a disadvantage with respect to societal decision makers, who are not always to be trusted.

At least one professional association, the American Anthropological Association, has suggested that its members have an obligation to make public statements relevant to societal issues. Its "Statements on Ethics" includes the following in the discussion of "responsibilities to the public" (American Anthropological Association, 1971, Paragraph 2[d]): "As people who devote their professional lives to understanding man, anthropologists bear a positive responsibility to speak out publicly, both individually and collectively, on what they know and what they believe as a result of their professional expertise gained in the study of human beings. That is, they bear a professional responsibility to contribute to an adequate definition of reality upon which public opinion and public policy may be based." It is significant that this statement speaks of providing descriptive information, presumably based on relatively objective observations and not specifically related to unique policy alternatives. Although it is implied that these public statements should reflect scientific observations and judgments, the degree of separation from personal political values is not made explicit.

The third strategy—providing statements that combine judgments on scientific-technical issues with opinions related to citizen-intellectual values—is adopted by many scientists, especially those who deal with social or human phenomena. But the eventual reactions to such statements are quite predictable. If the audience is unable to separate the evaluations and judgments related to scientific or technical issues from those related to citizen-intellectual values, the entire set of evaluations may be seen as politically motivated, despite the intentions of the scientist. This will be a particular problem where there is an honest difference of opinion on scientific issues; failure to present an objective rationale for such judgments will make it very difficult to identify the factors that account for the differences of opinion. The audience may assume that the differences are based on preexisting citizen-intellectual values rather than on variations in scientific judgment.

The fourth alternative is really the third alternative pushed to an extreme—complete subordination of scientific judgments to citizen-intellectual values. While it does not seem to occur very frequently, its effects could be detrimental for all scientists, since the audience would have no way to evaluate the basis for scientific or technical judgments and *any statements* by scientists might come to be viewed as a reflection of another political pressure group.

The second strategy may be the only satisfactory compromise—public comments on both scientific-technical issues and their relationship to citizen-intellectual values accompanied by an attempt to separate the two types of judgments and the rationales associated with each. This provides the audience, whether lay individuals, administrators, or political leaders, with both the technical judgments of the scientist and his or her views as a representative of an intellectual community. While such a distinction may, upon preliminary analysis, appear difficult for investigators closely involved and committed to the study of a particular problem or phenomena to make, it is the same type of distinction expected of many individuals who occupy special roles in society. Physicians, lawyers, police officers, teachers—to name only a few—are expected to discharge their "official" obligations without regard to the relationship between their personal political values and those of the patient, client, citizen, or student. It does not seem unreasonable to expect social scientists to develop the same degree of intellectual self-discipline and personal objectivity with respect to their scientific judgments and personal values as citizen-intellectuals.

Attempts to make distinctions between technical judgments and citizen-intellectual values may be more difficult when there is close similarity between the two, as in some areas of social science. It is difficult to deal with scientific knowledge related to social problems (such as health, education, crime, or equality of opportunity) without the emergence of a well-defined set of citizen-intellectual values related to these problems (Wax, 1971). It is certainly more difficult than when measures of the phenomena are relatively objective and reliable, as in safety standards for nuclear reactors, design of transportation systems, or problems related to pollution. Nevertheless, it seems reasonable to expect that social scientists will try to separate these two types of judgments, for the alternative would suggest that social scientists expect to exert greater influence with regard to their values as citizen-intellectuals than other citizens.

If societal decision makers come to the conclusion that it is impossible for them to acquire an unbiased evaluation of a scientific or technical problem—one that is not independent of the professional's political or moral preferences—there may be more substantial repercussions than just a loss of credibility. Since societal decision makers have a responsibility for allocating resources to support the scientific enterprise, they may begin to question whether or not this investment of public funds is providing an appropriate return—namely, unbiased knowledge that can be used to further the best interests of society, interests usually defined by legislatures and administrators. Hence, widespread and persistent convolution of technical and political opinions in the public statements of social scientists may not only lead to a reduction of credibility but may lead to a reduction in the public resources and privileges provided for the social science enterprise.

Regardless of which strategy is adopted by scientists in making their public statements, controversy over issues on which there is genuine technical disagreement may be quite confusing to typical citizens and societal decision makers, who may not understand the range or subtleties of the issues involved. The result may be confusion among the audience, a tendency to avoid the entire debate, and resolution of the problem on other, more familiar, grounds— perhaps legal. One suggestion has been to establish a "science court" that would provide for public, orderly discussion among scientists of a particular issue, resulting in a summary document suitable for public dissemination and designed to assist decision makers in clarifying policies affected by these scientific judgments. While there are some serious reservations about this method of producing "instant truth"—a major one being who will decide the "answers," since the usual procedure is for the entire scientific community to "choose among theories"—it might help to minimize the tendency to confound scientific judgments with personal political or moral positions (Presidential Advisory Group on Anticipated Advances in Science and Technology, 1976).

While new scientific knowledge may take longer to affect political judgments and policies than it takes to affect introductory textbooks, this may be an unavoidable consequence of having political systems in which the decision makers are periodically replaced and new knowledge related to the political, economic, and educational institutions of society is constantly being developed. Social scientists can certainly play a useful role in helping decision makers select and interpret information relevant to their decisions, but attempts to use this professional influence to exert undue influence with regard to political or moral issues may lead to suspicion, reductions in influence on scientific issues, and perhaps a loss of resources or privileges for the scientific enterprise.

Scientists and Organizational Dependence

Scientists who are part of an organization involved in basic research or development of an operational technique or device can also face serious dilemmas. If they feel that satisfaction of a moral obligation regarding the potential effects of an application requires them to influence those with the legitimate responsibility for implementation, they are placed in the position of attempting to exert influence on organizational officials (administrators or executives) beyond that normally anticipated. Further, if they go outside the organization and attempt to attract public attention and support for their position, they may create a "public relations" problem for the organization, subjecting it to unfavorable publicity. A frequent form of response to such actions is quite direct—"whistle-blowers" are punished or fired, while researchers who agree to a "conspiracy of silence" are quietly rewarded (Edsall, 1975a, 1975b; Jaroslovsky, 1977). There are numerous examples of such reactions involving all types of professionals (lawyers, accountants, scientists, and the like) and all types of organizations (prestigious universities, government agencies, and private corporations) in which the dominant pattern has been to quash dissent and promote the image of the organization as a benevolent "happy family." Since most professionals are aware of the risk of "whistle blowing," any scientists or investigators who choose to engage in a public controversy over an application of scientific knowledge can be assumed to be quite serious and confident that the potential negative effects for the public justify the risk to their careers.

Perhaps in response to this problem—and the risks it involves—there have been a number of attempts to develop standards for the treatment of social scientists as members of organizations. For example, national associations representing scientists have attempted to define the reciprocal rights and obligations that its members assume when they occupy certain types of occupational roles. This is most apparent with regard to associations that represent both applied professionals and scientific investigators. Medical and psychological associations, for example, have developed substantial and sophisticated sets of standards regarding the rights and privileges of applied professionals with respect to clients, society, and one other. In some cases, standards for activities pursued as investigators and applied professionals are combined.

In a similar fashion, many of the associations have chosen to adopt standards with regard to the relationship between social scientists who are college professors and academic organizations. In the United States this is reflected in the endorsement of the "Academic Freedom and Tenure: 1940 Statement of Principles" American Association of University Professors, 1974, by the national associations representing the major social sciences—anthropology, economics, political science, psychology, and sociology. These principles specify the conditions under which a faculty member can assume that tenure has been extended (after six years of full-time employment in the same institution if notice of termination has not been given) and a complex due-process procedure that must be followed if tenure is to be revoked.

A number of codes provided by national associations of social scientists refer to the relationship between social scientists and the organizations that employ them; almost all these codes are provided by associations representing psychologists. The composite of these codes in Appendix 6 was created by organizing the statements that appeared in these codes into a uniform format. Most of the statements are related to immediate, practical problems: autonomy in professional matters (such as intepreting test scores and data), respect of the rights of the organization, and issues related to the conditions and terms of employment and termination. However, not *one* of these principles is related to the actions a social scientist might take if he disagreed with the use of knowledge created within the organization. This is probably because most of the associations that created these statements are concerned with social scientists who contribute to organizations with an applied focus, such as industrial firms or public schools. The role of the social scientist is defined as one of interpreting and modifying existing knowledge for the purposes of the organization rather than assisting the organization in the creation of new knowledge (a similar perspective has been adopted by seventeen national engineering societies; Institute of Electrical and Electronic Engineers, 1973).

Standards regarding the rights and responsibilities of scientists in scientific organizations have been adopted by the United Nations Economic, Social, and Cultural Organization (1975) as a recommendation to all member nations. This document, designed to cover the research and development activity, part-time or full-time, of all scientific research workers (paragraphs 2 and 3), defines the responsibilities of scientists as related to mankind in general (paragraph 13) and mentions their right to publicly present views about the potential value of research and development and the actions they may take in response to projects they feel may not be "human or socially and ecologically responsible" (paragraph 4). The most relevant principle is expressed as follows (paragraph 14): "Member states should seek to encourage conditions in which scientific researchers, with the support of the public authorities, have the responsibility and the right: (c) to express themselves freely on the human, social, or ecological value of certain projects and in the last resort withdraw from these projects if their conscience so dictates." Further, the principles emphasize the scientist's right to publish, suggesting careful specification of this right in writing if it is to be restricted and a mechanism for appeal by the scientists if they object to restraints imposed upon them (paragraphs 35–37).

While these standards are intended to cover all scientific workers, they reflect a primary concern for the situation of scientists employed by public and private organizations. The standards suggest that the final choice of scientists should be to withdraw from projects they find "morally unacceptable" but provide no solution to the problem of the scientist's personal support or career disruption if withdrawal leads to termination of employment.

The American Association for the Advancement of Science (AAAS) organized a committee to review the same problem, eventually emphasizing the situation of the "whistle-blower" who creates public controversy about applications of science or technology by his or her organization (Edsall, 1975a; 1975b). While the committee concluded that it was appropriate for scientists to exercise their public responsibility by disclosing potentially "dangerous" situations, they were unable to develop recommendations that would lead to protection for the "whistle-blower." They suggested that due process become part of scientist-employer agreements, that professional associations move to represent the public interest (in addition to that of their members), and that the AAAS continue to support study of the problem. No unequivocal, immediate solutions are provided for the problems confronted by scientists who feel a public statement on a controversial issue is justified.

There are several examples of endangered scientists or engineers receiving assistance from their colleagues through professional associations. The most dramatic may be that of two engineers who worked on the design of a new mass transit system and were terminated after they publicized defects in the safety characteristics of the control mechanism. Their criticisms, which were consistent with the erratic operation of the actual system, led to a legislative investigation and eventually to redesign of the components under question. A local chapter of an engineering society provided funds to retain legal counsel to support these "whistleblowers" (Friedlander, 1973; Edsall, 1975a). In a similar fashion, several national associations representing social scientists (anthropologists, political scientists, and sociologists) filed a brief with the Supreme Court on behalf of a scholar jailed for contempt of a grand jury for not revealing his sources of information about the disclosure of confidential government documents—the "Pentagon Papers" (Carroll, 1973).

These examples might suggest that professional associations routinely assist members who take a public stance that promotes the public interest or the interests of the profession. There are several reasons why this does not always happen. Most basic is the marginal financial status of professional associations. Those representing social scientists are usually organized for the discussion of common intellectual concerns rather than as a serious attempt to represent professionals before the host society. A second problem is determining those conflicts where assistance is actually justified. Presumably, professional associations would prefer to assist only those members who take a responsible position (reflecting a competent professional analysis of a critical problem) related to the public interest, not just to their own personal predicaments. Involvement in controversy over personal or trivial professional issues would not further an association's credibility as a source of concern for the public interest. As currently constituted, associations representing social scientists probably cannot be depended on to provide assistance and support—other than encouragement—for scientists who challenge established authorities. They may again come to the defense of a besieged member but cannot be considered a certain source of support.

There are many sources of moral support from professional associations at the national and international levels, both disciplinary and multidisciplinary, for investigators who consider an application of scientific or technical knowledge as not in the best interests of society and inconsistent with their own personal values. For some scientists, public comments on such issues is not a major concern, for they have assured careers either as applied professionals with diverse clienteles or as tenured academics. However, for those with a career commitment to organizations—a relationship that may be terminated at the discretion of administrators—initiation of a public controversy is quite a different matter; such an action can pose severe risks for the investigator, including the loss of opportunity to pursue a career. Unfortunately, there is as yet no viable mechanism for helping such individuals share or minimize such a risk—or even receive an unbiased hearing.

A review of the issues associated with attempts to influence responsible officials with regard to the application of science and technology thus indicates that there are special problems associated with such actions. If the persuasive statements do not provide a clear separation of technical judgments from personal political or moral values, there is a strong possibility that the credibility of all scientists may be affected, as well as support for scientific activities. In short, all scientists—not just those who make public statements—may be affected by an inappropriate attempt at persuasion. The situation of scientists in untenable organizational positions is of special interest, for they may find their careers truncated if they initiate a public controversy, particularly if their stance is not eventually vindicated. Despite considerable attention to this problem, there are as yet no viable solutions for protecting "endangered scientists," those scientists who are dependent upon organizations but nevertheless publicly challenge decisions regarding the application of science.

Conclusion

A major concern of scientists—perhaps because of their strong identification with the knowledge they produce—is the implementation of science for practical objectives; they often assume that they should have an influence on applications to ensure that the best interests of society and their own personal values are reflected in these. However, a systematic review of the types of negative effects—harm or benefits forgone—and of the extent to which control over applications is considered the responsibility of the originating scientists suggests that opportunities for such influence are quite limited. The major conclusions were as follows:

1. Scientists can attempt to minimize failures to utilize new knowledge by publicizing the new advance and the possible benefits in the hope that this will influence the applied professionals who utilize scientific knowledge.
2. Unless scientists are, simultaneously, applied professionals, there is little they can do to minimize misapplication of existing knowledge. (Fortunately, most applied professionals have developed and support mechanisms to discourage such problems.)
3. A scientist may try to prevent the application of new scientific knowledge that produces effects inconsistent with his or her citizen–intellectual values through public statements on the dangers and disadvantages of the potential applications and through refusal to participate in the development of new knowledge that may be misused.
4. Misuse of data collected as part of a research project may be minimized if investigators obtain and organize data in such a way that all participants remain anonymous and unidentifiable, and if suitable interpretations, the inapplicability of alternate interpretations, and the limitations of the data are made clear by the original investigator so as to prevent, as far as possible, misinterpretations of aggregate data describing subgroups or special subcultures of society.

Most originating scientists are unable to have a major effect on the use of, or the failure to use, scientific knowledge; they usually do not control the application or have any direct, legitimated influence over those who do—applied professionals or decision makers in commerce and government, for example. As a result, their major influence takes the form of careful, relevant arguments designed to persuade those who control applications. They can, of course, also refuse to contribute to the development of knowledge that may be used in ways inconsistent with the scientist's values as a citizen-intellectual, but this will be an effective form of control only if all qualified scientists refuse to contribute to the project in question.

An additional dilemma may occur for scientists when legitimate societal decision makers, either political leaders or government administrators, request expert advice or contribution to research projects related to a societal problem. If the problem, or the particular application of scientific knowledge, may result in effects incongruent with the citizen-intellectual values of the scientist, there are only a few options available: (1) to refuse to make any statement on the issue, (2) to make a statement but clearly indicate opposition to the way the problem is defined or the application of the solution, or (3) to refuse to participate in any research related to the problem.

The action of one or more scientists to affect the utilization of scientific knowledge in practical applications may result in several types of negative effects—loss of credibility for scientists as a source of objective technical advice, loss of personal income or career opportunities for "unprotected" investigators, and a reduction of financial support for the scientific enterprise (if seen as support for narrow political values). There seems to be no obvious solution to this problem. Investigators who take controversial public positions may expect to receive substantial moral support but little assistance of substance (legal fees, guaranteed career opportunities, and so forth) if their presentations are inconsistent with the prevailing orientations of decision makers.

In the final analysis, a satisfactory relationship between the scientific enterprise and societal decision makers will probably be enhanced by mutual trust and respect. The following comment about the actions of atomic scientists would seem unlikely to further such a relationship: "It's like leaving long knives among small children and saying, 'Well, let them decide what to do with them.' The society has an immature mind, and is unable to digest complicated information and make complex decisions. The scientist, both because he has more information and because he causes the problem, has an extra responsibility" (Etzioni, 1973, p. 34). This statement has several unique characteristics. First, it employs a rather special concept of "responsibility," ignoring the key feature—ability and right to control an outcome—ordinarily associated with the term. Second, the anthropomorphization of "society" is unlikely to produce a useful analysis of the issues, since it ignores the mechanisms by which scientific knowledge is applied to societal problems. Finally, the assumption that the legitimated decision makers of society—elected leaders and their administrative staffs— are so naive and unsophisticated that they should be treated like irresponsible children is arrogant and probably inaccurate. In sum, such comments are unlikely to encourage consultation with scientists regarding the application of scientific knowledge.

13

Overview and
Future Developments

An intuitive feeling that a state of affairs should be otherwise—particularly if that feeling is associated with a sense of sorrow, regret, or anger—is the essence of a moral dilemma; its emotional aspects set it apart from a routine predicament or value quandary. While certain actions are universally and unambiguously condemned ("Thou shalt not kill"), there are a large number of situations where any alternatives (even no action) may be considered morally inappropriate by some. Three such dilemmas—conflicts between obligations as scientists and obligations as citizens, concern over the application of scientific knowledge, and involvement of human participants in risky but important research—may be confronted by serious, conscientious social scientists.

These dilemmas reflect inconsistencies between solutions developed to resolve several general issues in complex, modern societies, including the justification for a political state, criteria for selecting societal programs or policies, and individual standards for a moral or good life. The major solution to the first issue, justification for a political state, is associated with the idea of a social contract, which assumes that members of society give up certain privileges in return for a just and efficient administration of society and a guarantee of selected individual rights, rights that can be relinquished only with the informed consent of the individual involved. The most widely accepted strategy for evaluating societal activities is utilitarian analysis; such an analysis estimates the total positive and negative effects and then selects alternatives expected to provide the greatest net benefit to society. The distribution of effects among members of society may also be taken into account. Major criteria for guiding individuals toward a moral or good life are related to the direct effects for others, as reflected in the Golden Rule ("Do unto others as you would have them do unto you"); notions of charity and accepting responsibility for others may also be emphasized—some analyses focus upon personal rules that would lead to maximum benefits for society as a whole.

While these solutions are generally satisfactory for each specific type of problem, moral dilemmas occur in situations where more than one philosophy may apply, leading to a sense that, no matter what choice is adopted, it will not be consistent with some desired objective—respect for individual rights, increased benefits for society, or responding as a good or moral person. For example, scientific progress may require extreme dedication and concentration and thus encourage an investigator to ignore or avoid immediate, direct contributions to the welfare of others—this is the essence of the scientist-citizen dilemma. Scientists may feel that decision makers are considering applications of science that would not be best for society (or some of its members); attempts to influence such applications (as a moral person) may be ineffective and lead to career disruptions that would decrease a particular scientist's ability to make future contributions to science (or society), to say nothing of effects upon his or her personal welfare. Finally, to develop scientific knowledge that may improve the human condition, it may be necessary to expose human participants to risks that would be inconsistent with respect for the rights and welfare of others (the standard reflected in the Golden Rule). In sum, none of these dilemmas is unique or unprecedented, but increases in useful knowledge about important social and human phenomena have made them more salient for social scientists.

A number of strategies may be adopted by social scientists to resolve the citizen-scientist dilemma. A widely discussed position is that of the autonomous (or value-free) investigator, who emphasizes the study and understanding of natural phenomena without concern for current problems in society or the mechanisms by which scientific knowledge is applied to practical affairs. This may result in concern for the kind of rights that will promote scientists' ability to create scientific knowledge. Another alternative is the orientation of the applied scientist, who contributes to practical problems with theories, information, or techniques developed within the scientific community; this strategy requires explicit consideration of the definitions of problems and criteria for solutions adopted by nonscientists. Concern with current problems in society may lead a scientist to become a societal mentor, counseling or advising society by describing problems and suggesting solutions. Extreme distress may result in social activism—aggressive, direct attempts to change society either by becoming involved in the political process or through research. This may include the "use" of research to achieve political goals, at the expense of scientific objectives. Some social scientists may permanently adopt a particular strategy; others may shift perspectives depending upon the issues at hand and their estimates of the consequences of adopting each orientation as a solution to the moral dilemma.

The effectiveness of various strategies for minimizing the application of knowledge dilemma may depend upon the status and potential impact of the knowledge. If benefits are forgone because of the failure of those in applied roles to adopt the knowledge, there is little an investigator can do but inform them of the possible benefits. When concerned that a project may develop knowledge with a substantial potential for harm, investigators can refuse to become involved, but this will have a major impact only if no other scientists contribute to the project. If available scientific knowledge is to be utilized in ways an investigator considers detrimental, attempts to inform and persuade the responsible decision makers may be the only viable alternative; this may lead to serious career disruption or limitations on future influence if the issues are of substantial consequence and the investigator's actions are seen as extreme or highly political.

Dilemmas associated with the utilization of human participants in research are unique with respect to both the substantial recent attention they have received and the emergence of a number of mechanisms to resolve them. The dominant philosophical solutions—the emphasis on individual rights leading to informed consent and on utilitarian or risk-benefit analysis—were the basis for developing five issues to guide the analysis of research activities. These issues included attention to (1) the effects of a research program on intellectual objectives, (2) the effects of a specific project on a research program, (3) the effects for the research participants, (4) distribution of effects among participants and members of society, and (5) evidence that the procedure demonstrated consideration for the rights and welfare of participants. The value of these five issues as guides for the analysis of research activity was explored in Part One through applications to selected examples of research in three categories: experimental, descriptive, and covert.

Analysis of experimental research in both controlled and in natural settings (designed to affect "real-world" behavior) suggested that the major issues were related to the direct effects for the participants because of the investigator's responsibility for control of independent variables and, therefore, of effects on the participants. In those studies where informed consent could not be obtained without disruption to the objectives of research, concern for the participants could be demonstrated by the use of surrogate informed consent, careful postresearch debriefing, and surveillance during and after the research to ensure that negative effects were detected, minimized, and eliminated as far as possible

A major issue associated with descriptive research, that is, whether the information was obtained covertly or overtly, involved demonstration of respect for the participant's anonymity and the confidentiality of information. A large number of techniques has been developed to increase the possibility that participants' anonymity will be maintained. While covert research procedures provide a potential for a substantial infringement upon the privacy of participants, there have been no well-publicized cases in which disclosure of confidential information has occurred, much less caused embarrassment or damage to participants.

Special problems develop in the conduct of cross-cultural research; these problems are most complex when the host culture is a relatively primitive society under the supervision of another society. When the "crossed" culture is another economically advanced democracy, the analysis related to research may be quite similar to that for the "home" society. In less developed societies, the ability of participants to receive substantial benefits from new scientific knowledge may be quite limited. An equitable balance of effects may nevertheless be achieved if direct benefits to the participants are emphasized.

Concern over the research dilemma has resulted in a number of mechanisms designed to reassure the general public that investigators will not engage in unjustified infringement upon the rights and welfare of ordinary individuals. These include the principles adopted by professional associations, the federal guidelines and review procedures imposed upon the scientific community, and the general constraints embodied in legal standards. Unfortunately, none of these mechanisms is explicitly designed to assist investigators as they try to resolve the research dilemma. There is some provision for acquiring counsel or advice from ethics committees of professional associations or federally imposed institutional review boards, but these are not really organized or designed to assist investigators; they were developed to review complaints or evaluate proposed research as a means to discourage mistreatment of participants. It is clear that the legal principles applicable to social science investigators will continue to assume that they have a primary obligation as citizens; information gathered from participants (even if preceded by promises of confidentiality) will not be immune from legal subpoena except in very special situations (projects provided with immunity through special arrangements with federal sponsors).

Speculation on Future Developments

If viewed as emotional responses to incongruencies between reality and conceptions of an ideal, moral dilemmas may never be eliminated. As it will always be possible to elaborate the ideal as reality improves, there is an unlimited potential for dissatisfaction. As social scientists expand the scope of phenomena they study and develop new techniques for investigation, the range of situations and events under surveillance and capable of producing dilemmas will increase. As the scope of rights and individuals considered to have special rights expands, the potential for mistreatment will also expand; one recent proposal, for example, involves granting rights to groups.

The fundamental conceptualization used to justify the existence of a political state envisions a joint agreement among individuals—each person is to be treated as a unique and autonomous entity. Recent legal and government administrative actions have emphasized equal treatment for all individuals. Decisions are not to be made on the basis of sex, race, color, religion, and so forth. But it has been suggested that this antidiscrimination principle is inadequate to protect the interests of various disadvantaged groups, aggregates of individuals with a common social characteristic (ethnic identity and economic status receive the major attention). One alternative to the antidiscrimination principle has been referred to as the group disadvantaging principle, which states that the effect of a law or policy upon specially disadvantaged groups (social categories of people) should not be to aggravate or perpetuate such disadvantages (Fiss, 1976). In effect, this would preclude any actions affecting disadvantaged categories that would not clearly lead to an improvement in their position in society, including research upon individuals in such a category. Given this perspective, the informed consent of individual participants may not be considered adequate. If there could be indirect negative effects for the entire aggregate, the informed consent of the aggregate may be required before research can be conducted.

Extension of rights to social categories was advocated (approved by 58 percent of the 55 percent that voted; *Newsletter of the American Anthropological Association,* 1972b) by the fellows and voting members of the American Anthropological Association when they formally approved a motion condemming "theories of genetic inferiority of races, sexes, or classes" as "dangerous and unscientific" and because they "justify shifting the burden of the present economic crisis onto those who are already the most oppressed" and "attack the legitimate aspirations of oppressed people for a decent life" (*Newsletter of the American Anthropological Association,* 1972a, p.12). A major university has proposed prohibition of any research that entails "social risks" by placing the reputation or status of a social group or an institution in jeopardy (Hart, 1973; Irving, 1973). However, the changes required in the conceptual basis of the current legal system would be so great as to preclude the expectation that such group rights will be legally established in the near future. The decision in the Bakke case regarding reverse discrimination in medical school admissions suggests that the current Supreme Court will emphasize individual rights rather than group rights (Van Alstyne, 1978).

While the categories of human beings considered to have full rights may not be expanded much further (virtually all major categories seem to have been included), the expansion of rights to include nonhumans seems to be attracting substantial interest, usually associated with the condemnation of any procedure that involves mistreatment of animals. One attempt to justify this position is based on defining the moral community (those who have rights) as all sensate entities, those capable of experiencing pain or pleasure (Singer, 1975); hence, animals would be included—and plants as well if they could be shown to experience sensations (as some have suggested they do).

This is a somewhat different conception of rights than that developed from legal and political philosophies, where rights were formalized as a guarantee against abuses (unwarranted restraint, incarceration, loss of property, and so forth) that a societal leadership might impose upon the other parties to the social contract, the ordinary citizens. As it would be almost impossible to provide a convincing argument that nonhuman animals could take part in the development of a plan for organizing and administering society, it is necessary to assume that their rights are justified on some other basis, such as defining the moral community as including all sensate beings, mentioned above. The only ambiguity then becomes the categories of animals to be extended such rights; these generally include animals perceived to have human-like emotions or a complex social oganization (it also helps if they are "cute"). A young caretaker who released dolphins participating in research on man-dolphin communication attempted to utilize this argument in his defense (Turner, 1977); the circuit judge barred testimony relating to dolphin rights and the caretaker was convicted of first-degree theft by a jury (New York Times, 1977). Regardless of the basis, the use of animals in research may become more controversial; acceptable justifications may have to emphasize direct benefits for humans. Research utilizing animals only to expand scientific knowledge or reduce curiosity may become more difficult to defend (Loew, 1978).

      Major changes in the pattern of activity related to the resolution of the citizen-scientist dilemma are unlikely. A majority of social scientists will probably continue to adopt an autonomous investigator's or applied scientist's perspective as their major professional focus, with a smaller number acting as societal mentors or social activists. The pursuit of the social activist strategy is made difficult by the expense associated with most research; it will be hard to develop systematic and predictable funding from public sources for activities designed to promote a particular political perspective or the interests of a special group in society. While the professional associations may occasionally take political stands (as with the Vietnam conflict or equal rights for women) or encourage the involvement of their members in the politics of society (see the ethical codes of the American Anthropological Association and the American Political Science Association), it is unlikely there will be a major shift in the focus of these organizations away from the intellectual and professional interests of their scientist-investigator members. Of course, individual scientists may continue to shift from one strategy to another, depending upon the phenomenon being studied and the current political situation.

      As long as most investigators with a full-time commitment to science require resources for personal and research support, the alternatives for affecting the utilization of knowledge will not substantially change. Those with tenure in academic settings will have the freedom to make public statements without fear of personal retaliation, but may find that this limits their ability to affect decision makers and to gain funding. Those employed within government agencies or private organizations who make public statements inconsistent with the posture of organizational decision makers may continue to place their careers in jeopardy. The discharging or disciplining of "whistle-blowers" is one of the most difficult problems confronted by all professionals (accountants, lawyers, engineers, scientists, and so forth). Mechanisms to provide formal protection for "whistle-blowers" may soon be implemented within federal agencies (Gaines, 1978), but this would not guarantee protection from informal sanctions and subtle retaliation, lost promotions, or uninteresting work assignments. Those in private organizations may never receive any form of protection for speaking out in ways that demonstrate "disloyalty" to the organization.

While the research dilemma may never change, specific issues will vary; substantial public attention, particularly if isolated examples of participant abuse are newsworthy, will persist. Existing mechanisms to encourage public confidence that social scientists are not capriciously and callously misusing research participants will continue to be formalized and elaborated, although the basic features are unlikely to be altered. Professional associations have clearly demonstrated some capacity for controlling or standardizing the behavior of applied professionals (as lawyers, physicians, clinical psychologists, and so forth) but little ability to influence the actions of scientists and investigators. The legal system serves as a final arbitrator for the most extreme forms of abuse, but these are seldom found in either biomedical or social research, occurring more frequently in applied activities. The major mechanisms for controlling social science research will continue to be those of the federal government, which can use its financial resources to influence the conduct of investigations.

Up to 1979, the most systematic official attention given to the research dilemma has come from the National Commission for the Protection of Human Subjects of Biomedical and Behavioral Research. The bias represented by the title was incorporated in the original wording of Public Law 93–348—unfortunately, the commission was not established to examine both aspects of the research dilemma. Between 1974 and 1978 the commission composed of "individuals distinguished in the fields of medicine, law, ethics, theology, the biological, physical, behavioral sciences, philosophy, humanities, health administration, government, and public affairs"

(Public Law 93–348, Title II, Part A, Sec. 201, [b][1]) sponsored research and reports from consultants, held public hearings, and eventually produced reports on nine topics relevant to ethical dilemmas in research (each accompanied by a substantial appendix). Four of these reflect uncertainty about the implementation of informed consent with special categories of individuals involved in research: fetuses, prisoners, children and those institutionalized as mentally infirm (National Commission for the Protection of Human Subjects of Biomedical and Behavioral Research, 1975, 1976, 1977c, 1978a). They provide a review of major issues for those conducting research with participants in these categories.

The paternalistic bias of the commission toward participants is reflected in the recommendations for research with prisoners (National Commission for the Protection of Human Subjects of Biomedical and Behavioral Research, 1976). Despite the fact that their studies of contemporary practices could locate no evidence of investigators who failed to follow the letter and spirit of informed consent procedures, no evidence of any permanent negative effects for any prisoners (and modest evidence of temporary negative effects), and not one prisoner who said that opportunities to participate in research should not be made available (whether or not the prisoner had accepted such opportunities), the commission felt that, unless prison conditions were improved, a voluntary choice would be impossible and recommended that all research with prisoners be prohibited. But they thus denied all prisoners the opportunity to improve their situation during incarceration. These recommendations were adopted; only research with benefits to prisoners as individuals or as a social category are now permitted by federal regulations (*Federal Register, 43* (222): 53,652).

The remaining topics considered by the national commission include a research procedure with controversial benefits (psychosurgery), a review of the operation of the institutional review boards (the major empirical study was reviewed above in Chapter Nine), consideration of the orientation to be taken toward the delivery of health services by federal agencies (recommending it be considered a right, not a privilege, to receive medical care), a review of the major considerations associated with the involvement of human subjects in research, and attention to mechanisms that may reduce problems associated with unexpected biomedical or behavioral science advances with radical implications for society (National Commission for the Protection of Human Subjects of Biomedical and Behavioral Research, 1977a, 1978b, 1978d, 1978e, 1978f).

The penultimate report (National Commission for the Protection of Human Subjects of Biomedical and Behavioral Research, 1978e) was designed to provide a set of general principles for resolving the research dilemma, and it emphasizes three considerations: (1) respect for persons as individuals, (2) benefice (concern for individuals' welfare), and (3) justice ("fairness in distribution" or "what is deserved"). It suggests that the appropriate use of informed consent procedures will ensure that respect for persons is present, that careful attention to the assessment of the risks and benefits of research for the participants will ensure that benefice is achieved, and that judicious selection of participants is crucial for ensuring that justice is present. These concerns are similar to three issues developed for analysis of the research dilemma in this book; namely, 3) the nature of effects for participants, 4) distribution of effects among participants and members of society, and 5) evidence of consideration for the rights and welfare of the participants. However, the national commission emphasized "protecting subjects" and failed to provide any recommendations for, or attention to, the important prior issues that supply the major justification for any research (whether or not it involves human participants): (1) effects of a research program on achieving important intellectual objectives and (2) the nature of the effects of a research project on a research program. This inattention may have resulted partly from a belief that the federal government should not interfere with scientific freedom but only with the actual conduct of research (National Commission for the Protection of Human Subjects of Biomedical and Behavioral Research, 1978b), although any decision to allocate financial resources affects the potential to exercise scientific freedom and the federal government is very much involved in these decisions.

The activities of a typical investigator will probably be most affected by the procedures required by institutional review boards, the review committees designed to provide confidence that human participants are not being misused. The National Commission has made several recommendations, including expansion of the system to supervise as much research as possible, standardizing and coordinating the procedures utilized by all government agencies (in addition to HEW), providing for the systematic surveillance of institutional review boards to ensure compliance with the guidelines, and implementing mechanisms that will provide legal immunity for the members (this does involve recognition of a responsibility for risks to human participants of approved research). There is, in addition, a growing recognition that a large percentage of research does not involve a substantial risk for participants and that review of large numbers of low-risk projects might produce a genuine overload problem.

This has led to the recommendation that DHEW encourage "expedited review" procedures. A list of low-or no-risk research techniques would be developed and approved by an appropriate group; any project utilizing only procedures on such a list would then be spared the necessity for a full, formal review. Examples of "minimal risk" procedures included (National Commission for the Protection of Human Subjects of Biomedical and Behavioral Research, 1978b, p. 35):

F. Voice recordings made for research purposes;
G. Moderate exercise by healthy volunteers;
H. The use of survey research instruments . . . and psychological tests, . . . provided that the subjects are normal volunteers and that the data will be gathered anonymously or that confidentiality will be protected by procedures appropriate to the sensitivity of the data;
I. Program evaluation projects that entail no deviation for subjects from normal requirements of their involvment in the program being evaluated or . . . benefits related to their participation in such programs;
J. Research using standard protocols or noninvasive procedures generally accepted as presenting no more than minimal risk, even when done by students

While not yet officially adopted as DHEW policy, such a procedure could, if fully implemented, reduce both the resources required for review of projects, the delays confronted by investigators, and investigators' resentment at being subjected to supervision without a reasonable cause.

Federal regulation of research may continue to emphasize the process of review rather than the effects for participants (which are generally nil, as discussed in Chapter Three) or the importance of the research issues (an attempt to avoid encroachment upon scientific freedom). This emphasis is reflected in a hearing involving charges that the State University of New York at Albany (SUNYA) failed to ensure that proper prior review procedures had been followed for a research project conducted within the psychology department; that is, that the project had not received approval from an institutional review board (Smith, 1977a). Responding to allegations publicized by a graduate student dropped from the doctoral program, both the state health department and the National Institutes of Health investigated charges that individuals were coerced into participation and were not fully informed about the research experience and that in one study equipment used to administer electric shocks was unsafe. Immediately prior to the second public hearing on the matter, SUNYA officials agreed that there had been violations of procedure. A one-hundred-thousand-dollar state fine was suspended pursuant to the university's compliance with state and federal procedures during a monitoring period (Smith, 1977b). There was no charge or evidence of any direct negative effects for any research participant; the "offenses" attributed to the investigators and the institution were all related to violations of procedure. Further, there is good reason to suspect that the investigators demonstrated considerable respect for the rights and welfare of the participants (Tedeschi and Gallup, 1977), following the spirit, if not the form, of the federal guidelines; the research had been reviewed and approved by a committee within the psychology department.

Compared to the attention directed toward the supervision and control of investigators who conduct research incorporating human participants, the effort directed toward providing some form of assistance to those "damaged" by participation in research is quite modest. At the core of this issue is the need to clearly determine the source of negative effects for participants. This is considerably complicated by the wide range of social science research activities. Effects associated with natural phenomena are difficult to ascribe to the actions of investigators developing descriptions, particularly when the participants may not even know that data were collected for research purposes (as in some types of covert research). Least ambiguous is experimental research (the biomedical model that has been the basis for many of the government regulations), where the investigator may deliberately affect some aspect of the participant's context or personal attributes to examine the impact of such manipulations.

Effects for participants in research may be attributed to a number of sources, including:

1. Phenomena that may have unpredictable or unknown consequences;
2. The investigator who designed and supervised the project;
3. The host institution that provided facilities and encouraged the conduct of research;
4. The agency that provided financial support for the research;
5. The institutional review board that reviewed the project and determined it was worthwhile;
6. Society in general, which may have supported the investigator's training, the host institution, the sponsoring agency and provided members for the institutional review board;
7. The participant who provided competent, voluntary, informed, and comprehending consent to become involved, implying an acceptance of some responsibility for effects that may result.

Concern with preventing negative effects shifts emphasis to those causes that can be controlled and thus tends to exclude consideration of the phenomena; concern for determining blame emphasizes the responsibility of the investigator, host institution, sponsoring agency, or institutional review board; concern for providing recompense or correcting any negative effects leads to a different emphasis, an emphasis upon who can bear the costs.

Participants will bear some costs regardless of who else may be affected. Investigators are logical candidates to bear some costs, but unless the restitution for participants is restricted to professional attention or the investigators are privately wealthy, they will not be able to provide the needed resources—they are protected by their poverty, so to speak. The major source of responsibility with the resources to provide recompense or full corrective actions is society, and society clearly takes on responsibility through its support of host institutions, institutional review boards, and funding agencies. The idea that some form of insurance or a societal compensation program be initiated for the benefit of participants is not new; it was seriously discussed as early as 1969 (Calabresi), primarily in response to concern for participants in biomedical research. One review of the legal issues led to a proposal for a federally administered compensation fund to provide for the participants but no idemnification of investigators from suits initiated under common law; this latter feature was designed to discourage irresponsible or reckless investigators from misusing participants (Adams and Shea-Stonum, 1975).

There may be some movement in this direction in the near future, for a federal task force has recommended that participants injured in government-supported research be compensated for physical, psychological, or social injuries (1) if the injuries are in excess of those expected in the absence of research (those expected to be sustained from some phenomena or event if not mitigated by therapeutic treatment associated with the research); (2) if the research activity was the proximal cause of the injury; and (3) if the research was financially supported or conducted by the government (Department of Health, Education, and Welfare, 1977). This procedure would exclude all research not receiving federal financial support; the approval of research by government-mandated procedures would not lead to coverage by government-sponsored insurance. Perhaps such projects could purchase the needed insurance from the federal government.

Justification of Social Science to Society

A fundamental issue for all investigators, reflected in the increasing federal constraints on research, is their ability to maintain or increase public support for the social science enterprise. At least three different strategies are possible in attempting to achieve this objective: avoid any research topic or procedure that may be controversial, emphasize the traditional justification that any expansion of knowledge provides societal benefits, or shift emphasis to significant social phenomena where immediate benefits justify effects for participants.

Proponents of the first strategy tend to emphasize the activities of social scientists in terms of their relations to other members of society (the participants) and conclude that social scientists should avoid any technique or procedure that would diminish their stature as "model citizens":

> Research of this sort [covert participant observation] is liable to damage the reputation of sociology in the larger society and close off promising areas of research for future investigators [Erikson, 1967, p. 369].

> Social science must not become identified in the public mind with "snooping" and "prying"—that is, with unwarranted invasion of privacy [Conrad, 1967, p. 359].

> The treatment of persons as nonpersons inevitably erodes the trust and respect of citizens which the research enterprise requires to flourish, and inevitably results in withdrawal by the body collective of its cooperation and accessibility [Baumrind, 1977, p.10].

> His research tactics . . . reinforces an image already prevalent in some circles that social scientists are sly tricksters who are not to be trusted. The more widespread this image becomes, the more difficult it will be for any social scientists to carry out studies[Warwick, 1973, p.37].

This general line of argument, often associated with the idea that social scientists have an obligation to act as model citizens in their professional (and often personal) life, seems to rest on two inconsistent assumptions. One the one hand, the results of social science research are seen as so trivial and innocuous that no risks to the rights and welfare of the participants can ever be justified— at least not to those outside social science. On the other hand, the effects of social science research techniques are seen as so powerful that unless used with caution, they may create substantial detrimental effects for the participants. The extreme caution associated with this approach does not seem to be justified for numerous reasons; there is little systematic evidence that a substantial number (or percentage) of participants experience negative effects; participants seem to have considerable tolerance for mild discomforts or dislocations in their lives, more than social scientists seem to expect; and, if the social science enterprise is going to be considered an important source of information for society, the research emphasis should be upon human and social phenomena important to society (although the research procedure should minimize risks to the rights and welfare of participants).

A second strategy for obtaining public support is to emphasize the benefits to society from an expansion of scientific knowledge, usually defined in terms of increased knowledge and potential practical applications. It may be increasingly difficult for investigators to justify the conduct of individual projects with such arguments. Thus, major contributions to knowledge and societal benefits appear to derive from research programs—a series of studies related to a central intellectual (scientific) question; the specific benefits from any one study may not be large, but the cumulative impact of an integrated sequence of studies may be considerable. If evaluation focuses upon the cumulative effects of a research program, an isolated study without clear relevance to a more general problem or objective may not be given serious consideration.

In addition, there is the philosophical bias of the mechanisms that have significant control over research activity—the federally initiated review procedures and the legal system. The research problem is frequently considered in terms of the various rights of parties-at-interest (participants, investigators, sponsors, and so forth). Within legal structures, conflicts between the rights of individuals is a recurrent, important problem: the most widely accepted solution is to allow all parties-at-interest to present the evidence on their behalf and to use a procedure for resolving the conflict (such as a legislature, court, or institutional review board). In such a situation, those with well-explicated rights and direct representation have a considerable advantage over those with ambiguous rights and indirect (or surrogate) representation. Investigators seeking to pursue research with risk for present participants and ambiguous or uncertain benefits for future generations (which cannot be represented directly) will clearly be less persuasive.

While administrators and elected officials may feel comfortable with this form of resolution, the philosophical justification may seem unfamiliar to many scientific investigators, who find their position defined in terms of their right to scientific freedom. Some investigators may think that their goal is to develop useful knowledge—to advance scientific understanding and benefit mankind—and consider this as much an obligation as a right. They seek an opportunity to make a contribution to society; to interpret this as a desire to exercise rights gives it overtones of self-interest that may be awkward for an investigator to accept. Whether or not investigators will be able to convince societal decision makers to give more attention to their potential for making positive contributions rather than their rights is difficult to determine, but the future does not look promising in this regard.

Another factor is the change in attitudes toward social science knowledge. While there was a time when social science research was not considered of practical or political significance, it is now seen as a major basis for policy decisions and influential in affecting public opinion. In a sense, the success of social scientists, who are now taken seriously, has resulted in apprehension that research procedures and results may be misused, leading to greater public concern over the implementation of social science research. The increased respect for the importance of social science has resulted in measures to increase control of the investigators and reduce their autonomy.

A third strategy for acquiring public support for the social science enterprise is to emphasize phenomena that are significant for the conduct of people's lives and the organization of society or that have been explicitly defined as social problems. Rather than retreating to the study of trivial, innocuous phenomena or setting forth the importance of allowing investigators to satisfy their personal curiosity, this strategy emphasizes a comparison of the societal benefits and costs that research entails. Attempts to obtain societal support could take the form of preparing, in advance of the implementation of research, an analysis (preferably in written form) of the potential direct benefits to society from the conduct of a research project. Analyses could be organized around the five research dilemma issues—importance and effects of intellectual objectives, effects of a project and relevance to intellectual objectives, anticipated effects (positive and negative) for participants, a review of the possible distribution of effects and potential inequalities, and, perhaps most important, actions taken to demonstrate consideration for the rights and welfare of the participants (including any informed consent procedure).

Not only would such an analysis ensure that all major issues had been considered in advance of the research activity, minimizing the possibility that there would be unanticipated surprises for investigators or participants, but it would provide tangible evidence that the research had not been capriciously and thoughtlessly initiated. While this may appear to be a time-consuming bureaucratic chore—compared to the freedom to gather data in the spontaneous excitement of an intellectual inspiration—it will probably be necessary in one form or another for most projects of significance, a part of a proposal for funds or of a request for approval from a human subjects committee. A clear consequence of this strategy will be a shift toward research related to current social problems and away from research related to general intellectual objectives. There seems to be no way to avoid this, for projects that may provide immediate, direct benefits to all of society seem to be easier to justify than those designed to reduce intellectual curiosity but with uncertain present or future applications.

Appendix 1

Universal Declaration of Human Rights

◆━━◆━━◆━━◆━━◆━━◆━━◆━━◆━━◆━━◆

Preamble

Whereas recognition of the inherent dignity and of the equal and inalienable rights of all members of the human family is the foundation of freedom, justice and peace in the world,

Whereas disregard and contempt for human rights have resulted in barbarous acts which have outraged the conscience of mankind, and the advent of a world in which human beings shall enjoy freedom of speech and belief and freedom from fear and want has been proclaimed as the highest aspiration of the common people,

Note: This material taken from United Nations Economic, Social, and Cultural Organization, 1949, pp. 273–280. Complete text adopted on December 10, 1948, by the General Assembly of the United Nations at the Palais de Chaillot, Paris.

Whereas it is essential, if man is not to be compelled to have recourse, as a last resort, to rebellion against tyranny and oppression, that human rights should be protected by the rule of law,

Whereas it is essential to promote the development of friendly relations between nations,

Whereas the peoples of the United Nations have in the Charter reaffirmed their faith in fundamental human rights, in the dignity and worth of the human person and in the equal rights of men and women and have determined to promote social progress and better standards of life in larger freedom,

Whereas Member States have pledged themselves to achieve, in co-operation with the United Nations, the promotion of universal respect for and observance of human rights and fundamental freedoms,

Whereas a common understanding of these rights and freedoms is of the greatest importance for the full realization of this pledge,

Now, therefore, the General Assembly, proclaim this Universal Declaration of Human Rights as a common standard of achievement for all peoples and all nations, to the end that every individual and every organ of society, keeping this Declaration constantly in mind, shall strive by teaching and education to promote respect for these rights and freedoms and by progressive measures, national and international, to secure their universal and effective recognition and observance, both among the peoples of Member States themselves and among the peoples of territories under their jurisdiction.

Article 1

All human beings are born free and equal in dignity and rights. They are endowed with reason and conscience and should act towards one another in a spirit of brotherhood.

Article 2

1. Everyone is entitled to all the rights and freedoms set forth in this Declaration, without distinction of any kind, such as

race, color, sex, language, religion, political or other opinion, national or social origin, property, birth or other status.

2. Furthermore, no distinction shall be made on the basis of the political, jurisdictional or international status of the country or territory to which a person belongs, whether it be independent, trust, non-self-governing or under any other limitation of sovereignty.

Article 3

Everyone has the right to life, liberty and security of person.

Article 4

No one shall be held in slavery or servitude; slavery and the slave trade shall be prohibited in all their forms.

Article 5

No one shall be subjected to torture or to cruel, inhuman or degrading treatment or punishment.

Article 6

Everyone has the right to recognition everywhere as a person before the law.

Article 7

All are equal before the law and are entitled without any discrimination to equal protection of the law. All are entitled to equal protection against any discrimination in violation of this Declaration and against any incitement to such discrimination.

Article 8

Everyone has the right to an effective remedy by the competent national tribunals for acts violating the fundamental rights granted him by the constitution or by law.

Article 9

No one shall be subjected to arbitrary arrest, detention or exile.

Article 10

Everyone is entitled in full equality to a fair and public hearing by an independent and impartial tribunal, in the determination of his rights and obligations and of any criminal charge against him.

Article 11

1. Everyone charged with a penal offence has the right to be presumed innocent until proved guilty according to law in a public trial at which he has had all the guarantees necessary for his defense.
2. No one shall be held guilty of any penal offense on account of any act or omission which did not constitute a penal offense, under national or international law, at the time when it was committed. Nor shall a heavier penalty be imposed than the one that was applicable at the time the penal offense was committed.

Article 12

No one shall be subjected to arbitrary interference with his privacy, family, home or correspondence, nor to attacks upon his honor and reputation. Everyone has the right to the protection of the law against such interference or attacks.

Article 13

1. Everyone has the right to freedom of movement and residence within the borders of each State.
2. Everyone has the right to leave any country, including his own, and to return to his country.

Article 14

1. Everyone has the right to seek and to enjoy in other countries asylum from persecution.
2. This right may not be invoked in the case of prosecutions genuinely arising from non-political crimes or from acts contrary to the purposes and principles of the United Nations.

Article 15

   1. Everyone has the right to a nationality.
   2. No one shall be arbitrarily deprived of his nationality nor denied the right to change his nationality.

Article 16

   1. Men and women of full age, without any limitation due to race, nationality or religion, have the right to marry and to found a family. They are entitled to equal rights as to marriage, during marriage and at its dissolution.
   2. Marriage shall be entered into only with the free and full consent of the intending spouses.
   3. The family is the natural and fundamental group unit of society and is entitled to protection by society and the State.

Article 17

   1. Everyone has the right to own property alone as well as in association with others.
   2. No one shall be arbitrarily deprived of his property.

Article 18

   Everyone has the right to freedom of thought, conscience and religion; this right includes freedom to change his religion or belief, and freedom, either alone or in community with others and in public or private, to manifest his religion or belief in teaching, practice, worship and observance.

Article 19

   Everyone has the right to freedom of opinion and expression; this right includes freedom to hold opinions without interference and to seek, receive and impart information and ideas through any media and regardless of frontiers.

Article 20

   1. Everyone has the right to freedom of peaceful assembly and association.
   2. No one may be compelled to belong to an association.

Article 21

1. Everyone has the right to take part in the government of his country, directly or through freely chosen representatives.

2. Everyone has the right of equal access to public service in his country.

3. The will of the people shall be the basis of the authority of government; this will shall be expressed in periodic and genuine elections which shall be by universal and equal suffrage and shall be held by secret vote or by equivalent free voting procedures.

Article 22

Everyone, as a member of society, has the right to social security and is entitled to realization, through national effort and international co-operation and in accordance with the organization and resources of each State, of the economic, social and cultural rights indispensable for his dignity and the free development of his personality.

Article 23

1. Everyone has the right to work, to free choice of employment, to just and favorable conditions of work and to protection against unemployment

2. Everyone, without any discrimination, has the right to equal pay for equal work.

3. Everyone who works has the right to just and favorable remuneration ensuring for himself and his family an existence worthy of human dignity, and supplemented, if necessary, by other means of social protection.

4. Everyone has the right to form and to join trade unions for the protection of his interests.

Article 24

Everyone has the right to rest and leisure, including reasonable limitation of working hours and periodic holidays with pay.

Article 25

1. Everyone has the right to a standard of living adequate for the health and well-being of himself and of his family, includ-

ing food, clothing, housing and medical care and necessary social services, and the right to security in the event of unemployment, sickness, disability, widowhood, old age or other lack of livelihood in circumstances beyond his control.

2. Motherhood and childhood are entitled to special care and assistance. All children, whether born in or out of wedlock, shall enjoy the same social protection.

Article 26

1. Everyone has the right to education. Education shall be free, at least in the elementary and fundamental stages. Elementary education shall be compulsory. Technical and professional education shall be made generally available and higher education shall be equally accessible to all on the basis of merit.

2. Education shall be directed to the full development of the human personality and to the strengthening of respect for human rights and fundamental freedoms. It shall promote understanding, tolerance and friendship among all nations, racial or religious groups, and shall further the activities of the United Nations for the maintenance of peace.

3. Parents have a prior right to choose the kind of education that shall be given to their children.

Article 27

1. Everyone has the right freely to participate in the cultural life of the community, to enjoy the arts and to share in scientific advancement and its benefits.

2. Everyone has the right to the protection of the moral and material interests resulting from any scientific, literary or artistic production of which he is the author.

Article 28

Everyone is entitled to a social and international order in which the rights and freedoms set forth in this Declaration can be fully realized.

Article 29

1. Everyone has duties to the community in which alone the free and full development of his personality is possible.

2. In the exercise of his rights and freedoms, everyone shall be subject only to such limitations as are determined by law solely for the purpose of securing due recognition and respect for the rights and freedoms of others and of meeting the just requirements of morality, public order and the general welfare in a democratic society.

3. These rights and freedoms may in no case be exercised contrary to the purposes and principles of the United Nations.

Article 30

Nothing in this Declaration may be interpreted as implying for any State, group or person any right to engage in any activity or to perform any act aimed at the destruction of any of the rights and freedoms set forth herein.

Appendix 2

Nuremberg Code, 1946

1. The voluntary consent of the human subject is absolutely essential.

This means that the person involved should have legal capacity to give consent; should be so situated as to be able to exercise free power of choice, without the intervention of any element of force, fraud, deceit, duress, over-reaching, or other ulterior form of constraint or coercion; and should have sufficient knowledge and comprehension of the elements of the subject matter involved as to enable him to make an understanding and enlightened decision. This latter element requires that before the acceptance of

Note: This material taken from Katz, 1972, pp. 305–306. History of development and adoption (including by the United Nations General Assembly on December 11, 1946) is reviewed by Annas, Glantz, and Katz (1977, pp. 6–9).

an affirmative decision by the experimental subject there should be made known to him the nature, duration, and purpose of the experiment; the method and means by which it is to be conducted; all inconveniences and hazards reasonably to be expected; and the effects upon his health or person which may possibly come from his participation in the experiment.

The duty and responsibility for ascertaining the quality of the consent rests upon each individual who initiates, directs, or engages in the experiment. It is a personal duty and responsibility which may not be delegated to another with impunity.

2. The experiment should be such as to yield fruitful results for the good of society, unprocurable by other methods or means of study, and not random and unnecessary in nature.

3. The experiment should be so designed and based on the results of animal experimentation and a knowledge of the natural history of the disease or other problem under study that the anticipated results will justify the performance of the experiment.

4. The experiment should be so conducted as to avoid all unnecessary physical and mental suffering and injury.

5. No experiment should be conducted where there is an a priori reason to believe that death or disabling injury will occur; except, perhaps, in those experiments where the experimental physicians also serve as subjects.

6. The degree of risk to be taken should never exceed that determined by the humanitarian importance of the problem to be solved by the experiment.

7. Proper preparations should be made and adequate facilities provided to protect the experimental subject against even remote possibilities of injury, disability, or death.

8. The experiment should be conducted only by scientifically qualified persons. The highest degree of skill and care should be required through all stages of the experiment of those who conduct or engage in the experiment.

9. During the course of the experiment the human subject should be at liberty to bring the experiment to an end if he has reached the physical or mental state where continuation of the experiment seems to him to be impossible.

10. During the course of the experiment the scientist in charge must be prepared to terminate the experiment at any stage, if he has probable cause to believe, in the exercise of the good faith, superior skill, and careful judgment required of him that a continuation of the experiment is likely to result in injury, disability, or death to the experimental subject.

Appendix 3

Declaration of Helsinki, 1964

It is the mission of the doctor to safeguard the health of the people. His knowledge and conscience are dedicated to the fulfillment of this mission.

The Declaration of Geneva of the World Medical Association (1964) binds the doctor with the words, "The health of my patient will be my first consideration"; and the International Code of Medical Ethics which declares that "any act or advice which could weaken physical or mental resistance of a human being may be used only in his interest."

Because it is essential that the results of laboratory experiments be applied to human beings to further scientific knowledge

Note: This material taken from Beecher, 1970,p. 277–278. Originally issued in 1962, the Helsinki Declaration was revised in 1964; the revised version is presented here.

and to help suffering humanity, the World Medical Association has prepared the following recommendations as a guide to each doctor in clinical research. It must be stressed that the standards as drafted are only a guide to physicians all over the world. Doctors are not relieved from criminal, civil, and ethical responsibilities under the laws of their own countries.

In the field of clinical research a fundamental distinction must be recognized between clinical research in which the aim is essentially therapeutic for a patient, and clinical research the essential object of which is purely scientific and without therapeutic value to the person subjected to the research.

I. Basic Principles

1. Clinical research must conform to the moral and scientific principles that justify medical research, and should be based on laboratory and animal experiments or other scientifically established facts. (The use of animals is not always feasible or possible.)

2. Clinical research should be conducted only by scientifically qualified persons and under the supervision of a qualified medical man.

3. Clinical research cannot legitimately be carried out unless the importance of the objective is in proportion to the inherent risk to the subject.

4. Every clinical research project should be preceded by careful assessment of inherent risks in comparison to foreseeable benefits to the subject or to others.

5. Special caution should be exercised by the doctor in performing clinical research in which the personality of the subject is liable to be altered by drugs or experimental procedure.

II. Clinical Research Combined with Professional Care

1. In the treatment of the sick person the doctor must be free to use a new therapeutic measure, if in his judgment it offers hope of saving life, re-establishing health, or alleviating suffering.

If at all possible, consistent with patient psychology, the doctor should obtain the patient's freely given consent after the patient has been given a full explanation. In case of legal incapacity consent should also be procured from the legal guardian; in case of physical incapacity the permission of the legal guardian replaces that of the patient.

2. The doctor can combine clinical research with professional care, the objective being the acquisition of new medical knowledge, only to the extent that clinical research is justified by its therapeutic value for the patient.

III. Non-therapeutic Clinical Research

1. In the purely scientific application of clinical research carried out on a human being it is the duty of the doctor to remain the protector of the life and health of that person on whom clinical research is being carried out.

2. The nature, the purpose, and the risk of clinical research must be explained to the subject by the doctor.

3a. Clinical research on a human being cannot be undertaken without his free consent, after he has been fully informed; if he is legally incompetent the consent of the legal guardian should be procured.

3b. The subject of clinical research should be in such a mental, physical, and legal state as to be able to exercise fully his power of choice.

3c. Consent should as a rule be obtained in writing. However, the responsibility for clinical research always remains with the research worker; it never falls on the subject, even after consent is obtained.

4a. The investigator must respect the right of each individual to safeguard his personal integrity, especially if the subject is in a dependent relationship to the investigator.

4b. Any any time during the course of clinical research the subject or his guardian should be free to withdraw permission for research to be continued. The investigator or the investigating team should discontinue the research if in his or their judgment it may, if continued, be harmful to the individual.

Appendix 4

Composite Code:
Use of Human
Subjects in Research

The following composite is based on the statements appearing in twenty-four codes of ethics related to the conduct of research by social scientists. The majority represent codes adopted by national associations of social scientists, but several do not have that status (one was rejected by the national association, another was proposed by a group of social scientists as related to a special type of research endeavour—cross-cultural research). Terminology was standardized for this presentation, and the organization of the statements follows an examination of the principles and consideration of relevant issues. (The figure after each item represents the number of different codes in which the statement occurred.)

Note: This material taken from Reynolds, 1975b, pp. 563–611.

442

Principles

General Issues Related to the Code of Ethics

1. The social scientist(s) in charge of a research project is (are) responsible for all decisions regarding procedural matters and ethical issues related to the project whether made by themselves or subordinates (7).

2. Teachers are responsible for all decisions made by their students related to ethical issues involved in research (1).

3. All actions conducted as part of the research should be consistent with the ethical standards of both the home and host community (1).

4. Ethical issues should be considered from the perspective of the participant's society (2).

5. If unresolved or difficult ethical dilemmas arise, assistance or consultation should be sought with colleagues or appropriate committees sponsored by professional associations (2).

6. Any deviation from established principles suggests: (a) that a greater degree of responsibility is being accepted by the investigator, (b) a more serious obligation to seek outside counsel and advice, and (c) the need for additional safeguards to protect the rights and welfare of the research participants (2).

Decision to Conduct the Research

7. Research should be conducted in such a way as to maintain the integrity of the research enterprise and not to diminish the potential for conducting research in the future (3).

8. Investigators should use their best scientific judgment for selection of issues for empirical investigation (1).

9. The decision to conduct research with human subjects should involve evaluation of the potential benefits to the participant and society in relation to the risks to be borne by the participant(s)—a risk-benefit analysis (2).

10. Any study which involves human subjects must be related to an important intellectual question (4).

11. Any study which involves human subjects must be related to an important intellectual question with humanitarian im-

plications, and there should be no other way to resolve the intellectual question (2).

12. Any study which involves human participants must be related to a very important intellectual question if there is a risk of permanent, negative effects on the participants (2).

13. Any study involving risks as well as potential therapeutic effects must be justified in terms of benefits to the client or patient (2).

14. There should be no prior reason to believe that major permanent negative effects will occur for the participants (1).

15. If the conduct of the research may permanently damage the participants, their community, or institutions within their community (such as indigenous social scientists), the research may not be justified and might be abandoned (2).

Conduct of the Research

16. All research should be conducted in a competent fashion, as an objective, scientific project (4).

17. All research personnel should be qualified to use any procedures employed in the project (7).

18. Competent personnel and adequate facilities should be available if any drugs are involved (4).

19. There should be no bias in the design, conduct, or reporting of the research—it should be as objective as possible (4).

Effects on and Relationships with the Participants

Informed Consent
General
20. Informed consent should be used in obtaining participants for all research; investigators should honor all commitments associated with such agreements (10).

21. Participants should be in a position to give informed consent; otherwise it should be given by those responsible for the participant (2).

22. Informed consent should be used if the potential effects on participants are ambiguous or potentially hazardous (7).

23. If possible, informed consent should be obtained in writing (1).

24. Seek official permission to use any government data, no matter how it was obtained (1).

Provision of information

25. Purposes, procedures, and risks of research (including possible hazards to physical and psychological well-being and jeopardization of social position) should be explained to the participants in such a way that they can understand (7).

26. Participants should be aware of the possible consequences, if any, for the group or community from which they are selected, in advance of their decision to participate (1).

27. The procedure used to obtain the participant's name should be described to him or her (1).

28. Sponsorship, financial and otherwise, should be specified to the potential participants (2).

29. The identity of those conducting the research should be fully revealed to the potential participants (2).

30. Names and addresses of research personnel should be left with participants so that the research personnel can be traced subsequently (1)

31. Participants should be fully aware of all data gathering techniques (tape and video recordings), photographic devices, physiological measures, and so forth), the capacities of such techniques, and the extent to which participants will remain anonymous and data confidential (2).

32. In projects of considerable duration, participants should be periodically informed of the progress of the research (1).

33. When recording videotapes or film, subjects should have the right to approve the material to be made public (by viewing it and giving specific approval to each segment) as well as the nature of the audiences (1).

Voluntary consent

34. Individuals should have the option to refuse to participate and know this (1).

35. Participants should be able to terminate involvement at any time and know that they have this option (3).

36. No coercion, explicit or overt, should be used to encourage individuals to participate in a research project (6).

Protection of Rights and Welfare of Participants

General issues

37. The dignity, privacy, and interests of the participants should be respected and protected (8).

38. The participants should not be harmed; welfare of the participants should take priority over all other concerns (10).

39. Damage and suffering to the participants should be minimized through procedural mechanisms and termination of risky studies as soon as possible; such effects are justified only when the problem cannot be studied in any other fashion (8).

40. Potential problems should be anticipated, no matter how remote the probability of occurrence, to ensure that the unexpected does not lead to major negative effects on the participants (1).

41. Any harmful aftereffects should be eliminated (4).

42. The hopes or anxieties of potential participants should not be raised (1).

43. Research should be terminated if danger to the participants arises (3).

44. The use of clients seeking professional assistance for research purposes is justified only to the extent that they may derive direct benefits as clients (1).

Deception

45. Deceit of the participants should only be used if it is absolutely necessary, there being no other way to study the problem (3).

46. Deception may be utilized (1).

47. If deceit is involved in a research procedure, additional precautions should be taken to protect the rights and welfare of the participants (2).

48. After being involved in a study using deception, all participants should be given a thorough, complete, and honest de-

scription of the study and the need for deception (5).

49. If deception is not revealed to the participants, for humane or scientific reasons, the investigator has a special obligation to protect the interests and welfare of the participants (1).
Confidentiality and anonymity

50. Research data should be confidential and all participants should remain anonymous, unless they (or their legal guardians) have given permission for release of their identity (15).

51. If confidentiality or anonymity cannot be guaranteed, the participants should be aware of this and its possible consequences before involvement in the research (4).

52. Persons in official positions (studied as part of a research project) should provide written descriptions of their official roles, duties, and so forth, (which need not be treated as confidential information) and provided with a copy of the final report on the research (1).

53. Studies designed to provide descriptions of aggregates or collectivities should always guarantee anonymity to individual respondents (1).

54. 'Privacy' should always be considered from the perspective of the participant and the participant's culture (1).

55. Material stored in data banks should not be used without the permission of the investigator who originally gathered the data (1).

56. If promises of confidentiality are honored, investigators need not withhold information on misconduct of participants or organizations (1).

57. Specific procedure for organizing data to ensure anonymity of participants (details omitted)(1).

Benefits to Participants

58. A fair return should be offered for all services of participants (1).

59. Increased self-knowledge, as a benefit to the participants, should be incorporated as a major part of the research design or procedures (1).

60. Copies or explanations of the research should be provided to all participants (2).

61. Studies of aggregates or cultural subgroups should produce knowledge which will benefit them (1).

Effects on Aggregates or Communities

62. Investigators should be familiar with, and respect, the host cultures in which studies are conducted (1).

63. Investigators should cooperate with members of the host society (1).

64. Investigators should consider, in advance, the potential effects of the research on the social structure of the host community and the potential changes in influence of various groups or individuals by virtue of the conduct of the study (1).

65. Investigators should consider, in advance, the potential effects of the research and the report on the population or subgroup from which participants are drawn (1).

66. Participants should be aware, in advance, of potential effects upon aggregates or cultural subgroups which they represent (1).

67. The interests of collectivities and social systems of all kinds should be considered by the investigator (1).

Interpretations and Reporting of the Results of the Research

68. All reports of research should be public documents, freely available to all (4).

69. Research procedures should be described fully and accurately in reports, including all evidence regardless of the support it provides for the research hypotheses; conclusions should be objective and unbiased (14).

70. Full and complete interpretations should be provided for all data and attempts made to prevent misrepresentations in writing research reports (6).

71. Sponsorship, purpose, sources of financial support, and investigators responsible for the research should be made clear in all publications related thereto (3).

72. If publication may jeopardize or damage the population studied and complete disguise is impossible, publication should be delayed (2).

73. Cross-cultural studies should be published in the language and journals of the host society, in addition to publication in other languages and other societies (2).

74. Appropriate credit should be given to all parties contributing to the research (9).

75. Full, accurate disclosure of all published sources bearing on or contributing to the work is expected (8).

76. Publication of research findings on cultural subgroups should include a description in terms understood by the participants (2).

77. Whenever requested, raw data or other original documentation should be made available to qualified investigators (1).

78. Research with scientific merit should always be submitted for publication and not withheld from public presentation unless the quality of research or analysis is inadequate (1).

Appendix 5

Composite Code: Investigators Responsible for Sponsored Research

━━◆━━◆━━◆━━◆━━◆━━◆━━◆━━◆━━◆━━◆━━

This composite is based on the statements appearing in five codes of ethics, four adopted by national associations (Anthropology—U.S.; Political Science—U.S.; Sociology—U.K. and U.S.) and one drawn up by a group of psychologists from the U.S. with experience in cross-cultural research. (The figure after each statement represents the number of different codes in which the statement or its equivalent occurred.)

Principles

General Nature of Relationship

    1. Accept responsibility for research only if the way in which the knowledge will be used is consistent with personal values as citizen-intellectual (1).

Note: This material taken from Reynolds, 1975b, pp. 563–611.

2. Do not become involved in any secret research (1).

3. Do not become involved in, or accept responsibility for, research which involves any unethical practices (4).

4. Do not become involved in or use research activity as a cover or screen for any other activity, related to personal, professional, political, or other purposes (1).

5. Do not agree to terms and conditions which would undermine the freedom and integrity of other scholars or researchers (2).

6. Social scientists have the responsibility to ensure that the resources are adequate for completion of the project before initiating the research (1).

7. Social scientists representing different disciplines should be involved in interdisciplinary research from its inception; social scientists representing a new discipline may become involved at a later stage but should exercise caution regarding association with the endeavor (1).

8. Details of the relationship between the investigator and the sponsor should be as explicit as possible (1).

9. Investigators should be aware of the implications of the results of their research considering the nature of the sponsoring organization (1).

Limits of Competence

10. Be honest about limitations as an investigator or social scientist (2).

11. Maintain the right to determine the limits of expertise for personal professional activity or that of any research organization for which the investigator holds supervisory responsibility (2).

Management of Research Activity

12. Investigator should be responsible for all decisions related to the conduct of the research (1).

13. All conditions of relationship to the sponsor should be specific, explicit, and known to all members of the research staff (3).

14. Projects should be managed in a responsible, efficient, and conscientious fashion—meeting the standards for administration and accounting established by the funding agency (1).

15. Investigator should retain the right and responsibility for all ethical decisions related to the project (2).

Research Reports

16. The investigator(s) is (are) responsible for the content, form, and conclusions of the final report (1).

17. Investigator(s) should retain the privilege of free and open publication whenever possible (2).

18. Investigator(s) should insist upon and ensure that full disclosure of sponsorship occurs in all reports (3).

19. If anonymity of the sponsor is justified and does not endanger the integrity of the research, the character of the sponsor should be noted (1).

20. The purposes of the study should be fully disclosed in any report on the research (1).

21. Findings should be presented in an objective fashion (1).

22. The research report should be preserved intact by the sponsor, although conclusions may be treated as 'competent advice' (1).

23. Any distortions of the study by the sponsor should be publicly corrected by the investigator as soon as they occur (1).

Appendix 6

Composite Code: Social Scientists in Organizations

The following composite is based on statements appearing in a number of codes of ethics developed by national associations representing scientific investigators involved in research with human participants. The organization was developed after an examination of the relevant issues. (The figure after each item represents the number of different codes in which the statement occurred.)

Principles

I. Relationships to Individuals (Clients, Subjects, and so forth)
    1. Interests and welfare of individual clients always take precedence over those of the patron, organization, and the like (4).

Note: This material taken from Reynolds, 1975a.

2. Employed social scientists must assure themselves that the files on individuals are maintained in a fashion to ensure confidentiality (3).
3. Social scientists, employed or in practice, must respect the confidentiality of information exchanged with other professions (1).

II.   Relation to Organization

4. Employed social scientists should respect the rights and reputation of the employing organization (2).
5. Employed social scientists should respect the rights and ownership of the organization with regard to work produced for the organization (2).
6. Employed social scientists should be aware of the implications of their work as it is related to the purposes and goals of the organization (1).
7. Employed social scientists have an obligation for determining that resources are adequate before engaging in any research activity (1).
8. Social scientists engaged in a joint, private practice should have an explicit agreement on terms of relationship and procedures to be followed to terminate the relationship (1).
9. Social scientists should not engage in public criticism of the organization they work for (1).

III.   Principles Related to Independent Social Scientists

10. Social scientists should insist on independence and autonomy in professional matters, even though related to organizational interests (4).
11. Employed social scientists should be responsible for determining their own limitations and capacity (7).
12. Social scientists, employed or in joint practice, should respect the professional independence of other social scientists (3).
13. Employed social scientists must get permission to engage in outside activities as independent professionals (1).
14. Social scientists, employed or in joint practice, should not recruit clientele from the organizational clientele (1).

15. Employed social scientists should not present personal efforts as representing the organization (1).

16. Ambiguous issues related to personal and organizational rights and obligations with respect to any professional work should be specified in writing before the work is initiated (1).

17. Professional projects initiated by one social scientist should not be completed by a replacement if the original social scientist was terminated without just cause (1).

IV. Principles Relating to Seeking Employment

18. In seeking employment, social scientists should be honest in stating their limitations and qualifications (5).

19. Social scientists should solicit and consider offers of employment only if they are serious about considering a new position, not as a procedure to improve existing situations (1).

20. Employed social scientists must respect the rights of their employer when seeking another position (informing employer of intentions, providing adequate notice of termination, and so forth (1).

V. Social Scientists in Supervisory Positions

21. Senior social scientists in organizations or group practice are responsible for accuracy of information about the nature of services to be provided by social scientists (1).

22. Social scientists in supervisory positions should ensure that descriptions of new positions for social scientists are presented honestly and completely (2).

23. Social scientists in supervisory positions should ensure that there is no discrimination in the employment of social scientists (1).

24. An explicit agreement should be created to describe any supervisor-subordinate relationship between social scientists (1).

25. Social scientists in supervisory positions are responsible for ensuring that their subordinates conduct themselves in a responsible fashion in professional activities (1).

26. Social scientists in positions of responsibility should en-

sure that any subordinate social scientist is encouraged
to develop and advance professionally (2).

27. Social scientists in supervisory positions are responsible
for ensuring the professional independence of subordinate social science staff members (1).

28. Social scientists in supervisory positions should assist social scientists in subordinate positions to improve and
develop before resorting to termination of employment
(1).

29. Social scientists in supervisory positions should never
allow nonsocial scientists to conduct or take responsibility for social science activities or decisions (5).

References

Federal Laws Cited

Public Law 93–348. National Research Act of 1974. *United States Code Citations*

Title 5 USCS Statute 552 (1976). Administrative Procedure (Publication of Information, Rules, Opinions, Orders, and Public Records).

Title 13 USC Statute 8–9 (1976). Census Administration (Information as Confidential).

Title 20 USC Statute 1232g (1976). Education (Family Educational and Privacy Rights [Buckley Amendment]).

Title 42 USCA Statute 241 (1977). Public Health Service (Research and Investigations Generally).

457

Title 42 USCS Statute 1315 (1976). Public Health and Welfare (Demonstration Projects).

Title 42 USCA Statute 1862 (1977). National Science Foundation (Functions).

Title 42 USCS Statute 1891 (1976). Support of Basic Scientific Research (Authorization to Make Grants).

Title 42 USC Statute 3771 (1976). Law Enforcement Assistance (Information Available for Prescribed Purposes).

Code of Federal Regulations Citations

Title 20 Part 401 (1976). Social Security Administration (Disclosure of Official Records and Information).

Title 21 Part 310 (1976). Food and Drug Administration (New Drugs for Investigational Use).

Title 45 Part 46 (1976). Public Welfare (Protection of Human Subjects).

Federal Register Citations

Department of Health, Education, and Welfare; National Institutes of Health. Protection of Human Subjects: Policies and Procedures. *38* (221), November 16, 1973:31,738–31,749.

Department of Health, Education, and Welfare: Office of the Secretary. Protection of Human Subjects: Technical Amendments. *40* (50), March 13, 1975:11,854–11,858.

Department of Health, Education, and Welfare: Office of the Secretary. Protection of Human Subjects: Fetuses, Pregnant Women, and In Vitro Fertilization. *40* (154), August 8, 1975:33,526–33,551.

Rules and Regulations. Part 46—Protection of Human Subjects: Fetuses, Pregnant Women, In Vitro Fertilization. Correction. *40* (170), September 2, 1975:40,163.

Rules and Regulations. Part 46—Protection of Human Subjects: Fetuses, Pregnant Women, In Vitro Fertilization. Amendment. *40* (215), November 6, 1975:51,638.

Rules and Regulations. Part 46—Protection of Human Subjects: Secretary's Interpretation of "Subject at Risk." *41* (125), June 28, 1976:26,572–26,573.

Department of Health, Education, and Welfare: Office of the Secretary. Proposed Amendments Concerning Fetuses, Pregnant Women, and In Vitro Fertilization. *42* (9), January 13, 1977:2,792–2,793.

Department of Health, Education, and Welfare: Office of the Secretary. Protection of Human Subjects: Research Involving Prisoners, Report and Recommendations. *42* (10), January 14, 1977:3,076–3,091.

Department of Health, Education, and Welfare. Additional Protections Pertaining to Research, Development, and Related Activities Involving Fetuses, Pregnant Women, and In Vitro Fertilization. *43* (7), January 11, 1978:1,758–1,759.

Department of Health, Education, and Welfare: Office of the Secretary. Protection of Human Subjects: Research Involving Children. 43 (141), July 21, 1978:31,786–31,794.

Rules and Regulations, Part 46—Protection of Human Subjects: Informed Consent—Definition Amended to Include Advice on Compensation. *43* (214), November 3, 1978:51,559.

Rules and Regulations. Part 46—Protection of Human Subjects: Additional Protections Pertaining to Biomedical and Behavioral Research Involving Prisoners as Subjects. *43* (222), November 16, 1978:53,652–53,656.

Department of Health, Education, and Welfare: Office of the Secretary. Protection of Human Subjects: Proposed Regulations on Research Involving Those Institutionalized as Mentally Disabled. *43* (223), November 17, 1978:53,950–53,956.

Legal Cases Cited

Aguayo v. *Richardson*, 473 F. 2d 1090 (1973)

California Welfare Rights Organization v. *Richardson*, 348 F. Supp. 491 (1972)

Crane v. *Mathews*, 417 F. Supp. 532 (1976)

Griswold v. *Connecticut*, 381 U.S. 479 (1964)

Halushka v. *University of Saskatchewan*, 52 W.W.R. 608 (Sask, 1965)

People v. *Newman*, 298 NE 2d 651 (N.Y. 1973)

Washington Research Project v. *Department of Health, Education, and Welfare and others*, 366 F. Supp. 929 (1973); 504 F. 2d 238 (1975)

Authors Cited

Abelson, R. P., and Miller, J. C. "Negative Persuasion via Personal Insult." *Journal of Experimental Social Psychology*, 1967, *3*, 321–333.

Abrams, S. "A Response to Lykken on the Polygraph." *American Psychologist,* 1975, *30,* 709–711.

Acton, Lord (John Emerich Edward Dalberg). "Letter to Bishop Mandell Creighton," 1887. In J. Bartlett, *Familiar Quotations.* Boston: Little, Brown, 1955.

Adams, B., and Shea-Stonum, M. "Toward a Theory of Control of Medical Experimentation with Human Subjects: The Role of Compensation." *Case Western Reserve Law Review*, 1975, *25*, 604–648.

Allen, H. "Bystander Intervention and Helping on the Subway." In L. Bickman and T. Henchy (Eds.), *Beyond the Laboratory: Field Research in Social Psychology.* New York: McGraw–Hill, 1972.

Alston, W. P. "Comments on Kohlberg's 'From Is to Ought.' " In T. Mischel (Ed.), *Cognitive Development and Epistemology.* New York: Academic Press, 1971.

Altman, L. K. "New Rules Spark Controversy over Human Biologic Materials." *New York Times,* April 30, 1974.

American Anthropological Association. "Statements on Ethics: Principles of Professional Responsibility." Adopted, May 1971.

American Association of University Professors. "Academic Freedom and Tenure: 1940 Statement of Principles and Interpretive Comments." *AAUP Bulletin,* 1974 *60* 269–272.

American Psychological Association. *Ethical Principles in the Conduct of Research with Human Participants.* Washington, D.C.: American Psychological Association, 1973.

American Psychologist, 1965, *20* (2, entire issue).

American Psychologist, 1965, *20* (11, entire issue).

Amrine, M., and Sanford, F. H. "In the Matter of Juries, Democracy, Science, Truth, Senators, and Bugs." *American Psychologist,* 1956, *11,* 54–60.

Annas, G.J. "Confidentiality and the Duty to Warn." *Hastings Center Report,* 1976, *6* (6), 6–8.

Annas, G. J., Glantz, L. H., and Katz, B. F. *Informed Consent to Human Experimentation: The Subject's Dilemma.* Cambridge, Mass.: Ballinger, 1977.

Ashcraft, N., and Scheflen, A. E. *People Space: The Making and Breaking of Human Boundaries.* New York: Doubleday, 1976.

Astin, A. W., and Boruch, R. F. "A 'Link' System for Assuring Confidentiality of Research Data in Longitudinal Studies." *American Educational Research Journal,* 1970, *7* (4), 615–624.

Auger, P. "Science as a Force for Unity Among Men." *Bulletin of the Atomic Scientists,* 1956, *12* (6), 208–210.

Ayllon, T. "Behavior Modification in Institutional Settings." *Arizona Law Review,* 1975, *17,* 3–19.

Baratz, S. S., and Marvin, K. E. "Resolving Privacy, Access, and Other Problems in the Audit and Reanalysis of Social Research for Policy." *Evaluation: A Forum for Human Service Decision Makers,* 1978 (special issue), pp. 31–35.

Barber, B. "The Resistance of Scientists to Scientific Discovery." *Science,* 1961, *134,* 596–602.

Barber, B. *Drugs and Society.* New York: Russell Sage Foundation, 1967.

Barber, B., and others. *Research on Human Subjects.* New York: Russell Sage Foundation, 1973.

Barber, T. X., and Silver, M. J. "Fact, Fiction, and the Experimenter Bias Effect." *Psychological Bulletin,* 1968, *70* (6, Pt. 2), 1–29.

Barker, R. G., and Wright, H. F. *One Boy's Day.* New York: Harper & Row, 1951.

Barr, D. P. "Hazards of Modern Diagnosis and Therapy: The Price We Pay." *Journal of the American Medical Association,* 1955, *159,* 1452–1456.

Barth, F. "On Responsibility and Humanity: Calling a Colleague to Account." *Current Anthropology,* 1974, *15* (1), 99–102.

Baumrind, D. "Some Thoughts on Ethics of Research: After Reading Milgram's 'Behavioral Study of Obedience.'" *American Psychologist,* 1964, *19,* 421–423.

Baumrind, D. "Principles of Ethical Conduct in the Treatment of Subjects: Reaction to the Draft Report of the Committee on Ethical Standards in Psychological Research." *American Psychologist,* 1971, *26* (10), 887–896.

Baumrind, D. "Snooping and Duping: The Application of the Principle of Informed Consent to Field Research." Paper presented at meeting of the Society for Applied Anthropology, San Diego, April 1977.

Beals, R. L. "International Research Problems in Anthropology: A Report from the U.S.A." *Current Anthropology*, 1967, *8* (5), 470–475.

Beals, R. L. *Politics of Social Research*. Chicago: Aldine, 1969.

Becker, H. S. "Problems in the Publication of Field Studies." In A. J. Vidich, J. Bensman, and M. R. Stein (Eds.), *Reflections on Community Studies*. New York: Wiley, 1964.

Becker, H. S., and Horowitz, I. L. "Radical Politics and Sociological Research: Observations on Methodology and Ideology." *American Journal of Sociology*, 1972, *78*, 48–66.

Beecher, H. K. "Ethics and Clinical Research." *New England Journal of Medicine*, 1966, *274*, 1354–1360.

Beecher, H. K. *Research and the Individual*. Boston: Little, Brown, 1970.

"Behavior Modification and the Law." *Arizona Law Review*, 1975, *17* (1), 1–143.

Bell, E. H. "Freedom and Responsibility in Research: Comments." *Human Organization*, 1959, *18* (2), 49.

Bentham, J. *An Introduction to the Principles of Morals and Legislation*. Edinburgh: William Tait, 1789.

Berg, P., and others. "Potential Biohazards of Recombinant DNA Molecules." *Science*, 1974, *185*, 303.

Berkun, M. M., and others. "Experimental Studies of Psychological Stress in Man." *Psychological Monographs*, 1962, *76* (entire issue).

Bermant, G., Kelman, H. C., and Warwick, D. P. (Eds.). *The Ethics of Social Intervention*. New York: Wiley, 1978.

Bernal, J. D. *The Social Function of Science*. London: Routledge, 1939.

Bernal, J. D. *Science in History*. 4 vols. Middlesex, England: Penguin Books, 1965.

Berscheid, E., and others. "Anticipating Informed Consent: An Empirical Approach." *American Psychologist*, 1973, *28*, 913–925.

Black. C. L., Jr. *Perspectives in Constitutional Law*. Englewood Cliffs, N.J.: Prentice–Hall, 1963.

Black, H. C. *Black's Law Dictionary*. (4th ed., rev.) St. Paul, Minn.: West Publishing, 1968.

Blake, R. M. "On Natural Rights." *International Journal of Ethics*, 1925, *36*, 86–96.

Blasi, V. "Press Subpoenas: An Empirical and Legal Analysis." *Michigan Law Review*, 1971, *70*, 229–284.

Block, N. J., and Dworkin, G. "IQ, Heritability, and Inequality; Parts 1 and 2." *Philosophy and Public Affairs*, 1974, *3* (4), 331–409; *4* (1), 40–99.

Bok. S. "The Ethics of Giving Placebos." *Scientific American*, 1974, *231* (5), 17–23.

Boness, F. and Cordes, J. F. "The Researcher-Subject Relationship: The Need for Protection and a Model Statute," *The Georgetown Law Journal*, 1973, *62*:243–272.

Boruch, R. F. "Assuring Confidentiality of Responses in Social Research: A Note on Strategies." *American Sociologist*, 1971a, *6*, 308–311.

Boruch, R. F. "Education Research and the Confidentiality of Data: A Case Study." *Sociology of Education*, 1971b, *44*, 59–85.

Boruch, R. F. "Maintaining Confidentiality of Data in Educational Research." *American Psychologist*, 1971c, *26* (5), 413–430.

Boruch, R. F. "Strategies for Eliciting and Merging Confidential Social Research Data." *Policy Sciences*, 1972, *3*, 275–297.

Boruch, R. F. "Is a Promise of Confidentiality Necessary? Sufficient? A Review and a Bibliography" Research Report NIE–11/11X, Evaluation Research Program, Northwestern University, Evanston, Ill., 1975.

Bouchard, T. J., Jr. "Unobtrusive Measures: An Inventory of Uses." *Sociological Methods and Research*, 1976, *4* (3), 267–300.

Brandt, R. B. *Ethical Theory*. Englewood Cliffs, N.J.: Prentice–Hall, 1959.

Brandt, R. M. *Studying Behavior in Natural Settings*. New York: Holt, Rinehart and Winston, 1972.

Breger, M. J. "Legal Aspects of Social Science Research." Paper presented at symposium, "Ethical Issues in Social Science Research," at the University of Minnesota, Minneapolis, April 1976.

Bressler, B., and others. "Research in Human Subjects and the

Artificial Traumatic Neurosis—Where Does Our Responsibility Lie?" *American Journal of Psychiatry*, 1959, *116*, 522–526.

Brest, P. *Processes of Constitutional Decisionmaking: Cases and Materials*. Boston: Little, Brown, 1975.

Brody, J. "Study of Infants Suspended After Furor in Roxbury." *Boston Sunday Globe*, January 10, 1971, p. 64.

Brown, P. G. "Informed Consent in Social Experiments: Some Cautionary Notes." In A. Rivlin and P. M. Timpane (Eds.), *Ethical and Legal Issues of Social Experimentation*. Washington, D.C.: Brookings Institution, 1975.

Brown, S. M., Jr. "Inalienable Rights." *Philosophical Review*, 1955, *64*, 192–211.

Budrys, A. "The Politics of Deoxyribonucleic Acid." *New Republic*, 1977, *176* (18), 18–21.

Burton, R. "Honesty and Dishonesty." In T. Lickona (Ed.), *Moral Development and Behavior*. New York: Holt, Rinehart and Winston, 1976.

Cahn, E. "The Lawyer as Scientist and Scoundrel: Reflections on Francis Bacon's Quadricentennial." *New York University Law Review*, 1961, *36*, 1–12.

Calabresi, G. "Reflections on Medical Experimentation in Humans." *Daedalus*, 1969, *98* (2), 387–405.

Campbell, D. T., and others. "Confidentiality-Preserving Modes of Access to Files and to Interfile Exchange for Useful Statistical Analysis." Appendix A to *Protecting Individual Privacy in Evaluation Research: Report of the Committee on Federal Agency Evaluation*. Washington, D.C.: National Academy of Science, 1975.

Capron, A. M. "Social Experimentation and the Law." In A. M. Rivlin and P. M. Timpane (Eds.), *Ethical and Legal Issues of Social Experimentation*. Washington, D.C.: Brookings Institute, 1975.

Cardon, P. V., Dommel, F. W., Jr., and Trumble, R. R. "Injuries to Research Subjects: A Survey of Investigators." *New England Journal of Medicine*, 1976, *295*, 650–654.

Carroll, J. D. "Confidentiality of Social Science Research and Data: The Popkin Case." *P.S.*, 1973, *6* (3), 268–280.

Carroll, J. D., and Knerr, C. R. "The APSA Confidentiality in Social Science Research Project: A Final Report." *P.S.*, 1976a (Fall), 416–419.

Carroll, J. D., and Knerr, C. R. "Law and the Regulation of Social Science Research: Confidentiality as a Case Study." Unpublished report, Department of Public Administration, Syracuse University, Syracuse, N.Y., 1976b.

Carroll, J. D., and Knerr, C. R. "Confidentiality and Criminological Research: The Evolving Body of Law." Unpublished report, 1977.

Cassell, J. "Risk and Benefit to Subjects of Fieldwork." *American Sociologist*, 1978, *13*, 134–143.

Chalkley, D. T. "Requirements for Compliance with Part 46 of Title 45 of the *Code of Federal Regulations* as Amended March 13, 1975 and the Secretary of Health, Education and Welfare's Notice of May 20, 1975." Memorandum from Director, Office for Protection from Research Risks, Office of the Director, NIH, DHEW, May 22, 1975.

Christie, R. M. "Comment on Conflict Methodology: A Protagonist Position." *Sociological Quarterly*, 1976, *17*, 513–519.

Coburn, J. "Confidentality Is Not the Only Issue Causing Unrest Among Student Critics of the Effort to Study Protests," *Science*, 1969, *165*, 160–161.

Cohen, D. "Bathroom Behaviors: A Watershed in Ethical Debate." *Hastings Center Report*, 1978, *8* (2), 13.

Cole, S., Rubin, L., and Cole, J. R. "Peer Review and the Support of Science." *Scientific American*, 1977, *237* (4), 34–41.

Coleman, J. S. "Inequality, Sociology, and Moral Philosophy." *American Journal of Sociology*, 1974, *80* (3), 739–764.

Coleman, J. S. "Reply to Klees and Strike." *American Journal of Sociology*, 1976, *82* (1), 201–205.

Conrad, H. S. "Clearance of Questionnaires with Respect to 'Invasion of Privacy, Public Sensitivities, Ethical Standards, etc.' " *American Psychologist*, 1967, *22*, 356–359.

Cook, T. D., and others. "Demand Characteristics and Three Conceptions of the Frequently Deceived Subject." *Journal of Personality and Social Psychology*, 1970, *14* (3), 185–194.

Cook, V. G. *Shield Laws: A Report on Freedom of the Press*. Lexington, Ky.: Council of State Governments, 1973.

Cope, L. "AMA Urges Suspension for Unfit Doctors." *Minneapolis Tribune*, June 24, 1974, pp. 1, 5.

Coser, L. A. "A Question of Professional Ethics?" *American Sociological Review*, 1959, *24* (3), 397–398.

Council for Science and Society. *Scholarly Freedom and Human Rights*. Chichester, Sussex, England: Barry Rose, 1977.

Cowan, D. "Human Experimentation: The Review Process in Practice." *Case Western Reserve Law Review*, 1975, *25*, 533–564.

Cox, H. (Ed.). *The Situation Ethics Debate*. Philadelphia: Westminster Press, 1968.

Culliton, B. J. "Confidentiality: Court Declares Researcher Can Protect Sources." *Science*, 1976, *193*, 467–469.

Cunningham, R. L. (Ed.). *Situationism and the New Morality*. New York: Appleton-Century-Crofts, 1970.

Cuny, H. *Albert Einstein: The Man and His Theories*. (M. Savill, Trans.) London: Souvenir Press, 1961.

Curran, W. J. "Governmental Regulation of the Use of Human Subjects in Medical Research: The Approach of Two Federal Agencies." *Daedalus*, 1969, *98* (2), 542–594.

Davis, F. "Comment on Initial Interaction of Newcomers in Alcoholics Anonymous." *Social Problems*, 1961, *8* (4), 364–365.

"Declaration of Tokyo." *World Medical Journal*, 1976, *22* (6), 87–90.

De Kruif, P. *Men Against Death*. New York: Harcourt Brace Jovanovich, 1927.

DePalma, D. J., and Foley, J. M. (Eds.). *Moral Development: Current Theory and Research*. Hillsdale, N.J.: Earlbaum, 1975.

Department of Health, Education, and Welfare. *Guide for Laboratory Animal Facilities and Care*. Washington, D.C.: U.S. Government Printing Office, 1968.

Department of Health, Education, and Welfare. *Secretary's Task Force on the Compensation of Injured Research Subjects*. Publication No. OS–77–003. Bethesda, Md.: National Institutes of Health, 1977.

Deutscher, I. *What We Say/What We Do: Sentiments and Acts*. Glenview, Ill.: Scott, Foresman, 1973.

Diener, E., and Crandall, R. *Ethics in Social and Behavioral Research*. Chicago: University of Chicago Press, 1978.

Dornbusch, S. M. "The Military Academy as an Assimilating Institution." *Social Forces*, 1955, *33*, 316–321.

Dworkin, G. "Autonomy and Behavior Control." *Hastings Center*

Report, 1976, *6* (1), 23–28.

Edsall, J. T. *Scientific Freedom and Responsibility*. Washington, D.C.: American Association for the Advancement of Science, 1975a.

Edsall, J. T. "Scientific Freedom and Responsibility." *Science*, 1975b, *188*, 687–693.

Emerson, T. I., Haber, D., and Dorsen, N. *Political and Civil Rights in the United States*. Vol. 1. Boston: Little, Brown, 1967.

Epstein, L. C., and Lasagna, L. "Obtaining Informed Consent: Form or Substance." *Archives of Internal Medicine*, 1969, *123*, 682–688.

Epstein, Y. M., Suedfeld, D., and Silverstein, S. J. "The Experimental Contract: Subject's Expectations of and Reactions to Some Behaviors of Experimenters." *American Psychologist*, 1973, *28*, 212–221.

Erickson, M. "The Inhumanity of Ordinary People." *International Journal of Psychiatry*, 1968, *6*, 277–279.

Erikson, K. T. "A Comment on Disguised Observation in Sociology." *Social Problems*, 1967, *14* (4), 366–373.

Errera, P. "Statement Based on Interviews with Forty 'Worst Cases' in the Milgram Obedience Experiments." In J. Katz (Ed.), *Experimentation with Human Beings*. New York: Russell Sage Foundation, 1972.

Etzioni, A. "A Model of Significant Research." *International Journal of Psychiatry*, 1968, *6*, 279–280.

Etzioni, A. *The Genetic Fix*. New York: Macmillan, 1973.

Eysenck, H. J. "The Effects of Psychotherapy." In H. J. Eysenck (Ed.), *Handbook of Abnormal Psychology*. New York: Basic Books, 1961.

Farmer, L. *Master Surgeon: A Biography of Joseph Lister*. New York: Harper & Row, 1962.

Farr, J. L., and Seaver, W. B. "Stress and Discomfort in Psychological Research: Subject Perceptions of Experimental Procedures." *American Psychologist*, 1975, *30* (7), 770–773.

Fellner, C. H., and Marshall, J. R. "Kidney Donors—The Myth of Informed Consent." *American Journal of Psychiatry*, 1970, *126*, 1245–1251.

Festinger, L., Riecken, H. W., and Schachter, S. *When Prophecy Fails*. Minneapolis: University of Minnesota Press, 1956.

Feuillan, J. "Every Man's Evidence Versus a Testimonial Privilege for Survey Researchers." *Public Opinion Quarterly*, 1976, *40*, 39–50.

Findlay, B. A., and Findlay, E. B. *Your Rugged Constitution*. Stanford, Calif.: Stanford University Press, 1952.

Fiss, O. M. "Groups and the Equal Protection Clause." *Philosophy and Public Affairs*, 1976, *5* (2), 107–177.

Fletcher, J. *Situation Ethics*. Philadelphia: Westminster Press, 1966.

Fletcher, J. "Human Experimentation. Ethics and the Consent Situation." *Law and Contemporary Problems*, 1967a, *32*, 620–649.

Fletcher, J. *Moral Responsibility: Situation Ethics at Work*. Philadelphia: Westminster Press, 1967b.

Fletcher, J. "Realities of Patient Consent to Medical Research." *Hastings Center Studies*, 1973, *1* (1), 39–49.

Foss, D. C. *The Value Controversy in Sociology: A New Orientation for the Discipline*. San Francisco: Jossey-Bass, 1977.

Fost, N. C. "A Surrogate System for Informed Consent." *Journal of the American Medical Association*, 1975, *233*, 800–803.

Frankel, M. S. "The Development of Policy Guidelines Governing Human Experimentation in the United States: A Case Study of Public Policy Making for Science and Technology." *Ethics in Science and Medicine*, 1975, *2*, 43–59.

Frankel, M. S. "Ethical Issues Associated with Experimentation in Political Science." Unpublished paper, Wayne State University, 1976.

Frankena, W. K. "Symposium: The Concept of Universal Human Rights: II." American Philosophical Association (Eastern Division), *Science, Language, and Human Rights*. Vol. 1. Philadelphia: University of Pennsylvania Press, 1952.

Frankena, W. K. *Ethics*. Englewood Cliffs, N.J.: Prentice-Hall, 1963.

Freedman, B. "A Moral Theory of Informed Consent." *Hastings Center Report*, 1975, *5* (4), 32–39.

Freedman, J. L. "Role Playing: Psychology by Consensus." *Journal of Personality and Social Psychology*, 1969, *13*, 107–114.

Freedman, J. L., and Fraser, S. C. "Compliance Without Pressure: The Foot-in-the-Door Technique." *Journal of Personality and Social Psychology*, 1966, *4*, 195–202.

Fried, C. *Medical Experimentation: Personal Integrity and Social Policy.* New York: North-Holland, 1974.

Fried, C. *Right and Wrong.* Cambridge, Mass.: Harvard University Press, 1978.

Friedlander, G. D. "Bigger Bugs in BART?" *IEEE Spectrum*, 1973 (March), pp. 32–37.

Friedman, P. R. "Legal Regulation of Applied Behavior Analysis in Mental Institutions and Prisons." *Arizona Law Review*, 1975, *17*, 39–104.

Gaertner, S., and Bickman, L. "A Nonreactive Indicator Measure of Social Discrimination: The Wrong Number Technique." In L. Bickman and T. Henchy (Eds.), *Beyond the Laboratory: Field Research in Social Psychology.* New York: McGraw-Hill, 1972.

Gaines, R. "Whistle-blowing: Candor Brings Revenge from the Bureaucracy." *Minneapolis Tribune*, April 19, 1978, p. 13A.

Galliher, J. F. "The Protection of Human Subjects: A Reexamination of the Professional Code of Ethics." *American Sociologist*, 1973, *8*, 93–100.

Galliher, J. F. "Professor Galliher Replies." *American Sociologist*, 1974, *9*, 159–160.

Gard, S. A. *Jones on Evidence: Civil and Criminal.* Vol. 3 (6th ed.) Rochester, N.Y.: Lawyers Co-Operative Publishing Co., 1972.

Gellhorn, A. "Violations of Human Rights: Torture and the Medical Profession." *New England Journal of Medicine*, 1978, *299* (7), 358–359.

Gibbons, D. C. "Unidentified Research Sites and Fictitious Names." *American Sociologist*, 1975, *10* (1), 32–36.

Glynn, K. L. "Regulations Regarding the Use of Human Subjects in Research: Effect on Investigators' Ethical Sensitivity, Research Practices, and Research Priorities." Paper presented at annual meeting of American Sociological Association, San Francisco, 1978.

Gough, J. W. *The Social Contract.* (2nd ed.) Oxford, England: Clarendon Press, 1957.

Gouldner, A. W. *The Coming Crisis of Western Sociology.* New York: Basic Books, 1970.

Gray, B. H. *Human Subjects in Medical Experimentation.* New York: Wiley, 1975.

Gray, B. H., Cooke, R. A., and Tannenbaum, A. S. "Research Involving Human Subjects." *Science*, 1978, *201*, 1094–1101.

Groueff, S. *Manhattan Project*. London: Collins, 1967.

Haan, N., Smith, M. B., and Block, J. "Moral Reasoning of Young Adults: Political-Social Behavior, Family Background, and Personality Correlates." *Journal of Personality and Social Psychology*, 1968, *10* (3), 183–201.

Haney, C., Banks, C., and Zimbardo, P. G. "Interpersonal Dynamics in a Simulated Prison." *International Journal of Criminology and Penology*, 1973, *1*, 69–97.

Hart, H. L. A. "Are There Any Natural Rights?" *Philosophical Review*, 1955, *64* (2), 175– 191.

Hart, J. "Berkeley Scandal." *Daily Times-Advocate* (Escondido, Calif.), August 9, 1973.

Hendel, S., and Bard, R. "Should There Be a Researcher's Privilege?" *AAUP Bulletin*, 1973, *59*, 398–401.

Hicks, J. R. "The Foundations of Welfare Economics." *Economic Journal*, 1939, *49*, 696–712.

Hobbes, T. *Leviathan*. London: Andrew Crooke, 1651.

Hogan, R. "A Dimension of Moral Judgment." *Journal of Consulting and Clinical Psychology*, 1970, *35* (2), 205–212.

Hogan, R. "Moral Conduct and Moral Character: A Psychological Perspective." *Psychological Bulletin*, 1973, *79*, 217–232.

Holder, A. R., and Levine, R. A. "Informed Consent for Research on Specimens Obtained at Autopsy or Surgery: A Case Study in the Overprotection of Human Subjects." *Clinical Research*, 1976, *24*, 68–77.

Holstein, C. B. "Irreversible, Stepwise Sequence in the Development of Moral Judgment: A Longitudinal Study of Males and Females." *Child Development*, 1976, *47*, 51–61.

Homans, G. C. "The Small Warship." *American Sociological Review*, 1946, *11*, 294–300.

Honigfeld, G. "Nonspecific Factors in Treatment: I. Review of Placebo Reactors; II. Review of Social-Psychological Factors." *Diseases of the Nervous System*, 1964, *25*, 145–156, 225–239.

Horowitz, I. L. "The Life and Death of Project Camelot." *Transaction*, 1965, *3*, 3–7, 44–47.

Horowitz, I. L., and Rainwater, L. ". . . Journalistic Moralizers."

Trans-action, 1970, *7* (7), 5–8.

Humphreys, L. "Tearoom Trade: Impersonal Sex in Public Places." *Trans-action*, 1970a, *7* (3), 10–25.

Humphreys, L. *Tearoom Trade: Impersonal Sex in Public Places*. Chicago: Aldine, 1970b.

Ingelfinger, F. J. "The Unethical in Medical Ethics." *Annals of Internal Medicine*, 1975, *83*, 264–269.

Institute for Social Research. *Research in Prisons*. A Report to the National Commission for the Protection of Human Subjects of Biomedical and Behavioral Research. Ann Arbor: University of Michigan, 1976a.

Institute for Social Research. *Research on Children and the Mentally Infirm*. A Report to the National Commission for the Protection of Human Subjects of Biomedical and Behavioral Research. Ann Arbor: University of Michigan, 1976b.

Institute for Social Research. *Research Involving Human Subjects*. A Report to the National Commission for the Protection of Human Subjects of Biomedical and Behavioral Research. Ann Arbor: University of Michigan, 1976c.

Institute of Electrical and Electronic Engineers. "Guidelines to Professional Employment For Engineers and Scientists." *IEEE Spectrum*, 1973, *10* (4), 57–60.

Irving, C. "Showdown on Human Studies Nears at UC." *San Francisco Sunday Examiner & Chronicle*, August 19, 1973, pp. 1, 24.

Ivy, A. C. "The History and Ethics of the Use of Human Subjects in Medical Experiments." *Science*, 1948, *108*, 1–5.

Jaroslovsky, R. "Blowing the Whistle Begins a Nightmare for Lawyer Joe Rose." *Wall Street Journal*, November 9, 1977, pp. 1, 14.

Johnson, W. H. "Civil Rights of Military Personnel Regarding Medical Care and Experimental Procedures." *Science*, 1953, *117*, 212–215.

Jonas, H. "Philosophical Reflections on Experimenting with Human Subjects." *Daedalus*, 1969, *98* (2), 219–247.

Jung, J. "Snoopology." *Human Behavior*, 1975, *4* (10), 56–69.

Kaldor, N. "Welfare Propositions in Economics and Interpersonal Comparisons of Utility." *Economic Journal*, 1939, *49*, 549–552.

Kant, I. *The Fundamental Principles of the Metaphysic of Ethics*. (O. Manthey-Zorn, Trans.) N.Y.: Appleton-Century-Crofts, 1938.

(Originally published 1785).

Kant, I. *The Metaphysical Elements of Justice.* (J. Ladd, Trans.) Indianapolis: Bobbs-Merrill, 1965. (Originally published 1797.)

Kass, L. R. "Freedom, Coercion, and Asexual Reproduction." Reprinted in J. Katz, *Experiments with Human Beings.* N.Y.: Russell Sage, 1972, pp. 977–979.

Kassirer, L. B. "Behavior Modification for Patients and Prisoners: Constitutional Ramifications of Enforced Therapy." *Journal of Psychiatry and the Law,* 1974, *2*, 245–302.

Katz, J. "The Education of the Physician-Investigator." *Daedalus,* 1969, *98* (2), 480–501.

Katz, J. *Experimentation with Human Beings.* New York: Russell Sage Foundation, 1972.

Katz, J., and Capron, A. M. *Catastrophic Diseases: Who Decides What? New York: Russell Sage Foundation, 1975.*

Kaufman, H. "The Price of Obedience and the Price of Knowledge." American Psychologist, 1967, *22*, 321–322.

Kelling, G. L., and others. *The Kansas City Preventive Patrol Experiment: A Technical Report.* Washington, D.C.: Police Foundation, 1974.

Kelman, H. C. "Manipulation of Human Behavior: An Ethical Dilemma for the Social Scientist." *Journal of Social Issues,* 1965, *21*, 31–46.

Kelman, H. C. *A Time to Speak: On Human Values and Social Research.* San Francisco: Jossey-Bass, 1968.

Kelman, H. C. "The Rights of the Subject in Social Research: An Analysis in Terms of Relative Power and Legitimacy." *American Psychologist,* 1972, *27*, 989–1016.

Kennedy, E. C. (Ed.). *Human Rights and Psychological Research: A Debate on Psychology and Ethics.* New York: Crowell, 1975.

Kershaw, D. N. "A Negative Income Tax Experiment." *Scientific American,* 1972, *227* (4), 19–25.

Kershaw, D. N., and Small, J. C. "Data Confidentiality and Privacy: Lessons from the New Jersey Negative Income Tax Experiment." *Public Policy,* 1972, *20* (2), 257–280.

King, S. S. "23 in Chicago Street Gang Accused of Stealing Funds." *New York Times,* April 8, 1971, p. 25.

Kohlberg, L. "The Development of Modes of Moral Thinking and

Choice in the Years Ten to Sixteen." Unpublished doctoral dissertation, University of Chicago, 1958.

Kohlberg, L. "From Is to Ought: How to Commit the Naturalistic Fallacy and Get Away with It in the Study of Moral Development." In T. Mischel (Ed.), *Cognitive Development and Epistemology*. New York: Academic Press, 1971.

Kohlberg, L. "Continuities in Childhood and Adult Moral Development Revisited." In P. B. Baltes and K. W. Shaie (Eds.), *Life-Span Development Psychology: Personality and Socialization*. New York: Academic Press, 1973a.

Kohlberg, L. "Stages and Aging in Moral Development—Some Speculations." *Gerontologist*, 1973b, *13* (4), 497–502.

Kohlberg, L. "Moral Stages and Moralization: The Cognitive-Developmental Approach." In T. Lickona (Ed.), *Moral Development and Behavior: Theory, Research, and Social Issues*. New York: Holt, Rinehart and Winston, 1976.

Koocher, G. P. "Bathroom Behavior and Human Dignity." *Journal of Personality and Social Psychology*, 1977, *35* (2), 120–121.

Koopmans, T. C. *Three Essays on the State of Economic Science*. New York: McGraw-Hill, 1957.

Krasner, L., and Ullman, L. P. *Research in Behavior Modification: New Developments and Implications*. New York: Holt, Rinehart and Winston, 1965.

Kuhn, T. S. *The Structure of Scientific Revolutions*. Chicago: University of Chicago Press, 1962.

Kurtines, W., and Greif, E. B. "The Development of Moral Thought: Review and Evaluation of Kohlberg's Approach." *Psychological Bulletin*, 1974, *81* (8), 453–470.

Laforet, E. G. "The Fiction of Informed Consent." *Journal of the American Medical Association*, 1976, *235* (15), 1579–1585.

Lakatos, I., and Musgrave, A. (Eds.). *Criticism and the Growth of Knowledge*. London: Cambridge University Press, 1970.

Larsen, O. "Report of the Executive Officer." *ASA Footnotes*, 1975, *3* (6), 10.

Lassek, A. M. *Human Dissection: Its Drama and Struggle*. Springfield, Ill.: Thomas, 1958.

Latané, B. "Field Studies of Altruistic Compliance." *Representative Research in Social Psychology*, 1970, *11*, 49–60.

Latané, B., and Darley, J. M. "Social Determinants of Bystander Intervention in Emergencies." In J. Macaulay and L. Berkowitz (Eds.), *Altruism and Helping Behavior*. New York: Academic Press, 1970.

"Legal Implications of Psychological Research with Human Subjects." Duke Law Journal, 1960, *1960*, 265–274.

Leming, J. "Moral Reasoning, Sense of Control, and Social-Political Activism Among Adolescents." *Adolescence*, 1974, *9* (36), 507–528.

Levendusky, P., and Pankratz, L. "Self-Control Techniques as an Alternative to Pain Medication." *Journal of Abnormal Psychology*, 1975, *84*, 165–168.

Levick, M., and Wapner, A. "Advances in Mental Health: A Case for the Right to Refuse Treatment." *Temple Law Quarterly*, 1975, *48*, 354–383.

Levine, R. J. "The Institutional Review Board." Part 4 of Appendix to *Report and Recommendation: Institutional Review Board*. Washington, D.C.: U.S. Government Printing Office, 1978a. (DHEW Publication No. (OS) 78–0009).

Levine, R. J. "The Role of Assessment of Risk-Benefit Criteria in the Determination of the Appropriateness of Research Involving Human Subjects." Appendix to *The Belmont Report: Ethical Principles and Guidelines for the Protection of Human Subjects*. Vol. I. DHEW Publication No. (OS) 78–0013. Washington, D.C.: U.S. Government Printing Office, 1978b.

Lewis, O. *The Children of Sánchez: Autobiography of a Mexican Family*. New York: Random House, 1961.

Liell, J. T. "Comment." *American Sociologist*, 1978, *13*, 167–168.

Liska, A. E. (Ed.). *The Consistency Controversy*. New York: Halsted Press, 1975.

Locke, J. *Second Treatise of Government* (6th ed.) J. W. Gouth (Ed.). Oxford, England: Basil Blackwell, 1966. (Originally published, 1690.)

Lockhart, W. B., Kamisar, Y., and Choper, J. H. *Constitutional Rights and Liberties*. (4th ed.) St. Paul, Minn.: West Publishing, 1975.

Loew, F. M. "Animal Rights in the Laboratory." *Science*, 1978, *201*, 482, 484.

Lofland, J. F. "Reply to Davis." *Social Problems*, 1961, *8* (4), 365–367.

Lofland, J. F., and Lejeune, R. A. "Initial Interaction of Newcomers in Alcoholics Anonymous: A Field Experiment in Class Symbols and Socialization." *Social Problems*, 1960, *8* (2), 102–111.

Loftus, E. F., and Fries, J. F. "Informed Consent May Be Hazardous to Health." *Science*, 1979, *204*, 11.

Lundman, R. J., and McFarlane, P. T. "Conflict Methodology: An Introduction and Preliminary Assessment." *Sociological Quarterly*, 1976, *17*, 502–512.

Lykken, D. T. "Psychology and the Lie Detector Industry." *American Psychologist*, 1974, *29*, 725–739.

Lykken, D. T. "Lykken Replies." *American Psychologist*, 1975a, *30*, 711–712.

Lykken, D. T. "The Right Way to Use a Lie Detector." *Psychology Today*, 1975b, *8* (10), 56–60.

Lyons, R. D. "Periodic Relicensing Exams Urged for Doctors." *New York Times*, June 25, 1974, p. 20.

Macaulay, J., and Berkowitz, L. (Ed.). *Altruism and Helping Behavior: Social Psychological Studies of Some Antecedents and Consequences.* New York: Academic Press, 1970.

Macklin, R., and Sherwin, S. "Experimenting on Human Subjects: Philosophical Perspectives." *Case Western Reserve Law Review*, 1975, *25* (3), 434–471.

Mason, A. T., and Beaney, W. M. *American Constitutional Law.* (5th ed.) Englewood Cliffs, N.J.: Prentice-Hall, 1972.

Mead, M. "Research with Human Beings: A Model Derived from Anthropological Field Practice." *Daedalus*, 1969, *98* (2), 361–386.

Meglino, B. M. "Human Participants in Research: A Methodology for Determining Risk Through Subject Perceptions." Unpublished report, University of South Carolina, 1976a.

Meglino, B. M. "Human Participants in Research: Assessing Legal and Ethical Requirements Through Subject Perceptions." Unpublished report, College of Business Administration, University of South Carolina, 1976b.

Melmon, K. L., Grossman, M., and Morris, R. C., Jr. "Emerging Assets and Liabilities of a Committee on Human Welfare and

Experimentation." *New England Journal of Medicine*, 1970, *282*, 427–431.

Menges, R. J. "Openness and Honesty Versus Coercion and Deception in Psychological Research." *American Psychologist*, 1973, *28* (12), 1030–1034.

Merton, R. K. "Resistance to the Systematic Study of Multiple Discoveries in Science." *European Journal of Sociology*, 1963, *4*, 237–249.

Middlemist, R. D., Knowles, E. S., and Matter, C. F. "Personal Space Invasions in the Lavatory: Suggestive Evidence for Arousal." *Journal of Personality and Social Psychology*, 1976, *33* (5), 541–546.

Middlemist, R. D., Knowles, E. S., and Matter, C. F. "What to Do and What to Report: A Reply to Koocher." *Journal of Personality and Social Psychology*, 1977, *35* (2), 122–124.

Milgram, S. "Behavioral Study of Obedience." *Journal of Abnormal and Social Psychology*, 1963, *67*, 371–378.

Milgram, S. "Issues in the Study of Obedience: A Reply to Baumrind." *American Psychologist*, 1964, *19*, 848–852.

Milgram, S. "Some Conditions of Obedience and Disobedience to Authority." *Human Relations*, 1965, *18* (1), 57–76.

Milgram, S. "Reply to Critics." *International Journal of Psychiatry*, 1968, *6*, 294–295.

Milgram, S. "The Lost-Letter Technique." *Psychology Today*, 1969, *3* (1), 30–33, 66, 68.

Milgram, S. "The Experience of Living in Cities." *Science*, 1970, *167*, 1461–1468.

Milgram, S. "Interpreting Obedience: Error and Evidence." In A. G. Miller (Ed.), *The Social Psychology of Psychological Research*. New York: Free Press, 1972.

Milgram, S. *Obedience to Authority*. New York: Harper & Row, 1974.

Milgram, S., and Hollander, P. "The Murder They Heard." *Nation*, 1964, *198*, 602–604.

Mill, J. S. "Utilitarianism." In S. Gorovitz (Ed.), *Utilitarianism: With Critical Essays*. Indianapolis: Bobbs-Merrill, 1971. (Originally published 1863.)

Miller, R., and Willner, H. S. "The Two-Part Consent Form: A Suggestion for Promoting Free and Informed Consent." *New*

England Journal of Medicine, 1974, *290* (17), 964–966.

Mulford, R. D. "Experimentation on Human Beings." *Stanford Law Review,* 1967, *20* (1), 99–117.

Nader, R. "Thalidomide Children." *New Republic,* 1973, *168* (6), 10–11.

Nash, M. "Nonreactive Methods and the Law: Additonal Comments on Legal Liability in Behavior Research." *American Psychologist,* 1975, *30* (7), 777–780.

National Commission for the Protection of Human Subjects of Biomedical and Behavioral Research. *Report and Recommendations: Research on the Fetus.* DHEW Publication No. (OS) 76–127. (Appendix DHEW Publication No. [OS] 76–128) Washington, D.C.: U.S. Government Printing Office, 1975.

National Commission for the Protection of Human Subjects of Biomedical and Behavioral Research. *Report and Recommendations: Research Involving Prisoners.* DHEW Publication No. (OS) 76–131. (Appendix DHEW Publication No. [OS] 76–132) Washington, D.C.: U.S. Government Printing Office, 1976.

National Commission for the Protection of Human Subjects of Biomedical and Behavioral Research. *Report and Recommendations: Psychosurgery.* DHEW Publication No. (OS) 77–0001. (Appendix DHEW Publication No. [OS] 77–0002) Washington, D.C.: U..S. Government Printing Office, 1977a.

National Commission for the Protection of Human Subjects of Biomedical and Behavioral Research. *Report and Recommendations: Disclosure of Research Information Under the Freedom of Information Act.* DHEW Publication No. (OS) 77–0003. Washington, D.C.: U.S. Government Printing Office, 1977b.

National Commission for the Protection of Human Subjects of Biomedical and Behavioral Research. *Report and Recommendations: Research Involving Children.* DHEW Publication No. (OS) 77–0004. (Appendix DHEW Publication No. [OS] 77–0005) Washington, D.C.: U.S. Government Printing Office, 1977c.

National Commission for the Protection of Human Subjects of Biomedical and Behavioral Research. *Report and Recommendations: Research Involving Those Institutionalized as Mentally Infirm.* DHEW Publication No. (OS) 78–0006. (Appendix DHEW Publication No. [OS] 78–0007) Washington, D.C.: U.S. Government

Printing Office, 1978a.

National Commission for the Protection of Human Subjects of Biomedical and Behavioral Research. *Report and Recommendations: Institutional Review Boards.* DHEW Publication No. (OS) 78–0008. (Appendix DHEW Publication No. [OS] 78–0009) Washington, D.C.: U.S. Government Printing Office, 1978b.

National Commission for the Protection of Human Subjects of Biomedical and Behavioral Research. "Summary Analyses of Federal Policies and Procedures for the Protection of Human Subjects (by Agency)." In Appendix to *Report and Recommendations: Institutional Review Boards.* DHEW Publication No. (OS) 78–0009; pt. 2. Washington, D.C.: U.S. Government Printing Office, 1978c.

National Commission for the Protection of Human Subjects of Biomedical and Behavioral Research. *Report and Recommendations: Ethical Guidelines for the Delivery of Health Services by DHEW.* DHEW Publication No. (OS) 78–0010. (Appendix DHEW Publication No. [OS] 78–0011) Washington, D.C.: U.S. Government Printing Office, 1978d.

National Commission for the Protection of Human Subjects of Biomedical and Behavioral Research. *The Belmont Report: Ethical Principles and Guidelines for the Protection of Human Subjects of Research.* DHEW Publication No. (OS) 78–0012. (Appendices DHEW Publication No. [OS] 78–0013 and [OS] 78–0014) Washington, D.C.: U.S. Government Printing Office, 1978e.

National Commission for the Protection of Human Subjects of Biomedical and Behavioral Research. *Special Study: Implications of Advances in Biomedical and Behavioral Research.* DHEW Publication No. (OS) 78–0015. Washington, D.C.: U. S. Government Printing Office, 1978f.

National Safety Council. *Accident Facts.* Chicago: National Safety Council, 1972.

Nejelski, P. "Researchers in West German Survey Report Difficulty in Obtaining or Protecting Confidential Data." *ASA Footnotes,* 1973, *1* (8), 2.

Nejelski, P., and Finsterbusch, K. "The Prosecutor and the Researcher: Present and Prospective Variations in the Supreme Court's Branzburg Decision." *Social Problems,* 1973, *21* (3), 3–21.

Nejelski, P., and Lerman, L. M. "A Researcher-Subject Testimonial Privilege: What to Do Before the Subpoena Arrives." *Wisconsin Law Review,* 1971, (4), 1085–1148.

Nejelski, P., and Peyser, H. "A Researcher's Shield Statute: Guarding Against the Compulsory Disclosure of Research Data." Appendix B to *Protecting Individual Privacy in Evaluation Research.* Washington, D.C.: National Academy of Sciences, 1975.

Newsletter of the American Anthropological Association. "Two Resolutions to Go on Mail Ballot." 1972a, *13* (1), 11–12.

Newsletter of the American Anthropological Association. "Resolutions and Amendment Pass." 1972b, *13* (6), 1.

New York Times. "Ex-Lab Worker Convicted in Release of 2 Dolphins." December 10, 1977, 12.

Norris, N. "Impediments to Penal Reform." *University of Chicago Law Review,* 1966, *33,* 646–653.

Nozick, R. *Anarchy, State, and Utopia.* New York: Basic Books, 1974.

Olafson, F. A. (Ed.). *Society, Law, and Morality.* Englewood Cliffs, N.J.: Prentice-Hall, 1961.

Orne, M. T., and Holland, C. C. "On the Ecological Validity of Laboratory Deceptions." *International Journal of Psychiatry,* 1968, *6* (4), 282–293.

Pappworth, M. H. *Human Guinea Pigs.* Boston: Beacon Press, 1967.

Park, L. C., and others. "The Subjective Experience of the Research Patient." *Journal of Nervous and Mental Disease,* 1966, *143,* 199–206.

Patten, S. C. "The Case That Milgram Makes." *Philosophical Review,* 1977a, *88,* 350–364.

Patten, S. C. "Milgram's Shocking Experiments." *Philosophy,* 1977b, *52,* 425–440.

Peters, R. S. "Moral Development: A Plea for Pluralism." In T. Mischel (Ed.), *Cognitive Development and Epistemology.* New York: Academic Press, 1971.

Piaget, J. *The Moral Judgment of the Child.* New York: Free Press, 1932.

Piliavin, I. M., Rodin, J., and Piliavin, J. A. "Good Samaritanism: An Underground Phenomenon?" *Journal of Personality and Social Psychology,* 1969, *13* (4), 289–299.

Piliavin, J. A., and Piliavin, I. M. "Effect of Blood on Reactions to a Victim." *Journal of Personality and Social Psychology,* 1972, *23,* 353–361.

Podd, M. H. "Ego Identity Status and Morality: The Relationship Between Two Developmental Constructs." *Developmental Psychology,* 1972, *6* (3), 497–507.

Pound, R. *The Development of Constitutional Guarantees of Liberty.* New Haven, Conn.: Yale University Press, 1957.

Presidential Advisory Group on Anticipated Advances in Science and Technology. "The Science Court Experiment: An Interim Report." *Science,* 1976, *193,* 653–656.

Prichard, H. A. "Does Moral Philosophy Rest on a Mistake?" *Mind,* 1912, *21* (81), 21–37.

Queen, S. A. "No Garrison State—Difficulties, Yes: Replies to Coser and Roth." *American Sociological Review,* 1959, *24* (3), 399–400.

Quimby, F. H., McKenzie, S. R., and Chapman, C. B. *Federal Regulation of Human Experimentation, 1975.* Prepared by the Science Policy Research Division, Congressional Research Service for the Subcommittee on Health of the Committee on Labor and Public Works, U.S. Senate. Washington, D.C.: U.S. Government Printing Office, 1975.

Ragolia, W. E. "The FDA's Acceptance of Foreign Clinical Data." *Food Drug Cosmetic Law Journal,* 1975, *30* (7), 433–439.

Rainwater, L., and Pittman, D. J. "Ethical Problems in Studying a Politically Sensitive and Deviant Community." *Social Problems,* 1967, *14,* 357–366.

Rand Corporation. *Second Annual Report of the Housing Assistance Supply Experiment.* Report No. R–1959–HUD. Santa Monica, Calif.: Rand Corporation, 1976.

Rawls, J. *A Theory of Justice.* Cambridge, Mass.: Harvard University Press, 1971.

Rescher, N. *Distributive Justice.* Indianapolis: Bobbs- Merrill, 1966.

Resnick, J. H., and Schwartz, T. "Ethical Standards as an Independent Variable in Psychological Research." *American Psychologist,* 1973, *28* (2), 134–139.

Rest, J. R. "Moral Judgments Related to Sample Characteristics." Report to the National Institute of Mental Health. Minneapolis: University of Minnesota, 1976.

Reynolds, P. D. *A Primer In Theory Construction.* Indianapolis: Bobbs-Merrill, 1971.

Reynolds, P. D. "On the Protection of Human Subjects and Social Science." *International Social Science Journal,* 1972, *24* (4), 693–719.

Reynolds, P. D. *Value Dilemmas Associated with the Development and Application of Social Science.* Report prepared for UNESCO and the International Social Science Council. Paris, 1975a

Reynolds, P. D. "Ethics and Status: Value Dilemmas in the Professional Conduct of Social Science." *International Social Science Journal,* 1975b, *27* (4), 563–611.

Ring, K., Wallston, K., and Corey, M. "Mode of Debriefing as a Factor Affecting Subjective Reaction to a Milgram-Type Obedience Experiment: An Ethical Inquiry." *Representative Research in Social Psychology,* 1970, *1* (1), 67–88.

Rivlin, A. M., *Systematic Thinking for Social Action.* Washington, D.C.: Brookings Institute, 1971.

Rivlin, A. M., and Timpane, P. M. (Eds.). *Ethical and Legal Issues of Social Experimentation.* Washington, D.C.: Brookings Institution, 1975.

Robertson, J. A. "The Scientist's Right to Research: A Constitutional Analysis." *Southern California Law Review,* 1978, *51*(6), 1203–1280.

Robinson, G., and Merav, A. "Informed Consent: Recall by Patients Tested Postoperatively." *The Annals of Thoracic Surgery,* 1976, *22*(3), 209–212.

Rokeach, M. *The Nature of Human Values.* New York: Free Press, 1973.

Rosenthal, R. "Covert Communication in the Psychological Experiment." *Psychological Bulletin,* 1967, *67,* 356–367.

Rosenthal, R. "Experimenter Expectancy and the Reassuring Nature of the Null Hypothesis Decision Procedure." *Psychological Bulletin,* 1968, *70* (6, pt. 2), 30–47.

Rosenthal, R., and Rosnow, R. L. *The Volunteer Subject.* New York: Wiley-Interscience, 1975.

Rousseau, J. *The Social Contract.* In E. Barker (Ed.), *Social Contract: Essays by Locke, Hume, and Rousseau.* New York: Oxford University Press, 1972. (Originally published 1762.)

Roth, J. A. "Dangerous and Difficult Enterprise?" *American Socio-logical Review,* 1959, *24* (3), 398.

Roth, J. A. "Comments on Secret Observation." *Social Problems,* 1962, *9,* 283–284.

Rubin, Z. "Jokers Wild in the Lab." *Psychology Today,* 1970, *4* (7), 18–24.

Ruebhausen, O. M., and Brim, O. G., Jr. "Privacy and Behavioral Research." *American Psychologist,* 1966, *21,* 423–437.

Russell Sage Foundation. *Guidelines for the Collection, Maintenance, and Dissemination of Public Records.* New York: Russell Sage Foundation, 1970.

Rynkiewich, M. A., and Spradley, J. P. *Ethics and Anthropology: Dilemmas in Fieldwork.* New York: Wiley, 1976.

Sagan, L. A., and Jonsen, A. "Medical Ethics and Torture." *New England Journal of Medicine,* 1976, *294* (26), 1427–1430.

Sagarin, E. "The Research Setting and the Right Not to be Researched." *Social Problems,* 1973, *21* (1), 52–64.

Samoilovich, F. "Ideology and the Protest Movement in Science." *International Social Science Journal,* 1975, *27* (4), 703–720.

Savin, H. B. "Professors and Psychological Researchers: Conflicting Values in Conflicting Roles." *Cognition,* 1973a, *2* (1), 147–149.

Savin, H. B. "Ethics for Gods and Men." *Cognition,* 1973b, *2* (2), 257.

Schaps, E. "Cost, Dependency, and Helping." *Journal of Personality and Social Psychology,* 1972, *21,* 74–78.

Schimmel, E. M. "Hazards of Hospitalization." *Annals of Internal Medicine,* 1964, *60,* 100–110.

Schmidt, A. M. "The Drug Approval Process and the FDA." *Connecticut Medicine,* 1975, *39* (4), 237–240.

Schroeter, G. "Protection of Confidentiality in the Courts: The Professions." *Social Problems,* 1969, *16,* 376–385.

Schulman, A. D., and Berman, H. J. "On Berscheid et al." *American Psychologist,* 1974, *29,* 473–474.

Schulman, J. "Comment," *The American Scoiologist,* 1978, *13,* 169–171.

Schulman, J., and others. "Recipe for a Jury." *Psychology Today,* 1973, *6* (12), 37–44, 77, 79–84.

Scott, J. "Americans Enjoy Participating in Surveys, ISR Study Shows." *Institute for Social Research Newsletter,* 1978, *6* (1), 7.

Scott, W. R. "Some Implications of Organizational Theory for Research on Health Services." *Milbank Memorial Quarterly,* 1966, *44* (4), 35–59.

Seeman, J. "Deception in Psychological Research." *American Psychologist,* 1969, *24,* 1025–1028.

Shah, S. T. "Privileged Communications, Confidentiality, and Privacy." *Professional Psychology,* 1969, *1* (1, 2, 3) 56–69, 159–164, 241–252.

Sieghart, P. "A Corporate Conscience for the Scientific Community?" *Nature,* 1972, *239,* 15–18.

Sieghart, P., and others. "The Social Obligations of the Scientist." *Hastings Center Studies,* 1973, *2* (1), 7–16.

Silverman, I. "Nonreactive Methods and the Law." *American Psychologist,* 1975, *30* (7), 764–769.

Simmons, R. G., Klein, S. D., and Simmons, R. L. *Gift of Life: The Social and Psychological Impact of Organ Transplantation.* New York: Wiley-Interscience, 1977.

Singer, E. "Informed Consent: Consequences for Response Rate and Response Quality in Social Surveys." *American Sociological Review,* 1978, *43* 144–162.

Singer, P. *Animal Liberation.* New York: Random House, 1975.

Sjoberg, G. (Ed.). *Ethics, Politics, and Social Research.* Cambridge, Mass.: Schenkman, 1967.

Smith, M. B. "Of Prophecy and Privacy." *Contemporary Psychology,* 1957, *2* (4), 89–92.

Smith, M. B. *Social Psychology and Human Values.* Chicago: Aldine, 1969.

Smith, R. J. "Electroshock Experiment at Albany Violates Ethics Guidelines." *Science,* 1977a, *198,* 383–386.

Smith, R. J. "SUNY at Albany Admits Research Violations." *Science,* 1977b, *198,* 708.

Smith, R. H. " Ethics in Field Archeology," *Journal of Field Archeology,* 1974, *1,* 375–383.

"Social Research and Privileged Data." *Valparaiso University Law Review,* 1970, *4,* 368–399.

Sorenson, H. "Mate-Swapping Clubs: Family That Plays Together . . ."*Minneapolis Tribune*, September 16, 1977, pp. 1C, 4C.

Soewell, T. "The IQ Controversy." *Change Magazine*, 1973, *5*, 33–37.

Spece, R. G., Jr. "Conditioning and Other Technologies Used to Treat? Rehabilitate? Demolish? Prisoners and Mental Patients." *Southern California Law Review*, 1972, *45*, 616–681.

Stephenson, R. M. "The CIA and the Professor: A Personal Account." *American Sociologist*, 1978, *13*, 128–133.

Sternbach, R. A. *Pain: A Psychophysiological Analysis.* New York: Academic Press, 1968.

Stricker. L. J. "The True Deceiver." *Psychological Bulletin*, 1967, *68*, 13–20.

Sullivan, D. S., and Deiker, T. E. "Subject-Experimenter Perceptions of Ethical Issues in Human Research."*American Psychologist*, 1973, *28* (7), 587–591.

Sullivan, M. A., Jr. "Ethics and Difficulties: Replies to Coser and Roth." *American Sociological Review*, 1959, *24* (3), 398–399.

Sullivan, M. A., Jr., Queen, S. A., and Patrick, R. C. "Participant Observation as Employed in the Study of a Military Training Program." *American Sociological Review*, 1958, *23*, 660–667.

Symonds, C. L. "The Utopian Aspects of Sexual Mate Swapping: In Theory and Practice." Abstract of presentation to the Society for the Study of Social Problems. In *Sociological Abstracts*, 1970, *18* (5, supp. 12), 6.

Tapp, J. L., and Kohlberg, L. "Developing Senses of Law and Legal Justice." In J. L. Tapp and F. J. Levine (Eds.), *Law, Justice, and the Individual in Society: Psychological and Legal Issues.* New York: Holt, Rinehart and Winston, 1977.

Tapp, J. L., and others. "Continuing Concerns in Cross-Cultural Ethics: A Report." *International Journal of Psychology*, 1974, *9* (3), 231–249.

Tedeschi, J. T., and Gallup, G. G., Jr. "Human Subjects Research." *Science*, 1977, *198*, 1099–1100.

"The Nascent Right to Treatment." *Virginia Law Review*, 1967, *53*, 1134–1160.

Tropp, R. A. "What Problems Are Raised with the Current DHEW Regulation on Protection of Human Subjects as Applied to Social Science Research?" Chapter 18 of Appendix to *The Belmont Report: Ethical Principles and Guidelines for the Protection of Human Subjects.* Vol. II DHEW Publication No. (OS) 78–0014. Washington, D.C.: U.S. Goverment Printing Office, 1978.

Turnbull, C. M. *The Mountain People.* New York: Simon & Schuster, 1972.

Turnbull, C. M. "Reply." *Current Anthropology,* 1974, *15* (1), 103.

Turner, W. "2 Men, Facing Trial for Releasing Dolphins, Say the Creatures Have a Right to be Free." *New York Times,* July 5, 1977, p. 23.

United Nations Economic, Social, and Cultural Organization. *Human Rights: Comments and Interpretations.* New York: Allan Wingate, 1949.

United Nations Economic, Social, and Cultural Organization. "Recommendations on the Status of Scientific Workers." *International Social Science Journal,* 1975, *27* (4), 612–627.

United Nations. Universal Declaration of Human Rights. Appendix 3 to *Human Rights: Comments and Interpretations.* New York: Allan Wingate, 1949.

United States Senate. *Individual Rights and the Federal Role in Behavior Modification.* Prepared by staff of the Subcommittee on Constitutional Rights, Committee on the Judiciary. Stock No. 5270-02620. Washington, D.C.: U.S. Government Printing Office, 1974.

Van Alstyne, W. "A Preliminary Report on the Bakke Case." *AAUP Bulletin,* 1978, *64* (4), 286–297.

Vaughan, T. R. "Governmental Intervention in Social Research: Political and Ethical Dimensions in the Wichita Jury Recordings." In G. Sjoberg (Ed.), *Ethics, Politics, and Social Research.* Cambridge, Mass.: Schenkman, 1967.

Vasquez, A. L., and Resczczynski, R. "Ethical Questions to Psychologists: Techniques of Torture Used In Chile." Paper presented at the 21st International Congress of Psychology, Paris, 1976.

Veatch, R. M. "Human Experimentation Committees: Professional or Representative?" *Hastings Center Report,* 1975, *5* (5), 31–40.

Veatch, R. M. "Three Theories of Informed Consent: Philosophical Foundations and Policy Implications." Appendix to *The Bel-*

mont Report: Ethical Principles and Guidelines for the Protection of Human Subjects. Vol. II. DHEW Publication No. (OS) 78–0014. Washington, D.C.: U.S. Government Printing Office, 1978.

Vidich, A. J., and Bensman, J. *Small Town in Mass Society: Class, Power, and Religion in a Rural Community.* (2nd ed.) Princeton, N.J.: Princeton University Press, 1968.

Von Hoffman, N. "Sociological Snoopers and . . ." *Trans-action,* 1970, *7* (7), 4, 6.

Wallach, M. A., and Kogan, N. *Modes of Thinking in Young Children.* New York: Holt, Rinehart and Winston, 1965.

Walsh, J. "A.C.E. Study on Campus Unrest: Questions for Behavioral Scientists." *Science,* 1969a, *165,* 157–160.

Walsh, J. "Antipoverty R & D: Chicago Debacle Suggests Pitfalls Facing OEO." *Science,* 1969b, *165,* 1243–1245.

Walster, E., and others. "Effectiveness of Debriefing Following Deception Experiments." *Journal of Personality and Social Psychology,* 1967, *6,* 371–380.

Warwick, D. P. "Tearoom Trade: Means and Ends in Social Research." *Hastings Center Studies,* 1973, *1* (1), 27–38.

Warwick, D. P. "Who Deserves Protection?" *The American Sociologist,* 1974, *9,* 158–159.

Warwick, D. P. "Social Scientists Ought to Stop Lying." *Psychology Today,* 1975, *8,* 38, 40, 105–106.

Watson, J. D. "In Defense of DNA." *New Republic,* 1977, *176* (26), 11–14.

Wax, R. *Doing Fieldwork: Warnings and Advice.* Chicago: University of Chicago Press, 1971.

Webb, E. J., and others. *Unobtrusive Measures: Nonreactive Research in the Social Sciences.* Chicago: Rand McNally, 1966.

Welt, L. G. "Reflections on the Problems of Human Experimentation." *Connecticut Medicine,* 1961, *25,* 75–79.

Wexler, D. B. "Token and Taboo: Behavior Modification, Token Economies, and the Law." *California Law Review,* 1973, *61,* 81–109.

Whyte, W. F. "Freedom and Responsibility in Research: The Springdale Case." *Human Organization,* 1958, *17* (2), 1–2.

Wicker, A. W. "Attitudes Versus Actions: The Relationship of Verbal and Overt Behavioral Responses to Attitude Objects." *Jour-*

nal of Social Issues, 1969, *25* (4), 41–78.

Wigmore, J. H. *Evidence in Trials at Common Law* (J. T. McNaughton, Rev.) Boston: Little, Brown, 1961. (Originally published 1913.)

Wolf, E. P. "Some Questions About Community Self-Surveys: When Amateurs Conduct Research." *Human Organization,* 1964, *23* 85–89.

" *Wyatt* v. *Stickney* and the Right of Civilly Committed Mental Patients to Adequate Treatment." *Harvard Law Review,* 1973, *86,* 1282–1306.

Zimbardo, P. "The Human Choice: Individuation, Reason, and Order Versus Deindividuation, Impulse, and Chaos." In W. J. Arnold and D. Devine (Eds.), *Nebraska Symposium on Motivation.* Vol. 17. Lincoln: University of Nebraska Press, 1969, pp. 282–293

Zimbardo, P. G. "The Mind Is a Formidable Jailer: A Pirandellian Prison." *New York Times Magazine,* April 18, 1973a (sec. 6), pp. 38–60.

Zimbardo, P. G. "On the Ethics of Intervention in Human Psychological Research: With Special Reference to the Stanford Prison Experiment." *Cognition,* 1973b, *2* (2), 243–256.

Zuckerman, S. *Scientists and War. The Impact of Science on Military and Civilian Affairs.* London: H. Hamilton, 1966.

Name Index

Subject Index